CITIZENSHIP AND CITIZENSHIP EDUCATION IN A CHANGING WORLD

Edited by
ORIT ICHILOV
School of Education, Tel Aviv University

THE WOBURN PRESS
LONDON • PORTLAND, OR

First published in 1998 in Great Britain by
WOBURN PRESS
Newbury House, 900 Eastern Avenue
London IG2 7HH

and in the United States of America by
WOBURN PRESS
c/o ISBS
5804 N.E. Hassalo Street
Portland, Oregon 97213-3644

Website: http://www.woburnpress.com

British Library Cataloguing in Publication Data

Citizenship and citizenship education in a changing world.
    (The Woburn education series)
    1. Citizenship 2. Allegiance 3. Nationalism and education
I. Ichilov, Orit
323.6

ISBN 0 7130 0215 8 (cloth)
ISBN 0 7130 4035 1 (paper)
ISSN 1462-2076

Library of Congress Cataloging-in-Publication Data

Citizenship and citizenship education in a changing world / edited by
Orit Ichilov.
        p.   cm. – (Woburn education series, ISSN 1462-2076)
    Includes bibliographical references and index.
    ISBN 0-7130-0215-8 (cloth). – ISBN 0-7130-4035-1 (pbk)
    1. Civics–Study and teaching. 2. Citizenship–Study and
teaching. I. Ichilov, Orit. II. Series.
LC1091.C523 1998
321.8'071–dc21   98-29050
                                                            CIP

Printed in Great Britain by
Bookcraft (Bath) Ltd, Midsomer Norton, Somerset

CITIZENSHIP AND
CITIZENSHIP EDUCATION
IN A CHANGING WORLD

This book is to be returned on
or before the date stamped below

UNIVERSITY OF PLYMOUTH 8 NOV

EXMOUTH LIBRARY
Tel: (01395) 255331 3 0 NOV 2005
This book is subject to recall if required by another reader
Books may be renewed by phone
CHARGES WILL BE MADE FOR OVERDUE BOOKS

Woburn Education Series

General Series Editor: Professor Peter Gordon

ISSN 1462–2076

For over 20 years this series on the history, development and policy of education, under the distinguished editorship of Peter Gordon, has been evolving into a comprehensive and balanced survey of important trends in teaching and educational policy. The series is intended to reflect the changing nature of education in present-day society. The books are divided into four sections – educational policy studies, educational practice, the history of education and social history – and reflect the continuing interest in this area.

For a full series listing, please visit our website: www.woburnpress.com.

Educational Practice

Slow Learners. A Break in the Circle: A Practical Guide for Teachers
Diane Griffin

Games and Simulations in Action
Alec Davison and Peter Gordon

Music in Education: A Guide for Parents and Teachers
Malcolm Carlton

The Education of Gifted Children
David Hopkinson

Teaching and Learning Mathematics
Peter G. Dean

Comprehending Comprehensives
Edward S. Conway

Teaching the Humanities
edited by Peter Gordon

Teaching Science
edited by Jenny Frost

The Private Schooling of Girls: Past and Present
edited by Geoffrey Walford

International Yearbook of History Education, Volume 1
edited by Alaric Dickinson, Peter Gordon, Peter Lee and John Slater

A Guide to Educational Research
edited by Peter Gordon

CONTENTS

FOREWORD

In many parts of the world educationists are struggling to define or redefine education for citizenship. This is a difficult concept in the English language, which is made more difficult by the various shades of meaning the term acquires in different contexts and in different countries. Although this book does not aim to cover the whole world, the number of countries sampled is large enough to clarify the concept and to provide a good deal of information about what is happening in the field of citizenship education in a variety of education systems.

What emerges from the individual chapters is that it is not very difficult to define citizenship or even education for citizenship; what is difficult, however, is to convert these definitions into programmes in schools which stand a chance of working in practice. There are many curricula available, but are they teachable? And, if so, do they do any good?

The Editor, Professor Orit Ichilov, from Tel Aviv University, provides us with a helpful Introduction as well as two further chapters later in the book, and a Conclusion to summarize the main ideas from the other contributors. Her stance towards citizenship is to accept its past association with liberal democracy and nationalism but to try to move on from these limited perspectives. She also allows herself the luxury of speculating about possible future developments, which is also interesting and well informed. Wisely, she also warns us of the dangers of postmodernism, which is better at destroying traditions than proposing alternative solutions.

Professor Ichilov has managed to gather together in the volume many of the world experts on citizenship education. But not all of them are equally optimistic – at least about the immediate future. Shlapentokh, for example, is gloomy about the situation in Russia following the collapse of the Soviet Union: 'passivity' is the key word. Such frankness is refreshing in a book of this kind. Zsuzsa Mátrai is almost as pessimistic about contemporary Hungary, concluding that young people are being encouraged to be spectators rather than participants in the political process. But even in such well-established democracies as the USA there are no grounds for complacency: Mary Hepburn entitles her chapter 'A Disquieting Outlook for Democracy'.

So, has education for citizenship failed? Is this the message of the book? By no means: the underlying theme of this well-integrated collection of papers is that no society has yet approached the problem of citizenship education with the commitment that it deserves. This commitment would include not only adequate resources and massive programmes of teacher education but also paying much more attention to developing practical programmes firmly based in respectable theoretical frameworks. The latter requirement may be the most difficult of all: not only because politicians rarely see the need for educational theory but also because the kind of theoretical work needed for education for citizenship is difficult and complex. Elsewhere, Professor Ichilov has put forward a multidimensional theory of citizenship, which is referred to in this volume. This would provide a useful starting point for societies wishing to embark upon an ambitious programme of rethinking citizenship education.

But a multidimensional theory is not a ready-made solution. Every society has the task of working out a programme for itself. This book provides ideas, theories, even examples, but the problems of curriculum design and implementation remain. This collection of papers gives many clues about the future but also illustrates many of the problems.

Denis Lawton

INTRODUCTION

ORIT ICHILOV

Paramount political, economic, technological and cultural changes have taken place all over the globe in recent years, changes which have transformed the meanings of citizenship and citizenship education. 'Citizenship' has been closely associated with the ideas of liberal democracy, nationalism, and nation-states. Today's world is structured by contradictory social processes. There are powerful pressures towards the fragmentation of large political units, regional autonomy, localism and nationalism, while simultaneously there is a strive for globalism and unification. The breakdown of the Soviet Union and the growth of Islamic fundamentalism, for example, may reinforce nationalism. Communications, the globalization of capital and the acceleration of international migration, on the other hand, may alter the character of states and international relations (Tilly, 1993). Many Western democracies have witnessed growing cultural and ethnic heterogeneity, which rendered obsolete the concept of the nation-state: a state that is nationally homogeneous. Paradoxically, however, both growing localism and globalism have rekindled nationalism. For example, the disintegration of the Soviet Bloc and the formation of the European Community, resulted in more intense national sentiments. In the Middle East, some parts of Africa, South America and the Far East, the idea of the nation-state is very much alive.

Postmodernism declared obsolete all grand narratives, while at the same time new social movements such as feminism, environmentalism and peace movements are attempting to mobilize support for their causes, and offer a blueprint for a desirable future (Boyne and Rattansi, 1990).

The future of Western-style liberal democracy, and its adoption by former Soviet Union and Asian states remains unclear. Fukuyama proposes that liberal democracy may constitute the 'end point of mankind's ideological evolution' and the 'final form of human government', and as such constitutes the 'end of history' in the sense that liberal democracy, which rests on the twin principles of liberty and equality, could not be improved on (1992, p.xi). Havel expresses much less confidence in the blessings of modern democracy. He argues that democracy in its present Western form arouses skepticism and distrust in many parts of the world. On the one hand, people long for the prosperity they see in the West; on the other, they reject the importation of Western values and lifestyles as the work of the devil. Western culture and life styles are associated with:

> moral relativism, materialism, the denial of any kind of spirituality, a proud disdain for everything suprapersonal, a profound crisis of authority and the resulting general decay, a frenzied consumerism, a lack of solidarity, the selfish cult of material success, the absence of faith in a higher order of things or simply in eternity, an expansionist mentality that holds in contempt everything that in any way resists the dreary standardization of rationalism and of technical civilization. (Havel, 1995, p.7)

The present era of change brings to the fore many uncertainties and queries. Can and should a 'semi-direct democracy' be instituted using technological means to allow ordinary citizens more of a voice in politics? Will economy and technology increase homogeneity among all human societies, regardless of their historical origins and cultural heritage? Does the 'global village' become more fragmented as it becomes more unified by systems of communication? Will economic modernization result in the universal adoption of Western-style liberal democracy? Will Asia, and other parts of the globe, formulate a new kind of political-economic order that is different from Western capitalist democracy? Can a viable democracy be constituted in Russia and former Soviet Bloc countries, and in Asia or in the Muslim countries of the Middle East? How would citizenship be constituted and defined in a changing world? Will a single version of citizenship emerge, or could there be many diverse and different formulations of the citizenship principle? Should people be compelled into single identities? What alternatives are there for those who have multiple allegiances? No doubt that citizenship education, which is meant to prepare youngsters to assume the role of citizens, will have to change accordingly and to take on novel forms. The purpose of this volume is to describe and analyze changes which have taken place in a variety of countries, and to examine their implications for both citizenship and citizenship education.

AN OVERVIEW OF THE VOLUME

The volume includes 14 chapters. Some provide a comprehensive analysis of issues related to citizenship and citizenship education within a specific country (Ichilov on Israel, Mátrai on Hungary, Tsang on Hong Kong, for example) or region (Harber on Africa, for example). Others are dedicated to more specific issues concerning democratic citizenship and citizenship education (Sapiro on gender and world changes in citizenship; Hepburn on the impact of the mass media on citizenship education in the US, for example).

In Chapter 1, 'Patterns of Citizenship in a Changing World', Ichilov provides a broad framework for the analysis of the implications of the political, cultural, social and technological changes of the past few decades, for citizenship and citizenship education. Ichilov explores how changes related to such concepts as nationalism, patriotism, the nation-state, the welfare-state, postmodernism and technological change, affect the definition of citizenship and its various components, as well as citizenship attitudes and behaviors. She concludes that the affinity among nationalism, patriotism and citizenship will probably persist in the foreseeable future. In spite of trends such as globalization and the emergence of new supernational structures, and growing national, ethnic, and cultural heterogeneity within nation-states, nation-states seem to be diversifying and developing rather than fading away.

Postmodernism, as a negation of all grand narratives, could endanger the unity implied in citizenship, and become antithetical to emancipatory strategies of social movements toward greater equality and social justice. However, should it not evolve into indiscriminate pluralism, plural cultural forms may come to constitute a kind of restraint against all forms of total political ideology. Ichilov proposes a multidimensional approach to citizenship.

Chapters 2 and 3 describe changes in two former Soviet Bloc countries – Russia and Hungary. In Chapter 2, 'Russian Citizenship: Behavior, Attitudes and Prospects for a Russian Democracy', Shlapentokh reveals the shortcomings of civil society in Russia following the collapse of the Soviet Union in 1991. He characterizes citizenship behavior of Russians by radical alienation from the newly emerging state, which claims to be democratic, and analyzes the sources of these feelings. The manifestations of alienation from society include the disinterest of Russians in social values and the emergence of an ideological vacuum; the breakdown of community bonds and the growing feelings among individuals that they can only rely upon themselves and should give priority to their own selfish interests; political apathy; contempt for the political and economic élites; indifference to the army and attempts of young people to avoid military service by all means; and indifference to the fate of Russian citizens who reside in former Soviet republics.

Russian passivity, Shlapentokh claims, came as a surprise to scholars studying mass movements. The Russian situation of a brusque decline in the standard of living, of growing social inequality, of a breakdown of social services, and of growing rates of criminal violence, coupled with weak government and limited means for repression of rebellion, seems to meet virtually all the theoretical requirements for insurgence. Yet only marginal and sporadic actions of dissent have been taken by citizens. Shlapentokh attributes the passivity of Russian citizenry to several factors. First, in the name of their yearning for order, stability and security, Russians are ready to bear the harshest tribulations which would push most other people to the barricades. Second, Russians tend to be pessimistic and to believe that any actions undertaken can only make their situation worse. Third, Russians tend to be conservative, and regard changes as being too risky. Shlapentokh expresses great skepticism concerning the feasibility of restoring Russian civil society and citizenship feelings of solidarity in the decades to come.

In Chapter 3, 'Citizenship Education in Hungary: Ideals and Reality', Mátrai describes the change of regime and its consequences for citizenship and citizenship education in Hungary. As a result of the democratization of the political system, and the introduction of the free-market economy, the Hungarian population gained much in terms of civil, political and human rights, but lost a great deal in terms of social rights. Social services which were previously perceived as an integral part of citizenship rights, and were offered free of charge to everyone, no longer exist. In addition, the Hungarian economy is plagued by a mounting foreign debt and high inflation rates. Hungarian society is torn apart by ethnic conflicts, growing social inequalities (in income, for example), rising crime rates, and influx of immigrants and refugees from neighboring countries.

Using a modified version of Ichilov's (1990) model concerning dimensions and role patterns of citizenship, Mátrai provides a systematic content analysis of the Hungarian citizenship education curriculum and instructional materials. Her conclusion is that the image portrayed in the instructional materials is that of a knowledgeable citizen, capable of acquiring and evaluating information independently. However, youngsters are encouraged to become spectators rather than active participants in the political process.

Based on two recent studies of political attitudes and behaviors of Hungarian teenagers and young adults, Mátrai reports of very low rates of actual political participation, as well as of intentions to become active. This includes low rates of young people who said they would 'surely' or 'probably' vote in the parliamentary elections. Young Hungarians seem to dislike politics, distrust politicians, and possess a low sense of political efficacy. These attitudes have been deeply embedded in the Hungarian political culture. Mátrai concludes by saying that citizenship education should attempt to help reverse these trends. Hungarian citizenship education has taken significant strides in that direction, but much more must be done.

Chapters 4 and 5 are related to Israel, and to the Palestinian population of the West Bank during the recent Palestinian uprising. In Chapter 4, 'Nation-Building, Collective Identities, Democracy and Citizenship Education in Israel', Ichilov analyzes the central trends concerning citizenship education in Israel from the pre-state period until recently. She argues that citizenship education mirrors the social, political, and value changes within any given society. In Israel there has been a shift from the highly particularistic, emotional, and expressive 'Zionist citizenship' education, to apolitical 'civic education' from the mid 1950s. The educational system, which had been affiliated with rival political ideologies, became unified and depoliticized. Until 1967, civic education was restricted to the study of the structural and legal aspects of citizenship, excluding all controversial issues. Since 1967 politics was gradually introduced back into the schools, and students were exposed to the pluralistic and conflictual nature of the social and political reality in Israel. In 1985, a newly introduced policy concerning 'education for democracy', made the pendulum swing in the direction of universal humanistic values, marginalizing national-particularistic values.

In Chapter 5, 'Contested Regimes, Civic Dissent, and the Political Socialization of Children and Adolescents: The Case of the Palestinian Uprising', Mazawi argues that political socialization theory and research paid hardly any attention to processes of political learning within contested regimes. Unlike uncontested regimes in which regime legitimacy enjoys a wide consensus, no majority consent exists in contested regimes as to the exercise of power by a single authority. Instead, competing contenders to authority struggle (many times violently) against each other. Consequently, youngsters in many parts of the world grow up within unstable sociopolitical environments, and conflict situations. In contested regimes, thus, the centrality of conflict, and its reproduction at the various levels of action, become a basic feature of the political socialization process. Mazawi uses the case of the recent Palestinian Uprising (Intifada), to demonstrate how exposure to various experiences within a contested regime affects the structure of the political learning processes of children and adolescents. Palestinian youngsters acquired attitudes, behaviors, skills, and political ideologies and learned to identify themselves with symbols which were consistent with the Palestinian struggle. Mazawi concludes that 'the street' as the major agent and context of political socialization, and the peers became more significant in shaping youngsters' political world than the family and the school.

Chapters 6 and 7 deal with citizenship issues in the US. In Chapter 6, 'Citizenship and Citizenship Education in the United States in the 1990s', Braungart and Braungart point out that following changes in American life during the 1980s and 1990s, diverse experts have been claiming that national identity, civil behavior, the country's youth, and citizenship education are declining. Braungart and Braungart argue that before proceeding to redesign citizenship education, based on the aforementioned assumptions, it is necessary to assess objectively the status of American society, the beliefs and outlook of youth, and the way citizenship education is conducted in the United States.

The authors utilize national statistics to describe changes in American life, and seven national data sets are examined to determine young people's personal conduct and collective orientations in the 1990s. Overall, the authors report that while 1990s youth appear strong in areas of citizenship such as national identity, social equality and concern for the community, they are weak in political interest, exercising self-restraint, and acquiring knowledge. By evaluating recent societal trends and national data on youth, several widespread misconceptions about America's political culture, civil society, and depictions of its youth are identified, providing a clearer assessment of ways to enhance the education of a nation's upcoming generation of citizens. The authors provide a brief overview of citizenship education in the United States and its critics, and offer their recommendations for inculcating citizenship orientations.

In Chapter 7, 'A Disquieting Outlook for Democracy: Mass Media, News, and Citizenship Education in the US', Hepburn reviews the changing sources of news on public affairs in the USA, and discusses the implications for citizenship education. She maintains that, paradoxically, while the accessibility to clear communication of news and views has been heightened by advanced technology, the public seems to be less informed, less involved, and more distracted from public affairs. Drawing on a wide array of research, Hepburn seeks to explain this enigma.

Between 1961 and 1991 there has been a steady decline in the use of newspapers, while television has gradually and persistently increased in importance and became the predominant news source throughout the US. Hepburn labels the US a 'television society' – a society in which mass media, especially the TV, dominates much of the free time of its citizens.

According to Hepburn, TV use has a negative effect on the acquisition and processing of information. Much of it results from a rating system according to which a program is judged primarily by its commercial value – i.e., whether it can attract more viewers. Television conveys to the public an over simplistic, over dramatized, shallow and often one-sided image of occurrences in the political and social world around them. Television news is reported in short, fast-paced, dramatic episodes interspersed with advertising. Coverage of fundamental public issues, such as health care and unemployment, is often treated with a simplified 'story line' about an individual, instead of providing general information or analysis of the issue.

The public's lack of awareness of the power and pervasiveness of TV in their lives further complicates the situation.

Hepburn argues that formal school education and various forms of lifelong education must change if citizens are to become better equipped to deal with public affairs. This, she proposes, can be done in several ways. For example, by educating students for critical viewing; by making the various aspects of the mass-media-oriented society part of the content of social science knowledge and inquiry in school and college courses; and through teacher education.

In Chapter 8, 'Education for Democracy in Argentina: Effects of a Newspaper-in-School Program', Chaffee, Morduchowicz and Galperin examine the effects upon democratic perceptions and attitudes of fifth- and sixth-grade students throughout Argentina of an educational program introducing the use of newspapers into schools. They report that the program had significant effects in a country that is experiencing difficulty in establishing democracy after decades of political instability. Students whose teachers used local newsapers in class scored higher than a control group on political tolerance, support for democracy, expressing political opinions, discussing politics with family members, and reading the newspaper at home. Each of these effects was stronger among students from lower socioeconomic backgrounds, a notable 'gap-closing' phenomenon in a highly stratified country. A survey of the teachers and classroom strategies indicated that teaching about the free-press system enhanced political interest, knowledge, opinion holding, news reading, support for democracy, and interpersonal discussion of politics with friends and family. The second most powerful teaching method was assigning students to write essays on controversial issues they read about in the newspapers. This experience was related in students to heightened political interest, political knowledge, news reading, normative support for democracy, and tolerance for diversity. Should these outcomes endure through adulthood, they could be deemed of great importance for the establishing of a long-term viable democratic regime, and a democratic political culture in Argentina.

In Chapter 9, 'Democracy minus Women is not Democracy: Gender and World Changes in Citizenship', Sapiro explores the place of gender egalitarianism in democratic theory, and the extent to which it represents an analytical definition or a normative prescription. She maintains that 'democracy minus women' has been accepted as democracy throughout history. The measures that have been employed to determine whether a nation has crossed the threshold of democracy have usually required looking at men's but not women's relationship to the state. Sapiro demonstrates how the principle theories and practices of democracy developed in the United States and Western Europe during the past three centuries have been very basically gendered, and depended on specific notions of the distinct but functionally interdependent roles and characters of women and men. She also shows, using empirical studies, that attachment to democracy in many Western nations was not substantially related to whether people identified gender equality as a worthwhile social goal.

Sapiro argues that women's movements can play an important role in the incorporation of gender equality into democratic theory and practice. Such movements are not just agents of mobilization and conduits of pressure on political leaders: they are also agents of socialization and education.

In Chapter 10, 'Apolitical Patriotism and Citizenship Education: The Case of New Zealand', Hirshberg asserts that the gradual and non-conflictual breakaway of New Zealand from British colonialism, and the slow drift into a separate national identity, resulted in the development of apolitical nationalism and patriotism. Lingering British allegiance stunted the growth of full-fledged New Zealand nationalism, and indigenous national symbols very gradually replaced the symbols of the British Empire.

In the last couple of decades, citizens' relationship to the state have been altered by the decline of the welfare state. Hirshberg argues that the 'cradle to grave' arrangement in New Zealand, however benign, reinforced a paternalistic social compact whereby the state would look after citizens when in need, while citizens would passively obey the law. The waning of the welfare state activated the New Zealand citizenry, and made citizens more aware and better informed about politics.

Overall, citizenship education is far less salient and persistent in New Zealand than in other Western democracies, notably the United States. Early in this century, citizenship education was intended to produce loyal, patriotic subjects of the Crown. These particularist and nationalist notions of citizenship, have been replaced by transnational universalism. School-children are taught that they are citizens not just of New Zealand, but of a highly pluralistic world.

Hirshberg anticipates that as New Zealand approaches the twenty-first century, knowledge of political issues, electoral processes and avenues for participation will become increasingly relevant for New Zealanders. Greater attention to citizenship education is likely to play an important role in these developments.

In Chapter 11, 'Political Culture, Education and Democratic Citizenship in Africa', Harber claims that, in contrast with the early 1970s where most states of sub-Saharan Africa were ruled either by one party or military regimes, there has been a renewed interest in democracy in Africa. This trend has manifested itself in a rapid series of multi-party elections across the continent. He argues, however, that the extent to which these newly emerging democratic political institutions can be made sustainable in Africa will greatly depend on the political cultures in which they exist.

Harber explores some of the problems facing education as a potential mechanism for promoting democracy in Africa by examining two case studies of traditional political cultures – the Hausa/Fulani of northern Nigeria, and the Tswana of Botswana – and the patterns of child rearing in each. The Hausa culture does not seem to sit comfortably with democracy, whereas the Tswana culture is more compatible with democracy. Examining the role of the schools he argues that if schools in Africa wish to provide education for democracy in terms of peaceful debate, mutual respect and the protection of human rights, then the organization of both classrooms and schools must be more congruent with those aims.

In Chapter 12, 'Patronage, Domestication or Empowerment: Citizenship Development and Citizenship Education in Hong Kong', Tsang portrays Hong Kong as 'a borrowed place in borrowed time'. The Hong Kong citizenry is caught in a very peculiar situation regarding the political future of their country. They are captured, Tsang argues, between British patronage, and the attempts by the People's Republic of China (PRC) to domesticate the Hong Kong Chinese.

Hong Kong, which was a British colony for more than a century, was surrendered to the Chinese government in 1997. Anticipating the inevitable hand-over of the colony back to the PRC, the British started to democratize the political system. This has generally been viewed by citizens as a belated and patronizing handing-down-from-above of political rights. Similarly, the majority of the Hong Kong Chinese whose families sought refuge in the country when the Chinese Communists rose to power in 1949, still hold feelings of defiance to the PRC. Tsang examines the development of citizenship in Hong Kong in recent decades, focusing on the institutional and attitudinal levels. He also shows how modifications in the citizenship education curriculum in the Hong Kong school system reflect changes concerning citizenship and political configurations.

In Chapter 13, 'Citizenship and Citizenship Education in Britain', Lister analyzes the key factors which affected the crystallization of 'citizenship' in Britain. To mention a few, Lister shows that although the concept of citizenship is usually associated with republics and democracies, it has become a very meaningful idea within the British monarchy, without a written constitution or a bill of rights. British political culture, Lister argues, has been influenced by the fact that Britain is a multinational state made up of the English, Welsh, Scots, and Irish. The on-going civil strife in Northern Ireland makes Lister wonder how united is the United Kingdom, despite English dominance. The return of Hong Kong to China on 30 June 1997 marked the end of the Empire. Britain is still hesitant about how to relate to the new Europe.

In Britain, Lister argues, 'Education' had to come before 'Citizenship Education', because educational provision was divided and unequal. Between the Educational Acts of 1918 and 1944 most people in Britain had only elementary education, consisting mainly of training in the 'three Rs' (Reading, Writing and Arithmetic). Lister examines the factors which worked for and against the development of citizenship education in Britain. An important breakthrough occurred in 1974, when the Nuffield Foundation granted funds for a Programme for Political Education, a curriculum development and research project, which aimed to promote 'Political Literacy' and democratic values for all students in secondary schools. However, in spite of significant progress in the introduction of 'Citizenship Education' in the schools, there are many would-be citizens in search of a form of modern citizenship, appropriate for a democratic and pluralistic society.

In Chapter 14, 'Conclusion: The Challenge of Citizenship Education in a Changing World', Ichilov discusses the great variety of political contexts in which youngsters grow up today, and the challenge which these present for citizenship education. Examining trends and developments concerning citizenship education, she concludes that citizenship education is needed today perhaps more than ever to provide a sense of purpose, solidarity, and guidance in a fragmented and a rapidly changing world.

REFERENCES

Boyne, R. and Rattansi, A. (eds) (1990), *Postmodernism and society*. London: Macmillan.
Boyne, R. and Rattansi, A. (1990), 'The theory and politics of postmodernism: By way of an introduction', in R. Boyne and A. Rattansi (eds), *Postmodernism and society*, pp.1–46.
Fukuyama, F. (1992), *The end of history and the last man*. New York: Free Press.
Havel, V. (1995), 'Democracy's forgotten dimension', *Democracy*, 6 (2), 3–11.
Tilly, C. (1993), 'National self-determination as a problem for all of us', *Daedalus*, 22 (3–4), 29–47.

1

PATTERNS OF CITIZENSHIP IN A CHANGING WORLD

ORIT ICHILOV

The purpose of this chapter is to examine the processes which may transform the configurations and meanings of the ideological, cultural, political, and social components of 'citizenship'. The contents and patterns of citizenship education will, no doubt, have to be readjusted, in order to adequately prepare the younger generation to assume their role as citizens. One reason why this is a difficult task is that a mainstream theory of democracy is nonexistent today, and has been replaced by rather fragmented and isolated endeavors. The lack of a comprehensive theory of democracy further erodes the foundations of democracy because it becomes impossible to have reasons for existing institutions, and because democracies are not viable unless their citizens understand them (Sartori, 1987).

Citizenship is a complex and multidimensional concept. It consists of legal, cultural, social, and political elements, and provides citizens with defined rights and obligations, a sense of identity, and social bonds. The classical definition of citizenship rests on the assertion that citizenship involves a balance or fusion between rights and obligations. More recent definitions stress the affinity and identity dimensions of citizenship. According to Heater (1990), for example, citizenship is one among many identities of an individual, which 'helps to tame the divisive passions of other identities' (p.184). It does so by conveying to each individual citizen a society's collective memory; cultural togetherness and nationality and the collaborative sense of purpose in fraternity. These elements bind people together with a common identity of citizenship. Marshall (1977, 1981) differentiates among three dimensions of citizenship: civil, political and social, and emphasizes the social aspect. The civil element of citizenship is composed of the rights necessary for individual freedom, and the institution most directly associated with it is the rule of law and a system of courts. The political component consists of the right to participate in the exercise of political power. Political rights are associated with parliamentary institutions. Social rights represent the right to the prevailing standard of life and the social heritage of society. Included are entitlements such as unemployment benefits and provisions for health care and education. Citizenship in the social sense is based on an individual obligation to contribute taxation to a state system of provision, and to a method of redistribution of resources to those fellow citizens who are unable to provide for their own needs. All these forms of citizenship, in Marshall's view, have been institutionalized in the welfare state. The existence of a welfare state is, therefore, a requisite of modern democracy and democratic citizenship. From an economic vantage point, citizenship controls access to the scarce resources of society and hence this allocative function could also become the basis of a profound conflict in modern societies over citizenship membership criteria (Turner, 1990, 1997).

Potent social, political, and economic forces seem to be eroding the traditional foundations which are needed to form a social bond and to transform a random collection of consumers, or an aggregation of political, ethnic, and economic interests into citizens striving for the common good. In this chapter, some of these forces will be discussed.

CHANGING PATTERNS OF CITIZENSHIP

Citizenship and Nationalism

'Citizenship' as an expression of the political relations between the individual and the state is closely related to the concepts of nationalism and the nation-state (Janowitz, 1983). Nationalism, which is founded on ethnicity, religion, ideology and territory, has been viewed as a binding force, which provides people with collective and self-identities (Greenfeld, 1993; White, 1985; Kashti, 1994; Kelly and Ronan, 1987). Nationalism locates the source of individual identity within a 'people', which is seen as the bearer of sovereignty. The idea of the 'nation' becomes the central object of loyalty, and the basis of collective solidarity (Greenfeld, 1992).

The decline of nationalism as a result of economic and political globalization processes was predicted by Marx as early as 1848, during the time called 'the spring of nations', when nationalism was at its peak. Marx claimed that the speedy and imminent demise of nationalism was made inevitable by the globalization of the economy implied in the spread of capitalism (Greenfeld, 1993). The anticipation of the collapse of nationalism, often for reasons similar to those mentioned by Marx, remained a popular theme, and is gaining new popularity in the 1990s. For example, Brzezinski (1970) maintained that in the post-industrial world nationalism is ceasing to be the compelling force that determines social change. The emergence of newer and larger frameworks, such as the European Community, indicates that the autarkic ideas of the industrial age have lost their appeal. An inevitable consequence, he predicted, would be a rising global consciousness, with citizenship identity accentuating global awareness instead of nationalism. Hobsbawm (1990) maintains that the history of the late twentieth and early twenty-first centuries will be written as the history of a world which can no longer be contained within the limits of 'nations' and 'nation-states' as these used to be defined, either politically, or economically, or culturally, or even linguistically. Such units will be absorbed or dislocated by a new supernational structuring of the globe. Nations and nationalism will be present only in subordinate and minor roles.

Rifkin (1995) estimates that the shift from an economy based on material, energy, and labor to one grounded on information and communication further reduces the importance of the nation-state as a critical player in guaranteeing the fortunes of the marketplace. He considers global corporations to represent quasi-political institutions that exercise great power over people and places, by reason of control over information and communication. The use of military force, a primary function of the modern nation-state, he argues, is no longer needed to seize vital raw materials in a high-tech global economy. Standing armies cannot stop or slow down the 'invasion' of information and communication across national frontiers.

However, believed to be a spent force only a few years ago, nationalism has taken on rather a new life. Greenfeld (1993) argues that economic globalization is entirely consistent with nationalism, and does not erode its strength. People will never agree to be deprived of the dignity which they acquire through nationality unless alternative guarantees of dignity are offered. Marxism appealed to Jews, among other things, because it promised to deliver them from their nationality, which in those European countries where Marxism had an appeal, such as Germany and Russia, was associated with unbearable indignity (Greenfeld, 1993). The European Community (EC) is another case in point. So long as European unity was limited to economics, the idea aroused no protest and little sentiment in general. The Treaty of Maastricht, signed in December 1991, declaring EC control over virtually all policy areas, seemed to assault the distinctive national sovereignties and prestige of the member states. As a result, a substantial proportion of Western Europeans do not want unification, however interdependent their economies (Greenfeld, 1993; Hoffman, 1993; Mann, 1993; Brubaker, 1992a). The unification of Europe, it seems, may well rekindle national sentiments and old resentments instead of extinguishing them.

Janowitz (1983) examined the congruence and validity of concepts such as patriotism, nationalism and citizenship, which represent attachment and obligations to a country and a political community, in the face of a changing world. For him, citizenship consists of civil rights and obligations. However, he assigns special significance to obligations on the part of citizens – i.e., the contributions and sacrifices a citizen makes to keep the political system effective – for the viability of democracy. Citizens must be motivated to perform their duties willingly. In this respect, he considers citizenship to be closely linked with patriotism and nationalism because the latter provide an incentive to fulfill civic obligations. Janowitz defines patriotism as 'a primordial attachment to a territory and a society – a deeply felt and primitive sentiment of belonging; a sense of identification similar to religious, racial, or ethnic identifications. It has been historically associated with the ethos of modern national societies' (p.8). As nationalism and patriotism become battered notions, allegedly related to xenophobia or militarism, Janowitz offered the term 'civic consciousness' instead. It pertains to the positive and meaningful attachments a person develops to the nation-state, and involves elements of reason and self-criticism as well as personal commitment.

Some scholars advocate new and more universal concepts of citizenship. Soysal (1994), for example, supports one whose organizing and legitimating principles are based on universal personhood rather than national belonging. The institutionalization of rights through the UN charter of human rights can be regarded as a central aspect of this trend of globalization (Robertson, 1990). Citizenship defines bounded populations with a specific set of rights and duties, and excludes others on the grounds of nationality. 'Postnational' citizenship confers upon every person the right and duty of participating in the authority structures and public life of a polity, regardless of their historical or cultural ties to that community (Derrida, 1986).

These issues concerning citizenship patterns are not merely of a theoretical nature. The institutional growth of the European Community, for example, has raised important concerns about citizen status, not only for minorities, but also for all forms of transient and migrant labor. Issues associated with state membership for aboriginal communities, stateless peoples, and refugees have brought to the fore the implications of human rights in relation to citizenship. Turner (1993) suggests that human rights complement rather than replace citizenship rights. But, as politics become more global, human rights will have an expanded role in the normative regulation of politics.

Janowitz (1983) disputes the idea that a world allegiance needs to be substituted for national patriotism, and does not expect national citizenship to dissolve. He cautions that new communalism, such as the outbursts of ethnic/racial nationalism in the US in the 1960s and 1970s, and the desire of certain groups to become 'hyphenated Americans' (e.g., Mexican-Americans, Black-Americans, etc.), can only erode the foundations of civil obligation. Similarly, economic ideology – left, liberal, or right – is also incapable of supplying élites and democratic publics with the rationale for the values upon which democracies are founded. Civic consciousness is irreplaceable for collective problem solving in a democratic society, which rests on voluntarism, motivated by a sense of moral responsibility for the collective well-being. Furthermore, civic consciousness, Janowitz argues, is not only compatible with but required for both national and international responsibilities and obligations. The idea of citizenship, which is founded on the twin pillars of civil rights and obligations, is therefore necessary to support the dynamics of democratic political institutions.

It seems that the nation-state is not in any general decline anywhere else. The breakdown (in many instances violently) of multinational states into nation-states (for example, Czechoslovakia, Yugoslavia) is evident. Given the destruction of much of civil society in the former Soviet Bloc, nationalism is the most plausible and most easily available candidate for filling the resulting void (Gellner, 1993; Brubaker, 1992b; Duffy, Sullivan and Polakiewicz, 1993). Similar trends seem to characterize the Arab world. Kramer (1993), who describes and analyzes the fragmentation of the 'Arab Nation', argues that at present many Arabs openly doubt whether there is a collective Arab mission. Islamic activists prefer to think of themselves first and foremost as Muslims. Others prefer to be known as Egyptians, Syrians, Jordanians, Moroccans – citizens of over 20 independent states, each with its own flag and own interests.

Hobsbawm (1990), however, argues that the current wave of ethnic unrest does not represent the rebirth of nationalism. This unrest can be viewed as a response to the overwhelmingly non-national and non-nationalistic principles of state formation in the greater part of the twentieth-century world. He argues that multi-ethnic and multi-communal states are the norm, rather than the monolithic 'nation-state'. He also estimates that the role of national economies has been undermined by shifts in the international division of labor, whose basic units are transnational or multinational enterprises of all sizes, and by the development of international centers and networks of economic transaction which are generally outside the control of state governments.

In conclusion, it appears that nation-states in Europe and other continents seem to be diversifying, and developing rather than dying (Mann, 1993). There is a growing general concern with how a nation's citizenship and identities should be defined, preserved, or reinvented. The preoccupation is not solely related to economic growth, but to issues of culture, such as citizenship and education.

Nationalism and Democratic Citizenship

Is nationalism compatible with citizenship within modern democracies? Hobsbawm (1990) claims that while nineteenth-century nationalist movements were typically unificatory and emancipatory, late twentieth-century movements are essentially divisive, claiming ethnic, linguistic or religious uniqueness, and rejecting modern modes of political organization, both national and supernational. Thus, they are no longer associated with modernity and progress, unlike nineteenth-century nationalist movements, and are inappropriate within a democracy. Others, however, make distinctions among various forms of nationalism, showing that some may coexist in harmony with democracy. Barber (1995) considers all the extremist political forms which he terms 'Jihad' – referring to the fierce politics of religious, tribal and other zealots – a threat to democracy. Greenfeld (1992) differentiates between four types of nationalism along two axes: individualistic-libertarian vs collective-authoritarian, and civic vs ethnic nationalism. She argues that different forms of nationalism are grounded in different values, which in turn give rise to different patterns of social behavior, culture, identity and political institutions. The individualistic-libertarian type of nationalism, she claims, overlaps with the basic tenets of democracy: it locates sovereignty within the people, and it is because these individuals exercise sovereignty that they are members of a nation. Collective-authoritarian nationalism, on the other hand, implies the uniqueness of the people, as it is their very distinctness that makes people a nation. Unlike the former notion of nationality, this one is collectivist rather than individualist. Greenfeld (1992) also classifies nationalism according to the criteria of membership in the national collective which may be either 'civic' or 'ethnic'. 'Civic' implies that nationality is in principle open and voluntaristic, and can be acquired. 'Ethnic' implies that nationality is a generic characteristic which has nothing to do with individual will. She, therefore, asserts that certain types of nationality are more compatible with the ideas of liberal democracy than others.

The compatibility of nationalism and democracy greatly depends on the strength of civil society – an intermediary entity, standing between the private sphere and the state. Civil society is conceived as the realm of organized social life that is voluntary, self-generating, largely self-supporting, autonomous from the state, and bound by a legal order or set of shared rules. It involves citizens acting collectively in a public sphere to express their interests, passions, and ideas, exchange information, achieve mutual goals, make demands on the state, and hold the state officially accountable (Diamond, 1994; Keane, 1988; Pratte, 1988; Waltzer, 1991). By containing the power of governments, and by profoundly legitimating democracy among citizens, civil society plays a significant role in building and consolidating democracy. The feasibility of a stable democracy in the former Soviet Union has been in doubt mainly because seven decades of totalitarian rule obliterated not only private property and economic markets, but civil society and any real concept of citizenship as well. There are hardly any promising foundations on which to build democratic institutions (Gellner, 1993; Ordeshook, 1995). Given the enormity of the obstacles confronting it, Russia has made impressive strides toward democracy and market economy. Yet even these partial and precarious gains could be imperiled by the current tidal wave of crime and corruption (Cohen, 1995).

Technology and Democratic Citizenship

Technological advancements may profoundly change the reality of citizenship. Brzezinski (1970) coined the concept 'technotronic' to described modern society, a society which he claims, is shaped culturally, psychologically, socially, and economically by the impact of technology and electronics, particularly in the area of computers and communications. One of the impacts of globalization and technological developments, he argues, is that people in the 'technotronic' era will tend do identify themselves by tested criteria, such as IQ and aptitudes, rather than by reference to more personal standards and attributes.

Some scholars believe that technology can be used to invigorate the alienated citizenry of representative democracies, and to overcome its sense of being politically powerless and inefficacious. Through the Internet, telephone, cable, fax, television, and other modern means of communication, citizens may send and receive torrents of facts and ideas, they may lobby their representatives, discuss public issues, exchange views, mount campaigns, and become better informed and more influential (Wolff, 1976; Williams, 1982; Valaskakis and Annopoulis, 1982). Furthermore, instead of making their voice known once every few years at the polls, citizens may have an opportunity to participate more frequently in decision-making processes. 'Electronic town meetings' can be held, for example, and citizens can be asked to cast their votes periodically on issues concerning domestic and international policies. Technology could give people more of a voice in politics, and a 'semi-direct democracy' could be instituted shifting more political power from politicians to the people (Naisbitt, 1982; Toffler and Toffler, 1994).

Others are skeptical about the power of electronics to substitute for a deliberative process, including discussion with other citizens, developing a shared sense of social responsibility, and enhancing individual action and identity through mutual involvement (Gitlin, 1981; Malbin, 1982; Laudon, 1977, 1984; Arterton, 1987). The rates of citizens' participation in televoting and referendums also cast doubt on the feasibility of involving a sizable portion of the citizenry on a regular basis, and of sustaining their enthusiasm over a prolonged period of time. Turnouts in referendums are usually lower than in general elections, and the initially low participation in televoting declines even further as the novelty is wearing off (Malbin, 1982). It seems that it takes more than technology to convince and motivate citizens actively to participate in decision-making processes on a regular basis.

Democratic Citizenship and the Welfare State

Capitalist democracy is the predominant politico-economic system within many societies. Indeed, in 1960 Lipset wrote that 'democracy is related to the state of economic development. The more well-to-do a nation, the greater the chances that it will sustain democracy' (p.31). However, monetarism and an emphasis on markets has brought into question the foundations of the welfare state, and of citizens' social rights. Diamond (1992, 1994) demonstrated that improvements in the physical quality and dignity of people's lives better predict the presence and degree of democracy than does the level of per capita national wealth. To the extent that benefits are grossly maldistributed, he argues, economic development may do little to promote democracy or may even generate stresses and contradictions that are hostile to democracy. Likewise, when most of the population is literate and assured of minimal material needs, class tensions and radical political orientations tend to diminish. However, at present it is liberty rather than equality that even socialists now turn to with enthusiasm, with personal freedom given a greater prominence on most leftist agendas than the redistribution of wealth (Andrews, 1991, p.12).

For Marshall (1977, 1981) the social component of citizenship, which is embedded in the welfare state, is one of the corner stones of democracy. Held (1987, 1991) also considers citizenship to combine in rather unusual ways the public and social with the individual aspects of political life. The welfare state has been criticized by both left and right, and has eroded in many Western democracies. The left criticized the failure of the welfare state to bring about a fully egalitarian society, pointing to phenomena such as unemployment and gender inequality in the labor market. Mann (1987) went as far as suggesting that citizenship is merely a ruling class strategy for containing class conflict. The right, on its part, criticized the welfare state for undermining voluntarism, pluralism and self-help. For many critics, the contemporary reliance on the market to solve political and social problems is a savage attack on the principles of democratic citizenship. For others, the collapse of the command economies in Eastern Europe and the Soviet Union is a great triumph of liberalism and the rights of individual citizenships to shape their own future (Turner, 1993). There seems to be a general agreement, however, that social gaps among nations and within nations have been widening all over the world, and that this situation creates alienated and apathetic citizens, and great social unrest that may undermine democracy. Not surprisingly, there are differences of opinion concerning how the situation should be handled.

New right arguments suggest that economic deregulation would cut back on welfare bureaucracies, encourage welfare pluralism, and that the result would be a more efficient welfare system which would protect individual rights. Saunders (1993), for example, disputes Marshall's view that any erosion of the welfare state necessarily represents an erosion of citizenship rights. He argues that the emergence of widespread privatized consumption enhances rather than diminishes citizenship, and that a privatized mode of consumption endorses the freedom of choice and consumer accountability. He suggests that vouchers and other forms of cash-based enablement policies will insure that the poor can compete effectively as consumers in the non-welfare state. This indicates that social rights, unlike political and civil rights, are regarded as 'cash benefits' which can be revoked, rather than as a basic citizenship right in democracy.

Barber (1995) expresses his concerns about the detrimental consequences of consumerist capitalism (which he labels 'McWorld') for democracy. In his view, cosmopolitan companies tend to undermine the autonomy of individuals and nations alike. They do so primarily by creating global classes of haves and have-nots with no sense of local community. Consequently, democratic governments lose their ability to balance the interests of economic utility and social justice.

Rifkin (1995) presents a disturbing vision of 'the end of work' era. As a result of a high-technology revolution, he maintains, sophisticated computers, robotics, and other cutting-edge technologies are fast replacing human workers in every sector of the economy. The world is becoming polarized into two irreconcilable forces: an information élite that controls and manages the high-tech global economy, and masses of permanently displaced workers. Rising rates of unemployment have coincided with the lowering of the social security net in many countries around the globe. The result is growing political unrest, alienation, rising rates of crime and violence, and the re-emergence of neo-fascist and neo-Nazi movements. Rifkin is confident, however, that a new social contract can be reached, which would modify the negative consequences associated with the post-market era. He argues that as government has taken over many of the tasks previously performed by the community, these functions should be handed back to the volunteer sector, where action is guided by the altruistic motivation of serving others, and by a sense of a common bond. However, experience thus far concerning the privatization of social services, such as health care and education, suggests overwhelmingly that social gaps have become wider and that segregation based on social class and ethnicity has increasingly come to characterize schools and other client-serving organizations, which in the past catered to more mixed populations (Isaac and Armat, 1990; Willms, 1994; Ichilov and Mazawi, 1997). Furthermore, a large homeless population exists within Western democracies, notably in the US, a situation which infringes on human dignity and citizenship rights. Closing down mental health institutions magnified the homelessness phenomenon, and parks, alleys, vacant lots, steam grates and city pavements have become 'open air mental institutions' (Isaac and Armat, 1990). The decline of the welfare state in the

West seems to grant greater freedom of choice mainly to the affluent social echelons, unless one considers the 'liberty' of the sick and poor to sleep under the bridge a true freedom of choice. In a democracy the right to choose should also be allocated equally.

Citizenship and Postmodernism

Postmodernity is a newly proclaimed perspective for analyzing current developments in Western societies. One way of defining postmodernity might be in terms of the end of apprehension, the final arrival at the future and the end of revelation (Boyne and Rattansi, 1990). A vision of this kind lay behind the 'End of Ideology' thesis advanced by Bell, Lipset and others in the 1950s and early 1960s, and also behind various conceptions of post-industrial society (Brzezinski, 1970; Bell, 1974, 1988; Lipset, 1981). By the mid-1960s, 'Protestantism and Catholicism, fascism, capitalism, communism, and social democracy [had] all lost power to inspire Western people to work hard, to live normally, or to change the world' (Lipset, 1981, p.531). The dominant pattern seems increasingly to be that of highly individualistic, unstructured, changing perspectives, and compelling ideologies are giving way to compulsive ideas, but without the eschatology that characterized other historical eras (Brzezinski, 1970; Fukuyama, 1992). Bell (1988) argues that while the ideologies of the nineteenth century were humanistic, universalistic, and fashioned by intellectuals, the newly emerging ideologies in Asia and Africa are parochial, instrumental, and created by political leaders. The driving forces of the old ideologies were social equality and freedom, while economic development and national power underlie new ideologies.

The end of ideology thesis can be regarded as anticipating the thesis of the end of metanarratives proclaimed by the theorists of postmodernity (Boyne and Rattensi, 1990). Lyotard (1984), for example, continues some of the themes included in the end-of-ideology and post-industrialist-society theories. He describes the postmodern attitude as one of incredulity toward all statements which make out that things have to be done in one, and only one, particular way. He believes that all of the legitimate narratives of Western society, which provide valid and definitive principles, in any sphere, applicable across all societies, can now be seen to be defunct. The pattern of change is in the direction of fragmentation of old cultures and the proliferation of new values, attitudes, lifestyles and political movements in their place. The emerging character of contemporary political culture is pluralistic, anarchic, disorganized, rhetorical, stylized, ironic and abstruse (Kroker and Cook, 1988; Featherstone, 1988; Held, 1987, pp.241–2; Bourdieu, 1984; Baudrillard, 1980; Norris, 1990).

Crook (1990) argued that postmodernist theory itself resolves into a monistic metaphysics which is no more acceptable than the modernism it contests, and that its radical pretensions are flawed by the nihilistic implications of its monism.

Citizenship in the Postmodern Political Culture

Gibbins (1989, p.14) characterizes the postmodern political culture as follows:

> a. an affluent 'postmaterialist' middle class has created new alliances around environmental, peace and feminist issues, and new forms of political expression in symbolic and life-style politics; b. political order and legitimacy are threatened as objectivity, commensurability, unity and the integrated self are deconstructed and replaced by relativity, pluralism, fragmentation and polyculturalism; c. postmodernism signifies discontinuity between economy, society and polity; an information and consumer economy coincides with heightened conflict between public and private spheres, growing distrust of government, and realignments of party and class allegiances; d. an eclectic and amorphous culture of plurality and mixed life-styles is combined with an emphasis on leisure and consumption, and freedom, spontaneity and gratification take precedence over discipline, authority and predictability; e. the emerging character of contemporary political culture is pluralistic, anarchic, disorganised, rhetorical, stylized, and ironic.

The postmodern vision of society and the political culture may have adverse effects upon citizenship orientations and behaviors. Some believe that in their very plurality, these new cultural forms may come to constitute a kind of prophylactic against all forms of total political ideology. However, much radical thought, particularly Marxism and feminism, holds that the widespread hegemony of capitalist and/or patriarchal values still functions as total ideology, and thus continues to stands in need of opposition, demystification and dismantling. They have actually rejected post-modernism, considering it as antithetical to emancipatory strategies toward greater equality and social justice. Indiscriminate pluralism, they argue, may lead not to sharpened awareness of and increased respect for differences but to uncritical sponge-headedness. This could endanger mobilization and support for new social movements such as feminism, gay rights, anti-racism, anti-nuclear protest, the 'Greens' (Boyne and Rattansi, 1990; Gibbins, 1989; Lovibond, 1990). Boyne and Rattansi (1990) suggest that what is currently required is not the abandonment of the whole enterprise of grand narratives, but the replacement of obviously flawed ones with versions that can command both theoretical and political credibility.

Postmodernity may transform the meanings of citizenship and of citizenship education by introducing changes in the diffusion of information, the production of knowledge, the sense of identity, and the nature of politics itself (Gilbert, 1992). These changes raise many concerns with regard to the future and nature of citizenship in the postmodern society. For example, how, if at all, can order, meaning, legitimacy and morality exist once objectivity, certainty, foundations, commensurability, unity and the prioritized self are deconstructed? Put more positively, how are society, politics and morality possible when we accept partiality, relativity, uncertainty, the absence of foundations, incommensurability, pluralism, fragmentation and poly-culturalism (Gilbert, 1992)?

According to Heater (1990), the fragmentary and nihilist tendencies of the postmodern society threaten the commonness on which the concept of citizenship is founded. A truly good citizen in this new reality 'is he who perceives this sense of multiple identity most lucidly and who strives most ardently in his public life to achieve the closest concordance possible between the policies and goals of the several civic levels of which he is a member' (p. 326). In a context of radical pluralism the issue of contested and possibly conflicting collective identities becomes of central concern (Turner, 1990, 1997; Mouffe, 1992). Wexler (1990) argues that the decline in postmodernist culture of independent universal standards of judgement deprives the individual of autonomy by dissolving the ground for a unified self. Lacking an autonomous moral discourse comparable to religious or cultural tradition, individuals can no longer center their actions in a stable morality. Individual identity is decentered, diffuse and fragmented. Because societies are equally fragmented, the grounds for the contractual relation individual-society (on which citizenship is said to depend) no longer exist.

For Wexler the threat to citizenship lies also in the formation of the semiotic society which is characterized by processes of comodification and communication. Goods are valued for what they mean as much as for what they 'are' or what they are 'used' for. Advertising and product-images become goods in their own right consumed for their own sake, and are no longer only representations of 'real' products. Signs and codes acquire status in the fundamental dynamics of society. In the semiotic society citizenship may mean 'being a fan, who votes favorably for media products by purchasing them, extolling their virtues, or wearing their iconic packaging on one's bill cap or tee shirt' (p.72).

Class dynamics and identity in the semiotic society are based on the different positions of two classes *vis-à-vis* the means of production or participation in this semiotic society. The first class includes cultural creators and rationalizers, while the other class consists of consumers who find an imaginary solidarity in television. 'The other class gives its attention in exchange for solidarity, while the first class collects and rationalizes communicative artifacts – "signs" – in narrative self-reconstruction' (p.173).

Political attitudes become a part of lifestyle, a consumption in search for the new (Bourdieu, 1984). According to Wexler, collective identities which are needed for a solidary citizen action are difficult to construct in the face of class division and the different positions of the two classes with respect to the means of participating in the semiotic society. Gilbert (1992) disputes this pessimistic view and contends that postmodern developments offer new possibilities for citizenship, by extending the concept into the spheres of cultural expression and economic production. He agrees, nonetheless, that 'conventional' political action and citizenship are still essential elements of the social dynamic in postmodern societies.

MULTIDIMENSIONAL CITIZENSHIP

The analysis thus far suggests that there is no single version of citizenship, and that there can be many diverse and different formulations of the citizenship principle in different social contexts and cultural traditions. Turner (1993) suggests that a unitary theory of citizenship is inappropriate, and that different forms of citizenship have evolved under rather different circumstances of political and social modernization in contemporary societies. He, nevertheless, proposes a sociological model of citizenship. The following components are included in the model: legal status, cultural identity of individuals and groups, civic virtues which are regarded as necessary for the functioning of democracy, and redistribution of some scarce resources which lessen class conflict and creates a common form of solidarity in a political community (Turner, 1997).

Some of the conceptions of citizenship which have been discussed in previous sections suggest that citizenship should continue to be embedded at the national level, others recommend that it should become transnational and global, while others yet advocate a combination of both without proposing how this could be done.

Ichilov (1990) developed a multidimensional model, in an attempt to conceptualize and clarify the content and structure of the citizenship role in modern democracies, and also to incorporate both the national and transnational dimensions of citizenship. The model consists of ten different dimensions which could serve as building blocks for numerous conceivable citizenship profiles. These dimensions depict the relationships between individuals and their communities, as well as the quality of social life. The model includes participatory objectives, such as expression of consent and dissent; conventional and unconventional participatory means; the motivational orientations for participation – external/obligatory or internal/voluntary as well as other behavioral and attitudinal dimensions of citizenship. Of special relevance to our discussion is the distinction among different arenas and domains in which citizens may wish to participate. These include the political and the civic/social domains, and the national and transnational arenas.

The liberal and participatory models of democracy represent two ends of a continuum with regard to the domains of citizenship. Liberalism supposes a radical separation of the political from the civic, i.e., of politics from society. Citizens operate in the political domain, while persons' self-realization and fulfillment take place in the social/civic sphere. Participatory democracy, on the other hand, advocates citizens' participation in all social-political spheres. New social movements have been responsible for citizenship expansion in the post-war period. For example, in North America, the Black Movement, the Women's Movement, the anti-Vietnam war movement were all influential in expanding citizenship rights to minorities and in protecting individual social rights against state direction (Turner, 1993).

The introduction of transnational and global organizations marks the recognition that economic well-being, preservation of the environment, and security from nuclear war can only be promoted through international cooperation. Even though channels for broad citizen participation in international organizations have not been established, groups of citizens often organize to make their voices heard concerning international issues. Citizens increasingly want their opinion to count when global decisions are made which affect their lives physically and morally. Turner (1993) expresses the view that citizenship will have to develop to embrace both the globalization of social relations and the increasing social differentiation of social systems. Citizenship may, thus, be narrowly defined as related exclusively to the local and national political spheres, or more broadly as also related to a wide array of social concerns, which may be international in scope (Ichilov, 1990).

REFERENCES

Andrews, G. (ed.) (1991), *Citizenship*. London: Lawrence & Wishart.
Arterton, F.C. (1987), *Teledemocracy: Can technology protect democracy?* Newbury Park, CA: Sage.
Barber, B. (1995), *Jihad vs McWorld*. New York: Times Books.
Baudrillard, J. (1980), 'Forgetting Foucault', *Humanities in Society*, 3, 87–111.
Bell, D. (1974), *The coming of post-industrial society*. London: Heinemann.
Bell, D. (1988), *The end of ideology* (2nd edn with a new Afterword). Cambridge, MA: Harvard University Press.
Bell, D. (1989), 'American exceptionalism revisited: The role of civil society', *The Public Interest*, 95, 38–56.
Bourdieu, P. (1984), *Distinction: A social critic of the judgement of taste*. London: Routledge & Kegan Paul.
Boyne, R. and Rattansi, A. (eds) (1990), 'The theory and politics of postmodernism: By way of an introduction', in *Postmodernism and society* (pp.1–46). London: Macmillan.

Brubaker, R. (1992a), *Citizenship and nationhood in France and Germany*. Cambridge, MA: Harvard University Press.
Brubaker, R. (1992b), 'Citizenship struggles in Soviet successor states', *International Migration Review*, 26(2), 269–92.
Brzezinski, Z. (1970), *Between two ages*. New York: Viking Press.
Cohen, A. (1995), 'Reexamining Russia: Crime without punishment', *Journal of Democracy*, 6(2), 34–46.
Crook, S. (1990), 'The end of radical social theory? Radicalism, modernism and postmodernism', in R. Boyne and A. Rattansi (eds), *Postmodernism and society* (pp.46–76). London: Macmillan.
Derrida, J. (1986), 'Racism's last word', in H.L. Gates Jr (ed.), *Race, writing and difference*. Chicago: University of Chicago Press.
Diamond, L. (1992), 'Economic development and democracy reconsidered', in G. Marks and L. Diamond (eds), *Reexamining democracy*. Newbury Park, CA: Sage.
Diamond, L. (1994), 'Rethinking civil society: Toward democratic consolidation', *Journal of Democracy*, 5(3), 4–18.
Duffy, D.M., Sullivan J.I. and Polakiewicz, L.A. (1993), 'Patriotic perspectives in contemporary Poland: Conflict of consensus?', *The Polish Review*, 38(3), 259–98.
Featherstone, M. (1988), 'In pursuit of the postmodern: An introduction', *Theory, Culture and Society*, 5(2/3), 195–216.
Fukuyama, F. (1992), *The end of history and the last man*. New York: Free Press.
Gellner, E. (1993), *Nations and nationalism*. Oxford: Basil Blackwell.
Gibbins, J. (1989), 'Contemporary political culture: An introduction', in J. Gibbins (ed.), *Contemporary political culture: Politics in a postmodern age*. London: Sage.
Gilbert, R. (1992), 'Citizenship, education and postmodernity', *British Journal of Sociology of Education*, 13(1), 51–68.
Gitlin, T. (1981), 'New video technology: Pluralism or banality', *Democracy*, 60–76.
Greenfeld, L. (1992), *Nationalism: Five roads to modernity*. Cambridge, MA: Harvard University Press.
Greenfeld, L. (1993), 'Transcending the nation's worth', *Daedalus*, 22(3–4), 47–63.
Heater, D. (1990), *Citizenship: The civic ideal in world history*. London: Longman.
Held, D. (1987), *Models of democracy*. Cambridge: Polity Press.
Held, D. (1991), 'Between state and civil society: Citizenship', in Geoff Andrews (ed.), *Citizenship* (pp.19–26). London: Lawrence & Wishart.
Hobsbawm, E.J. (1990), *Nations and nationalism since 1780*. Cambridge: Cambridge University Press.
Hoffman, S. (1993), 'Thoughts on the French nation today', *Daedalus*, 22(3–4), 63–81.
Ichilov, O. (1990), 'Dimensions and role patterns of citizenship in democracy', in O. Ichilov (ed.), *Political socialization, citizenship education, and democracy* (pp.11–25). New York: Columbia University, Teachers College Press.
Ichilov, O. and Mazawi, A.E. (1997), 'The consequences of parental choice in education for the social periphery of Tel Aviv–Jaffa', in J. Gal (ed.), *Children and poverty in Israel*. Jerusalem: The National Council for Children's Care, Center for Research and Policy Making (Hebrew).
Isaac, R.J. and Armat, V.C. (1990), *Madness in the streets*. New York: Free Press.
Janowitz, M. (1983), *The reconstruction of patriotism: Education for civic consciousness*. Chicago: The University of Chicago Press.
Kashti, Y. (1994), 'Patriotism as identity and action', unpublished paper. Tel Aviv University, School of Education.
Keane, J. (1988), *Democracy and civil society*. London: Verso.
Kelly, R.M. and Ronan, B. (1987), 'Subjective culture and patriotism: Gender, ethnic, and class differences among high school students', *Political Psychology*, 8(4), 525–47.

Kramer, M. (1993), 'Arab nationalism: Mistaken identity', *Daedalus*, 22(3–4), 171–207.

Kroker, A. and Cook, D. (1988), *The post-modern scene*. New York: St Martin's Press.

Laudon, K.C. (1977), *Communications technology and democratic participation*. New York: Praeger.

Laudon, K.C. (1984), 'New possibilities for participation in the democratic process', in K.W. Grewlich and F.H. Pederson (eds), *Power and participation in an information society*. Luxembourg: Commission of European Communities.

Lipset, S.M. (1981), *Political man*. Baltimore, MD: Johns Hopkins University Press.

Lovibond, S. (1990), 'Feminism and postmodernism', in R. Boyne and A. Rattansi (eds), *Postmodernism and society* (pp.154–87). London: Macmillan.

Lyotard, J.F. (1984), *The postmodern condition*. Manchester: Manchester University Press.

Malbin, M. (1982, June–July), 'Teledemocracy and its discontents', *Public Opinion*, 57–78.

Mann, M. (1987), 'Ruling class strategies and citizenship', *Sociology*, 21(3), 339–54.

Mann, M. (1993), 'Nation-states in Europe and other continents: Diversifying, developing, not dying', *Daedalus*, 22(3–4), 115–39.

Marshall, T.H. (1977), *Class, citizenship and social development*. Chicago: University of Chicago Press.

Marshall, T.H. (1981), *The right to welfare and other essays*. London: Heinemann.

Mouffe, C. (ed.) (1992), *Dimensions of radical democracy*. London: Verso.

Naisbitt, J. (1982), *Megatrends: Ten new directions transforming our lives*. New York: Warner Brothers.

Norris, C. (1990), 'Lost in the funhouse: Baudrillard and the politics of postmodernism', in R. Boyne and A. Rattansi (eds), *Postmodernism and society* (pp.119–54). London: Macmillan.

Ordeshook, P.C. (1995), 'Reexamining Russia: Institutions and incentives', *Journal of Democracy*, 6(2), 46–61.

Porter, A. (ed.) (1984), *Principles of political literacy: The working papers of the programme for political education*. London: University of London Institute of Education.

Pratte, R. (1988), *The civic imperative*. New York: Teachers College Press, Columbia University.

Rifkin, J. (1995), *The end of work*. New York: G. P. Putnam's Sons.

Robertson, R. (1990), 'Mapping the global condition: Globalization as the central concept', in Mike Featherstone (ed.), *Global culture: Nationalism, globalization and modernity*. London: Sage.

Sartori, G. (1987), *The theory of democracy revisited*. Chatham, NJ: Chatham House.

Saunders, P. (1993), 'Citizenship in a liberal society', in B.S. Turner (ed.), *Citizenship and social theory* (pp.57–91). London: Sage.

Soysal, Y.N. (1994), *Limits of citizenship: Migrants and postnational membership in Europe*. Chicago: University of Chicago Press.

Toffler, A. and Toffler, H. (1994), *Creating a new civilization*. Atlanta, GA: Turner Publishing.

Turner, B.S. (1986), *Citizenship and capitalism: The debate over reformism*. London: Allen & Unwin.

Turner, B.S. (1990), 'Outline of a theory of citizenship', *Sociology*, 24(2), 189–217.

Turner, B.S. (1997), 'Citizenship studies: A general theory', *Citizenship Studies*, 1(1), 5–19.

Turner, B.S. (ed.) (1993), *Citizenship and social theory*. London: Sage.

Valaskakis, K. and Annopoulis, P. (1982), *Telecommunity democracy: Utopian vision or probable Future*. Montreal: McGill and Montreal Universities, Gamma Research

Service.

Waltzer, M. (1991), 'The idea of civil society', *Dissent* (Spring), 293–304.

Wexler, P. (1990), 'Citizenship in the semiotic society', in B.S. Turner (ed.), *Theories of modernity and postmodernity.* London: Sage.

White, P.L. (1985), 'What is a nationality?', *Canadian Review of Studies in Nationalism.* 12 (1), 1-24.

Williams, F. (1982), *The communications revolution.* New York: New American Library.

Willms, J.D. (1994, April), 'Ten years later: The effects of school choice in Scottish communities', paper presented at the Annual Meeting of the American Educational Research Association, New Orleans.

Wolff, R.P. (1976), *In defense of anarchy.* New York: Harper Colophon.

2

RUSSIAN CITIZENSHIP: BEHAVIOR, ATTITUDES AND PROSPECTS FOR A RUSSIAN DEMOCRACY

VLADIMIR SHLAPENTOKH

Russia is a country which continually amazes the world and confuses both domestic and foreign forecasters. One of the main sources of this confusion has been the behavior of the Russian people, which in the twentieth century has been very different from what politicians and scholars expected from them. The last time that the Russians astounded their own leaders, as well as foreign ones (not to mention sociologists and political scientists around the world), was during the developments in the summer and fall of 1992 and, to a lesser degree, in 1993. If one is to believe any of the theories concerning 'mass movements', 'collective action' and 'revolution' which have been advanced in the last two decades, be it the theory of 'relative deprivation' or 'resource mobilization theory', or any other theory combining both mass protest with a high level of violence, it would not have been expected to have occurred in Russia in 1992–93. Indeed, modern history seems to suggest that people whose material status has declined abruptly generally react immediately with various mass actions, and often alter the fundamentals of society. The post-medieval history of numerous countries abounds with mass strikes, riots and full-fledged rebellions of the people due to dissatisfaction with the drastic deterioration of their lives. However, nothing like this has happened in Russia.

One of the most important developments in Russia which also was not predicted was the radical alienation of Russians. This alienation was not only from the Communist state, but from the state which emerged after the collapse of the Soviet Union in 1991, and which claims to be democratic. Feelings of citizenship, involvement in public affairs, have not increased following the fall of the Soviet system with its repressive apparatus, as many had taken for granted, but have diminished drastically.

THE CATASTROPHIC FALL IN THE STANDARD OF LIVING IN 1992–93

The market reforms started by Boris Yeltsin and Egor Gaidar in the beginning of 1992 brought about a brusque decline in the quality of life. Such a decline has been unknown in Russia since the times of the war with Germany from 1941–45.

As a result of the release of prices on 2 January 1992, the national economy found itself in a state of shock. Probably no less than one half of all Russian workers stopped receiving their salary. Many of them were able to obtain their money only after waiting for four to six months. The delay in the delivery of pay checks for millions of people employed in various sectors of the economy continued in the following years. In 1993 the number of Russians who did not receive their salaries on time was never lower than 37 per cent, while in 1994 it never fell below 58 per cent (VTSIOM, 1995, No.1, p.28).[1] In addition to the delay in payment to workers, in 1992 the Russian government was unable to pay pensions on time. Millions of retired people arose in the early morning hours in order to stand in line in the hopes of being able to withdraw their meager pensions from the banks.

Moreover, in these months of 1992, it became evident to most Russians that their savings were rapidly being swallowed by soaring inflation. Already, by the end of 1992, official data indicates that 70 per cent of these savings were lost (Goskomustat, 1993, p.156).

Of course, the reaction of the 36 million retired people (25 per cent of the whole population and about one-third of all Russian adults) was particularly desperate. Similar responses were elicited from their children as well. In other words, the whole country was heavily stricken by the disappearance of the savings which had been arduously collected over many decades.

In 1992–93 the standard of living in the country declined catastrophically. There is no consensus among scholars about the magnitude of this decline. The views strongly influenced by the political position of the experts varied from the blunt denial of any significant fall of the quality of life to the opinion claiming that the whole population was being turned into beggars.

A sound estimate is difficult to achieve because the standard of living in Russia, as in any other country, depends on two components – personal income and expenditures on public goods (health services, individual security, the protection of nature, education, public transportation and culture). According to various, more or less objective sources, the decline in personal income was about 50 per cent. Coinciding with this drop was the drastic deterioration of services delivered by the public sector, particularly those regarding health, public transportation, cultural and health institutions for children,[2] and protection against criminals. The number of people who improved their housing conditions – a leading sphere of activity by the former Soviet state – dropped significantly, by 27 per cent in 1992 in comparison with 1990 (*Izvestia*, 29 June 1994). The number of people who were regarded as 'poor' in 1994 was about one-third of the population (*Argumenty i Fakty*, 1994, No.50).

Most Russians radically changed their style of life. Because of high prices, most Russians stopped utilizing the office or factory cafeteria at lunch time. The patronage of beauty salons and cleaning shops has declined as well.[3] Many Russians ceased to spend their vacations outside their place of residence, and they no longer send their children to summer camps. Of course, they were also buying fewer clothes and durable goods in comparison to the past.[4]

To some degree the drastic fall of their income has somewhat been compensated by the disappearance of lines – the plague of Soviet life – and the significant rise of assortments of goods and services offered to customers. Of course, the prices are much higher than in the past.[5] However, only a minority of Russians appreciate this progress. In the middle of 1994, 33 per cent of Russians surveyed considered their economic situation as 'bad' and 11 per cent as 'very bad'.[6]

In any case, most of them praised the Communist times as a Golden Age and voted for state control of prices. According to VTSIOM's survey in the middle of 1994, 43 per cent of the Russian city dwellers bemoaned the changes in the country and said that before 1985, 'life was better'. What is more, no less than 50 per cent of all Russians in 1992–93 expressed positive attitudes toward socialism (Gudkov, 1994; Grushin, 1993; *Argumenty i Fakty*, 1994, No.17; *Moskovski Novosti*, 8 May 1994; *Izvestia*, 30 December 1993; *Segodnia*, 24 June 1994).

THE EXPECTATION OF TURMOIL BY RUSSIAN POLITICIANS

Not only the experts who closely followed the developments in Russia in 1992–93 expected mass protests in Russia. Most Russian politicians in 1992–93 did not believe that the Russians would endure their sufferings without stormy reactions. This mentality was also prevalent among the reformers themselves. Egor Gaidar later mentioned that he and his team viewed themselves as kamikazes who were doomed to be ousted as soon as turmoil erupted in the country. Russian politicians and social scientists were divided only about the relative role of each of the two factors – absolute and relative deprivation – in abetting the stormy reaction of the masses. While some insisted on the crucial significance of the absolute decline in the standard of living, others pointed to social injustice as the most powerful factor which would cause the Russians to react violently against the state of affairs in the country in 1992–93.

The belief in Russia about the danger of mass protest was strongly influenced by the dogmas inherited from the political culture of the Soviet system. Such assumptions were shared by politicians as well as intellectuals prior to 1985. This culture supposed that the masses, especially industrial workers, were ready to go to the streets as soon as their material interests were seriously threatened. For this reason Soviet political culture supposed that under no circumstances could workers be denied the timely payment of their salaries, nor could they be fired from their jobs or evicted from their apartments. The attitudes of the Soviet leaders to a delay in the payment of salaries is a good illustration.[7] Apparatchiks who did not follow these norms would have been reprimanded or even fired as 'politically immature persons'.

These elements of Soviet political culture were determined not by genuine concern of the Soviet élite about the life of the masses: rather, it was their strong fear of riots by discontented workers, which they imagined would trigger a series of rebellions in the country and ultimately destroy their regime. The small Novocherkask riot of workers in 1963 produced an immense impact on the Kremlin.[8] This event was declared a classified state secret and, until Glasnost, it was virtually unknown to the Russian people. There is little doubt that Novocherkask contributed to Khrushchev's 'resignation'.

Thus, it is not surprising that when Brezhnev learned about labor unrest in Poland in the late 1970s he immediately ordered the revision of the next five-year plan in order to increase the production of consumer goods.

HOW RUSSIANS REACTED TO THEIR TRIBULATIONS, 1992–94

One can hardly imagine the surprise of the new Russian regime, as well as experts on mass movements in the world, when they watched the passivity of the Russian masses in 1992 and 1993.

Indeed, although there had been large miners' strikes in 1989 and 1991, such activity was virtually absent during this time. There were no assaults on any police stations or local governments, nor were there large protest marches or demonstrations. In the first half of 1993 there were only 34 strikes with 20,000 participants, and this in a country with hundreds of thousands of enterprises and millions of workers (*Moskovskii Komsomolets*, 15 October 1994). The participation of Russians in political meetings in 1993–94 even decreased in comparison with the previous period.[9]

The case of Khabarovsk, a city of 600,000 residents in the winter of 1991–92 is particularly characteristic of the national mood at this time. The heating systems of the city broke in the midst of the Siberian winter and people boiled water with public fires on the streets. There were no meetings, demonstrations or even the threat of deposing the local administration. The head of the local administration, Alexander Sokolov, could leave the city of suffering people for a trip to North Korea in order to congratulate 'the great leader', Kim Il Sung, on his jubilee.

The situation did not change significantly in 1993–95, even though at this time no less than one half of the Russian population considered themselves as victims of the changes. In this period there were no mass strikes of long duration, no riots or any other public actions which could endanger public order in the country. Using Durkheim's terminology, it is possible to say that the Russian masses in the period under consideration did not resort to either routine or non-routine collective action.

The miners in various coal basins were exceptions, and they went on strike several times during this time. However, the strikes were of relatively short duration, and workers in other industries generally remained passive, as did employees in various non-industrial sectors of society. The masses did not use the opportunity delivered by the clashes between the President and the parliament in 1993 for venting their anger against the authorities. In vain, the opposition desperately awaited the mass riots in their favor, but the masses remained mostly aloof from the political battles. The few demonstrations which took place in Moscow were quite small, with only a few thousand people, and they did not change the political or economic picture in the country.[10]

The situation in Ivanovo, one of the most depressed regions of the country, was typical. Here its main industry, textiles, is in a deep crisis. Its production had diminished in 1992–94 by four to five times in comparison with 1991. Most workers were getting a symbolic miserable salary and quite often could not get even that for months at a time. The desperation of the female weavers (some of them fainted from hunger) was extremely high. However, there was no example of a serious disturbance in the region.[11] Suffering from the delay in the payment of salaries and from the unemployment, most Russian workers ignored trade unions, which did not exist in 1994–95 at four-fifths of all enterprises. Those unions which formally functioned were mostly passive and did not enjoy the support of workers (Alexeieva, 1995).

Russians are fully aware of their passivity and unwillingness to participate in any public actions in order to defend their interests. The number of people who promised to take part in meetings or demonstrations of protest in the 1992–94 revolved all these years around 20–25 per cent (whatever negative developments occurred in these years), although the distance between the statement of verbal intentions and real behavior is in such cases extremely large.[12]

In stark contrast to the absence of violent or even non-violent protests of the Russian masses against the conditions of their life in 1992–94 was the outburst of violence on the part of criminals. In this period the number of murders increased twofold. Of special significance was the increase in the murders of 'New Russians' (bankers, managers and, in general, rich people). While the Russian masses manifested remarkable patience and forbearance, criminals were ready to resort to violence on any occasion.

RUSSIAN PATIENCE

The developments in 1992–94 showed that Soviet leaders who lived in a sort of fear of the masses rioting were totally wrong. Also wrong were the Soviet intellectuals who liked to repeat Pushkin's famous dictum from *The Captain's Daughter* about 'the Russian riot, meaningless and merciless'.

It is untrue that Gorbachev started his reforms because, as many Russian democrats as well as a number of Western experts suggest, the Russians were dissatisfied with their life and a storm was approaching the Kremlin. Nothing could be further from the truth. When Gorbachev received his scepter in March 1985 the masses were calm (Alexeieva, 1984). Their discontent only began when they were told that they had to be unhappy. In fact, the people with whom the Kremlin dealt were obedient subjects who were able to tolerate much more than the post-Stalin leaders realized (Shlapentokh 1986, 1988, 1990).

The Evaluation of Virtual Outcome: No Sense of Violence

Each theory dealing with mass movements reflects some factors accountable for their origin. As a matter of fact, the situation in Russia in 1992–93 met all of the requirements developed by resource mobilization theory (Tilly, 1978). It explains mass movements as an interaction between government, members of the polity (those who 'have routine low-cost access to resources controlled by the government') and contenders – 'any group which, during some period of time applies pooled resources to influence government' (Tilly, 1978, p.52). These major societal forces, in the course of political struggle, resort to collective action when they are presented with the opportunity for the creation of organizations and the mobilization of resources. Of course, the opportunity side of collective action depends on a degree of repression (or lack of political repression); thus, collective action can be suppressed or, on the contrary, facilitated, depending on the government's strength.

The advocates of 'resource mobilization theory', would expect that in the face of Russian discontent, the masses would have launched a major mass protest movement in 1992–94. The Russian case has virtually met 'the requirements' of this theory (weak government, limited resources available for repression of rebellion, and demoralization in the forces used for repression). The whole regime would have collapsed immediately if a chain of riots had broken out. From 3–4 October 1993 Yeltsin was unable to find even a regiment to fight a small rebellion put forth by the opposition. At the same time, the opposition had a powerful organization in the parliament, quite prestigious, even charismatic, and, what is more, legally elected leaders (Vice-President Alexander Rutskoi among them) and had many opportunities to foment general insurgence. So, in the light of all these circumstances, why did the Russians, when facing a drastic deterioration of their living conditions in 1992–93, not rebel in October 1993?

The inability to explain Russian passivity stems from the fact that the theory of resource mobilization underestimates one important factor. That is, it tends to disregard people's expectations of the possible outcomes of mass action. I feel that this is crucial if we are to understand the Russian situation in 1992–94.

Certainly, the role of this factor varies from one movement to another. However, people always have some ideas concerning what they can expect if their movement is successful. They tend to realize the implications which the direct goals of the movement will have on reality.

Some analysts of mass actions do not raise the question about how participants of mass actions or those who did not join them viewed the eventual outcome of their activities. They are mostly preoccupied with the macro-analysis of social movements and generally disregard how much the vision of this outcome influences the behavior of people (McCarthy and Zald, 1976; Klandermans and Oegema, 1987; Walsh and Warland, 1983; Hirsch, 1990; Zimmerman, 1982).[13] In some cases, as with Tilly, this disregard of the evaluation of the possible consequences of collective actions lies often implicitly, or by default, in the concept of irrationality. This, combined with the influence of utopian ideologies and a rejection of utilitarianism, can be seen as a key for understanding why some people involve themselves in protest activity while others do not (Tilly, 1978, pp.24–5).

Other authors hold rather contradictory positions. On the one hand, they are inclined to dismiss this issue with psychoanalytical considerations because 'angry men' can be satisfied from their self-assertiveness through violence. They also believe that 'calculations about the prospective benefits' are more likely to be made among leaders than followers, and that people are lured to mass actions with utopian slogans (Gurr, 1974, pp.210–11, 216). But, on the other hand, the same authors might also mention the role of such 'a determinant of perceived utility of political violence' and 'people's previous success in attaining their needs by such means'. Some speak of the role of such a factor as 'the proximity of goals' or even of the significance of 'the outcome'. Never, however, do they touch on this crucial issue: how people joining and not joining 'collective actions' increase the chances for success, and how much it influences their behavior (Gurr, 1974, pp.71–2, 218; Gamson, 1975, pp.31–7).

Indeed, in many cases people have joined mass movements stimulated by feelings of revenge and by the indomitable desire to vent their frustration, as well as by utopian hopes. On many occasions they become involved without thinking seriously about the movement's chances of success. In special cases, people will struggle for an admittedly 'lost cause' (Olson, 1971, p.161).

However, at the same time, people whose interests are presumably represented by a mass movement appear as being able to evaluate realistically the possible outcome of their actions. In such situations, a group presumably represents for its specific members the cost of their activity (repressions or fear of them, for instance) before making decisions to participate in its activities.[14]

In several cases people's negative attitudes toward possible forms of participation in collective actions is strongly determined by their belief that these actions have no chance of succeeding. Thus, they can only contribute to the deterioration of the situation through their participation. In some way this is an inverse 'free-rider' case, when people reject to being enrolled in mass actions not because they will be successful without their participation, as the free-rider theory suggests, but because these actions have no chances of success to begin with. In this respect, the role of the experience, for the individual as well as for a group or the nation, is of crucial importance.

This experience can make ordinary people skeptical about the utility of their protest actions and in this way prevent them from starting or joining a movement already in progress. The spread of education and media in recent times can only increase the role of 'collective utilitarianism' in the mass mind.

If people do not believe in the possibility of improving their life, even with potentially effective organizations and available resources, the chances for the emergence of collective action, especially those which use violence, are quite slim.

In the light of the facts mentioned above, it is reasonable to treat 'Russian patience' as a rational way for the people to adjust to their new reality. With this hypothesis in mind several variables can be advanced as independent ones in attempting to explain the present Russian situation. Three of them are of special importance and the discussion below will focus on them. These are Russian concern about the order in the country, pessimism, and the Russian ability to adjust to adverse circumstances.

THE AMERICAN (1929–41) AND GERMAN (1922–33) CASES

In no way is the current Russian case unique in the history of the twentieth century. The last hundred years have witnessed numerous national strikes, riots, rebellions and revolutions directly triggered by the deprivations of the masses. Besides Russia, two cases stand out as examples of when drastic decline in the quality of life did not produce any serious mass protests and violence. These two instances occurred in the United States in the period of the Great Depression and in the Weimar Republic in Germany after the First World War. In both cases the sufferings of the masses were enormous. There was a rapid decline in their standard of living, as well as a strong polarization of society. In both of these cases the hardships were much greater than those which post-Communist Russia has experienced.

However, in neither of these countries did the masses resort to collective action, riots or revolutions. In Weimar Germany, people tended to join one of two extremist parties, the Communists or the National Socialists. However, the Germans in general avoided any illegal or violent actions. In the United States during the Great Depression, the people were even closer to the Russians of today than were the Germans in the 1920s and early 1930s. The roles of trade unions and radical parties increased, but violence did not result.[15]

In both countries public order was generally upheld, even if in Germany there were individual cases of violence.[16] Again, as in the case of Russia, almost all possible conditions which were necessary for mass collective actions were met. For this reason the most powerful explanation for the lack of upheaval is the disbelief by the masses that they could achieve positive results with violent activities.

Russian Yearning for Order, Stability and Physical Security

The horror of the civil war of 1918–20, of the collectivization and hunger of the early 1930s, the mass purges of the mid-1930s and the war with Germany in 1941–45 instilled in the Russian people a great fear of any sort of violence. These events made order the highest value for them. With order being so cherished, the Russians are ready to bear the harshest tribulations which would push most other people to the barricades.

The vast amount of data collected by Russian sociologists confirm this conclusion. Asked by VTSIOM in September 1994, 'what is more important for Russia – order or democracy?', 76 per cent chose the first alternative, and only 9 per cent the second. Even among people with higher education the ratio was 4:1 (VTSIOM, No.6, 1994, p.49). In the economic sphere Russians also preferred 'stable and low income' to 'high and unstable', 60 per cent versus 19 per cent (VTSIOM, No.5, 1994, p.6).

With such a preoccupation with order and stability, most Russians, including the very frustrated, almost instinctively avoid disturbances which will disrupt the fragile stability of the country. It is in this way that it is necessary to interpret the attitudes of Russians toward Yeltsin in 1992–93. Indeed, in this period President Yeltsin was backed by 50–60 per cent of Russians, much more than any other politician in the country. However, as soon as new politicians with the promises of order emerged, the popularity of Yeltsin dropped enormously, and at the end of 1994 Yeltsin could garner no more than 10–15 per cent of the popular support for his re-election as president.

RUSSIAN PESSIMISM: THE LACK OF CONFIDENCE IN SOCIAL PROGRAMS

Along with a fear of a loss of order, Russian patience has also been influenced by Russian pessimism. This feeling has embraced the nation after the collapse of the Soviet Union, the discrediting of socialist ideology and the disintegration of the belief in the Soviet system as being superior to the West. The shock experienced by the Russians can only be compared to the reaction which medieval monks might have felt if the Pope had declared to them that God does not exist.

Since 1988–89 pessimism has been dominant in the country. The Russians began to believe that the future could only be worse than the present, and that any actions undertaken could only make their status worse.

No fewer than two-thirds of all Russians in 1992–94 described the situation in their country as gloomy, with no brighter outlook for the future.[17] The ratio of optimists to pessimists was, in these years, between 1:5 and 1:3. When asked at the end of 1994 'are hard times behind us or in the future?', 9 per cent in the VTSIOM survey of 3,000 respondents said 'in the past' and 52 per cent said 'in the future' (VTSIOM, No.5, 1994; VTSIOM, No.6, 1994). Russians were deeply pessimistic about each aspect of their life. Therefore, the number of people who believed in the improvement of the economic situation in the country in 1993–94 was never more than 10–20 per cent. The ratio of those who believed in its progress and those who believed in its deterioration were about 1:10 or even 1:24 (VTSIOM, No.6, 1993; VTSIOM, No.5, 1994). The ratio of Russians who are optimistic about the political processes in the country to those who are pessimists is between 1:6 and 1:18 (VTSIOM, No.6, 1993; No.6, 1994).

It is not amazing that the mood in the country in this period was evidently subdued. Of eight feelings which Russians were asked to choose as characteristic of the mood of the people, 90 per cent pointed to negative emotions (tiredness and indifference, 40 per cent; fear, 22 per cent; disorientation, 18 per cent; aggressiveness, 10 per cent). Only 23 per cent pointed to positive ones (hope, 16 per cent; human dignity, 7 per cent; pride in one's own people, 4 per cent).[18] By all accounts, pessimism and feelings of resignation did not encourage the Russian masses to embark on any collective actions.[19]

Ultimately, Russian pessimism in 1992–94 stemmed from the loss of belief in any ideology concerning how to make life better. No one public ideology with its own vision of the present and desirable future, be it a new democratic ideology (the disappointment of the Russians with democracy is overwhelming), or old ideologies such as Communist and nationalist, or any combination of any of these three, was popular among more than 5–10 per cent of the population. About two-thirds of all Russians in these surveys in 1993–95 could say nothing about their political preferences. The extremist versions of Communist and nationalist ideologies which in 1992–94 appealed to violence did not have any serious support among Russians.

CONSERVATISM: ALL CHANGES ARE TOO RISKY

With the lack of any ideology able to convince Russians to back its programs, the Russian people became not only pessimistic, but also very conservative. In 1992–94 Russians were strongly afraid that any radical changes in the country would bring about the worsening of the present situation rather than an improvement. This is their basis for supporting the existing regime and its policies. They truly fear that any radicals, on the left or right, will bring havoc and make life even more difficult. For this reason, most Russians in general dislike extremists on both sides, and prefer politicians who are, in their opinion, moderate. Because of their pessimism, most Russians have been very cautious in the last three years about radical changes in the economic and social structures of their society. The peak of genuine reformism in the mass conscience was probably reached in 1987–88, before the beginning of the deterioration of their living conditions. Later, most Russians were against revolutionary changes and supported the policy of the reforms, as was mentioned above, mainly because they deemed them necessary to bolster the supreme political power, which is a guarantee for order.

Their conservatism seems to have been mitigated by the necessity of adjusting to reforms. Understanding that it is impossible to return to the 'Golden Age' of the past (70 per cent of the Russians surveyed in 1993–94 shared this view – VTSIOM, No.4, 1994, p.16), the Russian people are trying to adjust to new social realities. Even though many Russian are enemies of market reforms, they attempt to establish their own businesses, purchase stocks, and speculate in dollars.[20]

THE MECHANISMS OF ADJUSTMENT

Having chosen patience as their social strategy, the Russian people have managed to adjust to their new situation in an almost miraculous way.

First of all, the Russians have managed to solve the problem of food shortages by increasing the production of food at their private plots. For three-quarters of all Russians private gardens are an important source of food. In 1994, young women and men spent, respectively, 1.6 and 2.0 times more time on them than in 1990 (Dzhaginova, 1994a; Levinson, 1993). The available statistics show that private plots make up to 70–80 per cent of potatoes, vegetables and fruits produced in the country while in the past their contribution to agricultural production of the country was significantly lower.

Private plots are the only developing sector of Russian agriculture. In contrast, collective and state farms are in a state of steady decline and private farmers are unable to make serious progress (*Izvestia*, 23 November 1994). What is more, Russians have turned their homes into factories, and they produce literally hundreds of canned food items. All members of the family, from school children up to the oldest babushka, are mobilized in the quest for affordable prices for the table and pantry. Most families, despite their small apartments, try to maintain stocks of food at a level that will permit them to survive emergencies.

Russians ceased to satisfy many of their wants. The majority drastically reduced the purchase of clothes and shoes. The acquisition of a new TV set or refrigerator, as well as furniture, is beyond the means of millions of Russians. Vacations out of town, most often at sea resorts, that were affordable for most people in the Soviet era now belong to memories of days past. With the small portion of income left after purchasing food, Russians have turned their homes into places where they fulfill many needs that are impossible to satisfy through state or private enterprises because of exorbitant prices. Russians have discovered the talents and skills of family members who now cut hair, make clothes, repair appliances, clean clothes with homemade chemicals and perform a myriad of other tasks.[21]

THE PRICE OF PATIENCE: ALIENATION FROM THE STATE

Having rejected mass protest actions and violence against the regime, the frustrated Russian people evidently reacted with wisdom to their changing conditions of life. This point of view will be supported by those who do not believe that violence is a necessary factor of progress. However, Russian society had to pay quite a high price for the patience of its members. This price was the strong alienation of ordinary people (and even those who adapted to the changing circumstances quite well) from the state and society in general.

In 1992–94 most Russians felt completely estranged from the existing political powers and major political institutions. No single institution, including the President, the Parliament and the courts, was able to garner more than 10–20 per cent of the people's trust. Only the church (48 per cent) and the army (before the Chechen war – 39 per cent) were exceptions (VTSIOM, No.4, 1993).[22] Of equal significance is the conviction of the Russians that the country is governed by mafias. Almost 50 per cent of all Muscovites at the end of 1994, according to a survey, believe that this is so.

Certainly, prior to 1991, the Soviet state and the Communist party, with all their central and local agencies, were not considered by Russians as democratically elected bodies. Of course, apparatchiks ('they' to the masses), were often hated and despised. However, Russians did not feel estranged from the state and the party, and regarded them as serving and defending their interests.

One of the many pieces of evidence proving this thesis is the data about the millions of letters of complaint which ordinary Russians regularly sent to the various institutions, as well as the millions of people who visited state and party officials with their concerns and problems. A large proportion of the Soviet people (60–80 per cent) believed that their contacts with authorities and the media were an effective way to solve their problems.[23] Of course, the frequency with which Soviet citizens addressed their complaints to authorities and media reflects first of all the paternalistic character of the Soviet state and the total dependence of the individual on the position of the state and party apparatus toward him or her. However, at the same time, this dependence was an important factor in the creation of the feeling of belonging to Soviet society and its institutions (Verkhvoskaia, 1972; Grushin and Onikov, 1980; Shlapentokh and Shlapentokh, 1990). In 1992–93 Russians almost stopped addressing the authorities for help. Newspapers abolished or radically curtailed their departments of letters to editors, which in the past were the largest sections in periodicals. What is more, they think that the present state is much more hostile to them than in Communist times and the level of arbitrariness in the decisions of governmental bodies related to ordinary citizens has increased.[24]

ALIENATION FROM SOCIETY

However, even more important is the estrangement of the masses from society. In 1992–94 Russians demonstrated their growing indifference to most social values necessary for the functioning of any society, dictatorial or democratic, and to any public ideology. According to data collected by VTSIOM in 1994, no more than 3–7 per cent supported any 'ideological slogan', including 'social justice' (no more than 3 per cent) or 'strong state' (7 per cent). From the list of 12 values, Russians chose mostly 'the conditions of the normal civil life' as it was formulated by the authors of this survey: 'order' was chosen by 19 per cent; 18 per cent chose 'stability'; and 'a decent life' was answered by 10 per cent. In another VTSIOM survey (1994) it was found that the number of people who said that they 'do not bear responsibility for the developments in their country' – a blatant support of 'jungle individualism' – increased between 1989 and 1994 twofold, from 17 to 33 per cent. Whereas no fewer than two-thirds of Russians in the past looked to 'the collective' (people in their firm) or to various party and state organizations for support in the case of emergency, now three-quarters of Russians when asked 'whose support you will hope to find in difficult circumstances' answered that they will 'count only on themselves'

(VTSIOM, No.5, 1994, p.58; No.1, 1995, p.11; Riabushkin and Osipov, 1982; Stepanova, 1994).[25] The social fabric weakened in 1992–94 in many other areas. The ties with relatives and friends, for instance, became less intensive too, and about 50 per cent of Russians met each other less frequently than in the past (VTSIOM, No.2, 1994, p.34).[26] Some growth in the tolerance of Russians toward behavior traditionally regarded as deviant also reflects, among other things, the growth of compassion, the growing 'individualization' of Russians, their indifference to the life of 'others', and to the impact of their behavior on social life (Levada, 1995a, p.12).

The disinterest of Russians in social values reflects the emergence of a sort of ideological vacuum. This makes it impossible for a consensus on major values to emerge among the population and among politicians.

Of course, the previous public ideology (a mixture of Communism and Russian nationalism) did not control the conduct or even the mentality of most Russians in the Soviet past. However, this ideology then exerted a significant influence on people's behavior, and on the evaluation of the public and individual activity of members of society. In post-Communist Russia public values as an influential factor of behavior have virtually disappeared from the human mind. A sort of consensus has emerged that everybody should be concerned only with individual survival and enrichment. Religion, as was hoped by many, did not replace the discarded ideology. In fact, its influence on Russians in the middle of the 1990s was less than modest.

POLITICAL APATHY

Political apathy is one of the evident manifestations of the alienation from the dominant political order in the country. As *Izvestia* wrote at the end of 1994, 'The results of sociological studies show the considerable alienation of the masses from authorities and its representatives in the center and regions, whatever their political affiliation' (16 November 1994).

One-half of the population ignored the most important political events in the country in 1993 – the referendum on the constitution and the parliamentary elections of December 1993. No more than 20–30 per cent of Russians took part in local elections, and in many regions the elections were canceled. At the same time, none of the political parties in the country can rely on more than 7–8 per cent of the popular vote, and by the end of 1994 no single leader could garner more than 10 per cent of the votes cast (VTSIOM, No.6, 1994, p.47; Levada, 1995b). The opposition leaders, despite the anger of the masses, could not earn any more support than the representatives of the regime. Some of them, especially those among the extremists, regularly complained that young people still 'do not storm McDonalds' (*Zavtra*, No.23, 1994).[27]

THE CONTEMPT FOR ELITES

The Russian alienation from the state also manifests itself in their contempt for élites – political and economic. Most Russians are sure that the majority of politicians are corrupt and that the majority of businessmen are crooks. No politician was able to garner more than 10–12 per cent of popular support in 1993–94. Only 3 per cent of Russians believed that Russian politicians 'are in essence honest people' (VTSIOM, No.6, 1994, p.5; see also *Moskovski Novosti*, 2 October 1994). In 1992–94 Russians rejected the idea that the Russian leaders, including those elected by them, are concerned about the interests of the country. Instead, they are confident that they are absorbed only with the enrichment and the preservation of their power.[28]

INDIFFERENCE TO THE ARMY

Indifference to the state, even to the fate of Russia's integrity, has been manifested in the people's attitudes toward the army. On the one hand, the army is more respected than any other institution, excluding the church. But, on the other hand, Russian young people are trying to avoid army service by all means. Their actions are supported by their parents and the population as a whole. According to the data of the Ministry of Defense, during the last recruitment campaign the army conscripted no more than 20 per cent of the potential draftees. Only ten years ago Nikita Mikhalkov's movie *Kinfolk* (1982) described the farewell party for a youngster going to the army as a celebration.[29] Currently, 53 per cent of Muscovites endorse desertion from the army and the refusal of military people to fulfill orders and take part in war. See, for instance, the data collected by the foundation 'Public Opinion' in February, as reported in *Moskovski Novosti*, 26 February 1995. Young people who were not able to avoid recruitment are viewed as misfits and failures because they did not have the resources (intellectual or financial) or decent social position to escape service. 'The movement of soldier's mothers' who are desperately fighting against hazing in the army and the participation of their children in local wars is another significant public sign of the unwillingness of Russians to sacrifice their children for any war, regardless of its official justification. But, of course, the most flagrant demonstration of the Russian indifference toward the army were the developments in Chechnya in December 1994–March 1995.[30]

INDIFFERENCE TO THE FATE OF RUSSIANS IN FORMER SOVIET REPUBLICS

Another visible manifestation of 'desocialization' of the Russians is their attitudes toward the Russian minorities in the former Soviet republics. It is evident that the status of Russians in all these republics has significantly diminished, and in most of them they suffer from some form of discrimination, especially in the realms of culture and education as well as in the bureaucracy. Thousands of Russians have been leaving the former Soviet republics and looking for happiness in the Russian Federation (Shlapentokh, Sendich and Pain, 1994).

However, as various surveys show, most Russians are indifferent to the plight of their countrymen and only a minority express a willingness to help them. The Russians who have returned to Russia receive very little protection or help in resettlement. Furthermore, local populations in Russia (especially local officials) are indifferent and even openly hostile to the arriving migrants. Russian immigrants in most cases are met with hostility by the local populations when they return. This is in stark contrast to the hospitality they expected to find.[31] A poll conducted by VTSIOM in 1994 also found that two-thirds of all Russians are against any Russian involvement in the developments of former Soviet republics; only 13 per cent supported such actions (Gudkov, 1995; Chorev, 1994; Dunlop, 1994; *Izvestia*, 14 August 1993; see also Gannushkina, 1994; Loizneau, 1994; Rotar, 1994; Terechov, 1994).[32] Ultimately, the attitudes toward minorities is only one of the signs of deep individualization of the Russian people in the aftermath of the collapse of the Soviet Union. According to the surveys conducted by VTSIOM during 1988–92, the number of people who answered positively to the statement, 'Most important to me is the fate of my own people' has declined from 34 per cent in 1988 to 26 per cent in 1992 (Levada, 1994a).

ELECTIONS AS A POTENTIAL WEAPON

At the time when this article was finished (beginning of April 1995), the most frustrated part of the Russian population was still relatively passive and avoided not only violent but also peaceful protests against the authorities. There are serious reasons to suppose that unless some new 'shock' events (a sudden deterioration in the food supply, a sudden great upsurge in inflation or mass unemployment) occurs, Russians in the coming years will behave as they did in the last three years and avoid collective protest actions.

However, Russians (as did the Germans in 1933) have already found a way to express their frustration with their life through a perfectly legal way. A portion of the Russian population may resort to the ballot box. In this case it is not necessary to resort to violence and it is possible to express their hatred of the regime with a low level of risk. This, apparently, was the view of many Russians. However, in this instance, the people's wisdom (for those who will participate in elections, as well as those who will avoid them) may fail to protect them from dangerous deeds, for they may vote for those who lambast the regime with special fervor.

In such a case, an election could bring to power, against the wishes even of those who voted for them, people who will deceive the electorate. It is possible that those who win the elections would eliminate democratic institutions, partially or completely, or become crass populists who will make the life of the people in the long term even more miserable. In such a context of frustration, particularly in a society with weak democratic traditions, an election could do what the masses refuse to accomplish in their refusal to go to streets: to open the way to violence through the installation of a dictator.[33]

Implicit here is another dimension of the people's passivity and their alienation from politics. In the case of a military coup, the people will be inert and will silently watch the change of the regime, even if they dislike its perpetrators. The impertinence of the new rulers will be dictated exactly by their confidence in the passivity of the masses.

CONCLUSION

Many changes can take place in the next few years in Russia. It is possible to imagine that the Russians will go to the streets when their unknown limit of patience is exhausted. It is not unlikely that Russians will reveal their frustration in voting for people dangerous to democracy and peace. It is also possible that a dictator will seize power and exploit the indifference of the masses for his benefit. However, in any case, the events of 1992–94 will enter history as another example of the ability of people to hold out in the most difficult times without resorting to acts of violence.

At the same time, as this chapter suggests, in the knowable foreseeable future, there is no chance of the growth of genuine feelings of citizenship in Russia. The alienation from the post-Communist state is so deep that not only this, but the next generation of Russians as well, will probably view their state with hostility and will try to avoid violating the laws of the country as much as possible. The deep social polarization of society, which will hardly change in the near future, will be an insurmountable obstacle to the restoration of feelings of citizenship which, as paradoxically as it may sound, existed in Soviet times. It will take decades for Russians, if the economic and social developments are positive, to eliminate (even partially) the gap which exists between them and the Russian state.

NOTES

1. In this paper I will rely heavily on data provided by the All-Russian Center of Public Opinion Studies (VTSIOM). This is because VTSIOM is the most authoritative polling firm in Russia today.
2. The number of children who spent the summer in camps declined in 1992 in comparison with 1991 by 30 per cent. In the same period 161 libraries for children were closed. The number of visitors to children's movie theaters declined by 2.2 million per year. See, for example, *Izvestia*, 29 June 1994.
3. The number of shops delivering various services declined in 1992 in comparison with the previous year by 30–50 per cent. See, for example, *Izvestia*, 29 June 1994.
4. According to VTSIOM's survey in 1994, responses to the question 'How often do you not have money for the satisfaction of one of your needs?', 43 per cent said they save money by not buying food; 22 per cent said they save by not buying clothes; 17 per cent save by not attending the theater; and 33 per cent by not buying newspapers. For instance, see *Izvestia*, 15 October 1994.
5. According to VTSIOM's survey (November 1994), 76 per cent of Russians appreciate 'the lack of a deficit' as a major achievement of post-Communist Russia. In comparison, 51 per cent of them consider the emergence of 'political freedoms' as being a major success of the new administration. See VTSIOM (1995), No.1, p.9.
6. These were the results of a national survey of 2975 respondents conducted by VTSIOM. See *Argumenty i Fakty* (1994), No.31.
7. Indeed, if any Soviet sociologist had been asked in the 1970s or early 1980s (when the country was completely calm) 'what would happen if, at the Kirov tractor factory in Leningrad, the payment of salary were postponed for two or three days?', he or she would have responded that this event was an emergency of national proportions. The General Secretary would have been informed of the situation immediately; the director of the enterprise and the director of the local banks would have been fired the next day; and the deputy Minister and possibly the Minister responsible for the tractor industry would have been strongly reprimanded. The workers would have received their salaries immediately, along with an accompanying apology.
8. In this southern city there was a strike and a protest march of 7,000 angry workers. They approached the police station demanding the release of their comrades. The Kremlin was so terrified by this event that two members of the Politburo, Anastas Mikoian and Frol Kozlov, were dispatched to the city, the whole military district under the command of General Issa Pliev was put on alert and troops were ordered to fire on the people. Twenty-four people were killed during this time, and seven were later executed. The potential for the riots to spread to other factories made Khrushchev and the other Kremlin leaders mad with fear. About the Novocherkask incident see Remnick (1993), pp.414–19.
9. So, according to the time budget studies of VTSIOM, the average Russian woman participated in political meetings three times in 1990 and once in 1994, while men participated on average once in both years. See Dzhaginova (1994a).
10. The few cases in which workers demonstrated their militancy are rather exceptional. For example, workers in the Kovrov factory, the builders of the power station in Chita, and miners in Chapaievsk stopped the movement of trains. In the Cherepovets' metallurgical complex, the workers ousted their director from the factory. See Alexeieva (1995).
11. As *Komsomolskaia pravda* (6 September 1994) stated, the head of the administration in one of the most depressed districts in the region, Iuzha, declared that, 'we will not permit a social outburst, even if hunger starts. We are accustomed to being patient, maybe we will hold out on these tribulations too.'

12. See VTSIOM (1993), No.1, p.55; VTSIOM (1995), No.1, p.4. In the survey conducted by the Vox Populi polling firm (March 1994), respondents were asked 'What manner of expressions of discontent in the critical situation are today admissible and proper?': 36 per cent said 'none'; 18 per cent preferred a talk at a meeting in the factory or office; 18 per cent said to send a letter to the authorities or the mass media; 14 per cent advocated participation in meetings and demonstrations; 9 per cent believed in strikes. Only 3 per cent would accept participation in violent actions. See *Megalopolis-Express*, 21 March 1994. In another survey (March 1995), 24 per cent of Russians supported the view that 'the demonstrations can improve their life'. See *Rossiiskaia Gazeta*, 31 March 1995. See also *Argumenty i Fakty*, July 1994, No.17.
13. Doug McAdam, John McCarthy and Mayer Zald (1988) clearly reject 'the rational choice' as an important factor in the formation of social movements. They contend that 'solidarity and purposive incentive are more important in explaining participation in a variety of voluntary associations ...than selective incentives'.
14. This view was discussed by Olson more profoundly than any other author. See Olson (1971), pp.1, 104–10, 161–2. See also Oberschall (1973); Klandermans and Oemega (1984).
15. For information concerning Germany at this time, see Abraham (1986); Hiden (1974); Eyck (1963). For the United States during this time, see Paradis (1967); Ellis (1970).
16. It is remarkable that the major theorists of mass movements practically avoided the developments in Germany and the United States in their theoretical formulations, especially when the conditions for mass protests were extremely favorable. See Gurr (1974); Gamson (1975); Tilly (1978).
17. So, in a survey conducted in August 1994, Russians described the situation in the country as 'critical' (40 per cent), 'alarming' (27 per cent), or 'catastrophic' (22 per cent). Only 6 per cent treated it as 'normal'. See *Nezavisimaia Gazeta*, 17 August 1994. At the end of 1994 only 6 per cent of Russians, according to VTSIOM, strongly believed in the improvement of life in the country. According to another survey conducted by VTSIOM, 25 per cent think that in 1995 'the country will continue to slide into an abyss', and 12 per cent expect 'anarchy'. See *Moskovskie Novosti*, 15 January 1995.
18. The respondents could choose their answer from a list. See Levada (1995b).
19. Andrei Konchalovsky's movie *Kurochka Riaba* (*Little Chicken*, 1994) reflects this deep pessimism of Russian society in the efficacy of market reforms. In the movie the single and successful entrepreneur in the village is the object of universal hatred and mockery. The peasants, most of them heavy drinkers, prefer 'the old regime', the life on the collective farm, and refuse to support reforms. Konchalovsky suggests that it is impossible to make Russians into admirers of a market economy, private property and a bourgeois style of life. Evstigneiev, in a movie *Limita* (1994), essentially develops the same idea and shows how rich people in Russia are mostly criminals and are unable to build a capitalist society.
20. Yurii Levada's survey data provided interesting information about how people inimical to reforms adjust to reality. Among those who denounced the privatization and marketization of the Russian economy in 1994, 20 per cent had or planned to have their own business. See VTSIOM (1994), No.6.
21. The amount of services (cleaning, beauty salons and others) declined in 1994 to 28 per cent of the level of 1993. See *Izvestia*, 19 October 1994.
22. According to the survey of 2,000 Russians carried out in April 1994, the differences between positive and negative estimates were negative (i.e., the negative estimates were more numerous than positive) for 10 of 11 official institutions (political parties – 57 per cent; the parliament – 53 per cent; the government – 40 per cent; the President – 30 per cent; the courts – 27 per cent; and the mass media – 11 per cent).

Only the army then had a positive balance – 16 per cent (see *Moskovski Novosti,* 8 May 1994).

23. No less than one-third of the Soviet population in the Russian Federation at least once in five years (one-quarter of the population 3–4 times a year) addressed the authorities and media with their complaints through various means (usually letters and meetings with officials). See Grushin and Onikov (1980), pp.376, 379. The newspaper *Izvestia,* with a circulation of 8.6 million, received in 1987 about 0.5 million letters from its readers. See Shlapentokh (1970), p.148.

24. According to the VTSIOM data, when Russians were asked about their fears in 1989, they put 'the arbitrariness of the authorities' in seventh place (after 'the illness of relatives', 'war', 'own illness', 'natural disasters', 'old age', and 'the demise of mankind'. In 1994, 'the arbitrariness of authorities' was in fifth place (after 'the illness of relatives', 'criminals', 'own illness', 'poverty' and before 'the return to mass repression', 'war', 'interethnic conflicts', 'public humiliation', and 'natural disasters)'. See VTSIOM, No.1, 1995, p.13.

25. The 'jungle individualism' manifested itself blatantly in offices and factories in 1992–94. Being asked in 1994 'How does the fear of being fired affect the behavior of your colleagues?', only 2 per cent pointed to 'increasing solidarity' and one per cent referred to 'the planning of collective actions against firing'. See VTSIOM, No.1, 1995, p.30. Lev Gudkov, a leading Russian liberal sociologist, cited with great satisfaction data showing the rejection of social values by Russians, evidence that Russians are abandoning Communist ideology and now concentrate only on their individual life. See Gudkov (1995). The same satisfaction was expressed by Yuri Levada, when he wrote about 'destatization' and 'privatization' of the average Russian. See Levada (1995); VTSIOM, No.1, 1995, p.11. See also *Moskovski Novosti,* 9 January 1994.

26. It is remarkable that the social contacts diminished particularly among 'losers' – those who lost their jobs and whose incomes were evidently insufficient for a decent life.

27. The political indifference is particularly blatant among young people. According to a recent survey, more than 80 per cent of Russian students declared their indifference to any political party and movement. See Olga Stepanova, 'Bolshinstvo vybiraiet skepsis', *Nezavisimaia Gazeta,* 13 October 1994.

28. Only 7 per cent of the Russians responded positively in the spring of 1994, only a few months after the election of the new parliament, to the statement 'the parties in the Parliament reflect the interests and views existing in society'. See VTSIOM, No.4, 1994, p.13.

29. According to the liberal Moscow newspaper *Moskovski Novosti,* in 1985–91 79 per cent of the mothers asked by the foundation 'The right of mothers' said that their son joined the army as a draftee 'with great wish' or 'with the feeling of duty'. See *Moskovski Novosti,* 11 November 1994.

30. According to various polls, only a quarter of all Russians supported the military operation in Chechnya. Only 12 per cent endorsed the use of aviation and artillery against Grozny, the capital of the republic. See VTSIOM, No.1, 1995, p.7. Reflecting on the mood in the country, only 42 per cent of the officers in the survey conducted at the military academies and army units in Moscow in February 1995 declared that they would follow the commands of the superiors and would go to war in Chechnya. Fifty-two per cent declared that they would refuse to do so openly or indirectly. See *Komsomolskaia Pravda,* 18 February 1995.

31. Numerous articles have appeared in the Russian press that depict an abysmal situation for some of the Russian refugees in Russia. Correspondents describe vividly numerous situations where refugees live under the threat of administrative harassment and violence, under the threat of being evicted from boarding houses and other places

where they have been temporarily placed. See Gannushkina (1994); Grafova (1994).

32. Solzhenitsyn's talk on TV on 30 January 1995 passionately attacked Russians for their indifference to the fate of their compatriots. He found such actions to be a dangerous sign of the moral collapse of the Russian nation. *Ostankino*, 30 January, 8:40 pm, 1995.

33. In any case, in the election held on 12 December 1993, a quarter of all Russians voted for Zhirinovsky's extreme nationalist party. Later, in 1994, the Russians supported Communists in the local elections.

REFERENCES

Abraham, David (1986), *The collapse of the Weimar Republic: Political economy and crisis.* New York: Holmes & Meier.

Alexeivea, L. (1984), *Istoria Inakomyslia v SSSR. Noveishi period.* Benson, VA: Khronika Press.

Alexeivea, L. (1995, 22 January), 'Nesvobodnyie profsouzy', *Moskovie Novosti.*

Argumenty i Fakty (1994), No.1.

Argumenty i Fakty (1994), No.31.

Argumenty i Fakty (1994), No.50.

Argumenty i Fakty (1994), No.52.

Argumenty i Fakty (1994, July), No.17.

Argumenty i Fakty (1995), No.8.

Bell, Daniel (1960), *The end of ideology: On the exhaustion of politics in the fifties.* Glencoe, IL: Free Press.

Belov, Vasilli (1994, 15 November), 'Tina veka', *Sovietskaia Rossia.*

Bohlen, Celestine (1994, 25 January), 'Nationalist vote toughens Russian foreign policy', *The New York Times.*

Chorev, Boris (1994, 19 November), 'Nezhelatel'nyje inostrantsy', *Pravda.*

Dunlop, John, B. (1994), 'Will the Russians return from the near abroad?', *Post-Soviet Geography*, 35(4), 205–15.

Durkheim, Emile (1964), *The division of labor in society.* New York: Free Press.

Durkheim, Emile (1982), *Rules of sociological method.* New York: Free Press.

Dzhaginova, Elena (1994a), 'Povsednevanaia zhizn Rossian: 100 – 1994', *Segodnia.*

Dzhaginova, Elena (1994b), 'Vino i sigarety v zhizni Rossian', *Segodnia.*

Ellis, Edward Robb (1970), *A nation in torment: The Great American Depression, 1929–1939.* New York: Howard-McCann.

Eyck, Erich (1963), *A history of the Weimar Republic.* Cambridge, MA: Harvard University Press.

Gamson, William A. (1975), *The strategy of social protest.* Humewood, IL: Dorsey Press.

Gannushkina, Svetlana (1994, 28 April), 'Priniat' svoich brat'ev', *Express-Chronika.*

Goskomustat (1993), *Rossiiskaia Federatsia v 1992 godu.* Moscow: Respublikanskii informarzionno-izdatekskii Zentr.

Grafova, Lidija (1994, 30 March), 'Migratsija. Shtorm deviat' balov', *Literaturnaia Gazeta* (p.10).

Grushin, Boris (1993, 17 April), 'Rossia – 93: Novyie Mify – novaia realnost', *Nezavsaiama Gazeta.*

Grushin, Boris and Onikov, L. (1980), *Massovaia Informnatsia v Sovietskom Promyshlennom Gorode.* Moscow.

Gudkov, Lev (1994, 25 June), 'Mnohie gorozhane toskiut o proshlo', *Segodnia.*

Gudkov, Lev (1995, 23 February), 'Vlast i Chechenskaia voina v obshchestvennom mnenii Rossii', *Segodnia.*

Gurr, Ted Robert (1974), *Why men rebel.* Princeton, NJ: Princeton University Press.

Hiden, John (1974), *The Weimar Republic.* London: Longman.

Hirsch, Eric L. (1990), 'Sacrifice for the cause: Group processes, recruitment, and commitment in a student social movement', *American Sociological Review,* 55, 243–54.

Izvestia, (1993, 20 February).

Izvestia, (1993, 30 December).

Izvestia, (1993, 24 May).

Izvestia, (1994, 29 June).

Izvestia, (1994, 14 August).

Izvestia, (1994, 16 September).

Izvestia, (1994, 15 October).

Izvestia, (1994, 19 October).

Izvestia, (1994, 16 November).

Izvestia, (1994, 23 November).

Klandermans, Bert and Oegema, Dirk (1987), 'Potentials, networks, motivations, and barriers: Steps towards participation in social movements', *American Sociological Review,* 52, 519–31.

Komsomolskaia pravda (1994, 6 September).

Komsomolskaia pravda (1995, 18 February).

Levinson, Aleksei (1990, 1 July), 'Moskvichi i bezhency', *Moskovskie Novosti.*

Levinson, Aleksei (1993, 29 May), 'Goroda i Ogorody', *Izvestia.*

Levada, Yuri (1992, 21 September), 'Zhizn trudna no bolshinstvo tribuiet prodolzhemia reform', *Izvestia.*

Levada, Yuri (1993, 24 April), 'Chto lezhit na vesakh', *Izvestia.*

Levada, Yuri (1994a), 'Vectora izmenenii', *Sociological Research* (July–August), 22–34.

Levada, Yuri (ed.) (1994b), *Sovietskii Porstoi chelovek.* Moscow: VTSIOM.

Levada, Yuri (1995a, 15 January), 'Trevogi i ozhidania', *Moskovskie Novosti.*

Levada, Yuri (1995b), *Chelovek Sovietskii: piat let spustia (1989–94).* Moscow: VTSIOM.

Literaturnaia Gazeta (1994, 10 August).

Literaturnaia Rossiia (1994, 1 July).

Loizenau, Manon (1994, 4 September), 'Return to Mother Russia', *Guardian Weekly,* p.16.

McAdam, D., McCarthy, J.D. and Zald, M.N. (1988), 'Social movements', in Neil Smelser (ed.), *Handbook of sociology.* Newbury Park, CA: Sage Publications.

McCarthy, J.D. and Zald, M.N. (1976), 'Resource mobilization and social movements: A partial theory', *American Journal of Sociology,* 82(5), 1212–41.

Megalopolis-Express (1994, 21 March).

Merton, Robert (1957), *Social theory and social structure.* New York: Free Press.

Moskovskii Komsomolets (1994, 15 October).

Moskovski Novosti (1993, 28 February).

Moskovski Novosti (1994, 8 May).

Moskovski Novosti (1994, 2 October).

Moskovski Novosti (1994, 11 November).

Moskovski Novosti(1995, 15 January).

Nezavisimaia Gazeta (1994, 9 January).

Nezavisimaia Gazeta (1994, 6 June).

Nezavisimaia Gazeta (1994, 16 August).

Nezavisimaia Gazeta (1994, 17 August).

Oberschall, Anthony (1973), *Social conflict and social movements.* Englewood Cliffs, NJ: Prentice-Hall.

Olson, Mancur (1971), *The logic of collective action.* Cambridge, MA: Harvard University Press.

Paradis, Adrian A. (1967), *The hungry years: The story of the great American depression.* Philadelphia, PA: Chilton Book Co.

Petrenko, Elena (1995, 11 January), 'Pianstvo – norma zhizni', *Segodnia.*

Pravda (1994, 21 December).

Remnick, David (1993), *Lenin's tomb.* New York: Random House.

Riabushkin, Timon and Osipov, Gennadii (eds), (1982), *Sovietskaia Sotsiologia*, 1, Moscow: Nauka.

Rossiiskaia Gazeta (1995, 31 March).

Rotar, Igor (1994, 7 June), 'Russkich pereselencev pytajutsia ispol'zovat' kak politicheskuju silu', *Nezavisimaia Gazeta.*

Scull, Andrew T. (1988), 'Deviance and social control', in Neil Smelser (ed.), *Handbook of sociology.* Newbury Park, CA: Sage Publications.

Sedov, Leonid (1995), 'Peremny v strane i otnoshenie k peremenam', in *VTSIOM*, No.1, p.24.

Segodnia (1994, 24 June).

Segodnia (1994, 30 October).

Shlapentokh, Dimitry and Shlapentokh, V. (1990), 'Letters to the editor on ideologies in the USSR during the 1980s', in A. Jones (ed.), *Research on the Soviet Union and Eastern Europe* (Vol.1). Greenwich, CT: Jai Press.

Shlapentokh, Vladimir (ed.) (1970), *Problemy sotsiologii pechati*, 2. Novosibirsk: Nauka.

Shlapentokh, Vladimir (1986), *Soviet public opinion and ideology.* New York: Praeger.

Shlapentokh, Vladimir (1988), *Soviet ideologies in the period of Glasnost.* New York: Praeger.

Shlapentokh, Vladimir (1990), *Soviet intellectuals and political power: The post-Stalin era.* Princeton, NJ: Princeton University Press.

Shlapentokh, Vladimir (1994a), 'The Russian fallout', *Foreign Service Journal* (February), 32–9.

Shlapentokh, Vladimir (1994b), 'Review: The Russian pollster debacle, 1993', *Public Opinion Quarterly* (Winter).

Shlapentokh, Vladimir, Sendich, Maurice, and Pain, Emil (eds) (1994), *The New Russian diaspora.* Armonk, NY: M.E. Sharpe.

Soloukhin, Vladimir (1995), 'V demokratiou ia ne veriu', *Zavtra*, 4 (January).

Sovietskaia Rossia (1993, 21 December).

Stepanova, Olga (1994, 13 October), 'Bolshinstvo vybraiet skepsis', *Nezavisimaia Gazeta.*

Terechov, Vladimir (1994, 29 November), 'Rabotat' golovoi stanovit'sia neprestizhno [Prestige of intellectual work is on the decline]', *Nezavisimaia Gazeta.*

Tilly, Charles (1978), *From mobilization to revolution.* Reading, MA: Addison-Wesley.

Vecherniia Moskva (1995, 5 January).

Verkhvoskaia, A. (1972), *Pismo v redaktsiu i chitatel.* Moscow: Izdatelstov Moskovskogo Universiteta.

VTSIOM (various years). *Ekonomicheskie i Sotsilanyie Peremeny: monitoring obshchestvennogo mnenia.*

VTSIOM (1993), No.1

VTSIOM (1993), No.2.

VTSIOM (1993), No.4.

VTSIOM (1993), No.5.

VTSIOM (1993), No.6.

VTSIOM (1993), No.8.

VTSIOM (1994), No.1.

VTSIOM (1994), No.5

VTSIOM (1994). No.6

VTSIOM (1995), No.1.

Walsh, Edward J. and Warland, Rex H. (1983), 'Social movement involvement in the wake of a nuclear accident: Activists and free riders in the TMI area', *American Sociological Review*, 48, 764–81.

Zavtra (1994, December).

Zimmermann, Ekkart (1982), *Political violence, crises, and revolutions: Theories and research*. Boston, MA: G.K. Hall.

3

CITIZENSHIP EDUCATION IN HUNGARY: IDEALS AND REALITY

ZSUZSA MÁTRAI

DEFINITIONS OF CITIZENSHIP

In his classical theory published in 1950, T. H. Marshall envisaged citizenship as involving three elements that have evolved gradually throughout centuries. The first of these, civil rights, was the product of the eighteenth century and consists of such rights as the freedom of speech, thought and faith, the right to own property and the right to justice. These rights of freedom are ensured by the institutions of justice. The second element, political rights, was added to the notion of citizenship in the nineteenth century and has come to mean the right to participate in the political power, the right to vote and to be elected. The institutions corresponding to these rights are the parliament and the councils of local governments. As the third element, Marshall mentions social rights which developed in the twentieth century. He associates it with economic welfare and social security which are guaranteed by the educational system and social services.

The Marshallian theory is an interesting starting point in two respects. First, it confronts us with the question of whether social rights still have relevance today. Second, it requires us to investigate whether or not these three elements exhaust the meanings of citizenship at the end of the twentieth century.

Many experts regard social rights as an integral part of citizenship (see, for example, Barbalet, 1988; Report of the Commission on Citizenship, 1990; Weale, 1991; Parry, 1991). In addition, there has been Hungarian research into the civic and political attitudes of the population towards the so-called big change: the political and economic changes of the regime. Research focused on the definitions of democracy as well (Bruszt and

Simon, 1992), identifying three definitions of democracy: political democracy, social democracy and individual rights. Most of those who were asked emphasized the political aspects of democracy but half of the respondents also mentioned social and economic aspects, such as, for example, moderate differences in people's incomes or secure employment. In a comparative study, British citizens emphasized the need for social rights even more powerfully. People who were asked associated citizenship with a minimum standard of living and the right to medical care, a job and education (Conover and Searing, 1991).

Marshall considers the existence of legal relationships between the individual and the state as a necessary arrangement which ensures civil, political and social rights. Other scholars do not regard the nation-state as the only possible custodian of civil rights. J. P. Gardner (1990), for example, makes a distinction between 'nationality citizenship' and 'new citizenship'. Lynch (1992) argues for the internationalization of citizenship and for 'global citizenship'. According to his approach, human rights are added to the definition of democracy. Human rights, it has been argued, are better maintained by international organizations and covenants than the laws of individual countries, although more and more states may adapt them.

In Hungary today, as a result of political and economic changes, people's attitudes towards citizenship have changed with regard to all four types of rights which were mentioned above. The Hungarian population gained much in terms of civil, political and human rights but suffered great losses concerning social rights. Many social services, previously free of charge for everybody and perceived as part of citizenship rights, no longer exist. This has also resulted in a change in citizenship education, but not to the extent that one could expect.

In the present chapter I will first outline the process and the consequences of the 1989–90 changes in Hungary. Then I will introduce Hungarian citizenship education as a school subject, focusing on the citizenship behavior model it represents. Finally, I will compare the participation component of the model with the actual citizenship behavior of Hungarian youth.

THE CHANGE OF REGIME AND ITS CONSEQUENCES

From the mid-1960s to the end of the 1980s Hungary was the 'happiest barrack' in the Eastern Bloc. In political terms this meant a soft dictatorship where the one-party regime did not directly restrict the sovereignty of private life but expropriated all areas of political life 'in exchange'. Thus, only those who violated the unwritten law of 'mutual non-interference' and openly declared themselves as 'political opposition' came into conflict with the authorities.

The vast majority of Hungarian society was not disturbed by the change of the regime, partly because the system seemed to endure, and partly because everyday life showed signs of consolidation. The majority of the population saw new opportunities for building careers and new ways for economic growth to develop, and were willing to put up with continuing restricted civil liberties.

As in other East European countries, it was the change in the external political circumstances – the dramatic falling away of the cementing force of the ex-Soviet Union – that created the opportunity for the change of regime. Gorbachev's politics resulted in the gradual release of the external dictatorship's pressure. Internally, the predominance of the monolithic political power also eased. At the same time, the number of opposition groups that openly turned against and constantly defied the authorities increased significantly. The so-called 'hard democratic' opposition and the nationalist groups had a secret meeting as early as 1985, in order to exchange views. The support of the party bureaucracy became less and less unified, and the majority agreed that the leader of the system, Janos Kadar, had to go.

The struggle for power soon began and events followed each other rapidly. In 1987, Imre Pozsgay, one of the leaders of the Communist party's reform wing, came to a compromise with the nationalist group, in an attempt to isolate the hard democratic opposition. In 1988, Janos Kadar was ousted from his secretary-generalship, and was replaced by Karoly Grosz, who once again tried to consolidate the situation. Meanwhile, different opposition groups turned into political parties, forming the so-called Opposition Roundtable, and in March 1989 negotiations started between the authority and the opposition. In October, the Hungarian Socialist Workers' Party (MSZMP), after having been in power for 40 years, split in two, and the reform wing established the Hungarian Socialist Party (MSZP). At the same time the government, lead by Miklos Nemeth, turned into an independent, so-called 'expert government' and reached an agreement with the opposition about the constitutional steps needed for political change. As a part of this, Hungary was proclaimed a republic and the first democratic parliamentary elections were held in the spring of 1990.

The first democratic parliamentary election was conducted in two rounds, with more than 40 participating parties. Six of them got into parliament: the Hungarian Democratic Forum (MDF), which represented the nationalist sector, got 165 mandates; the Alliance of Free Democrats (SZDSZ), formed from the hard democratic opposition, received 91 mandates; the Independent Smallholders' Party (FKGP), the legal successor of the similarly called pre-Communist party, obtained 44 mandates; the Hungarian Socialist Party (MSZP), which was formed out of the reform wing of the former Communist party, got 33 mandates; the liberal Alliance of Young Democrats received 21 mandates; and the Christian Democratic People's Party (KDNP), which aimed to reintroduce historical traditions, also received 21 mandates. In the first round of the elections 65 per cent, and in the second round 45 per cent, of those eligible to vote actually voted. The new multi-party parliament held its first session in May 1990. The MDF, the FKGP and the KDNP formed a coalition government, Jozsef Antall became the Prime Minister, Arpad Goncz became President of the republic.

The constitutional framework of the new democratic system had already taken shape before the elections, under the rule of the expert government lead by Miklos Nemeth. This marked the end of the one-party state, and the peaceful establishment of multi-party parliamentarism. The establishment of a Constitution Court supported this trend. Negotiations concerning the withdrawal of the Russian troops from Hungary were also started by the Nemeth government. The Antall government completed these talks in the summer of 1991 and Hungary finally won back its sovereignty.

However, the new government was a disappointment to the constituency from the very start. The new political élite that named itself Christian-national touched the wrong chord. The social vision it sought to implement was very similar to pre-war 'gentry' Hungary. As a result, people considered the change of regime as merely a change in the ruling élites, the result of a total lack of social sensitivity on part of the new government. Indeed, at the local elections the parties associated with the central government coalition suffered a dramatic defeat. In most villages the majority of the people elected 'independent', socialist-inclined candidates. The MDF won only one mayoral mandate in the 22 districts of the capital. In spite of the opposition and stormy domestic politics, the government survived and completed its four-year term. The results of the 1994 parliamentary elections were no surprise: the Christian-national coalition was replaced by a social-liberal coalition of the MSZP (209 mandates) and the SZDSZ (69 mandates), elected by a vast majority (72 per cent of the voters).

As a result of the changes, conditions for a free market system were established, putting an end to the previous centralized economy. These economic changes were and are still occurring amidst an economic crisis. The country's foreign debt is mounting from year to year and through its economic policy the government is trying hard to find a balance between monetary restriction and economic intensification. The Hungarian economy is burdened with inflation, unemployment and high taxes; the salaries of employees are low; and the huge income differences are close to tearing the society apart. The welfare state that had developed under the socialist regime is also breaking up. There has been a drastic reduction in state subsidies for health care, education and culture.

With the opening of the borders and as a result of the protracted war in neighboring Bosnia, immigrants entered the country, refugee camps were set up, and there emerged a black labor market and organized crime, on both an international and a national level. National, ethnic and minority conflicts also rock Hungarian society. The steady marginalization of the gypsy population – the main losers of the process of change – creates sharp domestic conflict, while in foreign politics Hungary faces the problem of granting minority rights to Hungarians living in neighboring countries.

CHARACTERISTICS OF CITIZENSHIP EDUCATION

Citizenship education in Hungary constitutes a special field and a distinct school subject. This has not always been the case. Prior to 1978, citizenship education was diffuse and was taught mainly through humanities. Civics, as a distinct school subject, was created in the 1978 curriculum reform. The reform changed the traditional past-centered nature of social science education, and topics dealing with the present became included in the curriculum alongside history. Civics became a normative-type subject aimed at maintaining the ideological character of social science education in Hungary.

Curricular changes, however, lagged behind political change. As a result, there has been a transitional period during which the centralized curriculum did not cater to the needs of growing pluralism within Hungarian society. The traditional 8+4 grade school structure broke up and new school types were established on the secondary level (6 and 8 grade academic secondary schools), while private schools run by churches and foundations also appeared in both primary and secondary levels. The decentralization process resulted in a growing number of school-based local curricula which replaced the former central curriculum. Privatization in the realm of textbook-publishing also occurred. State publishers and private publishers now determine the content of textbooks.

Under these circumstances, educational aims have become diversified and the public has become suspicious of and opposed to ideology-inclined education. The ideological struggles among Christian-national, socialist and liberal forces have only reinforced these trends. During the first four years following the political reform, Christian-national values won state support. They advocated, among other things, making religious education a compulsory subject. Although this particular effort failed, the new regime clearly showed that politics are not divorced from ideology. The value-debates about the different versions of the National Core Curriculum are an example of the great public sensitivity to the issues involved, especially regarding citizenship education.

During the transitional period following the change of regime all political parties were in favor of decentralization and privatization processes in the educational system. Simultaneously, however, it was feared that the end of uniform curricular control would lower educational standards and make it impossible for students to transfer between schools. Educators suggested a compromise between total state control and total decentralization: a national core curriculum would be introduced in all the schools offering compulsory education (i.e., up to age 16). Schools would be free to implement their chosen curriculum alongside the core curriculum. The National Core Curriculum should specify topics and general requirements in the various fields of knowledge but not the specific subjects or the number of hours to be devoted to them. These should be decided by the schools themselves. Schools should also be free to decide which textbooks to use.

The Educational Act (1993), including the National Core Curriculum, was passed. However, owing to political disagreements, implementation did not materialize during the rule of the Christian-national coalition. The government wanted to push through a National Core Curriculum based on their own ideology. However, these attempts failed because of the resistance of the opposition parties and educational experts.

The new social-liberal government set about preparing for the implementation of the National Core Curriculum in the first year of its term. In order to avoid value-debates it tried to free the restructured document from all ideological connotations. A wide-ranging expert poll also helped to legitimize the document through modification of the content and phrasing. The last version of the National Core Curriculum is currently under government consideration. If the government approves the present version, its implementation in the schools will take about three years.

The present situation is that the schools actually teach whatever they want. There is no available national data concerning the actual structure and content of education. Characteristics of citizenship education in Hungary can thus be described only on the basis of indirect information.

The Subject Structure of Citizenship Education

Most subjects, but especially the teaching of history, literature, philosophy and ethics, provide opportunities for citizenship education. Citizenship education in a more specialized form appears only in two school subjects in Hungary: civics and social studies. Both of these subjects deal with the present, and their contents often overlap. However, while legal-political elements are dominant in civics, economic-social elements predominate in social studies.

Looking at the Hungarian curriculum and textbooks on the market it is evident that civics is mostly taught in grade 8 in the general schools, and social studies in the final grade of secondary schools. Information concerning the implementation of these subjects in the school can be obtained only indirectly, using publishers' reports of the sales of textbooks. A private publisher in 1994 published a textbook for 8th-grade students. Out of 3,771 schools around the country, 2,265 ordered the book.[1] Peli, Bozoki and Jakab, published a textbook for secondary schools. In 1993, the publisher registered orders from 675 out of 866 secondary schools.[2] The schools that did not order these books either do not teach these subjects or use other social studies or civics textbooks or alternative programs.[3] The number of these schools is low and varies between 100–150 each year.[4] Schools using alternative programs teach social studies during more than one year, in grades 1–4 or 1–6. However, the general practice definitely is, that after a chronological overview of history, citizenship education is dealt with in the framework of an independent, present-centered subject in the final grade of the general school and in the final grade of the academic and vocational secondary schools.

The not yet implemented National Core Curriculum designates ten areas of education. The area entitled 'Man and Society' covers the content of civic education. In grades 1–4 and 5–6 this content is transmitted through social studies; in grades 7–8 through social studies and civics; while in grades 9–10 it is studied through civics (National Core Curriculum, 1995). The National Core Curriculum does not address schooling after compulsory education (grades 11–12), this will probably be regulated by the national exam requirements. The reform of the final examination (matriculation) has just started, and plans concerning the subjects and requirements of the examinations have not been finalized. Thus, we cannot know how the final examination will affect the various school subjects and the content of civic education.

The Contents of Citizenship Education

In order to obtain insights into the contents of citizenship education in Hungary, I did a content analysis of the relevant sections of the National Core Curriculum, using Ichilov's (1990) sophisticated approach. Ichilov creates a ten-dimensional model (see Table 3.2) to map role patterns of citizenship, and examines the alternative possibilities within these dimensions to make up frameworks for the analysis of several combinations of individual citizen attitudes. The model describes the dimensions and alternatives gathered under the following facets: theoretical vs practical orientation; attitudinal orientation (affective, cognitive, evaluative); motivational orientation (obligatory, voluntary); action orientation (inactive, passive, active); means/ ends orientation (instrumental, diffuse); value orientation (particularistic, universalistic); participatory objective (consent, dissent); participatory means (conventional, unconventional); political or civic/social domains; national or transnational arenas.

The author herself suggests several possible uses for the model. Besides the analysis of role patterns of citizenship common in political socialization studies, she believes that it might also be useful in research and development

TABLE 3.1
CITIZENSHIP EDUCATION THROUGH SCHOOL SUBJECTS BY SCHOOL GRADE:
A COMPARISON OF GENERAL PRACTICE AND THE NATIONAL CORE CURRICULUM

Grade	Present General Practice	Future Plans National Core Curriculum
Grades 1–4		Social studies
Grades 5–6		Social studies
Grades 7–8		Social studies, civics
Grade 8	Civics	
Grades 9–10		Civics
Grade 12	Social studies	

TABLE 3.2
ICHILOV'S DIMENSIONS OF CITIZENSHIP

1. Theoretical vs Practical 1a. Verbal adherence to principle 1b. Actual behavior	6. Value Orientations 6a. Particularistic 6b. Universalistic
2. Attitudinal Orientation 2a. Affective 2b. Cognitive 2c. Evaluative	7. Participatory Objectives 7a. Expression of consent 7b. Expression of dissent
3. Motivational Orientation 3a. External/obligatory 3b. Internal/voluntary	8. Participatory Means 8a. Conventional 8b. Unconventional
4. Action Orientation 4a. Inactive 4b. Passive 4c. Active	9. Domains of Citizenship 9a. Political 9b. Civic/social
5. Means/Ends Orientation 5a. Instrumental 5b. Diffuse	10. Arenas of Citizenship 10a. National 10b. Transnational

Source: Ichilov (1990), p.19.

of textbooks, teaching practices and teacher-training programs.

Going back to the original topic, I will now try to describe the content structure of Hungarian citizenship education using the above model.

Referring to the two most commonly used textbooks and the National Core Curriculum as the sources of my analysis, I will focus on what role patterns of citizenship they transmit to students, and how much they resemble and differ from each other. However, to carry out this task, I have to modify the model a little.

The following modifications were made to Ichilov's model. The width or narrowness of citizenship orientations (dimensions nine and ten in Ichilov's model), will hold the first places in the modified model. In addition, the two original alternatives in the ninth dimension will be extended to four: civil rights, political rights, social rights and human rights. The institutions protecting these rights will be considered as well.

Ichilov's fourth dimension (action orientation) comes next in the modified model. I will examine only two alternatives here: passive and active. With some modification, the first dimension, which investigates whether the documents require merely theoretical knowledge or the corresponding praxis as well, will be included.

I will also examine participatory objectives (the seventh dimension in Ichilov's model), focusing on expressions of consent and dissent.

Ichilov's second dimension will be last, examining whether the documents address the affective, the cognitive or the evaluative dimensions of citizenship. This dimension basically covers the categories which are customarily used in the analysis of such documents, namely, whether a document can be described as normative, descriptive or multiperspective. Ichilov's third dimension, motivational orientation, will be used to assess the representation of external-obligatory or internal-voluntary orientations in the documents.

The fifth, sixth and eighth dimensions in Ichilov's model will not be used for the content analysis of the above-mentioned documents.

The first two dimensions will be used to examine the topics of the documents, the next two for exploring their methodological apparatus and educational requirements, while the last one will be used to analyze their general character. Ichilov's model has an advantage over conventional tools used for the purpose of content analysis of educational materials. It enables a more sophisticated analysis of each citizenship orientation as well as of the interrelationships among the various orientations.

Domains of citizenship: The content analysis revealed that 26 out of the 31 items in 8th-grade civics deal with the national situation of Hungary; within this category ten topics deal with society, 16 with the Hungarian state; five of the topics concerning society are distinctly economic and sociological in nature, the other five are closely connected to citizen rights and to the institutions ensuring them. The 16 topics dealing with the Hungarian state apply basically to the four groups of citizen rights and the corresponding institutions.

TABLE 3.3
THE MODIFIED MODEL OF CITIZENSHIP ORIENTATIONS BROKEN INTO FACETS

1. Domains of Citizenship
    1a. Civil rights
    1b. Political
    1c. Social rights
    1d. Human rights
	2. Arenas of Citizenship
	    2a. National
	    2b. Transnational

3. Action Orientation
    3a. Passive
    3b. Active
	4. Participatory Objective
	    4a. Expression of consent
	    4b. Expression of dissent

5. Attitudinal Orientation
    5a. Affective
    5b. Cognitive
    5c. Evaluative	

Civil rights appear under two topics: basic rights and jurisdiction. The introduction of political rights gets the greatest emphasis, being present in ten topics: government systems (democracy, dictatorship), the democratic state (constitution), citizenship, political rights, parliamentary and local government elections (right to vote), the state and the division of power, the parliament, the President of the republic, the government, local government. Social rights are represented in seven topics: local community (support system), diversification of the Hungarian society (professions, wealth, age groups), the world of work (realization of interests, labor laws, unemployment, social security system), economic, social and cultural rights, education, health care and social politics. Human rights appear in four topics: human rights and their international protection (children's rights included), equal rights of citizens, Hungarian minorities living abroad and minority groups (ethnic, religious) in the Hungarian society.

We can draw the conclusion that the 8th-grade civics textbook which has been analyzed, although dealing thoroughly with all four groups of rights, primarily stresses newly gained political rights and the corresponding institutions, with social rights which were significantly cut down following the political reform taking second place.

The social studies textbook taught in the final grade of secondary schools, as its name indicates, focuses on social issues rather than on legal-political ones. Only seven out of the 25 topic units involve some kind of citizen rights directly. Civil and political rights are involved in two topics: politics as a system, democracy and dictatorship. Social rights appear in four topics: social-cultural disadvantages, social diversification, social politics, distribution policies in social politics. Human rights are mentioned only in the section describing disadvantaged ethnic groups. Thus, at present, students in secondary schools learn a lot more about citizen rights than students in the general schools.

Social studies required in grades 1–4 and 5–6 in the planned National Core Curriculum do not involve citizen rights directly. Certain elements, such as Hungarian national symbols, nationalities, ethnic groups, Hungarian minorities living abroad, are included. Social studies in grades 7–8 directly discusses citizen rights – with the exception of civil rights. Political rights and especially the institutions ensuring them are dealt with in two out of the five major topics, in the section about local communities (student self-government in the school) and in the section about political divisions (parties, representative organizations, chambers, parliamentary democracy). Trade unions are also mentioned under topics of another unit dealing with social issues such as professions and wealthy groups, impoverishment, unemployment, social inequalities. Human rights are dealt with primarily under the heading of social divisions, which includes such issues as nationalities and ethnic groups, gypsies in Hungary, churches and religious communities, and gender. Xenophobia, as a socio-psychological factor influencing human rights, is also included.

The requirements of grades 7–8 and 9–10 civics aim explicitly at citizenship education. Of the 17 topics designated for these grades, two units are dedicated to civil rights and corresponding institutions (basic rights, jurisdiction), nine units deal with political rights and institutions (constitution, the system of election, government, parliament, Prime Minister, local government, the sovereignty of the state), three units mention social rights and institutions (education, health care, social politics) and three

TABLE 3.4

MENTIONS OF CITIZENSHIP RIGHTS IN TEACHING MATERIAL[a]

	Civil rights	Political rights	Social rights	Human rights
Civics Grade 8	2	10	7	4
Social Studies Grade 12	2	2	4	1
National Core Curriculum Grades 1–10	2	11	5	5

[a] Based on their frequency of appearance in the topic units.

units address human rights (equal rights of citizens, Hungarian minorities living abroad, human rights and their international protection).

All in all, the National Core Curriculum treats the four groups of citizen rights exhaustively: they are planned to be taught in four grades instead of one, and they are taught continually within the domains of these two school subjects.

Table 3.4 clearly shows that the teaching of the four groups of citizen rights and the institutions ensuring them is balanced neither in the present practice, nor in the National Core Curriculum. In both instances political rights are dominant, perhaps as a natural consequence of the recent events associated with the political reforms.

Arenas of citizenship: Of the 31 topics in 8th-grade civics only six units discuss transnational questions, such as foreign policy and diplomatic relations between Hungary and Europe, or the UN, European security, global problems. These topics deal mainly with international organizations and with global, social, economic, political and ecological issues.

Of the 25 topics in secondary school final-grade social studies, four deal with transnational questions. One of them discusses different cultures from a multicultural approach. The other three investigate ecological questions and the relationship between man and nature.

Grades 1–4 and 7–8 social studies in the National Core Curriculum cover only the national arena. At the same time, one out of five major topics for grade 5–6 material deals exclusively with transnational topics from a multicultural approach (comparison of people's ways of living in different cultures). In grades 7–8 the section of civics dealing with Hungary's foreign affairs and international organizations is the only one relating to transnational issues. In the case of grades 9–10 topics, four out of five major topics are clearly transnational, including topics like international protection of human rights, European and international organizations and global issues.

Table 3.5 reveals that all three documents deal similarly with national and transnational topics, and put much greater emphasis on national issues.

TABLE 3.5
FREQUENCY OF NATIONAL AND TRANSNATIONAL TOPICS

	National topics	*Transnational topics*
Civics Grade 8	25	6
Social Studies Grade 12	21	4
National Core Curriculum Grades 1–10	32	6

Action orientation: This dimension has been interpreted in our content analysis as a distinction between theoretical and practical knowledge.

In Hungary, the distinction between the dimensions concerning passive and active citizenship education refers to the methodology of teaching: it may either be restricted to the conveyance of information, or cultivate students' ability to independently acquire and transmit knowledge. Active teaching could include library work, textual and statistical analysis, fieldwork, and the use of sociological, economic, and political research methods. It also includes simulations and role-play in investigating a problem. Though in this respect we can find some differences among the three analyzed documents, basically the goal of all of them is that students should not be satisfied with ready-made information, and that they should try to take an independent attitude in gathering information.

In Table 3.6, the frequencies of the different forms of active teaching are presented. In order to interpret Table 3.6, one must keep in mind that it incudes only practices related to citizenship education topics. As such these practices represent about 25 per cent of all the learning strategies in grade 8 civics, about 70 per cent in secondary school social studies and about 60 per cent in the National Core Curriculum. Table 3.6 reveals that theoretically oriented inquiry outweighs fieldwork and games simulation in all three documents.

TABLE 3.6
THE RATIO OF EXERCISES AIMING AT INDEPENDENT ACQUISITION OF INFORMATION

	Inquiry	*Fieldwork*	*Game simulation*
Civics Grade 8	31	17	12
Social Studies Grade 12	15	1	2
National Core Curriculum Grades 1–10	17	7	8

Participatory objectives: In Table 3.7 the frequencies of activities encouraging free discussion are shown.

After these figures are compared with the sum total of exercises and requirements in citizenship education topics, expression of free opinion makes up about 13 per cent of grade 8 civics, about 40 per cent of secondary school social studies textbooks, and about 30 per cent of the National Core Curriculum.

TABLE 3.7
FREQUENCY OF EXERCISES ENCOURAGING FREE DISCUSSIONS

| Civics
Grade 8 | Social Studies
Grade 12 | National Core Curriculum
Grades 1–10 |
|---|---|---|
| 31 | 13 | 14 |

Attitudinal orientation: The attitudinal orientation expressed in the documents can be inferred mainly from the generic characteristics of the documents. The two textbooks represent two different genres. Grade 8 civics is an exercise-textbook with equal amounts of descriptive and statistical text and pictorial sources, exercises and summarizing questions. Secondary school social studies, on the other hand, uses a collection of readings with hardly any descriptive texts and with exercises for the analysis of the readings.

The genre of the National Core Curriculum – just like that of any other curriculum – is determined by the types of requirements it contains. The educational requirements of the National Core Curriculum focus on ability development, with the emphasis on information acquisition and evaluative skills.

Our analysis of the exercises reveals that in all three documents there is a considerable number of exercises that require independent information acquisition or evaluative skills. These add up to about 30 per cent in grade 8 civics textbook, about 80 per cent in secondary school social studies and about 65 per cent in the National Core Curriculum.

None of the documents can be characterized by an affective orientation, in other words, none of them is normative. Grade 8 civics is cognitive oriented. Secondary school social studies is, however, basically evaluatively oriented, considering its multi-perspective sources. The National Core Curriculum seems to aim at some balance between cognitive and evaluative orientation.

PARTICIPATORY ORIENTATIONS OF YOUTH: MODELS AND REALITY

In conclusion, what is the overall picture? What kinds of citizenship attitudes do Hungarian curriculum and instructional materials display? What are the citizenship models youngsters are recommended to follow? Our analysis seems to reveal a general agreement concerning the desire not to encourage active, participatory citizenship attitudes. Instead, the materials are aimed at preparing knowledgeable citizens. The instructional materials focus primarily on domestic issues and on Hungarian democracy, and attempt to develop skills for independent information acquisition and evaluatation, and for free expression of opinions, including dissenting ones. Youngsters, however, are encouraged to become spectators rather than active participants in the political process. They are entitled to their opinions, but are not urged to translate them into action. This is the model, the ideal of citizenship education. But to what extent does this model describe the actual citizenship orientations of Hungarian youth? This question clearly is not within the scope of the present chapter, nor do Hungarian political socialization studies as yet provide sufficient information. I shall, therefore, narrow down the question, and try to determine only if the lack of active-participatory citizenship orientations indeed characterizes the attitudes of Hungarian youth in reality.

Two recent studies offer some clues. One study was carried out among a representative sample of 14 to 18-year-olds (Garami and Tóth, 1994). The other was conducted at a teachers' training college (Civizmus, 1994).[5] A questionnaire was administered to 500 prospective elementary school teachers (ages 18–25) about issues that influence their civic activities. In both studies respondents were asked about their participatory behavior and about their intentions to participate in political life.

Regarding the actual political participation of youth, only one per cent of the 14 to 18-year-old respondents reported participation in political organizations, or in other types of political activities. Similarly, more than 80 per cent of the young adults reported not having taken part in any kind of political activity during 1993.

The situation regarding intentions to participate is somewhat more encouraging. Youngsters aged 14–18 years indicated their intention to participate in such peaceful political activities as signature collection (58 per cent), and 42 per cent were willing to protest by signing a petition. However, the percentage of those who intend to participate in the parliamentary elections was quite low. Only 26 per cent declared that they would surely go to vote, and 33 per cent said that they probably would. Concerning the prospective teachers, 83 per cent did not intend to be active politically, and at most were willing to take part in the work of charity organizations (76 per cent), human rights organizations (73 per cent), or students' self-government activities (61 per cent).

Both studies asserted that the reasons for the low participation rates among young people are mainly little interest in politics, a dislike for politics, distrust in politicians, and a low sense of political efficacy. The majority of the 14–18-year-old respondents felt that political parties care the least about their problems, and 57 per cent of the young adults felt that they have hardly any influence in political matters.

A great correspondence therefore seems to exist between the citizenship model as represented in citizenship education, and the actual political attitudes and behavior of young people in Hungary. Rather than claiming a causal relationship between the two, it should be pointed out that active participation has not characterized Hungarian political culture. During the pre-war era, politics was the prerogative and the exclusive domain of the élite, and at the present stage of Hungarian democracy, civil society is just begining to emerge. The question remains whether citizenship education could be expected to encourage youngsters to be more active in shaping their own future. Hungarian citizenship education has taken significant strides in that direction, but much more must be done.

NOTES

1. I took the data from the Korona Publisher's written account on book orders.
2. Here again, I took the data from the textbook publisher's written account on book orders.
3. There are several such alternative programs. Two of these programs have social studies textbooks for the lower grades (grades 1–4) of general school. One is the Zsolnai program (Hölgye, 1992), the other is the Fifty–Fifty program (Mátrai, 1994–95). Besides these, there are two projects for working out a new teaching conception for secondary school social studies and civics (Arató, 1992; Balla and Szebenyi, 1994). The former was initiated with the support of the World Bank, the latter enjoys the support of the US and is financed by The Joint Eastern Europe Center for Democratic Education and Government.
4. This estimation is based on oral information from the Association of Textbook Publishers.
5. I wish to acknowledge the help of Ildikú Szabú and Janos Kriskú who put the questionnaire and the survey data at my disposal before writing their final study.

REFERENCES

Act LXXIX of 1993 on Public Education of the Hungarian Republic (1993). Budapest: Ministry of Culture and Education.
Arató, L. (1992). '*Társadalomismeret*' (Social studies), *Iskolakultœra*, 13/14, 116–38.
Balla, Á. and Szebenyi, P. (1994a). '*A jó polgár*' (The good citizen), A Civitas program iskolai tanterve (The curriculum of the Civitas program) (unpublished).
Balla, Á. and Szebenyi, P. (1994b). *Állampolgári ismeretek az általános iskola 8. osztálya számára* (Civics for grade 8 of general school). Budapest: Korona Kiadó.
Barbalet, J.M. (1988). *Citizenship: Rights, struggle and inequality*. Minneapolis: University of Minnesota Press.
Bruszt, L. and Simon, J. (1992). '*A Nagy Átalakulás*' (The big change), *Politikatudományi Szemle*, 1, 75–98.
Civizmus (1994). Kérdöív (Questionnaire). Kecskemét, Tanitóképz Föiskola.
Commission on Citizenship (1990). *Encouraging citizenship*. London: HMSO.
Conover, P.J., Crewe, I.M. and Searing, D.D. (1991). 'The nature of citizenship in the United States and Great Britain: Empirical comments on theoretical themes', *Journal of Politics*, 23(3), 800–32.
Garami, E. and Tóth, O. (1994). *Ifjúság 1993. Társadalmi, csal.di helyzet és politikai attitüdök* (Youth, 1993: Social and family conditions, political attitudes). Budapest:

Népjóléti Minisztérium.

Gardner, J.P. (1990). 'What lawyers mean by citizenship', in *Report of the Commission on Citizenship: Encouraging citizenship* (pp.63–77). London: HMSO.

Hölgye, L. (1992). *Társadalomismeret 4. osztály* (Social studies grade 4). Budapest: Calibra Kiadó.

Ichilov, O. (1990). 'Dimensions and role patterns of citizenship in democracy', in O. Ichilov (ed.), *Political socialization, citizenship education, and democracy* (pp.11–25). New York: Teachers College Press.

Lynch, J. (1992). *Education for citizenship in a multicultural society* (pp.9–24). London: Cassell.

Marshall, T.H. (1950). *Citizenship and social class* (pp.10–11). Cambridge: Cambridge University Press.

Mátrai, Z. (1994/95). *Társadalomismeret 1–2* (Social studies 1–2). Budapest: Calibra Kiadó.

Nemzeti A. (1995). National Core Curriculum (unpublished).

Parry, G. (1991). 'Conclusion: Path to citizenship', in U. Vogel and M. Moran (eds), *The frontiers of citizenship*. New York: St Martin's Press.

Péli, G., Bozóki, A. and Jakab, G. (1991). *Társadalomismeret a középiskolák IV. osztálya számára* (Social studies for grade 4 of secondary schools). Budapest: Tankönyvkiadó.

Weale, A. (1991). 'Citizenship beyond borders', in U. Vogel and M. Moran (eds), *The frontiers of citizenship*. New York: St Martin's Press.

4

NATION-BUILDING, COLLECTIVE IDENTITIES, DEMOCRACY AND CITIZENSHIP EDUCATION IN ISRAEL

ORIT ICHILOV

INTRODUCTION

The state of Israel is now half a century old. Yet, Israeli society today is more deeply divided than ever. No consensus exists concerning issues such as the separation of state and religion, what should be the final destination of the current peace process with the Palestinians and neighboring Arab countries, and the price that Israel is willing to pay in exchange for peace. So deep and unbridgeable have the rifts between orthodox and non-orthodox Jews become that articles published recently in daily newspapers suggested that the only solution is perhaps to divide Israel into two states: a religious and a secular one.

Educating the younger generation for citizenship where little consensus exists regarding a vision of what Israeli society should be, and what binds citizens together, is an extremely difficult task. Citizenship is, after all, a complex and multidimensional concept. It consists of legal, cultural, social, and political elements, which provide citizens with defined rights and obligations, a sense of identity, and social bonds. Citizenship is considered one among many identities of an individual which 'helps to tame the divisive passions of other identities' by conveying to each individual citizen a society's collective memory: cultural togetherness and nationality and the collaborative sense of purpose in fraternity (Heater 1990, p.184). However princely, these elements which bind people together with a common identity of citizenship are controversial within Israeli society today.

In addition, Israel continues to absorb immigrants, mainly from the former Soviet Union and Ethiopia. These immigrants arrive from non-democratic countries, and lack experience in democratic citizenship.

Citizenship education is also problematic among the Arab citizens of Israel, who find it difficult to form an affinity with a Jewish nation-state.

Examination of the Israeli context of citizenship education must take into account changes regarding the election system as well. Voters today are entitled to participate in primary elections within each party to elect the party's representatives to the Israeli parliament (Knesset), and the Prime Minister is elected by direct personal vote. This is a change from the past where parliament membership was determined by a special committee within each party, and where voters could not split their ballot and vote separately for Prime Minister and for a political party. These changes may foster a stronger sense of political efficacy and participation among citizens. The great exposure of Israeli citizens to international TV channels and press may promote greater global awareness in spite of citizens' preoccupation with regional affairs.

The purpose of the present chapter is to investigate the central trends concerning citizenship education in Israel, and to examine how they are related to changing values and to a changing sociopolitical reality. We begin by providing an historical overview, and proceed to examine current trends.

ZIONIST EDUCATION IN THE THE PRE-STATE (YISHUV) PERIOD

The institutional foundations of the state of Israel were laid by Zionist pioneers prior to the establishment of the state in 1948. Although these institutions lacked sovereignty, they provided many public services, such as education, and performed various governmental functions. 'Citizenship' is conventionally perceived and defined with reference to an existing state. It is, therefore, interesting to note that citizenship education[1] preceded the establishment of the state of Israel and was entitled 'education for Zionist citizenship'.

During the Yishuv period national symbols were restored, developed and articulated. The main functions of the emerging national symbols were to erase two thousand years of Diaspora, erect a bridge over time and space, and amalgamate Jewish immigrants from all over the globe into one nation. The newly instituted progressive and modern Hebrew educational system took an active part not only in transmitting national values and symbols to the younger generation, but also in the revival and affirmation of these values and symbols.

There was a general consensus among educators regarding the aims of Zionist education. It was expected to inculcate in the younger generation a strong loyalty to the ideas of national rebuilding, and of the redemption of the land. The ideal was to produce 'pioneers' dedicated to the rebuilding of the foundations for the state to come, willing to postpone the fulfilment of their personal wishes and to give precedence to the achievement of collective goals.

However, there was a debate among educators between two opposing pedagogical philosophies concerning the implementation of Zionist education in the schools. Many educators held the opinion that the study of Zionism should form the core of the curriculum with the social sciences occupying a marginal place: 'If vision [is our guide] – we cannot be content with rational Socratic teaching of legislation and social and historical problems. Vision is embodied in experiences, events, and impressions; in personalities, images and legends' (Urinovsky, 1929, pp.112–17). It was also believed that primacy should be given to emotions and impressions and not to the cognitive aspects in the learning process. According to the other approach, which was less popular, the curriculum should mainly provide conceptual tools for analyzing the complex social reality. Its advocates held the opinion that although 'National-political emotions are of central importance', and 'symbols and symbolic acts [such as] raising and saluting the flag, singing the national anthem... are suggestive means that political education anywhere cannot and should not do without, a moderate use of these means is appropriate, while an excessive use is harmful' (Riger, 1929, pp.57–63). The first approach finally won. Zionist education became part of the schools' curriculum, was incorporated into every school subject, and was taught as a separate subject as well. All school subjects and the various aspects of school life were turned into a passing parade of national symbols, and every occasion became an identification rite. Educators proudly declared that: 'Today each school subject opens its pages and hours to the Zionist enterprise. Each reader today contains a selection of the legacy of the founders, leaders, and dreamers of Zionism. Every arithmetic book uses the rebuilding of the land as a subject for problem solving and exercises' (Ben-Yehuda, 1949, p.77).

A central characteristic of the education for Zionist citizenship was the primacy given to emotional and expressive components, over cognitive and rational ones. There had been a general understanding among educators that 'deeply rooted and undisputed Zionist convictions are not acquired through rational deliberation, but through the development of healthy emotions during childhood and youth' (Ben-Yehuda, 1949, p.78). Educators were nonetheless aware of the dangers entailed in emotionally centered education and attempts were made to prevent this: 'not to bring into the schools the emotionalism of propaganda, but the vital national emotions. To stay away from the sensational character of propaganda, and stress instead emotional maturity through education' (Bistritzki, 1948, p.25).

Celebration of holidays in the schools presented ample occasions for the inculcation of nationalist emotions. In the Diaspora the celebration of Jewish holidays had had mainly religious connotations. New ways of celebrating the holidays were conceived, with an emphasis on national themes. These were claimed to represent the revival of ancient customs dating back to periods of independent Jewish statehood preceding the two thousand years of exile. New holidays related to the Zionist settlement were also instituted. These included, for example, the birthday of Herzl, the founder of Zionism. The celebration of holidays and national ceremonies in the schools came to function as a rite of identification with national symbols and Zionist ideology. All children took an active part in these festivities, dancing, singing, reciting, not merely as passive spectators.

The ancient Hebrew calendar was introduced in the schools, replacing the one which took the birth of Jesus Christ as the chronological reference point in relation to which events were 'dated'. The introduction of a unique dating system has a symbolic function very similar to that of introducing a unique national anthem or flag (Zerubavel, 1977). Such symbols and systems are internalized during early socialization and become part of the most basic concepts shared by all members of a society.

Zionist education also included the recruitment of students for various national projects and tasks. For example, the schools organized 'work camps' to assist agricultural settlements, especially during harvest periods. In addition, the students cultivated vegetable and flower gardens around the schools and contributed their fruits to the Jewish National Fund[2] (JNF) on Shavuoth (Festival of the giving of the Torah). The students also collected money for the JNF. They made money, for example, by cleaning up the neighborhood and by selling products which they made in arts and crafts classes. Youngsters often donated money that they had received as birthday gifts. The educational philosophy of encouraging students to contribute to the JNF was not 'sheer philanthropy'. It was believed that 'by contributing to the JNF youngsters are educated to participate in voluntary national activities of self redemption' (Ben-Yehuda, 1949, p.98).

CITIZENSHIP EDUCATION DURING THE FIRST YEARS OF STATEHOOD

The establishment of the state of Israel was a turning point which brought about ideological and institutional changes. These affected citizenship education as well. One of the first and major objectives of the leadership of the newly born state was to create a strong central government that would transcend partisan interests and affiliations. The institutional framework that had operated during the pre-state period lacked sovereignty, and consequently depended on the voluntary compliance of citizens. In addition, these institutions were fragmented and affiliated with the various factions within the Zionist movement. There were, for example, several military organizations, and the educational system was divided into so-called 'streams'. The three major Hebrew educational sub-systems were: the religious, the general Zionist, and the socialist-labor stream. The tasks of centralization and depoliticization of various organizations and institutions, and the creation of an effective central government to take charge of the former, dominated the first years of statehood.

The first years of statehood were also marked by mass immigration of Jews into Israel. From Europe came survivors of the holocaust, and from Arab countries in the Middle East came many refugees. Immigrants arrived mainly from non-democratic countries and countries in which Jews had limited citizenship rights. They, therefore, lacked the experience of participatory citizenship. This situation presented a challenge to Israel as a young democracy: there was a need to re-socialize the immigrants to function effectively within a democracy.

Concerning citizenship education, it became clear that what was adequate prior to the establishment of the state must be reconsidered and adapted to the new social and political reality. The major goal of citizenship education was now perceived to be the inculcation of citizenship awareness and skills in people who had been stateless for two thousand years, and who often did not hold full citizenship rights in exile. It was believed that Jews must readjust to a life of independence and sovereignty, and learn to fulfill their civic obligations and rights voluntarily.

Educators considered democratic ideas such as equality, liberty and justice to be part of the legacy of the prophets and the Bible. They introduced these ideas to students through the exposure to Jewish heritage, rather than by reference to non-Jewish external sources.

Much of the ideological fervor of the pre-state period continued to dominate the first years of statehood. Educating for Zionism and pioneering remained central goals. Developing a sense of common destiny and affinity between Jews in Israel and Jews all over the world was another goal. Many of the textbooks which had been used during the Yishuv period continued to be used for most school subjects.

In 1953 the State Education Law was passed. The educational system was unified and centralized administratively, and it was dissociated from the various political parties with which it had previously been linked. The depoliticization of the school system was accompanied by strict instructions to the effect that politics and ideological controversy should not enter the schools. Instead, schools should emphasize consensus and unity, and avoid partisanship and divisiveness.

However, in spite of the organizational unification of the educational system, depoliticization did not occur overnight. Great diversity of curriculum continued to exist, and political influences were not completely eliminated. After all, the same teachers, the same administrators, the same constituency were involved, and thus true unification and depoliticization were postponed. Gradually, however, 'politics' became banned, and civic education came to focus solely on the structural and legal characteristics of state institutions. Furthermore, the emotional components which were dominant in education during the Yishuv period became marginal and cognitive, and evaluative components became pre-eminent. Citizenship education came to rely mainly on concepts rooted in the social sciences, and Jewish heritage lost its hegemony as a source of both national and universal ideas.

Citizenship Identity of Israeli-Arabs

A national minority within a Jewish-Zionist state: The presence of a large Arab minority within Israel makes citizenship education a highly sensitive task, in both Arab and Jewish state schools. Arabs who remained in Israel following the establishment of the state came to constitute a minority within a Jewish nation-state (Ackerman *et al.*, 1985). This is a unique situation because Israel is the only country in the Middle East where Arabs constitute a minority. The Arab population of Israel became citizens of a state whose creation they had forcefully opposed, together with their brothers in the neighboring Arab countries, regarding it as an illegitimate infringement upon their national rights. It is, therefore, not surprising that Palestinian Arabs who remained in Israel were initially treated by the Jewish majority as an enemy-affiliated, untrustworthy minority. Moreover, until 1966, they were subjugated to a military administration and martial law, which limited their civil liberties. This meant, among other things, that their movement was restricted and special permits were needed in order to look for jobs or education outside their home towns or villages (Zureik, 1979; Lustick, 1980; Smooha, 1985). Nevertheless, Israeli-Arabs proved to be loyal to the state, and hardly ever took part in hostile and violent acts, not even during the recent Palestinian uprising (Intifada).

The end of the military administration in 1966 did not solve the issue of Arab integration into Israeli society, and the problem of their civic, cultural, and national identities as citizens of a Jewish-Zionist state (Smooha, 1985). It is fair to state that except for fringe elements on both sides, neither Jews nor Arabs ever really aspired to integration. The model for Arab integration into Israeli society was that of a cultural pluralism which encouraged the creation of ethnic enclaves, allowing minorities to preserve their native culture, and allowing them partial or full participation in the affairs of the larger community. However, it turned out to be problematic to secure the necessary basic conditions for achieving cooperative coexistence (Smooha, 1985; Ichilov, 1988). Arab cultural autonomy, which has been perceived as capable of fostering an alien national identity, has been discouraged. Nor has there been any proportional equality of resources between Jews and Arabs in

Israel while most of the state's resources have been allotted, and still are, to national security, immigration absorption, and settlement.

Institutional separateness and minimalistic demands upon the Arab citizen have characterized the relations between the central government and the Israeli-Arab minority. For example, unlike other Israeli citizens, including minorities such as the Druze for whom military service is obligatory, Arabs do not serve in the army. This is done both for security reasons and in order to avoid a situation whereby the Israeli-Arabs would fight against their own kin. Israeli-Arabs did not choose to substitute military service by other forms of national service, such as volunteer work in the community. Arabs' exemption from this central civic duty limits their equality, because army veterans enjoy special privileges in housing, loans, and work and study opportunities. Enduring interpersonal contacts between Jews and Arabs have been difficult to achieve in a situation where no common ideology exists, the issue of national identity is salient to both national groups, and there is a general atmosphere of mutual alienation and distrust.

The national symbols of the state of Israel represent Jewish themes which are not an acceptable form of civic identity for the Arab minority. The flag shows the Star of David, and the national emblem is made up of the Menorah of the Temple. The national anthem describes the yearnings of the Jewish people during two thousand years of exile to return to their homeland; its last verse is: 'to be a free nation in our land, the land of Zion and Jerusalem'. The lack of a general, sufficiently diffuse Israeli identity makes it difficult to create an ideology that can be shared by both Arab and Jewish Israeli citizens.

Israel's protracted occupation of the West Bank and the Gaza Strip, the recent Palestinian uprising (Intifada), and the prolonged state of war between Israel and its Arab neighbors represent persistent obstacles to the emergence of an Arab-Israeli identity (Rekhes, 1989). At the same time, Arabs in Israel have adopted increasingly militant forms of national identity (such as Islamic fundamentalism) which are opposed to integration into the Jewish state. While Jewish youngsters are raised on the glorification of Israel's wars against its Arab neighboring countries, Israeli-Arabs cannot identify with national holidays, such as Independence Day, which mark for them defeat and despair, nor can they share in the glorification of wars in which Israel emerged victorious over its Arab neighbors (Smooha, 1976, 1985).

The difficulties of Israeli-Arabs to identify with the State have been documented over the years. In 1974, for example, only 40 per cent of Arab respondents recognized without reservation Israel's right to exist, while 55 per cent of them viewed the establishment of the state in 1948 as illegitimate. Similarly, only 25 per cent of Arab respondents felt more at home in Israel than they would in an Arab country (Smooha and Hoffman, 1976/77), and only 22 per cent thought that young Arabs have a future in Israel (Hoffman, 1976). Arab adolescents expressed minimal commitment to the state, and much greater commitment to their families and community (Ichilov, 1989). These feelings are reinforced in the schools as well. An Arab educator expressed his feelings and views saying: 'Independence Day is a sad day for me'. Others mentioned that Independence Day is not celebrated or mentioned in their schools: 'it's merely a vacation day, it has nothing to do with us' (Ichilov, 1996).

On the Jewish side, too, great ambivalence toward the Arab minority is evident. Jewish Israelis' image of Arabs is generally negative, and people do not make a distinction between fellow Arab citizens, Arab citizens of enemy countries, or members of terrorist organizations (Biniamini, 1969; Zohar, 1972). Feelings of hatred and distrust toward Arabs were found to be fairly common among Israeli respondents (Levy and Guttman, 1976; Stock, 1968; Peres, 1971, 1976; Slann, 1973; Meisles, 1989). In one study only 45 per cent of the respondents would find it acceptable to have an Arab mayor in a mixed population city, and only 12 per cent would allow Arabs to run for any political office on an equal footing with Jewish political leaders (Pukan and Moskovitz, 1976).

CITIZENSHIP EDUCATION AFTER THE SIX DAY WAR

The Six Day War (1967) created a new social and political reality. Israel emerged victorious from a war which had been imposed upon it by its Arab neighbors. Since then Israel has been occupying Judea, Samaria (the West Bank) and the Gaza Strip. The outcomes of the war rekindled ideologies and national aspirations which had lain dormant since 1948. Now there were new possibilities for expanding Jewish settlement into the newly occupied territories, which some Jews regard as the heart of the Biblical Land of Israel. The 1967 victory also introduced the political alternative of trading land for peace. Israeli society became greatly polarized around the future of the West Bank and the Gaza Strip. The political map shows two blocs which consist of two large parties and their satellites: the Likud and small parties to its right, supporting Jewish sovereignty in the West Bank; and Labor and its left-wing allies, who are more willing to exchange land for peace. These controversies represent the revival of old rivalries. Already during the Yishuv period there had been no consensus concerning the ideal new state. Some advocated socialism, others liberalism and a free-market economy. Some were in favor of the separation of state and religion, while others supported orthodox Jewish rule. There was also disagreement concerning the relationships with the neighboring Arab countries, and the desirable borders of the future Israel.

During the first years of statehood ideological rivalry became less conspicuous. It was muted by the formidable national tasks which confronted the new polity, such as defence and the absorption of mass immigration. Until

1967 the boundaries of Israel were determined by the armistice agreements made at the conclusion of the War of Independence. Following the Six Day War, these controversies resurged in the public arena.

The Six Day War was a turning point for the Israeli-Arabs as well. They were no longer isolated from their brothers in Samaria, Judea and the Gaza Strip, and more militant types of national identity, such as Islamic fundamentalism, began to develop.

The awakening of old ideological rivalries within the Zionist establishment rendered pre-1967 'neutral' civic education irrelevant. Schools could no longer ignore the new social reality and their responsibility to help students comprehend it and cope effectively. What began as an individual initiative of educators – bringing politics into the schools – won the official support of the Ministry of Education and Culture in 1983. For example, educators now could and did invite public officials representing the entire political spectrum to talk to students. Mock elections were held in schools during general election periods, and teachers began discussing the daily news and controversial issues with their students.

During the 1970s and 1980s many new textbooks were published for most school subjects, including civic education and social sciences. In a study of 183 items of instructional materials for civic education and the social sciences, content analysis was carried out using several categories (Ichilov, 1993).[3] These included types of citizenship behavior – active participation vs passive compliance; types of value orientations – particularistic vs universalistic; and the arenas of citizenship – local vs international, and political vs civic. The results of this study are shown in Table 4.1.

Overall, the instructional materials emphasized active citizenship behaviors more often than passive ones and a balance was observed between particularist and universalist values. However, discussion of the international arena is missing, and citizenship is portrayed mainly as related to the political arena and not as a broader commitment to the community.

In 1985, the Ministry of Education and Culture circulated a directive nationwide, setting down the basic principles that education for democracy should follow. The approach presented in the directive is an almost complete reversal of the ideas which had dominated Zionist and civic education in earlier periods. The directive introduces three propositions. The first one, entitled the 'principle of universalism', affirms that 'individuals should be treated as the center of social processes'. The second, the 'particularist principle' emphasizes 'an expression of Jewish-Zionist national values and culture'. These two principles are considered to be supportive of each other because 'Racism and anti-democracy contradict both humanistic values, and the essence of Judaism, Zionism, and Israel's charter of Independence'. However, should there be a conflict between the two, the Ministry categorically ruled that universalism should triumph over particularism

TABLE 4.1
CONTENT EMPHASIS IN INSTRUCTIONAL MATERIALS (PERCENTAGES)

	Social sciences	Civic education
Behavior		
Active	4.3	21.0
Passive	3.7	11.0
Values		
Particularist	3.2	15.5
Universalist	5.9	15.3
Arenas		
National	3.9	34.6
International	–	–
Political	3.1	53.1
Civic	7.1	14.3

(Ministry of Education and Culture, 1985). In other words, national values and interests should always be marginalized in favor of humanistic universal values. This approach suggests that the pendulum had swung away from citizenship orientations of the Yishuv and early statehood years, which gave precedence to Jewish and Zionist interests and values.

The directive also stressed the need to educate both Arabs and Jews in Israel for mutual respect and peaceful coexistence. Research findings which revealed that youth were intolerant of opinions that differed from their own, that they were ready to deprive rivals of their civil rights (Zin, 1984; Van Leer Institute, 1987), underlined the urgent need for these new guidelines. The Ministry of Education and Culture became alert to the existence of anti-democratic attitudes among youth and decided to dedicate the academic years 1986 and 1987 to democracy as a central theme in all the schools around the country.[4] Educators were urged to discuss in class current political events and daily occurrences.

The implementation of this theme in schools was not a simple task, given the time allocated for the purpose, the lack of instructional materials, and the fact that teachers were not properly trained for conducting class discussions over controversial issues. Following the eruption of the Palestinian uprising, the Ministry of Education and Culture instructed both Arab and Jewish educators to deal in class with the violent events in an 'educational manner' (Ministry of Education and Culture, 1988a). A special guide was put out instructing teachers in Arab state schools how to deal in class with 'actualities', i.e., daily occurrences and events (Ministry of Education and Culture, 1988b). The guide also addressed issues relating to the various components of the national identity of Israeli-Arabs, and encouraged Arab educators to discuss sensitive political issues in class. On the whole, however, the guide did not provide teachers with practical solutions and tools for the task. Democratic education is also made difficult by the autocratic and conservative nature of Arab schools (Al-Haj, 1993).

CITIZENSHIP EDUCATION AND PEACE

Israel concluded a peace treaty with Egypt in 1979 and with Jordan in 1994, and embarked on a rocky road which, one hopes, will lead toward peace with the Palestinians. The prospects for a comprehensive peace in the Middle East rekindled both old hopes and fears among Israelis.

The first peace treaty with an Arab nation was signed between Israel and Egypt in 1979. Israel exchanged the Sinai desert for peace, evacuated Jewish settlements and relocated the settlers. Many settlers refused to leave of their own free will and were forcefully evacuated by Israeli soldiers. Heart-breaking scenes were shown on TV. These wounds seemed to have healed over the years, as the peace with Egypt proved to be a stable peace.

Nevertheless, a great many Israelis are extremely distrustful about the outcomes of a peace treaty with the Palestinians. A study that was conducted shortly after the outbreak of the Palestinian uprising revealed reserved optimism concerning the feasibility of peace among both Israeli-Arab and Jewish youth. Arab youngsters, however, were more pessimistic than their Jewish counterparts. Jewish respondents considered Palestian positions to be the major obstacle on the road to peace. Arab respondents viewed Israeli positions similarly (Ichilov et al., 1994). The polarization within Israel grows as the peace talks progress in the direction of a signed treaty. Active protest against the Israeli government's policy has taken on the form of signed petitions, occupation or liberation (depending on one's political views) of hill sites on the West Bank, and demonstrations. Occasional acts of terror within Israel by Palestinian extremists fuel opposition and distrust.

A recent study (Barzilai and Inbar, 1996) has shown that the current political atmosphere of reconciliation with the Palestinians and neighboring Arab countries had a limited effect on Israeli public opinion regarding the use of military force. In the study two extremist groups were identified. One refuses to use large-scale force under any circumstances, regardless of the scope of threat. The other, in contrast, endorses the most hawkish options and advocates the most extensive use of force. The centrist position, which characterizes the majority, indicates potential for a 'rally around the flag' phenomenon, particularly in the case of defensive or pre-emptive war, with large public support for short military actions with few casualties.

Should peace finally reign in the Middle East, peace education will have to become an integral part of citizenship education. Today, much of this is sporadic and carried out mainly by institutions outside the educational system.

In summary, the Israeli case clearly demonstrates that it is impossible to engage in citizenship education in isolation from its social and political context. Citizenship education mirrors the social, political and value changes within a society.

NOTES

1. In this work I have used the concepts 'citizenship education' and 'political education' alternately. For a distinction concerning these and other related concepts, see O. Ichilov, 'Political education' (1994), in T. Husen and T.N. Postlethwaite (eds), *The international encyclopedia of education* (2nd edn). Oxford: Pergamon Press.
2. The Jewish National Fund was the financial arm of the Zionist movement, which collected money for the purchase of land in Palestine on which Jewish settlements were built.
3. For more details about these categories, see O. Ichilov, 'Dimensions and role patterns of citizenship in democracy', pp.11–25 in O. Ichilov (ed.), *Political socialization, citizenship education, and democracy*. New York: Columbia University, Teachers College Press, 1990.
4. The Ministry of Education and Culture regularly designates an annual central theme for the educational system.

REFERENCES

Ackerman, W., Carmon, A. and Zucker, D. (eds) (1985). *Education in an evolving society*. Tel Aviv and Jerusalem: Ha'Kibbutz Ha'Meuchad, and Van Leer (in Hebrew).

Al-Haj, M. (1993). 'Democratic education in the Arab school system', in O. Ichilov (ed.), *Citizenship education in democracy* (pp.10–23). Tel-Aviv: Tel-Aviv University, School of Education, Unit of Sociology of Education and the Community, and Massada Publishing House (in Hebrew).

Azar, E.E., Jureidini, P. and McLaurin, R. (1978). 'Protracted social conflict: Theory and practice in the Middle East', *Journal of Palestinian Studies*, 29, 41–60.

Barzilai, G. and Inbar, E. (1996). *The use of force: Israeli public opinion on military options*. Ramat Gan: BESA Center for Strategic Studies, Bar-Ilan University.

Ben-Yehuda, B. (1949). *The teachers' movement for the redemption of Zion*. Jerusalem: The Jewish National Fund (in Hebrew).

Biniamini, K. (1969). 'The images of the Israeli, the American, the German and the Arab as viewed by Israeli youth', *Megamot*, 16(4), 305–14 (in Hebrew).

Bistritzki, N. (1948). 'Beshulei Ha'Yovel' (Summary of 20 years of activity of the teachers' movement), *Shorashim* (Roots), 3 (in Hebrew).

Bowles, S. and Gintis, H. (1976). *Schooling in capitalist America*. New York: Basic Books.

Carnoy, M. and Levin, H.M. (1985). *Schooling and work in the democratic state*. Stanford, CA: Stanford University Press.

Collins, R. (1979). *The credential society*. New York: Academic Press.

Erlich, A. (1987). 'Israel: Conflict, war and social change', in C. Creighton and M. Shaw (eds), *The sociology of war and peace* (pp.121–43). London: Macmillan.

Heater, D. (1990). *Citizenship: The civic ideal in world history*. London: Longman.

Hoffman, Y. (1976). *Identity and intergroup perceptions in Israel: Jews and Arabs* (Occasional papers on the Middle East No. 7). Haifa: The Institute of Middle Eastern Studies.

Ichilov, O. (1988). 'Citizenship orientations of two Israeli minority groups: Israeli-Arab and Eastern-Jewish youth', *Ethnic Groups*, 7, 113–36.

Ichilov, O. (1990). 'Dimensions and role patterns of citizenship in democracy', in O. Ichilov (ed.), *Political socialization, citizenship education, and democracy*. New York: Columbia University, Teachers College Press.

Ichilov, O. (1993). *Citizenship education in Israel.* Tel Aviv: Sifriat Poalim (in Hebrew).

Ichilov, O. (1996). 'Citizenship education in Israel'. Research report submitted to the International Educational Association Civic Education Project, National Case Studies. December.

Ichilov, O., Mazawi, A. and Dor, O. (1994). *Perceptions of peace and war by Jewish and Arab adolescents in Israel.* Tel Aviv: Tel Aviv University, School of Education, Unit of Sociology of Education and the Community. Publication No. 1.94 (in Hebrew).

Levy, S. and Guttman, L. (1976). *Values and attitudes of Israeli youth.* Jerusalem: Institute for Applied Social Research (in Hebrew).

Lustick, I. (1980). *Arabs in the Jewish State: Israel's control of a national minority.* Austin, TX and London: Texas University Press.

Meisles, O. (1989). *Perceptions and attitudes of high school students concerning security and the military.* Zichron Yaakov: Israeli Institute for Military Studies (in Hebrew).

Ministry of Education and Culture (1985). *Educating for democracy.* Special Directive No. 5 (in Hebrew).

Ministry of Education and Culture (1988a). *Special Directive No. 10* (in Hebrew).

Ministry of Education and Culture (1988b). *Events in the territories* (in Hebrew).

Peres, Y. (1971). 'Ethnic relations in Israel', in M. Curtis (ed.), *People and politics in the Middle East*. New Brunswick, NJ: Transaction Press.

Peres, Y. (1976). *Ethnic relations in Israel.* Tel-Aviv: Sifriat Poalim (in Hebrew).

Pukan, J. and Moskowitz, A. (1976). *Teaching the Arab–Israeli conflict: A study of attitudes.* Jerusalem: Ministry of Education and Culture (in Hebrew).

Rekhes, E. (1989). 'Israeli Arabs and Arabs of the West Bank and the Gaza Strip: Political ties and national identification', *Hamizrah Hehadash* (The New East), 32, 165–91 (in Hebrew).

Riger, E. (1929). 'Yesodot le'Chinuch Chevrati' (Foundations for Social Education), *Shorashim* (Roots), 3, 57–63 (in Hebrew).

Slann, M. (1973). 'Jewish ethnicity and integration of an Arab minority in Israel: A study of the Jerusalem incorporation', *Human Relations*, 26, 359–70.

Smooha, S. (1976). 'Arabs and Jews in Israel: Majority–minority relations', *Megamot*, 22, 397–422 (in Hebrew).

Smooha, S. (1985). 'Existing and alternative policy toward the Arabs in Israel', in E. Krauz (ed.), *Politics and society in Israel* (Vol.2, pp.334–61). New Brunswick, NJ: Transaction Books.

Smooha, S. and Hoffman, J.E. (1976/77). 'Some problems of Arab–Jewish coexistence in Israel', *Middle East Review*, 5–14.

Stock, E. (1968). *From conflict to understanding.* New York: Institute of Human Relations Press.

Urinovsky, A. (1929). 'What is Zionist education', *Shorashim* (Roots), 1(in Hebrew).

Van Leer Institute (1987). 'Political and social attitudes among youth: A public opinion survey'. Jerusalem (in Hebrew).

Zerubavel, E. (1977). 'The French republican calendar: A case study in the sociology of time', *American Sociological Review*, 42(6), 868–77.

Zin, R. (1984). *Attitudes of youth concerning democratic values.* Jerusalem: Van Leer Institute.

Zohar, N. (1972). 'The Arab image in Israeli readers', unpublished MA Thesis. Jerusalem: Hebrew University.

Zureik, E. (1979). *The Palestinians in Israel: A study in internal colonialism.* London: R & KP.

5

CONTESTED REGIMES, CIVIC DISSENT, AND THE POLITICAL SOCIALIZATION OF CHILDREN AND ADOLESCENTS: THE CASE OF THE PALESTINIAN UPRISING

ANDRÉ ELIAS MAZAWI

INTRODUCTION

The present chapter explores the extent to which the Palestinian uprising (Intifada) in the Israeli-occupied West Bank and Gaza Strip (hereafter: WB&GS) affected the political socialization of Palestinian children and adolescents. The more general aim is to clarify the relative contribution of conflict and dissent situations to the political learning process of children and adolescents in contested regimes.

Contested regimes are characterized by the absence of institutionalized and accepted norms by which a single group effectively claims a 'right to rule'. Furthermore, in such cases no majority consent exists as to the exercise of power by a single political authority, within a defined territory. Instead, competing contenders for authority struggle against each other within a territorially divided political unit, thus retarding and/or preventing regime legitimacy (Merelman, 1990, pp.47–8).

Political socialization has been studied within uncontested regimes, mainly in European and North American countries (Torney et al., 1975). Consequently, theoretical approaches within political socialization have tended to marginalize the contribution of civic dissent and political conflicts to the political socialization process of children and adolescents.

First, students of political socialization have stressed the developmental aspect of political learning (Allen et al., 1989). The acquisition of political concepts is perceived as presenting some form of linear development, from simpler to more complex and elaborate structures (Belsky et al., 1991; Sonnert and Commons, 1994). Such a conceptualization is influenced by the work of Piaget, Kohlberg and others (Piaget, 1970; Rosenau, 1975; Vosniadou and Brewer, 1987). The basic assumption is that the individual evolves in a relatively stable sociopolitical environment, where political figures and processes gradually uncover their multidimensional features as the individual acquires the necessary cognitive abilities (Conway *et al.*, 1977; Renshon, 1977; Torney-Purta, 1989). However, children and adolescents across the world experience a wide – and extremely diversified – array of unstable sociopolitical environments and often get directly socialized into conflict situations. This is the case, for instance, in Afghanistan, Algeria, Bosnia-Herzegovina, Cambodia, Cuba, East Timor, Haiti, India, Iraq, Kuwait, Mexico, Northern Ireland, the Palestinian Occupied Territories, Rwanda, Somalia, South Africa, the Spanish Basque region, Sri Lanka, Tibet, regions and states of the former USSR, Vietnam and Western Sahara. In these and other settings, children and adolescents experience global threats (Klingman *et al.*, 1991), wars (Tolley, 1973; Punamaki, 1982), military occupation (Punamaki, 1987), immigration (Goodnow and Espin, 1993), political instability (Chan, 1993) and ethnic and racial antagonisms (Cross, 1993). How do such experiences affect the structuration of the political learning process of children and adolescents? How are such experiences integrated at the level of attitudes' formation and acquired civic behaviors?

Second, researchers have stressed the relative contribution of various socialization agents to the political learning process of children and adolescents (Ichilov, 1984; DiRenzo, 1990a, p.25). However, the modality of this process was not systematically studied in contested sociopolitical orders (Merelman, 1990). The process of political socialization is rather perceived as taking place within institutional settings, such as the school (Banks and Roker, 1994) and the family (Phinney & Chavira, 1995), or through the media (DiRenzo, 1990b, pp.158–64). Few attempts were undertaken to understand it within the context of global social movements – such as revolutions, uprisings, protest movements – and to investigate the way such processes recurrently affect the political consciousness and behaviors of individuals and groups (Sapiro, 1990). Ichilov (1990, pp.12–13) observed that this conceptual shortcoming has inevitably reduced the concept of political socialization to fit mainly within a functionalist-structuralist mold: the functions and objectives of political socialization having been equated, the very experience of being socialized and its effects on the process of political learning have thus remained largely unaccounted for.

Recently, several authors have attempted to conceptualize the mechanisms through which civic dissent and conflict affect political learning processes. Ichilov (1990) argued that dissent, via conventional and/or unconventional means, contains the very prerequisites and antecedents which determine the structuration, and change, of citizenship roles over time. Etzioni (1970) has remarked that demonstrations and other manifestations of civil disobedience have played a central role in mobilizing large sections of the public into political action. Merelman (1990) observed more particularly that the perception of historical circumstances in which conflicts originate ('awareness to history'), and their transformation ('mythologizing') into meaningful interpretive frameworks, mediate the political socialization of individuals and groups in contested regimes. Thus, from a political socialization perspective, dissent and conflict are equally relevant dimensions of political learning, not only in what is considered as democracy, but in what is perceived and experienced as contested and/or oppressive regimes as well. Dissent, as such, mediates political learning and socializes individuals and groups into alternative sociopolitical visions of citizenship relations (Ichilov, 1990, pp.17–18; Merelman, 1990, p.58).

The above conclusion is central to the case of the Palestinian uprising which erupted in early December 1987 in the Israeli-occupied WB&GS. In the present chapter the uprising is addressed as a Palestinian mass civic dissent in a highly contested Israeli politico-military regime. In this context, it is argued, citizenship orientations of Palestinian children and adolescents were comprehensively restructured in terms of acquired civic participatory behaviors and the modalities through which political concepts and attitudes are learned.

To probe the above contention, this chapter proceeds in four parts. The first part outlines the major characteristics of the uprising as an act of mass civic dissent. The second part examines the participation of children and adolescents in the uprising, and the outcomes of this in terms of the development of more generalized participatory behaviors and skills. The third part focuses on the relative contribution of uprising-related dissent activities to the learning of sociopolitical concepts by children and adolescents. The fourth part examines the extent to which uprising-related emotional experiences affect citizenship orientations of Palestinian children and adolescents. The concluding discussion analyzes the contribution of the Palestinian case to the understanding of political socialization processes in contested regimes.

THE UPRISING: A TOTAL ENVIRONMENT OF CIVIC DISSENT

From the vantage point of Palestinians, Israeli military occupation and rule of the WB&GS constitute a highly contested regime, lacking legitimacy. Israeli rule is structurally and inherently opposed to the concept and reality of Palestinian self-determination within the frame of an independent Palestinian state. The causes of the uprising are, therefore, deeply rooted in the experience of Palestinians under Israeli military rule since June 1967, and express a continued national struggle for statehood. Israeli rule over the WB&GS is secured mainly through the presence and imposition of military power. All powers are vested in military commanders who act as the legislature, the judicial and the executive branches of the government. Palestinians have no institutionalized channels at their disposal through which they can choose their government or otherwise freely change it by way of elections or through other democratically established procedures (Moffett, 1989; Playfair, 1992). Unconventional means, namely, armed struggle and mass civic insurrection, were considered by Palestinians as the ultimate political means available through which the power structure regulating Israeli–Palestinian relations could be affected.

Since its outbreak in early December 1987, the uprising manifested itself primarily in the breakdown of public routine in the WB&GS, and in a generalized confrontation with Israeli occupation apparatus. As a result, the role of traditional socialization agents was comprehensively affected. With frequent and prolonged periods of imposed closures by the Israeli military authorities, educational institutions at all levels were unable to conduct a regular school year (Jerusalem Media and Communication Centre, 1990). Family structure, and gender roles and relations were deeply affected as the consequence of Israeli military and economic reprisals, imprisonments, deportations, house demolitions, general strikes and the worsening conditions of daily life (Peretz, 1990).

Uprising-related anti-occupation activities exposed Palestinians in general, and children and adolescents in particular, to civic dissent on a large scale, both as observers and as participants (Schiff and Yaari, 1990). In his review article, Lustick (1993, pp.566–7) notes that '[i]n the first two years of the uprising [i.e. 1988–89] the army demolished 350 Arab homes and arrested 60,000 Palestinians. Sixty people were deported and 40,000 were held in administrative detention, that is without indictment or trial. One Israeli lawyer estimated that about 25 per cent of the WB&GS Palestinian population passed through the military court system in the first years of the uprising.' Lustick further adds that about 13,100 Palestinians were wounded in the first thousand days of the uprising (the rate of uprising-related casualties standing at 43 per 100,000), 2,500 Israeli soldiers and 1,100 Israeli civilians.

Lustick (1993, p.561) also observes that 'in addition to being unprecedented in the Palestinian context itself, the intifada was also the first of many-based, illegal, nonviolent or semi-violent challenges to nondemocratic governing structures to burst upon the world scene at the end of the 1980s'. Others, such as historian Yehoshua Porath, remarked that the uprising presents a 'popular action, covering all social strata and groups ... The whole population is rebelling, and this is creating a common national experience' (quoted in Peretz, 1990, p.78).

If some observers viewed the uprising as a popular and largely spontaneous act of mass civic dissent, others have stressed the contribution of Palestinian grass-root organizations to its occurrence and continuance

(Schiff and Yaari, 1990; Lustick, 1993, p.587). Hiltermann (1991, pp.174–5) notes in this respect that

> grass-roots activists had been organizing and mobilizing sectors of the population for years prior to the outbreak of the uprising. They had a clear sense of strategy and tactics, and were astute in their evaluation of the conditions that would be necessary to sustain prolonged mass action … When mass demonstrations broke out, spontaneously, throughout the Gaza Strip, spreading to areas of the West Bank, including East Jerusalem, and even to inside Israel for a day (20 December [1987]), activists could capitalize on their accumulated experience and credibility in the eyes of the masses, and deploy their organizations, including the trade unions and women's committees, to mobilize people further and channel the insurrection.

In sum, the Palestinian uprising evolved into a total environment of civic dissent and insurrection, comprehensively challenging the legality and legitimacy of Israeli occupation over the WB&GS. This mainly took place within the bounds of a society seeking alternative forms of political legitimacy by which to govern itself. Generalized confrontation with established occupation apparatuses became, therefore, the rule rather than the exception, mobilizing large social strata into different types of anti-occupation activities.

THE PARTICIPATION OF CHILDREN AND ADOLESCENTS IN THE UPRISING

The participation of children and adolescents soon became a central feature of the uprising (Kuttab, 1988). In December 1987, with the eruption of the uprising, more than 60 per cent of the 1.5 million Palestinian inhabitants of the WB&GS were below 20 years of age. The overwhelming majority was born under Israeli occupation and knew no other, or previous, forms of government. In 1992, five years later, 21 per cent of the 1.8 million WB&GS Palestinians were below 5 years of age. Children and adolescents between the ages of 5 and 19 constituted an additional 38 per cent of the total population (State of Israel, Central Bureau of Statistics, 1994, pp.786–7, 27.1 to 27.3). For Palestinian children and adolescents, the uprising and the permanent confrontation with Israeli occupation apparatus, were the major forms of social order, and political rule, experienced on a daily basis.

The participation of children and adolescents in the uprising extensively affected their exposure to various socialization agents. 'The street' soon became the primary setting for their socialization, whether as spectators or as participants. In a study conducted in 1990–91 among a sample of 36 refugee-camp children aged 6–8 and their mothers, Merizian-Khazin (1995, p.293) found that all children reported having watched a political march and a demonstration, with more than half the boys participating in a march, and more than 80 per cent in a demonstration (compared to less than one-fifth of the girls). Further, half the children mentioned having witnessed a wounded Palestinian receiving first aid. About 43 per cent of the boys and 14 per cent of the girls participated in a martyr's funeral (*shaheed*). One-third of the children reported having one imprisoned family member, and about 25 per cent reported having more than three. Further, around 80 per cent of the mothers reported that their children spent an average of five hours per day for boys and three hours per day for girls, playing war games on the streets. A war game was described as follows by one of the mothers:

> There is a leader who is responsible for deciding roles, his duties are to plan and prepare for a demonstration, and to hide the equipment once it is over. The Palestinian resistance would throw stones at soldiers and run away very fast. The child who takes the role of soldier carries a wireless phone, has two body guards one on each side, looks for wanted guys and most of the time is protected by an armored vehicle.

Toys used by children during war games included wooden guns, empty cola bottles (simulating molotov cocktails), objects simulating wireless phones and guarded areas symbolizing prisons in which arrested Palestinians were incarcerated. Other play objects would include plastic guns and binoculars (Merizian-Khazin, 1995, p.292). War games were played with 'complete military terminology, Hebrew and Arab curses, legalistic repartees, and V-signs' (Rouhana, 1989, p.118).

Children under 6 years of age were willing to simulate the role of Israeli soldiers while playing 'war games'. Children above 6 were less enthusiastic to do so. The latter would rather opt for the role of the youth (*shabab*), simulating stoning and molotov-throwing scenes in their confrontation with Israeli soldiers (Rouhana, 1989). Games, therefore, presented children with actual channels of socialization through which they were being initiated into modes of pictorial rehearsals (Merelman, 1990, p.52) concurrent with the uprising. Learning through simulation and role-play constituted therefore the primary mechanisms through which younger age-groups acquired basic behavioral skills which they integrated into actual uprising-related activities. Rouhana (1989, pp.110–11) writes in this respect about a phenomenon that came to be popularly known as 'Children of the Stone' (*atfal al-hijara*):

> By their own choice, children are the ones on the front lines of the intifadah – throwing stones, blocking roads, burning tires, spraying graffiti and participating in strike forces. Children who decide to be actively involved are assigned different roles according to their ages: the seven- to ten-year-olds burn tires and stand as look-outs; the eleven-

to fourteen-year-olds block roads with large boulders and use sling-shots to fire small stones; the fifteen- to nineteen-year-olds are the actual stonethrowers and they also distribute food during curfews. Those over nineteen coordinate the team and direct the attacks.

Yet, if 'the street' became the major space in which children and adolescents acted, it did not remain the only one. Some writers have indicated that the participation of children and adolescents in dissent activities was mobilized by various civic and political institutions and popular committees (Peretz, 1990, p.84). Thus, identification with different political factions (their ideologies, tactics and strategies) enabled adolescents to become aware of points of convergence and divergence existing among various segments of Palestinian society. This type of learning was further intensified through personal experiences such as stone-throwing, getting beaten by soldiers, experiencing detention, participating in commemorative days and strikes, or as a result of the death of peers or family members (termed *shuhada'*, or martyrs) in confrontations with Israeli troops. Consequently, if direct anti-occupation activities enabled the acquisition of new behaviors and skills, enrollment into, or exposure to, various sociopolitical movements provided for children and adolescents a channel through which they were able to gradually differentiate between competing sociopolitical platforms within Palestinian society. Peretz (1990, p.84) has observed in this respect that '[c]hildren's participation in the uprising involved much more than stone throwing or provoking Israeli soldiers. Nationalist or popular committees affiliated with the PLO or Islamic fundamentalist factions organized youth in a variety of educational and volunteer programs, from street or building construction in refugee camps to lessons in Palestinian history.' The fact that schools remained closed for prolonged periods of times, intensified the relative exposure of youth to the socializing effects of various factions and informal settings.

The role of young people in the confrontation with Israeli occupation apparatus was clearly visible in the proportional representation of young age-cohorts among uprising casualties. Between December 1987 and October 1988, of 287 Palestinians killed by Israeli troops, about 39 per cent were below 19 years old, and an additional 40.4 per cent were between the ages of 19 and 25. The mean age was 23.1 years (Stockton, 1989, pp.102, 104). Between November 1988 and December 1989, out of 357 casualties, about 9 per cent were below 13 years of age, and about 62 per cent were between 17 and 35. The mean age dropped to 20.5 years (Stockton, 1990, p.88). Between December 1987 and 8 June 1993, 232 Palestinians below the age of 16 were killed in the confrontation with Israeli troops (B'Tselem, 1993, p.147).

In sum, the uprising presented both children and adolescents with the opportunity to acquire new, unconventional, modes of political action and skills. The participation of children and adolescents in the uprising comprehensively transformed their perception of citizenship relations. In this respect, on the one hand, the uprising did considerably enhance behaviors related to collective social solidarity and cohesion, in defiance of military regulations and prohibitions (e.g., food distribution under curfews, distributing leaflets, and opposing the military). On the other hand, the increased exposure of youth to various sociopolitical currents and movements, in a wide array of institutional frames, further presented children and adolescents with new opportunities for political learning. Such experiences affected their world-view and their affective group evaluation (Merelman, 1990, p.53), intensively shaping their identification with collectively shared (national) symbols.

PERCEPTIONS OF AUTHORITY

The active participation of Palestinian children and adolescents in the uprising broke with previous modes and products of political socialization which were mainly based upon a protective parental attitude (Peretz, 1990, p.84). If previous socialization to the Israeli–Palestinian conflict relied on accounts by members of older generations, the uprising provided both children and adolescents with a channel through which they were being socialized into, and took part in, the structuration of an alternative sociopolitical order and new forms of family relations.

First, experiences of dissent against Israeli occupation were generalized towards other agents of authority as well, such as teachers (Yair and Khatab, 1995) and parents (Dockser-Marcus, 1994). A number of professionals have argued that active involvement in daily confrontation with the Israeli occupation apparatus constituted an empowering factor as younger generations discovered, in the words of psychoanalyst Francis Azraq, that 'the adult power over them was a myth, both the power of the family and that of the soldiers [and that they actually] broke the most terrible military force which was dominating the patriarchal society and family policy' (quoted in Rouhana, 1989, p.120).

In the web of confrontation, many sociopolitical concepts, such as the perception of 'authority', were radically transformed and had their divergent meanings conflated. Roy (1993, p.28) observes in this respect:

> Thirty fifteen-year-old boys were asked, 'What does authority mean?' All answered that 'authority means the enemy.' When told, 'But authority can mean your teacher as well,' several of them replied, 'You mean our teacher is a collaborator?' 'Do you have authority at home?' was another question. 'Yes', they replied, 'the authorities have entered our homes many times.' Children in the Gaza Strip are increasingly

incapable of conceptualizing authority in traditional terms since parents and teachers, unable to protect the youth from constant abuse and threat, have ceased to exist as authority figures. Authority is now the enemy and is inherently evil. Law and order do not exist in Gaza, in concept or in practice, and therefore children have no boundaries and no markers for distinguishing good behavior from bad. Children are fearful in Gaza, but they are also feared.

'Authority' was thus perceived as being inherently evil and was opposed as such when exercised. One of the major consequences of this process was visible at the level of classroom teacher–pupil interaction. Fieldwork carried out by Yair and Khatab (1995, pp.104–5), though limited to Arab schools in the Israeli-annexed territory of East Jerusalem, provides nonetheless insights into this process as it reveals that,

> Before the intifada, the classroom was an authoritarian kingdom, a realm full of respect and personal fulfillment for many teachers. It was a secure place, both physically and psychologically. Teachers' dominance was normatively and structurally embedded within the traditional patriarchal system.
>
> The intifada, however, reversed this supremacy–obedience polarity … [t]he increasingly prominent status of students led to a change in their attitude toward the school as a seat of authority. At the onset of the intifada, students were protesting against the traditional authority of teachers and began to demand more rights than had been customarily granted them. In addition, they usually determined the order of the day, the material to be learned, and the level and rate at which it would be taught.

All in all, while the dynamics of dissent engendered by the uprising altered the perception of authority by younger generations, their participation in uprising-related activities constituted an empowering factor, and thus had comprehensive repercussions on the whole Palestinian social fabric.

EMOTIONAL CONSEQUENCES OF THE UPRISING

The psychological effects of the uprising on Palestinian children and adolescents were studied primarily regarding the traumatic consequences on their personality development. Less attention was given to the way uprising-related emotional experiences affected their acquisition of citizenship orientations.

The apprehension of uprising-related experiences seem to be highly conditioned by the child's cognitive level of development. Traumatizing experiences of uprising-related violence seem to affect, most of all, children below the age of 7. This age-group, characterized by entirely concrete thinking, was found to have difficulties in coping with reality. Children at this stage, being unable to 'grasp abstract concepts such as nation, occupation, land' (Rouhana, 1989, p.119), showed signs of behavioral disturbance expressed through unruly and aggressive behavior. When asked what the uprising was, a 4-year-old refugee-camp boy replied: 'We throw stones on soldiers'. Children aged between 7 and 10, while being aware of their national identity as Palestinians and able to identify with the Palestinian flag, nonetheless 'still lacked the full ability to conceptualize political thoughts that would enable them to cope better with reality'. However, they seemed to stress peer-group solidarity and support as a fear-reducing mechanism. Both age-groups appear to express their fears mainly through anxiety-ridden dreams, bedwetting and psychosomatic illnesses. Age-groups above 12 seem to be more adept at grasping the full political and national meaning of the uprising, thus gaining most in self-esteem, group identity and social support (Rouhana, 1989, p.120). Somewhat similar findings were reported by Baker (1990) who conducted a survey among 300 Palestinian families (200 in the WB and 100 in the GS) with a total of 796 children examined. Results indicated that exposure to political and military violence within the context of dissent activities may be associated with the onset of behavioral problems and fears (11.3 per cent were reported to have suffered from depression). Yet, it was noted that a certain level of active participation in conflict may enhance self-esteem and shield children from developing psychological symptoms.

Other studies provide evidence of changes in children and adolescents' internalization and coping with the occupation as a result of uprising-related emotional experiences. Drawings by children aged 4–5, examined before and after the beginning of the uprising, revealed significant changes in their perception of the wider sociopolitical reality, as Rouhana (1989, p.118) notes:

> In a developmental test administered by the [Early Childhood Resource Center in Jerusalem] before and after the [beginning of the] intifadah, children ages four and five drew houses, trees and family members in the first sample, and flags, soldiers, Palestinians and stones after the intifadah began. Early on, said developmental psychologist Cairo Arafat, who works with the ECRC, the children were apt to draw themselves very small and rather faceless, with towering soldiers whose faces were well detailed. The flags in these pictures were also large and often erroneously drawn. A few months later, the same children's drawing featured the same subject matter, but this time the children were proportionately larger, the same size as soldiers, and it was the soldiers' faces that were less clearly delineated. The flags, she says, were smaller but accurately drawn.

For older age-cohorts, over 13 years of age, the experience of the uprising was differently patterned as, in the words of Rouhana (1989, p.120), they were 'galvanized, learning responsibility, accountability, cooperative effort, and battle strategy', and that 'leadership is earned, not inherited'.

Nevertheless, prolonged experiences of uprising-related violence appears to have had traumatizing effects on children's feelings, self-perception, the perception of various elements in their sociopolitical environment and of others (Roy, 1993; Merizian-Khazin, 1995). Speaking particularly of the Gaza Strip in the post-1991 Gulf war period, Roy (1993, p.28) states:

> The children of Gaza are psychologically damaged, some beyond repair; others, while scarred, are more resilient. All are affected. The death of a child, a brother or sister, is no longer an extraordinary event; injured and maimed children are increasingly common as well. Gaza is a society devoid of childhood. Children have left the home and classroom, two critical sources of socialization, and the impact has been devastating.

All in all, the assessment of the emotional effects of uprising-related violence on children's and adolescents' citizenship orientations still needs sounder research strategies. Available fieldwork and data are at best provisional. On the one hand, the participation of children and adolescents in the uprising may have enhanced their self-esteem, their sense of political efficacy and their identification with the national collectivity. Yet, on the other hand, it remains rather true that, for these younger generations of Palestinians, the traumatizing effects of such experiences have radically transformed their personality and their perception of social relations. This point, although critical, unfortunately still awaits careful research. Furthermore, future research will have to examine how uprising-related emotional consequences will affect the interaction of youth with authority structures within Palestinian society, rather than as a reaction against an outside occupier.

DISCUSSION

This chapter has examined the contribution of dissent to the political socialization process of Palestinian children and adolescents. The main trends depicted suggest that the political socialization of Palestinian children and adolescents was comprehensively affected by the dynamics of dissent engendered through the uprising.

The case under review has three major implications for the study of political socialization in contested regimes. First, it corroborates Merelman's (1990, pp.52–3) contention that conflict situations in contested regimes are often visualized by younger generations as presenting a set of heroic and emotionally evocative undertakings. The latter constitute the basic bricks of gradually elaborated interpretive frameworks in which affect-laden symbols are hierarchically constructed 'so that episodes of conflict become necessary parts of an increasingly dramatic and powerful group history' (Merelman, 1990, p.58). Consequently, in contested regimes, the centralization of conflict, and its reproduction at various levels of action, becomes a main feature of political socialization. Affective group evaluation determines, in such cases, the primary political socialization of children, with later analytical learning having only a limited effect on its modification (Merelman, 1990, p.53).

Second, political socialization approaches have remained limited in their ability to explain how changes in the broader political culture affect political socialization patterns, and vice versa. The present case is much more instructive as it pertains to political socialization in contested regimes. The Palestinian case implies that individuals in contested regimes take a much more active part in their own political socialization than established socialization approaches would lead us to believe. Political socialization far exceeds being the mere structural and relative effect of various socialization agents. It reflects, in addition, the ability of human beings to pursue the implications of their own perception and understanding of sociopolitical reality in their attempts to construct new modes of sociopolitical legitimacy (Sapiro, 1990, p.278). This conclusion inevitably raises the necessity of devising new conceptual and methodological approaches in political socialization studies. This is imperative if our understanding of political socialization is to be meaningfully integrated into a broader theory of social action.

Third, the studies surveyed provide evidence of the relationship between cognitive level and the perception of conflict. This pattern seems to coincide with classical developmental theories of political learning (Connell, 1971; Moore et al., 1985). Nonetheless, little attention has been given in current developmental research on political socialization to the cultural expressions of this process in contested regimes. As mentioned above, different age-groups coped with sociopolitical reality through the production of various artefacts, such as the invention of games, toys, drawings, discursive clichés etc. These artefacts are contextually situated in the sense that children would usually select them from among the available resources within their direct environment, in the hic et nunc of the conflict. Few studies were undertaken to the effect of clarifying how children and adolescents select the objects they incorporate into their learning process. Moreover, how do such objects, and their incorporation, affect the political learning process? In contested political regimes, this dimension has a particularly relevant contribution to the political socialization process, as the cultural productions of children and adolescents are active mediators and bearers of meanings, and of affect-laden collectively defined symbols.

Future research in political socialization will have to elaborate extensively on these and other dimensions, which were only tentatively discussed. In fact, the study of political socialization in contested regimes will significantly contribute to our understanding of the emergence of political cultures. Yet, one of its most important contributions is the opportunity to theorize about how political cultures and the political learning of children and adolescents – while mediating broader sociopolitical changes – transform and structure the formers' citizenship orientations.

REFERENCES

Allen, J., Freeman, P. and Osborne, S. (1989). 'Children's political knowledge and attitudes', *Young Children*, 44(2), 5–61.

Baker, A. (1990). 'The psychological impact of the intifada on Palestinian children in the occupied West Bank and Gaza: An exploratory study', *American Journal of Orthopsychiatry*, 60(4), 496–505.

Banks, M. and Roker, D. (1994). 'The political socialization of youth: Exploring the influence of school experience', *Journal of Adolescence*, 17(1), 3–15.

Belsky, J., Steinberg, L. and Draper, P. (1991). 'Childhood experience, interpersonal development, and reproductive strategy: An evolutionary theory of socialization', *Child Development*, 62(4), 647–85.

B'Tselem (1993). 'The killing of Palestinian children and the open-fire regulations', *Journal of Palestine Studies*, 89, 144–8.

Chan, D. (1993). 'A new civic education for Hong Kong in a time of transition', *Education and Society*, 11(2), 51–65.

Connell, R. (1971). *The child's construction of politics*. Carleton: Melbourne University Press.

Conway, M., Ahern, D. and Feldbaum, E. (1977). 'Instructional method, social characteristics, and children's support for the political regime', *Simulation and Games*, 8, 233–54.

Cross, M. (1993). 'Youths, culture, and politics in South African education: The past, present and future', *Youth and Society*, 24(4), 377–98.

DiRenzo, G. (1990a). 'Socialization for citizenship in modern democratic society', in O. Ichilov (ed.), *Political socialization, citizenship education, and democracy* (pp.25–46). New York and London: Teachers College Press, Columbia University.

DiRenzo, G. (1990b). *Human social behavior: Concepts and principles of sociology*. San Francisco: Holt, Rinehart & Winston.

Dockser-Marcus, A. (1994). 'Generation gap: Young Palestinians vow to derail Accord, level attacks on Israel ...', *The Wall Street Journal*, Vol. XII (No. 224).

Etzioni, A. (1970). *Demonstration democracy*. New York: Gordon & Breach.

Goodnow, C. and Espin, O. (1993). 'Identity choices in immigrant adolescent females', *Adolescence*, 28 (No. 109), 173–84.

Hiltermann, J. (1991). *Behind the Intifada: Labor and women's movement in the Occupied Territories*. Princeton, NJ: Princeton University.

Ichilov, O. (1984). *The political world of children and adolescents*. Tel Aviv: Yahdav (in Hebrew).

Ichilov, O. (1990). 'Dimensions and role patterns of citizenship in democracy', in O. Ichilov (ed.), *Political socialization, citizenship education, and democracy* (pp.11–20). New York and London: Teachers College Press, Columbia University.

Jerusalem Media and Communication Centre (1990). *Palestinian education: A threat to Israel's security?* (2nd edn). Jerusalem: JMCC.

Klingman, A., Goldstein, Z. and Lerner, P. (1991). 'Adolescents' response to nuclear threat: Before and after the Chernobyl accident', *Journal of Youth and Adolescence*, 20(5), 519–30.

Kuttab, D. (1988). 'A profile of the stonethrowers', *Journal of Palestine Studies*, 67, 14–23.

Lustick, I. (1993). 'Writing the intifada: Collective action in the occupied territories', *World Politics*, 45(4), 560–94.

Merelman, R. (1990). 'The role of conflict in children's political learning', in O. Ichilov (ed.). *Political socialization, citizenship education, and democracy* (pp.47–65). New York and London: Teachers College Press, Columbia University.

Merizian Khazin, A. (1995). 'Palestinian child play during the uprising', *Bulletin of the Palestinian Child Society*, 1(3), 291–7.

Moffett, M. (1989). *Perpetual emergency: A legal analysis of Israel's use of the British Defense (Emergency) Regulations 1945, in the Occupied Territories.* Occasional Paper No. 6. Ramallah (West Bank): Al-Haq.

Moore, S., Lare, J. and Wagner, K. (1985). *The child's political world: A longitudinal perspective.* New York: Praeger.

Peretz, D. (1990). *Intifada: The Palestinian uprising.* Boulder, CO: Westview Press.

Phinney, J. and Chavira, V. (1995). 'Parental ethnic socialization and adolescent coping with problems related to ethnicity', *Journal of Research on Adolescence*, 5(1), 31–53.

Piaget, J. (1970). 'Piaget's theory', in P. Mussen (ed.), *Carmichael's manual of child psychology*, Vol.1, pp.703–32 (3rd edn). New York: J. Wiley.

Playfair, E. (ed.) (1992). *International law and the administration of occupied territories: Two decades of occupation of the West Bank and Gaza Strip.* Oxford: Clarendon Press.

Punamaki, R. (1982). 'Childhood in the shadow of war: A psychological study of attitudes and emotional life of Israeli and Palestinian children', *Current Research on Peace and Violence*, 5(1), 26–41.

Punamaki, R. (1987). 'Psychological stress responses of Palestinian mothers and their children in conditions of military occupation and political violence', *The Quarterly Newsletter of the Laboratory of Comparative Human Cognition*, 9(2), 76–83.

Renshon, S. (1977). 'Assumptive frameworks in political socialization theory', in. S. Renshon (ed.), *Handbook of political socialization* (pp.3–44). New York: Free Press.

Rosenau, N. (1975). 'The sources of children's political concepts: An application of Piaget's theory', in S. Schwartz and E. Schwartz (eds), *New directions in political socialization*, pp.163–87. New York: Free Press.

Rouhana, K. (1989). 'Children and the Intifadah', *Journal of Palestine Studies*, 72, 110–21.

Roy, S. (1993). 'Gaza: New dynamics of civic disintegration', *Journal of Palestine Studies*, 88, 20–31.

Sapiro, V. (1990). 'The women's movement and the creation of gender consciousness: Social movements as socialization agents', in O. Ichilov (ed.) *Political socialization, citizenship education, and democracy* (pp.266–80). New York and London: Teachers College Press.

Schiff, Z. and Yaari, E. (1990). *Intifada.* New York: Simon & Schuster.

Sonnert, G. and Commons, M. (1994). 'Society and highest stages of moral development', *Politics and the Individual*, 4(1), 31–55.

State of Israel, Central Bureau of Statistics (1994). *Statistical Abstract*, 45, Jerusalem.

Stockton, R. (1989). 'Intifadah deaths', *Journal of Palestine Studies*, 70, 101–8.

Stockton, R. (1990). 'Intifada deaths', *Journal of Palestine Studies*, 7, 86–95.

Tolley, H. (1973). *Children and war: Political socialization to international conflict.* New York: Teachers College Press.

Torney, J., Oppenheim, A. and Farnen, R. (1975). *Civics Education in ten countries.* New York: John Wiley.

Torney-Purta, J. (1989). 'Political cognition and its restructuring in adolescents', *Human Development*, 32, 14–23.

Vosniadou, S. and Brewer, W. (1987). 'Theories of knowledge restructuring in development', *Review of Educational Research*, 57, 51–68.

Yair, G. and Khatab, N. (1995). 'Changing of the guards: Teacher–student interaction in the Intifada', *Sociology of Education*, 68, 99–115.

6

CITIZENSHIP AND CITIZENSHIP EDUCATION IN THE UNITED STATES IN THE 1990s

RICHARD G. BRAUNGART and MARGARET M. BRAUNGART

PERCEPTIONS OF CITIZENSHIP

A cornerstone of American democracy is citizenship, with the well-being and survival of the country's institutions and traditions largely dependent on the successful education and integration of each new generation of children and youth. Citizenship involves the rights and duties of individuals and the constitutional state. Rooted in the Enlightenment and social contract, membership status in the modern democratic state confers certain rights and privileges upon its citizens, who, in return, are expected to exercise both personal control and collective responsibility for the common good (Barbalet, 1988; Bottomore, 1993; Dahrendorf, 1994; Seligman, 1993). While these are the basic tenets of citizenship, the way citizenship is practiced is strongly influenced by political culture – the shared values, beliefs, traditions, and knowledge that affect the political order (Almond and Verba, 1965; Berger, 1989; Femia, 1993). As the twentieth century comes to a close, the political culture in the United States is changing, and concerns about citizenship have moved to the forefront of public discourse, generating considerable criticism and pessimism about the country's future.

Citizenship under Threat

Citizenship in the United States appears to be threatened by several recent trends. In a nation whose motto is *E Pluribus Unum* ('one out of many'), Americans worry that pluralism, multiculturalism, and ethnic diversity are dividing rather uniting the citizenry and undermining national identity and allegiance to the state (Beiner, 1995; Schlesinger, 1992). To pollsters and journalists, the low voter participation, political disinterest and loss of party support indicate civic responsibility is lagging, with the American electorate frequently characterized as politically alienated and disaffected (Lipset, 1995).

Moreover, the surge of social problems in the United States – violence, pornography, abortion, poverty, and the lack of gun control – elicits general agreement that there is too much emphasis on individual freedom and not enough attention to personal and collective responsibility. Solutions to many of these problems cannot be found, however, because the major political factions are too concerned with blaming each other for policies that promote irresponsible behavior (Kymlicka and Norman, 1995). Brzezinski (1993, p.69) notes that citizen responsibility requires an 'inner spirit that prompts the willingness to serve, to sacrifice, and to exercise self-restraint' – qualities that he says are difficult to develop in America's materialistic, self-indulgent culture.

While the fundamental task of the adult generation is to transmit political values and the national heritage to its offspring, the task is made more difficult when the political culture is perceived as fragmented and contentious, the electorate is alienated from politics, and Americans' passion for individual freedom overrides their sense of civic or collective responsibility. Exacerbating the political socialization process, young people's attitudes and behavior in the United States appear at odds with traditional American values.

Novelists, film-makers, and journalists labeled youth in the 1990s 'Generation X' because they have no real identity or future, 'slackers' because they are lazy and irresponsible, and 'clueless' because they appear mindless and materialistic. The first downwardly mobile generation in American history, 1990s youth have been portrayed as cynical, politically apathetic and disconnected from their communities (Coupland, 1991; Howe and Strauss, 1993; People For the American Way, 1989). America's young people do not look like promising citizens, and as former Carnegie Commission President Ernest Boyer (1990, p.5) observed, 'Unless we find better ways to educate ourselves as *citizens*, America runs the risk of drifting unwittingly into a new dark age.'

Currently under national scrutiny, citizenship education in the United States is criticized for being ineffective. American students perform poorly on tests of knowledge about history and civics, and many young people claim there is little they can do to make a difference politically. Civics courses in American middle schools and high schools are reputed to be dry and dull, and in a crowded curriculum and school day, teachers readily admit that they are too overwhelmed by demands on their time and energy to do a better job teaching civics courses to their disinterested students (Eveslage, 1993; Neisler, 1994). As education critic Richard Remy described, 'There is a deep malaise in citizenship education K-12 [kindergarten through 12th grade] right now' (O'Neil, 1991, p.1). Gagnon (1995, p.66), attributes much of the malaise to the 'vast inertia of an educational establishment ... more engrossed in the means rather than the academic content of education'.

According to these accounts, the outlook for America's future is problematic, if not bleak. It must be asked, however, whether these descriptions of American society and its youth are accurate? An objective examination is needed to gain a clearer perspective on citizenship and citizenship education in the United States. In order to address this need, information has been gathered about the changes in American society during the 1980s and 1990s, the attitudes and behavior of 1990s youth, and the conduct of citizenship education in American schools. The results are used to assess young Americans' attributes of citizenship and to explore ways to educate children and youth more effectively for their role as citizens.

Examining Citizenship and Citizenship Education

Citizenship and citizenship education are examined by piecing together national statistics, surveys and educational information in a two-part study. The first part of the study focuses on *citizenship* in the United States. An initial question is: What changed in American society that promoted the widespread criticism and concern about citizenship? To assess this question, recent economic, social and political changes are identified that have influenced Americans in general and youth in particular. Next, young Americans' attitudes toward themselves and their country are explored. An explanation of the procedures is required.

National surveys of youth conducted from 1990–95 have been gathered from seven prominent research organizations that questioned samples of young people from households, high schools, and colleges and universities throughout the country. Youth is defined broadly by the age levels included in these surveys, which range from 13–29 years of age. Survey items were selected that tap the two central dimensions of citizen rights and responsibilities. One set of items concerns youth's personal conduct and views, involving their aspirations for themselves as well as their attitudes and behavior toward the family, education, work and religion; also examined are young people's health and well-being, their cultural pursuits, and their views and actions related to the community and politics. Another set of response items involves youth's collective orientations and beliefs, such as their attitudes toward the American economy, society and politics, and their beliefs about citizenship. Where possible, the responses of youth in the 1990s are compared with adult responses or with earlier surveys of young people in the 1970s and 1980s. A focus-group study of college students' views of citizenship at ten universities is included to supplement the survey findings.

The second part of this study is concerned with understanding *citizenship education* in the United States. The conduct of citizenship education is described first. Much of the information pertains to how citizen education is approached and carried out in American primary and secondary schools; some mention is made of other settings that provide citizenship education experiences. Principal criticisms and difficulties in conducting citizenship education in the United States are noted. Then, on the basis of the national survey results, young Americans' strengths and weaknesses as citizens are identified, and suggestions are offered for improving citizenship education in American schools.

CITIZENSHIP IN THE UNITED STATES

The contemporary status of citizenship in the United States is explored by identifying recent changes in American life, followed by an examination of the 1990s national youth surveys.

American Society

Economic, social and political trends from the 1980s and 1990s are briefly described. These trends influenced America's political culture and citizenship and provided the societal context within which young Americans came of age and formulated their orientations toward themselves and their country.

Economic life: During the 1980s and 1990s, economic changes had a profound impact on American society and its youth. The globalization of the market economy heightened economic competition and, as a result, the balance of trade in the United States went from slightly favorable in 1980 to highly unfavorable by 1990, and the US dollar declined in value against Japanese and most European currencies. With the success of the political conservatives in the 1980 national election, economic policies were implemented that decreased federal taxation while increasing military spending, shifted federal expenses to state and local governments, and produced tax legislation that benefitted the wealthy at the expense of the middle class. During the 1980s, economic growth slowed in the United States, the manufacturing sector of the economy declined while the service sector grew, and union membership fell. In the attempt to improve their economic position and shareholder profits, American corporations downsized their workforces, and although corporate profits more than doubled from 1980 to 1994, fewer new businesses incorporated in 1991 than in 1980 and were eight times more likely to fail by 1991. During the 1980s, federal, state, local, and consumer debt soared, and the federal public debt went from $908 billion dollars in 1980 to over $4 trillion dollars by 1992 (Cassidy, 1995; Famighetti, 1994; Johnson 1995; Kennedy, 1993).

The economic upheavals of the 1980s and 1990s had an especially detrimental impact on young people. For example, over half of America's youth who held jobs in the 1990s worked in the less well-paying service and technical-sales sectors. Unemployment for 16–24 year olds in 1994 was 27 per cent, three times higher than the national average (much higher for African-American youth than for white youth). From the late 1960s through the late 1980s, the median income (in 1993 dollars) of Americans aged 35 and older rose and then dropped slightly by 1991. However, the 15–24 year old age group steadily lost ground, with a 14 per cent decline in median income from 1967–91 (Famighetti, 1994; Mitchell, 1995).

Social life: Shifts in population, family, health, education and crime from the 1980s to the 1990s changed the texture of America's social life. The age composition of the US population had important consequences for youth. During the 1980s and 1990s, the national population became significantly older. Moreover, Mitchell (1995, p.11) reported that young people aged 19–30 comprised a small percentage of the population (17 per cent) relative to the much larger percentages of adults aged 31–49 (30 per cent), children under 19 (27 per cent), and older adults aged 50 and over (26 per cent). As Ryder (1965) noted, a small-size cohort is at a decided disadvantage in the competition for society's resources and attention. The ethnic composition of the American population shifted as well during the 1980s and 1990s to become more and ethnically diverse, largely due to higher fertility rates among certain ethnic groups than others, an increased rate of immigration from non-European countries, and an influx of illegal immigrants (Famighetti, 1994; Mitchell, 1995; Snyder and Fromboluti, 1993).

Over the last two decades, American family life appeared to decline. For example, from the 1980s to the 1990s, fewer couples married, and the average number of children in a family decreased, while the workforce participation of mothers with children rose, especially for mothers of young children under the age of three. Although the abortion rate declined in the 1990s, particularly worrisome to many Americans has been the high divorce rate and the growth in teenage and out-of-wedlock births. As a result, increased percentages of children in the United States are growing up in single-parent families (24 per cent of American children in 1992, and 57 per cent of African-American children), and the percentage of poor children coming from female-headed households has increased steadily to 59 per cent in 1991 and to 83 per cent for African-American children (Johnson, 1995; Snyder and Fromboluti, 1993).

A particularly important aspect of any country's well-being is the health of its citizens. Although average life expectancy continued to increase for Americans to 75.8 years of age by 1992, the health of children and youth did not fare as well as it should. Violence was the number one killer of adolescents and youth in the United States (including motor vehicle accidents and other accidents, suicide and homicide), with much higher rates for young males than females, and an alarming escalation in homicide deaths for young African-American males in the late 1980s and early 1990s. Partly because of their riskier life styles, sexually transmitted diseases, AIDS and HIV infection, posed serious threats to the health of youth and young adults. Ironically, although the United States spends more money on health care than any nation in the world, it is the only advanced industrial country without a comprehensive national health insurance system. Those without health coverage are most apt to be children, youth and young adults, with one study reporting that nearly half of 18–24 year olds in America were without health insurance for a month or more between 1990 and 1992 (Johnson, 1995; Mitchell, 1995; Snyder and Fromboluti, 1993).

Educational trends in United States during the 1980s and 1990s produced mixed results for youth. On the positive side, the teacher–student ratio declined, per pupil expenditure rose, and higher percentages of 14–17 year olds enrolled in school and committed themselves to college preparatory programs. Although proficiency scores in reading, writing, mathematics and science remained stable or rose, the achievement test performance of American pupils ranked relatively low in international comparisons. And while the overall high school drop-out rate declined by 1991, it remained high for Hispanics and some inner-city schools. America's colleges and universities generally have received high ratings, but in the 1990s higher education has been threatened by escalating tuition costs and sizable state budget cuts (Famighetti, 1994; Kennedy, 1993; Snyder and Fromboluti, 1993).

An especially discouraging aspect of social life in the 1980s and 1990s has been the rising crime rate in the United States, with the steepest rise in the area of violent crime (murder, forcible rape, robbery, and aggravated assault) and the smallest increase in property crimes. How rapidly violence is escalating in America is evidenced by a three per cent overall increase in the number of murders in the 1992–93 year alone. Although there are no reliable statistics on gun ownership, estimates are that at least half of American families own a gun; more alarming is a study that reported nearly half of the high school students surveyed thought they could obtain a gun without trouble. Violence is also indicated by the large number of substantiated child abuse and neglect cases, which equaled more than 800,000 in 1991 (1.8 million cases reported). Over 14 million arrests were made in 1992, with a notable increase in arrests for those under age 18 from 1991–92. By 1992, the United States had a record high prison population in federal and state correctional facilities, and by 1995, one out of three African-American males spent time in prison (Johnson, 1995).

Political life: The 1980 national election initiated a new era of political conservatism in the United States – what Schlesinger (1986) terms a cycle of privatist rather than public interest. In 1980, former Hollywood movie actor and Republican Ronald Reagan became President, and the Republican Party gained control of the Senate and captured 33 seats from the Democrats in the House of Representatives. Immediately after Reagan's inauguration, the Americans who had been held hostage in Iran (during the Carter administration) were suddenly released, and Congress quickly raised the military budget and legislated the largest tax-cut in American history. The women's equal rights amendment was defeated after a ten-year struggle, and legislation was passed that virtually ended school busing as a means to achieve racial integration. Reagan's second term in office was marred by Wall Street scandals and public hearings of the White House's involvement in the Iran-Contra affair. Although Reagan built his political reputation as a staunch anti-communist, relations with the Soviet Union and communist China eased considerably during his second term (Dye, 1986, 1990).

In 1988, Reagan's Vice-President, George Bush, was elected President. Bush's popularity peaked during the brief Gulf War against Iraq's invasion of Kuwait. For the most part, the Bush years were marked by ups and downs in the stock market and unemployment figures, the Government Accounting Office's revelation of banking improprieties in the House of Representatives, and the savings and loan scandal that cost the United States billions of dollars in government bailout money. During the 1980s, political party support continued to weaken, the cost of running for political office rose sharply, and Political Action Committees (PACs) and lobbying organizations increased their power and influence over the legislative process. By the end of the 1980s, the cold war had virtually ended, and the United States struggled to define its role in the new world order (Dye, 1990; Flanigan and Zingale, 1994).

Promising to attend to jobs and domestic problems, Bill Clinton won a plurality (43 per cent) of the Presidential vote in 1992, including a sizable percentage of the youth vote. Although Clinton's plans for economic stimulation and health care reform were defeated by Congress, his initiatives were passed for deficit-reduction, a waiting period for handgun purchases, the North American Free Trade Agreement (NAFTA), and a national service program for youth called 'Americorps'. Tarnishing Clinton's presidency were charges of character flaws, the Whitewater real estate scandal, and the puzzling suicide of his friend and White House lawyer, Vincent Foster. Conflicts in Bosnia, Russia, the Middle East, Haiti, Somalia and Rwanda focused much of Clinton's attention on foreign policy (Dye, 1995).

In pursuit of economic and cultural freedom, the 1980s and early 1990s have been characterized as an era of self-interest, greed and hedonism in the United States, with little emphasis on moral restraint or concern with the public good. Americans were enamored with business and market sector values, and political conservatives attempted to downsize social welfare and the federal government, deregulate industry and finance, and decrease taxes while privatizing services such as health care, education and transportation. The end of the cold war was a relief but left many Americans uncertain about who the enemy is and what direction foreign policy should take (Bellah *et al.*, 1991; Brzezinski, 1993; Verba *et al.*, 1995). The next questions are: How did these societal trends affect the perceptions and behavior of the youth generation? How did young people evaluate themselves and their country in the early 1990s?

Youth and Citizenship

Citizenship is both a status and a role. As specified in the 14th Amendment to the Constitution, the status of citizen is conferred to any child born in the United States, with the exception of foreign diplomats' children. The Immigration and Nationality Act of 1952 outlines conditions of citizenship for children born outside the United States if one parent is an American citizen. Foreigners may acquire American citizenship by becoming naturalized. As citizens, children and adolescents receive protection from the state, including special laws that pertain only to juveniles. Full rights as citizens begin at age 18 with the right to vote and serve in the military, but young people are subject to the laws of the state in which they reside for a variety of privileges such as driving a car, marrying without parental consent, the legal age for drinking, and numerous other activities.

In this study, the interest is how American youth view their role as citizens, both in the present as well as the future. Young people's perceptions of citizenship are assessed on the basis of their responses in the six national survey reports and a focus group study. Table 6.1 presents the percentages of youth endorsing a series of attitude and behavior items related to their personal conduct and views and to their collective orientations to society, politics and citizenship. General trends and the direction of findings are emphasized in the reporting of these data, although specific percentages are given in some instances. For the precise percentage distribution, refer to Table 6.1. The effects of recent societal trends on young people's perceptions of themselves and their country are explored as well.

Personal conduct and views: The economic aspirations of youth in the 1990s are examined first. According to Table 6.1, despite the lagging US economy, high school seniors in the Monitoring the Future survey claimed to be satisfied with their standard of living, and slightly fewer than in 1980 thought that times ahead would be tougher. In addition, young Americans did not appear to be downtrodden and 'slackers'. Quite the contrary. As suggested by several surveys, the majority of youth had high aspirations, hoping to be successful and find steady work (CIRP/ACE survey and Official Guide). When asked about their objectives in life, college freshmen in the CIRP/ACE

TABLE 6.1
PERSONAL CONDUCT AND COLLECTIVE ORIENTATIONS OF YOUNG AMERICAN
CITIZENS IN THE 1990s

Themes, Surveys, Attitudes and Behavior	1990s %	(comparison)
PERSONAL CONDUCT AND VIEWS		
1990 Monitoring the Future Survey		
Satisfied with own standard of living	73	(75% in 1980)
Think times ahead will be tougher	48	(55% in 1980)
Argued or fought with parents 5 or more times this year	46	(41% in 1980)
Am not too happy	13	(29% Blacks)
Other students would not care if I cheated on test	77	(79% in 1980)
This past year have:		
gotten into serious fight in school or at work	19	(16% in 1980)
fought with friends against another group	1	(18% in 1980)
used a knife/gun/weapon to take something	4	(3% in 1980)
taken something not belonging to you under $50	32	(33% in 1980)
taken something from a store without paying	32	(31% in 1980)
damaged school property on purpose	14	(13% in 1980)
gotten into trouble with police	24	(22% in 1980)
had something stolen from you under $50	45	(44% in 1980)
Watch TV almost every day	72	(72% in 1980)
Read books, magazines, newspapers almost every day	47	(59% in 1980)
Probably will (or have):		
vote in a public election	87	(87% in 1980)
write to public officials	26	(36% in 1980)
give money to political candidate/cause	18	(22% in 1980)
work in a political campaign	11	(16% in 1980)
participate in lawful demonstration	25	(22% in 1980)
boycott certain products	28	(30% in 1980)
1991–92 Gallup International Institute Surveys		
Get along with parents very well or fairly well	96	
Likely to marry	88	(84% in 1977)
Want to have children	84	(79% in 1977)
Satisfied with personal life	86	(88% in 1985)
Grade their high school A or B	70	
Grade their teachers A or B	76	
Discipline in school very or somewhat strict	84	(64% in 1984)
A great deal or fair amount of cheating in school	55	(66% in 1986)
Personally have cheated	46	(59% in 1986)
Fear for physical safety at school	24	(18% in 1977)
Classroom disturbances a (very, fairly) big problem	69	
Fighting in class is a big problem	23	(10% in 1985)
Students bring guns and knives to school	28	
Drug abuse is biggest problem facing teens	40	(27% in 1977)
Peer pressure is biggest problem facing teens	15	(5% in 1977)
AIDS is biggest problem facing teens	11	(5% in 1987)

Themes, Surveys, Attitudes and Behavior	*1990s %*	*(comparison)*
Greatest personal problem is school grades	33	
Greatest personal problem is career uncertainties	25	
Favorite pastime:		
visit with friends	34	(28% in 1988)
watch TV	14	(22% in 1988)
sports and exercise	12	(3% in 1988)
dating, partying, dancing	5	(10% in 1988)
Plan to join political party	21	
Plan to run for public office	6	
1993 CDC National Survey		
Carried a weapon (gun, knife, club) during past month	22	(8% a gun)
Engaged in a physical fight during past year	42	
Seriously contemplated suicide during past year	24	
Attempted suicide during past year	9	
Regular cigarette use	25	
Episodic heavy drinking	30	
Current marijuana use	18	
Current cocaine use	2	
Claimed to be overweight	34	
Attempting weight loss	40	
Had sexual intercourse during lifetime	53	
Intercourse with 4 or more partners	19	
Condom used last intercourse	53	
1994 CIRP/ACE Freshman National Norms Survey		
Become authority in my field	65	(78% in 1977)
Be very well-off financially	74	(66% in 1977)
Be successful in own business	41	(56% in 1977)
Develop a philosophy of life	43	(56% in 1977)
Rated self above average for emotional health	52	(65% in 1985)
Rated self above average for physical health	52	(72% in 1985)
Felt overwhelmed	24	(6% in 1985)
Felt depressed	10	(12% in 1985)
Help others in difficulty	62	(57% in 1977)
Influence social values	40	(29% in 1977)
Plan to participate in community action	24	(27% in 1977)
Classify self as:		
liberal/left	25	(28% in 1977)
conservative/right	22	(19% in 1977)
middle-of-the-road	53	(53% in 1977)
Keep up with politics	32	(45% in 1977)
Discuss politics	16	(22% in 1988)
Want to influence political structure	19	(19% in 1977)
Be involved in environmental clean up	24	(31% in 1977)
Have participated in a demonstration	40	(16% in 1978)
1994 Roper/ISI National Poll		
Satisfied with job	78	(adults 83%)

Themes, Surveys, Attitudes and Behavior	1990s %	(comparison)
Family shaped beliefs a great deal	75	(adults 84%)
Values pretty much same as parents	67	(adults 76%)
Quality of life at home good or wonderful	82	(adults 87%)
Believe in God and always have	88	(adults 89%)
Pray once a day or more	49	(adults 58%)
Performed volunteer work in past year	51	(adults 53%)
Volunteered during past month	44	(adults 55%)
Identify as a Republican	31	(adults 31%)
Identify as a Democrat	27	(adults 31%)
Identify as an Independent	36	(adults 35%)
Petitioned government during past year	38	(adults 50%)
Attended public meeting	33	(adults 44%)
Attended political rally or speech	20	(adults 23%)
Written congressman or state representative	16	(adults 34%)

1995 Official Guide to the Generations
Very important to me:

being successful at work	89	(85% in 1972)
being able to find steady work	88	(78% in 1972)
having lots of money	37	(18% in 1972)
having strong friendships	80	(79% in 1972)
marrying and having a happy family	79	(82% in 1972)
give children better opportunities	76	(67% in 1972)
Registered to vote in 1992	52	(adults 73%)
Voted in 1992 election	42	(adults 66%)

COLLECTIVE ORIENTATIONS AND BELIEFS

1990 Monitoring the Future Survey

People are too concerned with material things	83	(78% in 1980)
Our system of doing things still best in world	58	(64% in 1980)
Satisfied with the way government is operating	24	(10% in 1980)
Government in Washington can be trusted to do right	46	(37% in 1980)
Government wastes a lot of the tax money	51	(61% in 1980)
People running government smart and know what they do	67	(58% in 1980)
US puts too much emphasis on profits, not enough on human well-being	72	(72% in 1980)
Way people vote has major impact on how country run	71	(64% in 1980)
People who get together in citizen action have effect	65	(58% in 1980)
Good citizen tries to change government policies	58	(61% in 1980)
You can't be a good citizen unless you obey the law	44	(48% in 1980)
Good citizen should go along with government even if they disagree with government	15	(21% in 1980)

1991–92 Gallup International Institute Surveys
Too little respect for:

Native Americans	73
Hispanic Americans	60

Themes, Surveys, Attitudes and Behavior	*1990s %*	*(comparison)*
Gays	57	
Illegal aliens	56	
Asian-Americans	53	
Blacks	52	
Whites	5	
Oppose equal opportunity programs	7	
Three greatest problems facing US:		
drugs	32	(13% in 1988)
AIDS	15	(8% in 1988)
economics	13	(16% in 1988)

1991–92 Harwood Group Focus-Groups Study

	Critical Views	*Positive Views*
Politics	'Politics as usual' seen as narrow, negative, irrelevant Big interests dominate	Politics could be better More cooperation Solution-oriented
Political debate	Partisan politics too acrimonious Dominated by extremes Excessive views and behavior	Tone down rhetoric Need to truly listen Genuine idea exchange Searching for the center Common language needed plus pluralism
Citizenship	Too much emphasis on rights, entitlements, and freedom rather than responsibility, obligations, and duty	'Want to participate in meaningful ways, but don't know how' Feel sense of responsibility

1994 CIRP/ACE Freshman National Norms Survey

The wealthy should pay more taxes	67	(77% in 1977)
Racial discrimination not a problem	17	
There is too much concern for criminals	73	(69% in 1977)
Should abolish death penalty	20	(27% in 1978)
Government should do more to control handguns	80	(67% in 1989)
Government not protecting consumer	72	(68% in 1977)
Government not controlling pollution	84	(79% in 1977)
National health care plan needed	71	(60% in 1977)

1994 Roper/ISI National Poll

There should not be a top limit on incomes	80	(adults 72%)
Each individual should have opportunity, even if some people are more successful	75	(adults 73%)
If you work hard, you can get ahead	75	(adults 73%)
Children should be brought up practicing a religious faith – very or somewhat important	89	(adults 94%)

Themes, Surveys, Attitudes and Behavior	1990s %	(comparison)
Black Americans have equal chance to succeed	49	(adults 60%)
Affirmative action programs are good idea	60	(adults 39%)
Ethics and honesty have fallen	61	(adults 63%)
Dissatisfied with way things going in the US	63	(adults 64%)
Congress more concerned with own political future	87	(adults 89%)
Big government is a threat to country	72	(adults 66%)
Big business is a threat to country	13	(adults 14%)
Approve of Bill Clinton's character and policies	30	(adults 28%)
America is still the best place to live	72	(adults 82%)
'In God We Trust' is appropriate motto for the US	72	(adults 87%)
Prefer more government services and more taxes	23	(adults 12%)
Prefer less government services and less taxes	40	(adults 55%)
1995 Official Guide to the Generations		
Groups and institutions having good influence:		
people who run their own business	93	(adults 91%)
computers and technology	92	(adults 87%)
women's movement	86	(adults 67%)
environmentalists	86	(adults 74%)
the churches	85	(adults 85%)
CNN (TV network)	85	(adults 76%)
newspapers	84	(adults 70%)
unions	70	(adults 48%)
local and state governments	66	(adults 59%)
police	64	(adults 71%)
business executives	55	(adults 40%)
Congress	55	(adults 35%)
movies and TV shows	49	(adults 28%)
investors from foreign countries	43	(adults 32%)
rock music	43	(adults 27%)

Note: The 1990 'Monitoring the Future' survey, conducted by the University of Michigan Institute for Social Research, included 15,676 seniors at 137 high schools; a comparable sample comprised the 1980 survey (Bachman *et al.*, 1981, 1993). The 1991–92 Gallup Youth Surveys interviewed national probability samples of American households with youth between the ages of 13–17 (Bezilla, 1993). The 1993 Centers for Disease Control and Prevention (CDC) surveyed 16,296 high school students in grades 9–12 (between the ages of 14–18) (Centers for Disease Control and Prevention, 1995). The 1994 Cooperative Institutional Research Program/American Council on Education (CIRP/ACE) survey is based on a sample of 237,777 freshmen attending 461 colleges and universities. CIRP/ACE comparisons are made with similar size samples (Cooperative Institutional Research Program/American Council on Education, 1991, 1994). The Roper Center/Institute for Social Inquiry National Poll surveyed 1,053 adults nationwide 18 years and older (Institute for Social Inquiry, 1994). The results of national polls conducted in the 1990s on all age-groups were taken from *The Official Guide to the Generations* (Mitchell, 1995). The Harwood Group studied focus groups at ten universities located throughout the United States in 1991–92. Focus-groups consisted of approximately 12 students between the ages of 18–24, representing a cross-section of American college students (Harwood Group, 1993).

survey expressed much greater concern with being well-off financially (74 per cent) and becoming an authority in their field (65 per cent) than with developing a philosophy of life (43 per cent). The shift away from philosophical values in favor of materialism has been pronounced for American college freshmen over the past 30 years. In contrast to the 1990s, 83 per cent of college freshman in 1967 wanted to develop a philosophy of life, and 44 per cent wanted to be well-off financially (see Cooperative Institutional Research Program/American Council on Education, 1991, p.122).

What impact did the much-discussed decline and break-up of the family in the 1980s have on this generation of youth? According to these survey results, the family is highly valued by young people. Despite the increasing divorce and illegitimacy rates, more than nine out of ten teenagers said they got along well or fairly well with their parents, and most youth hoped to marry, have children, and give children better opportunities (Gallup surveys and Official Guide). And although almost half of high school seniors in the Monitoring the Future survey reported that they argued or fought with their parents five or more times a year, such arguments did not appear to dampen youth's appreciation for family life. According to the Roper poll, over three-quarters of 18–29-year-olds maintained that their home life was good or wonderful and claimed the family had a great deal of influence on shaping their beliefs; a majority also agreed that their values were similar to those of their parents.

Another myth challenged by these youth survey data is that young people are miserable and unhappy, with little appreciation for conventional American values. Most youth reported being satisfied or happy with their personal lives, although it is worth noting that 29 per cent of African-American high school seniors reported they were not happy, a percentage twice that for the national sample of youth (Gallup and Monitoring the Future surveys). Besides endorsing family values, young people in the 1990s upheld the American traditions of religion and work. Nearly nine-tenths of youth in the Roper poll said that they believe in God, and almost half said they pray once a day or more. While much has been written about worker dissatisfaction in the 1990s, most youth and adults expressed satisfaction with their jobs.

When it comes to education and school, the findings are mixed. On the positive side, the Gallup surveys found that most adolescents gave high grades of 'A' or 'B' to their school and teachers, and characterized their schools as 'very' or 'somewhat' strict. Yet, while youth in the early 1990s appeared to like their schools, they faced alarming problems of cheating, disruption, and even violence. For example, while 55 per cent of the respondents in the Gallup survey said there was a great deal or a fair amount of cheating in school – a decrease since 1986 – 77 per cent of high school seniors in the Monitoring the Future survey claimed that other students would not care if they (the respondent) cheated on a test. In addition, 69 per cent of the Gallup respondents maintained that classroom disturbances are a big or fairly big problem, 28 per cent reported that others students brought knives and guns to school, and 23 per cent claimed that fighting in class is a big problem (more than twice the per centage in 1985). The percentage of students fearing for their physical safety at school increased to 24 per cent by 1992.

The trend toward violence at school is symptomatic of much wider violence and crime in American society. Perhaps some small comfort may be taken by the finding in the Monitoring the Future survey that self-reports of adolescent stealing and vandalism have not changed substantially – from 22–24 per cent of high school seniors got themselves into trouble with police in 1980 and in 1990. According to the CDC survey, violence and self-abuse are escalating: 22 per cent of American students reported carrying weapons, and 42 per cent engaged in physical fighting during the year of the survey. Sad to say, violence against others is accompanied by violence against the self, with one out of four teens reporting seriously contemplating suicide in the past year, and almost one out of ten actually attempting suicide. Substance abuse is another form of damage to the self, with 18–30 per cent of adolescents reporting that they smoke cigarettes, use marijuana, or engage in episodic heavy drinking. Although adolescents in the Gallup survey said that their greatest personal problems were routine issues of school grades and career uncertainties, these youth thought that drug use and peer pressure were the biggest problems for their generation – to a much greater extent than in the 1970s.

In addition to violence, the physical and emotional health of American youth is jeopardized by weight problems and sexual promiscuity (CDC survey). An important health change for young people is that they do not see themselves as healthy as they did in the past, with fewer freshmen in the CIRP/ACE survey rating their physical or emotional health as 'above average' in 1994, compared to freshmen in 1985. While there is little increase in the percentage of freshmen saying they are depressed, there has been a four-fold jump in the percentage claiming to feel overwhelmed.

What about the cultural pursuits of 1990s youth? Although the Monitoring the Future survey reported that nearly three-quarters of high school seniors watched television every day, the Gallup surveys found that television viewing has declined as a favorite leisure pastime since 1988, whereas the desire to visit with friends and participate in sports and exercise had increased by 1994. Clearly, reading has decreased as a pastime for 1990s youth (Monitoring the Future survey). And although having strong friendships remained of significant importance to most youth (Official Guide), for some reason, young people in the 1990s were much less likely to list 'dating, partying, and dancing' as favorite activities than they were in 1988 (Gallup survey).

One of the most pervasive notions about 1990s youth is that they are self-centered, unconcerned and uncaring about the larger society. These 1990s surveys document a significant change in youthful attitudes and behavior related to social values and the community. Compared to 1977, increased percentages of freshmen in the 1994 CIRP/ACE survey wanted to help others in difficulty and to influence social values. Though less than a quarter of these freshmen said they plan to participate in community action, the Roper poll found that half the 18–29-year-olds had performed volunteer work in the past year, and many during the past month. In fact, young people's rate of community voluntarism resembled that of adults in 1994.

While concern with social values and the community gained interest among youth in the 1990s, politics clearly lost ground. Although most high school seniors in the Monitoring the Future survey maintained that they intend to vote, the percentages likely to take other kinds of political actions are much smaller and have declined since 1980. Do not look to Generation X for political support or contributions. A mere 18 per cent claimed they might give money to political candidates or causes, and only 11 per cent would work in a political campaign. Few teens in the Gallup survey plan to join a political party, and only six per cent were willing to run for political office. Furthermore, compared to college freshmen in the previous CIRP/ACE surveys, those going to college in 1994 are less likely to want to keep up with politics or discuss politics, and, in contrast to the 40 per cent of freshmen in 1994 who wanted to influence social values, only 19 per cent wanted to influence the political structure. Yet, despite their apparent lack of political interest, 40 per cent of freshmen in 1994 claimed to have participated in a demonstration, which was more than twice as high as the 1978 cohort.

What about young people's political identification? Although they grew up during a politically conservative era, only a minority of youth in the 1990s identified with political conservatism or the Republican Party. Many shied away from conventional political labels. Slightly over half of college freshmen in the CIRP/ACE survey classified themselves as political moderates, with one-quarter identifying themselves as liberal or far left and somewhat fewer claiming to be conservatives or on the far right. The pattern was similar for political party identification, with a plurality of youth in the Roper poll choosing an Independent (36 per cent) political affiliation, versus 31 per cent who said they were Republicans and 27 per cent who claimed to be Democrats. Youth, however, were not much different from adults in their political party identification – or lack of it. But they were less likely than adults to engage in political actions such as registering to vote, voting, petitioning the government, going to public meetings or rallies, and they were much less likely to have written to a Congressman or state representative (Official Guide and Roper poll).

Collective orientations and beliefs: The next issue in this study involves young people's collective orientations to society, politics and citizenship in the 1990s. In an era marked by economic declines and heightened ethnic and religious group divisiveness, what are young people's perceptions about America's economy and political system, what are their views about social equality, and what is their conception of citizenship? An important issue is whether the collective orientation of 1990s youth is similar to or different from the adult generation. Novels and films give the impression that 1990s youth are at odds with the adult generation's conceptions of society and politics. See Table 6.1 for the percentage distribution of youth's collective orientation and beliefs.

Despite the economic losses for the United States in general and youth in particular, young people in the early 1990s were highly supportive of America's economic system and preoccupation with business. Although many high school seniors agreed that people are overly concerned with material things and that there is too much emphasis on profits and not enough on human well-being, close to three-fifths endorsed the idea that our system of doing things is the best in the world (Monitoring the Future survey). And, when asked which groups and institutions have a 'good' influence on the country, the two groups receiving the strongest endorsement from youth were (1) people who run their own business, and (2) computers and technology – both ranked slightly higher than support for churches (Official Guide). Corroborating the strong support for capitalism among youth, there was a decline in the percentage of college freshmen who thought the wealthy should pay more taxes (CIRP/ACE survey). Moreover, the generations share enthusiasm for America's economic system, individualism and, to some extent, social darwinism. Most youth and adults concurred that there should not be a top limit on incomes and that individuals should have opportunities, even if some people are more successful. The generations also agreed that the work ethic is strong in the United States, believing that if you work hard, you can get ahead. Only a minority of youth and adults thought that big business was a threat to their country (Roper poll).

Generational differences appeared more evident in the area of social life than in economics. As the country became more ethnically diverse, young people in the 1990s viewed equality and discrimination more of a problem in the United States than did adults. According to the Gallup surveys, from 52–73 per cent of 1990s youth believed there is too little respect for Native Americans, Hispanic Americans, gays, illegal aliens, Asian-Americans, and Blacks. And, despite the conservative argument that white males do not get enough respect and that equal opportunity and affirmative action programs need to be dismantled, only five per cent of young people said whites are not respected, and a mere seven per cent opposed equal opportunity programs. Similarly, a minority of freshmen in the 1994 CIRP/ACE survey claimed that racial discrimination is not a problem. Moreover, the Roper poll indicates that adults were more likely to say that Blacks have an equal chance to succeed than were youth, whereas many more youth than adults thought that affirmative action programs are a good idea. Higher percentages of young people viewed the women's movement and environmentalists as 'good influences' on society when compared to adults (Official Guide).

While many 1990s youth have liberal attitudes toward equality and discrimination, their views about crime and morality are more conservative. America's social problems and morality have youth worried. College freshmen thought that there is too much concern for criminals, and only a minority wanted to abolish the death penalty (CIRP/ACE survey). Moreover, adolescents ranked drugs and AIDS over economics as the major problems facing the country in 1992 (Gallup surveys). The generations tended to agree that 'ethics and honesty have fallen in the United States' and were generally dissatisfied with the way things are going in the country (Roper poll). Both youth and adults firmly believed that children should be brought up practicing a religion.

When it comes to American political life, youth were highly critical of government and politics in the early 1990s, although youth in the 1980s appeared to be critical as well. In 1990, only 24 per cent of high school seniors said they were satisfied with the way government was operating, less than half thought the government in Washington could be trusted to do the right thing, and slightly over half said the government wastes a lot of tax money. Although young people agreed that the people running government are smart and know what they are doing (Monitoring the Future survey), youth and adults lack confidence in Congress. On a list of institutions that youth thought were 'good for society', Congress was rated low – only somewhat higher than rock music (Official Guide). But, if youth are critical of Congress, adults are more so, with 55 per cent support for Congress among youth compared to only 35 per cent of adults. Moreover, nearly nine out of ten youth and adults agreed that the US Congress is more concerned with its own future than with passing good legislation (Roper poll).

Youth in the early 1990s appear suspicious of government – even more than adults – with nearly three-quarters of young people viewing big government as a threat to this country, compared to slightly more than three-fifths of the adults. Less than a third of young people and adults approved of President Bill Clinton's character and policies in 1994, and 40 per cent of youth and 55 per cent of adults maintained they would like to see fewer government services and less taxes (Roper poll).

Does this mean that young people and adults are alienated from America's political system? Not so, according to the 1994 Roper poll, which found that 72 per cent of youth and 82 per cent of adults agreed that America is still the best place to live. And it is not entirely clear that young people would actually like to see less government. For example, from 71–84 per cent of college freshmen in the CIRP/ACE survey said they wanted the government to do *more* to control handguns, the environment and consumer protection, and an increased percentage wanted a national health-care plan.

To supplement the quantitative survey findings, the Harwood Group study of college students across the country provides qualitative data supporting the generalization that young people in the 1990s are disenchanted and dissatisfied with politicians and government. In addition, the focus-group responses give an indication why young people were disgusted with politics in the early 1990s. For example, many college students associate 'politics' with endless, rancorous political campaigns, self-seeking politicians, and an ineffective government and bureaucracy, while 'citizen participation' is viewed as largely confined to individual voting, signing petitions and writing to officials. As students see it, the average person does not count for much in American politics, partially because powerful financial and lobbying interests prevail. No one cares about politics anyway, many youth said. Politicians merely placate voters in order to pursue their personal agendas, and public officials insulate themselves from citizens. '"London Bridge is Falling Down",' one student responded, 'and we cannot change how things are going' (Harwood Group, 1993, p.18).

Another pervasive complaint among college students, according to the Harwood Group study, is that political extremes, negative advertising and excessive behavior receive an undue amount of media attention in the United States. As one student remarked, 'There's no solutions discussed, it's all rhetoric.' Another stated, 'I think our political system is becoming impotent. It's becoming so partisan … it's coming to the point where it seems to be losing its effectiveness' (Harwood Group, 1993, pp.16–17). Students also complained that political moderates receive little attention, with several students observing that people do not know the middle-of-the-road exists in the United States.

Like the survey results, these focus-group findings should not be interpreted to mean that youth are alienated from their country. Young people's disgust and frustration with politics appear to be rooted in their firm belief that politics could be much better. For example, while the Harwood Group study indicated that youth were disgruntled with 'politics as usual', young people also expressed the view that the political process in the United States could be more thoughtful and productive. What is needed both on and off campus, students concurred, is a genuine, *civilized* exchange of political views, with a full range of perspectives represented. Most of all, the emphasis should be on solving society's problems based on cooperation rather than unnecessary conflict. Across the country, college students reacted against social and political divisiveness and political correctness; instead, they wanted a common language that pulled the country together, yet respected diversity.

What do these surveys suggest about young people's beliefs regarding citizenship in the 1990s? According to the Monitoring the Future survey, most youth (71 per cent) believed that people's voting behavior has a major impact on the how the country is run and that citizens who get together can make a difference (64 per cent). Many youth agreed that good citizens try to change the government (58 per cent), while only 15 per cent said that good citizens should go along with the government even if they disagree with it.

A somewhat clearer picture of what youth think about citizenship is provided by the Harwood Group study results, which found that when most college students talked about citizenship, they referred to individual rights, entitlements and freedom, with little mention of responsibility, duty and obligation. Moreover, students did not connect citizenship with politics. Typifying students' notions of citizenship is the student who said, 'Being a citizen is your God-given right. Politics doesn't have anything to do with being a citizen' (Harwood Group, 1993, p.42). Another common belief is that public demonstrations and civil disobedience are among the only ways to attract attention in the United States, yet students said they were tired of the haranguing. As one student observed, 'Someone on campus is always protesting something' (Harwood Group, 1993, p.15).

The Harwood Group study highlights two problems related to youth and citizenship in the 1990s, which have important implications for conducting citizenship education. First, while youth in the 1990s valued community service, they did not view it as an aspect of citizenship and politics, reflected by the remark, 'I don't really see a connection between community service and politics' (Harwood Group, 1993, p.35). Second, although young people claimed to feel a sense of citizen responsibility and wanted to participate in making the community better, they lamented they did not know how, commenting: 'We don't see what it is that we can do' and 'What they need to do is teach us how to be involved' (Harwood Group, 1993, p.33).

CITIZENSHIP EDUCATION

Before evaluating 1990s youth as citizens, a brief overview of the conduct of citizenship education in the United States is provided, including some principal criticisms. The results of the survey findings are analyzed in the light of what they suggest about American youth's areas of strength and weakness as citizens and their implications for improving citizen education in the United States.

Citizenship Education in the United States

Unlike many advanced nations, the United States has no national citizenship goals, curriculum, standards, examinations, or ways to evaluate citizen education. Instead, American youngsters attend school in a decentralized public education system comprising approximately 15,200 school districts, each of which largely determines its own policies and practices for conducting citizenship education from kindergarten through the twelfth grade. Not surprisingly, wide variations exist among the districts in state-mandated curricula, teacher salaries, per pupil expenditure, the quality of education, and graduation rates (Eveslage, 1993; Famighetti, 1994).

The primary and secondary school system is chiefly responsible for teaching citizenship to American youth. Citizenship courses and curricula tend to emphasize either the structure of government in the United States and major historic events, or the problems and issues associated with democracy and American culture. In general, elementary school children are exposed to American symbols and the rudiments of American history and government. In many states children are also taught about their state government, history, and symbols (state flag, song, mascot and flower). Indirect efforts in the public schools to socialize youngsters to American democracy include elections of class officers, voting on classroom or school decisions, and school and teacher attempts at moral education directed toward getting along and working with each other in the school and in the playground (O'Neil, 1991).

The most intensive formal instruction in citizen education usually takes place at the middle school (junior high school) or early high school level. Many states and localities require that all students take a designated citizenship education course – variously titled Civics, Principles of Democracy, Government, and Problems of Democracy, etc. This basic course is supported by previous and subsequent courses, mostly from social studies and history. The course content is drawn primarily from the fields of American history, political science, government, economics, social problems, law, and sociology. Course objectives and teacher efforts are most likely to be directed toward the knowledge component, but, increasingly, affective and behavioral objectives are included (Braungart and Braungart, 1994; Reische, 1987; Zevin, 1992).

In addition to the primary and secondary schools, several other formal settings in the United States undertake citizenship education. Although colleges and universities are not typically considered training grounds for citizenship education, a number of course offerings and concentrations pertain to citizenship. Some research has suggested, however, that extracurricular activities are more effective ways to learn citizenship skills (i.e., group participation, leadership, taking responsibility, applying democratic principles, and conflict resolution) for college students. Adult education is another avenue for promoting citizenship education. A variety of groups and organizations (i.e., labor unions, government-sponsored associations, political parties, public interest and voluntary organizations, religious groups, philanthropic foundations, professional organizations, and advocacy groups) offer formal training or workshops that enhance adults' knowledge, skills, attitudes, and behavior about themselves and their citizen role. In many countries, the military and public service programs are considered highly effective for promoting a strong sense of national loyalty and civic obligation. However, currently conservatives in the US Congress are threatening to severely curtail or dismantle America's recently implemented national youth service program as a way to cut government spending (Braungart and Braungart, 1994; Sigel, 1989).

Citizenship education in American schools is criticized by almost everyone: students, teachers, parents, and experts. Many courses have the reputation of being tedious and boring to students. Teachers may not be well prepared to deliver the course, and often find themselves treading a fine line between offering a course that is objective or neutral versus one that is stimulating but considered too controversial.

Redesigning and implementing citizen education in American schools is difficult because all of the controversies inherent in democracy (freedom versus equality, majority rule versus minority rights, communitarianism versus libertarianism) are likely to surface in arguments over how students should be taught. For example, while many school administrators, teachers, and parents believe that the principal goal of citizenship education is to produce well-informed, conventional and conforming citizens, other adults demand a critical, issue-oriented, problem-solving approach intended to develop an activist citizenry. As another example, civics and history textbooks may be scrutinized by various politically correct advocates for possible white, male Anglo-European bias as well as by the fundamentalist Christian right demanding that their religious values and beliefs be represented in the texts. Little wonder civics textbooks are denounced for being so impartial that they are lifeless, so controversial that advocate groups demand they be banned, or so cluttered with disparate details and discussions of various perspectives that the subject matter does not cohere (Eveslage, 1993; Reische, 1987).

1990s Youth as Citizens and Implications for Education

Based on this brief overview of American society and the attitudes and behavior of its youth, the principal recommendation of this study is to build on young people's citizenship strengths and attempt to address their weaknesses in citizenship education programs. More specifically, the following analysis and suggestions are offered.

A significant source of civic strength is young Americans' positive identification with their country and its fundamental ideals. A central finding of this investigation is that *youth and adults share a similar set of meanings and orientations toward the political culture in the 1990s: they strongly endorse their country and its traditional values, and are highly critical of politics, politicians, and the way the federal government operates.* Americans' collective orientation in the early 1990s reflects the principal characteristics that de Tocqueville ([1835] 1956) observed in the United States well over a century ago: a love of wealth, personal freedom, equality, individualism, pragmatism, and a keen distrust of authority and government. Such persistent themes suggest there is a 'center' or core set of traditional values shared by youth and adults, an underlying patriotic albeit critical spirit, and a deep commitment to the American system. However, while the political system is perceived as fundamentally legitimate, youth and adults concur that currently it is not effective. Americans are skeptical of the way the government operates and are weary of extremists and ideologues dominating the media and political agenda.

The implication for citizenship education in the United States is that adolescents, college students and adults need information about what citizens can do when they think democratic values are threatened. Yet, a plethora of objections are likely to be raised. Although promoting critical thinking and an activist orientation toward politics appear to be relatively innocuous educational goals – goals that certainly would be supported by America's founding fathers – some educational experts, school boards and parents today have argued that emphasizing critical thinking in education produces self-centered, negative, cynical students who cannot agree to any other position than their own (Janowitz, 1983). Adults who view the primary function of citizenship education in the schools as system-maintenance are likely to object to an emphasis on reflective criticism and reforming the *status quo* (Reische, 1987).

A second source of civic strength identified in this study is the viability of civil society in America. Viewed as mediating the forces of the market and those of the state, civil society is based on the voluntary associations of individuals whose actions are directed toward self-help, the public good, and the well-being of the larger community (Bendix *et al.*, 1987; Kumar, 1993). When compared to youth in the 1970s, *young people in the 1990s appear more interested in committing themselves to improving social values and volunteering in the community.* American youth in the 1990s believe that community service is worthwhile and exhibited high rates of voluntarism, similar to adults.

Although both youth and adults in the 1990s view politics as corrupt, divisive, and ineffective, civil society holds promise as the sector where youth may prefer to exercise active citizenship. Civil society is the arena where citizens can exert pressure on both the economy and polity to improve the quality of community life. However, recent research indicates that Americans tend to view the state rather than the economy as the major source of societal problems, whereas Europeans see both the market and state as equal threats to community life (Dekker and van den Broek, 1995). Despite America's tightening economy and young people's declining economic status over the past 15 years, youth surveyed in the 1990s were remarkably uncritical of the economic sector and reflected Americans' penchant for blaming big government instead. These results suggest that educators will have to work harder to expand the definition of citizenship, focus on the various dimensions of individual responsibility, and demonstrate the linkages among economics, civil society and politics.

Citizenship education programs in American schools that include community service participation are likely to be evaluated favorably by youth and represent a worthwhile socialization experience for active political learning and lessons in civic responsibility. Until establishment politics is perceived as improving and politicians genuinely address society's problems, participatory politics appears to be the legitimate route to integrate youth into society and to promote political and economic reform. Having students volunteer in the community, work in a political campaign, engage in fund-raising for the school, and help with grass-roots projects have been found to be exciting and effective ways to teach democracy, responsibility, and to foster positive feelings in the adolescent (Eveslage, 1993; Reische, 1987; Remy, 1980; Zevin, 1992). Yet, the United States is a litigious society, and some parents have sued school districts because they contend that the state cannot 'require' their child to participate in community activities, however worthwhile.

A third area of citizenship strength identified in this study is *young Americans' increasing concern with solving social problems, equality, and the environment.* It should not have come as a surprise that when the University of California Board of Trustees recently decided to dismantle affirmative action programs, students rose up in protest. The youth generation in the United States has the potential to act as a balancing force for adults' penchant for ideological polarization and destructive ingroup-outgroup partisanship. Young people today also want social problems corrected – gun control, a clean environment, consumer protection, health care, and crime. An implication is that despite the likelihood of some adults' objections, youth are more apt to see the relevance of citizenship education programs that include a social problems perspective and attention to issues of equality and discrimination. Unfortunately, focusing on issues such as social and environmental problems, gender and multiculturalism, global citizenship, and biological and human rights may generate friction, criticism, and perhaps an organized backlash by some adults. All too often, school systems and teachers in the United States tend to shy away from controversy and emotionally charged debates (Braungart and Braungart, 1994; Zevin, 1992).

While American youth in the early 1990s evidenced a number of desirable attributes of citizen responsibility, an important question is how can some of their shortcomings be addressed in citizen education? First of all, this study suggests that much of the current discussion about Generation X and alienated youth has been misleading: the problem of young Americans is not a lack of national identification or patriotism. The primary need is to *give a clear focus to citizenship responsibility at the individual-behavioral level, particularly exercising the kind of self-restraint that will promote the health and emotional well-being of oneself and others.* Brzezinski (1993, p.60) observed that civic freedom has become divorced from civic responsibility partially because of America's emphasis on personal gratification at the expense of social need and moral restraint. Though young Americans in the 1990s show interest in social justice, the community, and attending to society's ills, their difficulty with self-gratification and impulse control undermines their personal and collective health. A dual approach in education is suggested: (1) incorporate health as a dimension of citizenship, and (2) teach students to exercise personal responsibility and self-control.

As an illustration, the Carnegie Council on Adolescent Development (1995) offered a number of recommendations to deal explicitly with the many problems associated with young Americans' health in the 1990s. First, promote young people's knowledge and understanding of their health by integrating health into the science curriculum, such as focusing on a life sciences curriculum, providing life-skills training, and offering social support programs. Second, improve students' academic performance through health and fitness by establishing developmentally appropriate health facilities for adolescents that are related to the curriculum and housed in or near the school. Third, include the media in educational efforts: introduce media literacy as part of the standard curriculum; utilize the media as part of comprehensive health-promotion campaigns; and incorporate young people's viewpoints and involvement in media production. Fourth, encourage business and government sponsorship of healthy youth activities and curriculum development, making certain these efforts are conducted in the spirit of responsible adult citizenship rather than as opportunities to foster youthful allegiance to commercial products or to partisan politics.

Young people's worries about their generation (drugs, AIDS, peer pressure) may provide a starting point in citizenship education programs to gain their attention and direct them toward more responsible behavior; then follow-up with topics such as personal decision-making, the self-in-relation-to-society, and conflict resolution. For example, educational programs in conflict resolution are being attempted in some of the toughest, crime-ridden neighborhood schools, and the more successful programs make a concerted effort to link their message to the home and the community in order to reinforce what is being taught in school (Carnegie Council, 1995; Gallup, 1995).

A number of American schools are implementing character education training to address an array of ethical and interpersonal problems from cheating to violence. Peer-focused rather than teacher-driven, students learn to take responsibility for themselves and each other, while teachers are trained to listen and act as facilitators. To reinforce character development and self-restraint, schools may want to incorporate the topic of emotional intelligence into the curriculum. Adolescents need direct information about their feelings that they can use to monitor themselves and cope more effectively when they become emotionally excited or distressed (Gallup, 1995; Goleman, 1995).

Besides focusing on self-restraint, the findings of this study also indicate *more emphasis needs to be given to acquiring accurate knowledge and information in citizenship education.* Being well-informed is a fundamental citizen's responsibility. Suspicious of authority, Thomas Jefferson (1969, p. 10) argued that democracy largely rests on a well-informed citizenry and that effective mass education and a free press are essential to producing critical, active citizens: 'When the people are well-informed, they can be trusted with their own government; whenever things get so far wrong as to attract their attention, they may be relied on to get them right.' This recommendation supports Gagnon's (1995) assertion that greater emphasis should be given to academic content and high standards in American education. In addition, Bellah and colleagues (1991) advise on teaching students how to weigh the moral implications of knowledge and expert testimony.

Emphasizing knowledge acquisition, substantive content, and judgment of technical information in citizenship education will be a challenge, since American youth in the 1990s expressed little interest in reading, knowing about politics, or developing a philosophy of life. Besides the distraction of America's pervasive popular culture (Yankelovich, 1991), young people's lack of interest in acquiring knowledge may be partially due to the passive learning experiences American schools and teachers often provide in citizenship courses – rote memorization, reading dull textbooks, listening to lectures, and watching films.

Integrating knowledge, coordinating curricula, and promoting active student learning are strongly encouraged by educators (Carnegie Council, 1995; Eveslage, 1993; Remy, 1980). Socialization research as well as educational psychology studies highlight the effectiveness of active approaches to teaching and learning, particularly if the goal is to have students internalize what they learn (Handel, 1990; Ichilov, 1990). Rather than being reactive, a proactive approach to teaching and learning is more compatible with the goals of democratic citizenship and education. Another suggestion is to create communities for learning that provide stability and opportunities for personal relationships between teachers and students. Small group learning is recommended, such as 'schools-within-schools' and teacher–student teams (Carnegie Council, 1995).

Knowledge acquisition, objectivity, critical thinking and problem-solving also may be enhanced by having students employ the scientific method to investigate political and social issues related to citizenship. Working with the scientific method is a practical way to encourage young people to take a systematic, unbiased approach toward gaining information about a social or political problem. In addition, youngsters obtain active, hands-on experience and, one hopes, an appreciation for what is involved in data design, gathering and reporting (Remy, 1980). Computer-generated information and utilization can aid the process. Moreover, using the scientific method may be a way to help students question some of the misinformation and misperceptions gained from the media, government, and business.

Incorporating a Developmental Perspective

For any of these suggestions to be effective, a developmental approach is needed when designing and implementing citizenship education programs. Assessing the cognitive functioning of adolescents and youth is a fundamental consideration. For example, although Piaget (Piaget and Inhelder, 1969) contended that adolescents are in the stage of formal operations and able to reason abstractly, Adelson's (1986) work demonstrated that (1) adolescents have difficulty grasping many of the abstract ideas associated with politics, and (2) more sophisticated, complex thinking is acquired gradually over the life course. Since the basic civics course, typically, is taken during mid-adolescence in the United States, citizenship education programs need to allow for a wide range of cognitive functioning at any adolescent grade level. Providing opportunities for *active* student learning at each stage is another hallmark of cognitive developmental theory (see Torney-Purta, 1990).

Besides cognitive functioning, educators must consider the socioemotional development of adolescents and youth in citizenship programs. For example, Erikson (1968) noted that adolescents are idealistic and searching for fidelity – trying to find someone or something to be 'true'. Thus, adults involved with citizenship education programs must be genuine in their communication efforts with youth as well as strong role models for exhibiting appropriate behavior. In addition, adolescents and youth are striving for independence from adults, likely to be experimental in their personal conduct, and, unfortunately, often think of themselves as indestructible (Elkind, 1985; Karsh, 1987). Young Americans' greater concern with freedom than with responsibility no doubt enhances the youthful inclination to engage in risky behavior. In the permissive United States, it is going to be especially difficult to encourage adolescents to be less experimental and more accountable in their personal conduct (violence, sexuality and substance abuse). A third developmental consideration is to recognize that young people are part of a different generation than adults, with a tendency for youth to deauthorize the previous generation. The consequences may be positive, such as American youth's rejection of adults' ideological, contentious style of politics – reminiscent of the 1960s; or more problematic, such as the difficulties age groups have in communicating and understanding each other in a rapidly changing society like the United States (Braungart and Braungart, 1986; Feuer, 1969).

CONCLUSION

Identifying recent societal trends and American youth's strengths and weaknesses can be a useful way to assess the effectiveness of citizenship education. Comparing the responses of young people in the 1990s with those of adults and with previous youth cohorts helps to anchor the findings and give them perspective. Contrary to popular images and stereotypes of contemporary youth, the personal views and collective orientations of young people today are not much different from adults. And, although young Americans are becoming more violent, unhealthy, and materialistic, they are also more concerned about community issues than their youthful predecessors. These national survey findings, in turn, provide the basis to make recommendations for improving citizenship education in the future. Given the decentralized nature of American education, school districts may want to examine their students' conduct, local beliefs, and levels of civic awareness in order design citizenship education programs tailored to their community needs (Rogers, 1995).

In piecing together the national surveys, several unexpected findings resulted. First, America's political culture appears more cohesive than reported in the popular press. Though sometimes ignored, a persistent moderate political center exists, providing the necessary ballast and support for political cooperation. The challenge is to keep this tradition alive for successive generations of Americans. A second unanticipated finding is that young Americans are committed to improving the quality of life in their communities. But, given their disdain for 'politics as usual', civil society appears to be the most appropriate sector to foster their integration into the polity. A 'pragmatic generation' is taking form among young people in the United States. Deauthorizing the 1960s divisive style of politics exhibited by many adult leaders, the youth generation of the 1990s is sorting out its own style of politics, searching for balance, compromise, and solutions.

There are some disturbing features of young Americans' personal conduct threatening their well-being. Youth's greatest needs appear to be in the areas of knowledge, health, and controlling violence. The 1990s youth generation in the United States is at risk, and citizenship responsibility is at the heart of the problem. The task for older Americans is to adequately prepare the younger generation for citizenship, but many adults abdicate or ignore their civic responsibility. During the 1980s and 1990s, the US Congress passed legislation that benefitted the rich and the elderly while shortchanging children and youth, and downplayed the value of public education (Kennedy, 1993).

Though criticisms have been leveled and doubts raised about the effectiveness of citizenship education in the United States, a recent survey of over 15,000 Americans found that education was the strongest predictor of Americans' political involvement, efficacy, and activity. In addition, participation in school government and clubs while young was related to political activity and skills later in life (Verba *et al.*, 1995). In the 1990s, however, critics contend that American youth are not responding to routine approaches to citizenship education (Eveslage, 1993; Gagnon, 1995).

This study of citizenship and citizenship education recommends a fresh approach to the subject, better suited to the attitudes and behavior of contemporary American youth. In *fin de siècle* America, citizen education needs to be directed toward active personal responsibility and self-restraint; the acquisition of accurate knowledge about the economy, society, and polity; and information about how citizens can make politics more civilized and solution-oriented. As Verba *et al.* (1995) conclude, responsible participation is the key to making democracies more effective and education is the principal avenue for developing a competent citizenry.

REFERENCES

Adelson, J. (1986). *Inventing adolescence*. New Brunswick, NJ: Transaction Books.
Almond, G. and Verba, S. (1965). *The civic culture*. Boston: Little, Brown.
Bachman, J.G., Johnston, L.D. and O'Malley, P.M. (eds) (1981). *Monitoring the future, 1980*. Ann Arbor, MI: Institute for Social Research, University of Michigan.
Bachman, J.G., Johnston, L.D. and O'Malley, P.M. (eds) (1993). *Monitoring the future, 1990*. Ann Arbor, MI: Institute for Social Research, University of Michigan.
Barbalet, J.M. (1988). *Citizenship*. Minneapolis, MN: University of Minnesota Press.
Beiner, R. (ed.) (1995). *Theorizing citizenship*. Albany, NY: State University of New York Press.
Bellah, R.N., Madsen, R., Sullivan, W., Swidler, A. and Tipton, S. (1991). *The good society*. New York: Knopf.
Bendix, R., Bendix, J. and Furniss, N. (1987). 'Reflections on modern Western states and civil societies', in R.G. Braungart and M.M. Braungart (eds), *Research in political sociology*, 3, pp.1–38. Greenwich, CT: JAI Press.
Berger, A.A. (1989). *Political culture*. New Brunswick, NJ: Transaction Publications.
Bezilla, R. (ed.) (1993). *American youth in the 1990s*. Princeton, NJ: Gallup International Institute.
Bottomore, T.B. (1993). 'Citizenship', in W. Outhwaite and T. Bottomore (eds), *The Blackwell dictionary of twentieth-century social thought* (p.75). Cambridge, MA: Blackwell Reference.
Boyer, E.L.(1990). 'Civic education for responsible citizens.', *Educational Leadership*, 48, 4–7.

Braungart, R.G. and Braungart, M.M. (1986). 'Life-course and generational politics', in R. Turner and J. Short (eds), *Annual review of sociology*, 12, pp.205–31. Palo Alto, CA: Annual Reviews.

Braungart, R.G. and Braungart, M.M. (1994). 'Political socialization and education', in T. Husen and T.N. Postlethwaite (eds), *The International Encyclopedia of Education*, 8, pp.4575–81. Oxford: Pergamon.

Brzezinski, Z. (1993). *Out of control*. New York: Charles Scribner's Sons.

Carnegie Council on Adolescent Development (1995). *Great transitions: Preparing for a new century.* New York: Carnegie Corporation of New York.

Cassidy, J. (1995). 'Who killed the middle class?', *New Yorker*, 16 October, 113–24.

Centers for Disease Control and Prevention (1995). 'Youth risk behavior surveillance – United States, 1993', *Morbidity and Mortality Weekly Reports*, 44, 24 March, 1–17.

Cooperative Institutional Research Program/American Council on Education (1991). *The American freshman: Twenty-five year trends.* Los Angeles: UCLA Graduate School of Education.

Cooperative Institutional Research Program/American Council on Education (1994). *The American freshman: National norms for fall 1994.* Los Angeles: UCLA Graduate School of Education.

Coupland, D. (1991). *Generation X*. New York: St Martin's Press.

Dahrendorf, R. (1994). 'The changing quality of citizenship', in B. van Steenbergen (ed.), *The condition of citizenship.* Thousand Oaks, CA: Sage.

Dekker, P. and van den Broek, A. (1995). 'Citizen participation in civil societies: Cross-national inquiries into the social and political correlates of volunteering', paper presented at the annual meeting of the International Society of Political Psychology, Washington, DC, July.

Dye, T.R. (1986). *Who's running America? The conservative years* (4th edn). Englewood Cliffs, NJ: Prentice-Hall.

Dye, T.R. (1990). *Who's running America? The Bush years* (5th edn). Englewood Cliffs, NJ: Prentice-Hall.

Dye, T.R. (1995). *Who's running America? The Clinton years* (6th edn). Englewood Cliffs, NJ: Prentice-Hall.

Elkind, D. (1985). 'Egocentrism redux', *Developmental Review* 5, 218–16.

Erikson, E. (1968). *Youth: Identity and crisis.* New York: W.W. Norton.

Eveslage, T.E. (1993). 'The social studies and scholastic journalism: Partners in citizenship education', *Social Studies Education*, 57, 82–6.

Famighetti, R. (ed.) (1994). *The world almanac and book of facts.* New York: St Martin's Press.

Femia, J.V. (1993). 'Political culture', in W. Outhwaite and T. Bottomore (eds), *The Blackwell dictionary of twentieth-century social thought* (pp.475–7). Cambridge, MA: Blackwell Reference.

Feuer, L.S. (1969). *The conflict of generations.* New York: Basic Books.

Flanigan, W.H. and Zingale, N.H. (1994). *Political behavior of the American electorate* (8th edn). Washington, DC: Congressional Quarterly Press.

Gagnon, P. (1995). 'What should children learn?', *The Atlantic Monthly*, December, 65–78.

Gallup, G.H. (1995). *Growing up scared in America*. Princeton, NJ: The George H. Gallup International Institute.

Goleman, D. (1995). *Emotional intelligence.* New York: Bantam Books.

Handel, G. (1990). 'Revising socialization theory', *American Sociological Review*, 55, 463–6.

Harwood Group (1993). *College students talk politics.* Dayton, OH: Kettering Foundation.

Howe, N. and Strauss, B. (1993). *13th Gen: Abort, retry, ignore, fail?* New York: Vintage Books.

Ichilov, O. (ed.) (1990). *Political socialization, citizenship education, and democracy.* New York: Teachers College Press.

Institute for Social Inquiry. (1994). *The Roper Center/Institute for Social Inquiry national poll.* Storrs, CT: Roper Center for Public Opinion Research.

Janowitz, M. (1983). *The reconstruction of patriotism.* Chicago: University of Chicago Press.

Jefferson, T. (1969). *Democracy.* New York: Greenwood Press.

Johnson, O. (ed.) (1995). *1995 information please almanac* (48th edn). Boston, MA: Houghton Mifflin.

Karsh, E. (1987). 'A teen-ager is a ton of worry', *New York Times*, 3 January, 23.

Kennedy, P. (1993). *Preparing for the twenty-first century.* New York: Random House.

Kumar, K. (1993). 'Civil society', in W. Outhwaite and T. Bottomore (eds), *The Blackwell dictionary of twentieth-century social thought* (pp.75–7). Cambridge, MA: Blackwell Reference.

Kymlicka, W. and Norman, W. (1995). 'Return of the citizen: A survey of recent work on citizenship theory', in R. Beiner (ed.), *Theorizing citizenship* (pp.283–322). Albany, NY: State University of New York Press.

Lipset, S.M. (1995). 'Malaise and resiliency in America', *Journal of Democracy*, 6, 4–18.

Mitchell, S. (1995). *The official guide to the generations.* Ithaca, NY: New Strategist Publications.

Neisler, O.J. (1994). 'Inside social studies at Castleton High: Young citizens discuss their citizenship education', unpublished doctoral dissertation, Syracuse University, Syracuse, New York.

O'Neil, J. (1991). 'Civic education: While democracy flourishes abroad, U.S. schools try to reinvigorate teaching of citizenship', *Curriculum Update* (Association for Supervision and Curriculum Development), January, 1, 8.

People For the American Way (1989). *Democracy's next generation.* Washington, DC: People for the American Way.

Piaget, J. and Inhelder, B. (1969). *The psychology of the child.* New York: Basic Books.

Reische, D.L. (1987). *Citizenship: Goal of education.* Arlington, VA: American Association of School Administrators.

Remy, R.C. (1980). *Handbook of citizenship competencies.* Alexandria, VA: Association for Supervision and Curriculum Development.

Rogers, E.M. (1995). *Diffusion of innovations* (4th edn). New York: Free Press.

Ryder, N.B. (1965). 'The cohort as a concept in the study of social change', *American Sociological Review* 30, 843–61.

Schlesinger, A.M., Jr (1986). *The cycles of American history.* Boston, MA: Houghton Mifflin.

Schlesinger, A.M., Jr (1992). *The disuniting of America: Reflections on a multicultural society.* New York: W.W. Norton.

Seligman, A.B. (1993). 'The fragile ethical vision of civil society', in B.S. Turner (ed.), *Citizenship and social theory* (pp.139–61). Newbury Park, CA: Sage.

Sigel, R.S. (ed.) (1989). *Political learning in adulthood.* Chicago: University of Chicago Press.

Snyder, T.D. and Fromboluti, C.S. (1993). *Youth indicators 1993.* Washington, DC: US Government Printing Office.

Tocqueville, A. de ([1835] 1956). *Democracy in America* (Vols 1 and 2). New York: Knopf.

Torney-Purta, J. (1990). 'From attitudes and knowledge to schemata: Expanding the outcomes of political socialization research', in O. Ichilov (ed.), *Political socialization, citizenship education, and democracy* (pp.98–115). New York: Teachers College Press.

Verba, S., Schlozman, K.L. and Brady, H.E. (1995). *Voice and equality: Civic voluntarism in American politics*. Cambridge, MA: Harvard University Press.

Yankelovich, D. (1991). *Coming to public judgment: Making democracy work in a complex world*. Syracuse, NY: Syracuse University Press.

Zevin, J. (1992). *Social studies for the twenty-first century*. New York: Longman.

7

A DISQUIETING OUTLOOK FOR DEMOCRACY: MASS MEDIA, NEWS AND CITIZENSHIP EDUCATION IN THE US

MARY A. HEPBURN

The relationship between the news media and citizen participation is critical in a democratic society. It is essential that the public have ready access to information and discussions about government and public issues. These sources of news must be free from interference by the government, and they must provide a means for citizens to express their views. Citizenship education in democracies, therefore, is based on assumptions that information on public affairs is freely disseminated, open to various viewpoints, and widely available. Democratic education is also tied to assumptions that the public news media can be readily utilized by citizens to gain awareness, gather information, and find paths to participation in decisions on public issues.

These are the ideals. Unfortunately, the situation in the US in the mid-1990s falls far short of the ideals. The potential for extensive, rapid, and clear communication of news and views has been heightened by advancing technology. However, researchers from several disciplines are finding that the mass communication media, dominated by television, are not generally serving our democracy well. Instead, there is considerable evidence of dysfunction. The public seems to be less informed, less involved, and more distracted from public affairs. According to one team of analysts, the news media 'promote apathy, cynicism, and quiescence rather than active citizenship and participation' (Gamson et al., 1992), conclusions that are of serious consequence to citizenship education in the United States and other democracies experiencing similar electronic media growth. This chapter will review the changing sources of news on public affairs, assemble from various pieces of research a picture of the characteristics of the new media environment, and discuss the implications for citizenship education.

BACKGROUND: THE CHANGE IN NEWS SOURCES

In the United States there is a long tradition of recognition of the importance of the role of news in citizen discourse. A free press protected from government interference was a value of such significance that when the Constitution was drawn up in 1787 without written assurance of a free press, the need to add this protection became a national issue. Appropriately, the issue was argued fervently in the young nation's newspapers, and public outcry helped bring about the First Amendment to the Constitution.

Newspapers and news magazines were the main vehicles of information and exchange of citizens' viewpoints on local and national public issues for about 170 years. Advances in the speed and range of news gathering were furthered by the inventions of the telegraph and telephone, and by the early 1900s the American public could read daily about happenings in other regions and on other continents as well as in their home towns. By the 1930s, radio became a popular source of information, and many American families gathered to listen to the evening news. In 1933 President Franklin D. Roosevelt broadcast the first of 18 'fireside chats', involving millions of Americans in his discussions of national affairs. Radio news, however, did not displace newspaper readership but supplemented it with speedy transmission, especially during the Second World War.

The greatest change in the dissemination of news in the US came about in the 1960s. Fledgling television stations of the 1950s began to offer local and regional broadcasts of special documentary programs on news events and public issues, but TV network news programs of that period were short. The first daily 30-minute national news program was broadcast by CBS in 1962, and soon viewing such broadcasts became a daily evening routine in American homes.

In 1963 there was an important change in the main source of news for Americans. For the first time, national polls showed that among the news sources television exceeded newspapers. TV had become the most used and the most believed news medium. In 1986 half of American adults stated that they relied totally on television for news (Hudson, 1987; Roper, 1989). Even college-educated Americans, who persistently relied on newspapers as their main news source into the 1980s, had shifted to television as their main source by 1984 (Roper, 1985). By 1991, 69 per cent of Americans were depending mainly on television for news. The steady decline in the use of newspapers is striking. Television has gradually and persistently increased in importance and become the predominant news source throughout the United States. (See Table 7.1: note respondents were allowed to name more than one source, and the use of multiple sources has declined as well.)

Television is not just the main source of news and information, it has become a way of life in the US. Nearly 100 per cent of households have

TABLE 7.1
WHERE DO YOU USUALLY GET MOST OF YOUR NEWS ABOUT WHAT IS GOING ON
IN THE WORLD TODAY?

	Nov. 1961	Nov. 1963	Nov. 1968	Dec. 1978	Dec. 1986	Feb. 1991
Newspapers	57	53	49	49	36	35
Television	52	55	59	67	66	69
Radio	34	29	25	20	14	14
Magazines	9	6	7	5	4	4
People	5	4	5	5	4	6
All Mentions	157	147	145	146	124	128

Source: *The 1989 Roper Report* and *America's Watching – Public Attitudes Toward Television, 1993.*

TABLE 7.2
AVERAGE WEEKLY TV VIEWING IN THE UNITED STATES

Children	
2–11	23 hours 01 minutes
Teenagers	
12–17	21 hours 50 minutes
Men	
18–24	23 hours 31 minutes
25–54	28 hours 44 minutes
55+	38 hours 47 minutes
Women	
18–24	28 hours 54 minutes
25–54	31 hours 05 minutes
55+	44 hours 11 minutes

Source: *Nielsen Report on Television, 1993.*

television; 69 per cent have two or more sets. Most viewers (85 per cent) use remote control devices to select programs, and with these push-button controls the inclination is to 'surf' or skim over the programs looking for the most exciting offering. The average daily viewing per household reached 7 hours and 13 minutes in 1993 (Nielsen, 1993). Neither small children nor teenagers are the heaviest viewers as is commonly thought. The largest consumers, according to Nielsen market surveys, are women and men over 55 (see Table 7.2.). Presumably many of these older people are retirees with time to spare. However, the significant number of hours of weekly TV viewing across all other age groups shows that watching television is central to the American lifestyle.

The advent of pay cable television has meant that the numbers of networks that can be accessed has increased considerably: 32 were served by Nielsen media research in 1993. Although cable gives the consumer clearer pictures and more choices, there is much similarity in the types of programs offered. Among the most popular programs are action movies, personal talk shows, murder mysteries, sports, police stories, situation comedies, and weekly news programs that dramatically present results of investigative reporting. About 62 per cent of the households with television subscribe to cable today, a tenfold increase since 1970 (Nielsen, 1993).

Among ethnic groups in the United States there are significant differences in viewing time. African-Americans were the heaviest viewers in every time segment surveyed in 1992–93. TV sets were turned on for two additional hours during 'prime time' (8–11 pm) in African-American households compared to all other groups; African-American children (aged 2–11) viewed 55 per cent more TV; and in the daytime, men 18 and over in African-American households viewed 90 per cent more television (Nielsen, 1993).

One way of obtaining a sense of the significance of the media in daily life is to examine comparatively how time is spent. Compared with job, sleep, and other activities, the largest share of time (on average 3,256 hours per year) in the lives of Americans involves 'media' including television, cable, car radios, recorded music, newspapers, home videos, movies, and various print media (Harwood, 1992). Mass media, especially the TV screen, not only takes up much of the free time of Americans, but media consumption is a major expense: about $109 billion was spent by adults in 1991. Also, it is a big business: about $80 billion was spent on advertising in that same year. There is little doubt that, for the majority of Americans, both home life and public life have become intricately linked to electronic media.

CHARACTERISTICS OF THE TELEVISION SOCIETY

What difference does it make in the lives of the large majority of Americans who are so tied to the electronic tube? What are the features of a society that relies on television for news on public affairs? Research from several disciplines provides a means to piece together a picture of apparent effects on citizens and thus raise appropriate questions related to citizen education and citizen participation in the US.

Depth and Credibility

The enormous popularity of the electronic media does not necessarily mean that today's citizens will be better informed. News is likely to reach the public rapidly, but not necessarily in any depth. For example, only two per cent of the national prime time evening TV audiences view Public Broadcasting Service television programs including the news. Of the 2.5 million teenagers who tune in to radio, only about 10,000 listen to Public Radio. Both of these public-supported networks are more oriented toward communicating information, news on public affairs, and scientific news. Younger people are not the chief viewers of other types of news programming either. Of Americans under 30, only one in five is a regular viewer of Cable News Network (CNN). One press analyst assesses youth attitudes toward political news not as alienation but as a lack of interest. 'Young Americans may have tuned the political system out ... they don't seem terribly concerned about the direction in which it's heading' (Matlack, 1992).

Another change is in public perceptions of news credibility. In the 1960s, as television viewing increased, public trust began to shift away from other media toward TV. In 1991, a national survey showed that if there were conflicting news reports, 58 per cent of the public would be most inclined to believe television over newspapers, radio, and magazines (Stanley and Niemi, 1993). Apparently people do not consider the ways in which video cameras can mislead, nor do they realize that incorrect information can corrupt the pictures broadcast on TV as it does any other news source.

One aspect of credibility is addressed in survey research on public 'confidence' in the media. Media industry analysts found that 66 per cent of Americans have either the same or more confidence in the news media than they had five years before. But when asked specifically, the public did have criticisms of media news organizations. In 1992, a presidential election year in the US, 63 per cent of the public felt that in presenting political and social news, the media tend to favor one side. About two-thirds complained that the media put too much emphasis on negative news (Bowman and Ladd, 1993). So, we have some evidence that the American public is not completely satisfied with news reporting as they are receiving it in the 1990s. One appeal of television news is its immediacy. People can tune in to get quick summaries of news events in brief capsule form as the news is breaking, such as provided by CNN Headline News. Each evening they can obtain 30-minute summaries as provided by the older networks CBS, ABC, and NBC, and in one-hour summaries as offered by local stations. In all of these forms the news is reported in short, fast-paced, dramatic episodes interspersed with advertising.

Unlike the print news reader, who can obtain more depth of background material in the back pages of the paper or in a magazine, the electronic news consumer cannot control the extent or pace of information received. With television there are few opportunities to gain information in depth or to reflect on analysis of public affairs. There is little time or incentive to reflect on political issues or solutions. An exception is the C-SPAN public affairs network which provides complete unedited coverage of Congress in session plus various panel discussions of public issues. However, C-SPAN is available only on cable TV and only from some local cable companies.

Years of electronic news consumption, received in short, quick segments, have produced shorter attention spans and less understanding of public affairs, especially for those who have little background political knowledge (Postman, 1982; Chaffee and Tims, 1982; Garramone and Atkin, 1986). The widespread use of push-button remote control devices may be further reducing attention spans and contributing to a lack of patience with discourse on public issues.

Rapid-fire, on-the-spot broadcast of images of people and events in the news is common and quite seductive. Viewers can readily believe they are well informed as they watch news happen. Live coverage of the Gulf War not only sped pictures of war events and reporters in the area to millions of households, but it demonstrated how such on-site communication can dramatize and, at times, mislead. (Many Americans believed that gas attacks were occurring in Israel as they watched reporters trying on gas masks.) The live multi-network ground and helicopter coverage of police chasing runaway sports figure O.J. Simpson shows how crime coverage on TV can overemphasize personal episodes as 'news'. Likewise, it has demonstrated how sensational, impromptu coverage, including the opinions of reporters and various interviewees, tends to compromise legal protections and the justice system.

Image has always been a factor in political campaign news coverage as the public made its estimates of the honesty of a political candidate's looks. But, since the 1980s, 'image' has displaced candidate talk about the issues in TV news. Comparing the 1988 and 1968 presidential elections, a 300 per cent decline was found in candidate talk on TV networks in 1988. News managers want to keep up the fast pace so we hear little of a candidate's views (Adatto, 1993). Dramatic phrases spoken in short segments (sound bites) coupled with selected photos of the candidates are the mode of TV campaign coverage. Consequently, sound bites have become central to any candidate's campaign plan.

News reporters often have more commentary about the style of a campaign than they do about the substance of the candidate's views on issues

(Graber, 1990). According to Adatto (1993) American news viewers are fascinated with the mechanics of TV image-making, especially how particular political candidates work to create a public image. Yet this interest in the image game does not diminish public belief in the candidates. Rather, Adatto finds that the public has 'continuing confidence in the camera's ability to record reality and document facts' (p.167). It seems to be a current example of an old American adage: seeing is believing.

Television coverage of fundamental public issues such as health care, unemployment, and the national debt is most often treated with a simplified 'story line' about an individual. To some extent this type of dramatization via visual images becomes entertainment. Rather than general information or analysis of the issue, television news often presents a personal case. Each case is tendered as an individual human drama. Unfortunately, such reporting is unlikely to be adequately linked by viewers to the public policy questions. Experimental research conducted by Iyengar (1991) compared the effects of dramatic, personal story presentation ('episodic framing') with more general presentation which examines the problem or issue ('thematic framing'). He found that the difference in presentation affects viewers' opinions on who is responsible. Viewers of episodically framed news tended to attribute responsibility for the problem to the victim rather than to public conditions, public action, or public officials. Viewers of news presented in the less dramatic thematic frame attributed responsibility to society or societal factors. Citizen response and participation in efforts to seek solutions is likely to be discouraged by so much news coverage that gives the impression that social problems are the fault of the victims.

Another experimental study in which responses to dramatic and non-dramatic presentations were compared (Milburn and McGrail, 1992) found that sensational or dramatic presentation of network news has a negative effect on the viewers' cognitive complexity. Emotional vignettes in TV news tend to oversimplify complex political issues and conflicts. Oversimplification tends to suppress further thinking about the problems involved. Hence, it is evident that in using the limited news air time to present melodramas about individuals, TV news broadcasts are failing to probe the issues, and failing to give viewers insights into societal problems and possible alternative actions.

An extensive analysis of studies of news broadcasts and audience understanding of those broadcasts concluded that 'news generally and TV news in particular is failing to systematically inform the public about important issues and events' (Davis and Robinson, 1989). This research found that while considerable money and time are spent by networks to increase audience size, the news program developers are not concerned about what the audience learns from the news.

Violence and 'Market Share'

Sensational scenes of carnage in newscasts arouse what researchers call 'disruptive stress', which distracts and negatively affects information processing. Milburn and McGrail (1992) conclude that the extent of visual sensationalism on television news broadcasts is detrimental to the public and fails to fulfill 'the charter entrusted to the networks, that is, to inform and educate the public through means of the airwaves'.

The mingling of news and entertainment is characteristic of American television, and it is done in a subtle manner. Dramatic episodes, personal chatter, and human interest items are interspersed with news. They take up time that could be used for real news of national or international affairs. The problem is rooted in the commercial basis for making programming decisions. Rather than considering the public's need to know, news directors are often worried about the numbers of viewers, the 'market share', that the news program can offer to advertisers. To attract larger audiences, and thus be able to sell the audience size for product sales, news directors feel pressed to use amusing chatter and gory images and stories to hold viewer attention. Television news, according to Neumann (1987), operates on 'borrowed time' in a 'commercial, entertainment-oriented media system'.

United States' television is reputed to have the most violent programming in advanced industrialized nations. Violence is common in entertainment programs focused on stories about police, crime, emergency services, and war. Similar close-up camera focus on bloody violence is often seen in the news. Why do we see so many shootings, killings, stabbings, and rapes in dramas? And, why are we shown detailed photos of mangled victims in news of domestic crime and world conflict? Here again obtaining and maintaining public attention is important in gaining advertisers. A program has more commercial value, i.e., it achieves greater 'market share', if it can hold more viewers. Apparently, scenes of violence are expected to keep viewers awake and attentive and less likely to change channels.

During the first several decades of large-scale television viewing in the US, there were psychologists who estimated that viewing violence vicariously on television had a cathartic effect and would reduce actual aggressive behavior in the real world. But psychological researchers Huesmann and Eron (1986), who studied the effects of media violence on youngsters in the early 1970s, perceived how real the action on the TV screen is to children. They found that there was a connection to behavior and then decided to collect long-term data and test for cumulative effects. Following their original subjects into adulthood in the 1980s, they found that TV viewing in childhood served as a 'script' to learning behavior. From persistent, heavy viewing of TV violence students learned that aggressive behavior is appropriate in given life situations. The most aggressive youngsters identified with aggressive and violent figures in TV stories.

Among their adult subjects, those who had the most arrests for drunk driving, violent crime, and abuse of their spouses were the same individuals who were most vulnerable to TV violence and the most aggressive reactors when they were children.

In research that compared people in areas with and without television and also made comparisons in areas before and after the introduction of TV, Centerwall (1993) determined that homicide rates increased when TV was introduced. Acknowledging that other factors besides TV do influence the quantity of violent crimes, he argued, nevertheless, that quantitative evidence shows that by removing the negative effects of TV 'there would be 10,000 fewer homicides, 70,000 fewer rapes, and 700,000 fewer injurious assaults'.

Centerwall has also brought to light riveting research literature on violence little known among citizenship educators in the US. He reported results of studies from the 1970s that have been unavailable to the general public. These studies were commissioned by each of the three major networks in the United States: CBS, ABC, and NBC. The studies were initiated in response to public hearings and public concern over TV aggression and violence. (At that time, violence in programming was much less than currently found in entertainment shows.)

Similar to research by American tobacco companies on the ill effects of smoking, the results of these studies were disseminated only to small, select groups. Only in the mid-1990s are the outcomes of the network studies circulating and gaining the attention of social scientists and educators. The study commissioned by CBS was conducted in London and subsequently published in England. In this research, Belson (1978) studied the effects of viewing violent television programs on 1,565 teenaged boys. Many of the programs were imported from the US. Belson found that youths who watched above-average hours of TV violence committed a 49 per cent higher rate of serious acts of violence than the youths who had viewed below-average quantities of violent programming. Dramas and movies that showed violence in close, personal relationships and fictional violence presented in very realistic images were among the types of TV programs that Belson's research found to be most powerful in evoking violent behavior.

The NBC-sponsored study observed a large number of school children over a three year period to determine if watching television programs increased physical aggressiveness. NBC reported no effects. However, it should be noted that the study was conducted by a team of four researchers which included three NBC employees. The research commissioned by the ABC network was conducted by a Temple University research team. They surveyed young male felons imprisoned for violent crimes. The interviews revealed that up to 34 per cent of the criminals said they had consciously imitated crime techniques learned from television programs. These studies are two decades old and are yet to be disseminated to educators. In a society that protects the media from government interference, educators may ask how the public is to be protected from the media industry withholding news.

A revealing article in *The Chronicle of Higher Education* in January 1994 discussed the huge 'education gap' that exists between what psychological and medical researchers consider to be conclusively documented effects and what the general public knows. The article gives some insight into why the findings were not well known. 'Until recently, researchers' voices have been drowned out in the din of denial and disinformation coming from executives of the television and movie industries, whose self-serving defense of violent programming has prevailed' (Slaby, 1994). Accordingly, TV industry spokespersons have insisted that they are giving the public what they want. They also argue that it is a mere reflection of the society, and that any effort to modify programming would interfere with First Amendment guarantees of 'freedom of the press'. Another response is that parents or families must take the responsibility for preventing the viewing of violent programs. These responses are designed to derail research information that shows that an appetite for violence has been stimulated by the glorification of violence and a daily diet of violent programs.

The American Psychological Association Commission on Violence and Youth has tried to get the word out to researchers and educators in a 1993 report. It concluded that the research evidence was very clear and that there was no doubt that the high levels of violence seen on television programs, day after day, were clearly correlated with increased acceptance of aggression and outright aggressive behavior. Moreover, the highest consumption of television violence is by those most vulnerable to the effects (Slaby, 1994; Institute for Social Research, 1994; see also Holroyd, 1985; Zuckerman and Zuckerman, 1985). These deductions are especially disconcerting to citizenship educators in an era when television violence in the US is increasing and the imagery is becoming more intense.

While representatives of the television industry deny that violent images and violent dramas in their programming influence the behavior of youth and adults, on the other hand, the evidence they offer to advertisers is that television images and dramatic presentations about products *do* influence viewers. Critics of commercial television programs that contain heavy doses of violence have called for some type of regulation. Self-regulation from within the television industry is the answer most compatible with First Amendment guarantees of freedom of the press. However, the Congress of the United States is debating a law that would require that television sets contain a 'V-chip' a device that would allow parents to restrict their children's access to violent programs in the home. But perhaps the most effective means of reducing the infusion of violence into American households is education about the ill effects of viewing violence.

WHAT ARE THE IMPLICATIONS FOR CITIZENSHIP EDUCATION?

As stated in the introduction, citizenship education in the US democracy is assumed to be a means of developing informed, responsible political participation. To be more than a citizen who just expounds civic maxims; to be a motivated, informed, fair but critical participant is the ideal. To move toward the ideal requires ready access to news and information plus awareness, attitudes, and skills that promote reflection and evaluation. Now that television has become the key source for the needed news and viewpoints that come into play as citizens respond to their political environment, we have not only an educational problem but a societal issue.

The dominance of television as both the main news source and the chief entertainment medium, coupled with the general public's lack of awareness of the power and pervasiveness of TV in their lives, has made citizenship education problematic. Clearly, formal school education and various forms of lifelong education must change if citizens are to become better equipped to deal with public affairs.

Social Science Content

The characteristics of the television society briefly discussed above are the substance of the social sciences. Television, mass media as news sources, and the national television lifestyle should be key topics in social science and social studies courses in colleges and schools. It has become evident that the mass media affect the formal educational process by influencing, possibly dominating, the student's consciousness as well as home lifestyle and perceptions of community life. The electronic media cannot be understood by means of adding another paragraph or a chapter to the textbooks. It is an institution that now influences all other institutions (Hepburn, 1990, 1994, 1995) and requires critical examination in citizenship education.

For example, Shanahan and Morgan (1992), in cross-national research, have begun the documentation of the pivotal role television plays in family behavior and relationships. They find that television helps define the context within which family interactions take place in the several countries they studied. They point out that, in the US, television is 'not an occasional invited guest, but is a permanent visitor'. The American adolescents studied, compared to adolescents in China, Taiwan or Argentina, were much more likely to view television alone or with friends rather than with family. Yet, across national samples, it was co-viewing of TV with parents that was associated with feeling 'close' to parents. Overall they conclude that television is of 'enormous importance in understanding family relationships'.

Other research suggests that parent behavior regarding television viewing can make a difference with children. A study of television viewing and co-viewing in American families with children from three to seven years old indicates that children are gradually socialized into program preferences much like their parents (St Peters *et al.*, 1991).

How often do we examine or discuss such a topic in social science courses? Clearly, these aspects of the mass-media oriented society must become part of the content of social science knowledge and inquiry in school and college courses.

Media Literacy in Lifelong Learning

We must take care not to define citizenship education too narrowly. The process goes on and must not be neglected after schooling. Technological and social change is occurring too rapidly to expect education through secondary school or even college to be valid for many years. And here we must rely on the mass media to participate in the examination and review of itself. The sources of news and their relationship to the maintenance of democracy must become part of public discourse in magazines, newspapers, radio talk shows, and on television itself. CNN initiated some dialogue on the issue recently within a series on the decline of civility. Questions were raised about a society where students cannot pay attention long enough to learn to read. The television media were compared to individuals and other institutions which seek only their own profit, lack respect for others, and feel no sense of public trust. This kind of review of societal norms can greatly stimulate citizen awareness.

Concern about increasing violence and crime is generating forums among various professional and interest groups including law enforcement officials, educators, lawyers' organizations, community leaders, and parent organizations. As the pressure for discussion from media-literate interest groups grows, the subject will receive more media attention, but it will be up to a broader, active public to demand less superficial treatment in the media and greater depth in the discussion of alternatives.

Typically, the issue of violence on television is treated with the usual television news dichotomy: only two sides to the argument; good guys and bad guys; in favor of or against censorship. The issue need not be viewed only in terms of First Amendment legal guarantees of free speech in the US. The issue of censorship often squelches the discourse on media violence. We do not have to compromise our rights. There are other alternatives. Citizen education is one.

Increased information about the hazards and more consideration of alternatives could generate discourse on the consequences of using oversimplification and violence to attract advertising and viewers to TV. The television industry is likely to respond to pressures from large numbers of informed people. Like the decline in the promotion and use of cigarettes, with which an uninformed society poisoned itself for decades, the presentation and consumption of violence can be reduced by means of increased citizen knowledge and action. Television programming will respond to meet market needs.

Educating Students for Critical Viewing

Youth in the United States today, perhaps more than any generation before them, need training in the development of critical, evaluative skills. These young people have been raised in an electronically charged, fast-paced environment that does not encourage contemplation and deliberation. As children, they watched between 20 and 27 hours of TV a week; now they play video games, view movies and shows on videotape, and work and play using computer monitors. Do they have the orientation and the skills to evaluate critically what comes before them on the video screen? What can be discerned from the images? Do they perceive it all as equally valuable as long as it is engaging? Are opinion and factual information distinguishable? Can they determine why some video presentations are more engaging than others?

Some of these questions are the critical content questions that we have long applied to print media. But other questions move beyond content to address the television medium itself. Subtle and more obvious influences of any medium for news and entertainment should be reviewed. Educators should be ready to lead students into a critical examination of the effects of computer communication, virtual-reality programs, and other types of electronic communications that fiber optics and other new developments will bring into our lives. The task requires historical, sociological, psychological and mass-media knowledge. To help develop curriculum and revise courses to improve teaching of critical and analytical thinking about mass media, it is essential to have well-educated, media-literate and analytical teachers.

Teacher Education

For more than a decade, Neil Postman (1982, 1990) has been alerting the education profession about the potential negative effects of mass media on youth. But his message has not had a strong reach into social studies teacher education. Typically, the education of social studies teachers has focused on the more traditional content of history and the social sciences and discussions of how to teach that content. I examined several secondary social studies teaching methods books currently in use in teacher education (Banks, 1990; Martorella, 1991; Ellis et al., 1991; Zevin, 1992) and found that not one had a section on teaching about mass media generally or about television specifically. Television videotape is mentioned as a tool of learning in school in two of the books. The mass media are not discussed as social science content, e.g., in regard to their efficiency in delivering information. Neither is the issue of the medium as message (à la Marshall McLuhan) discussed as a social issue. Social critique concerning television in our lives in the US apparently has not yet been adapted from the social sciences to teacher education.

I have heard teachers reflect on and comment on ubiquitous television viewing and the decline in reading among their students. Teachers could be assisted and fortified professionally by opportunities to study how changes in the quantity and pacing of news communication affects the society and their students. Likewise, teachers could address how these changes might be studied in the curriculum.

Only one of the teacher education textbooks I examined had a section on political socialization. It presented in some detail the multi-agency model of political socialization that citizenship educators have used since the late 1960s to show students how family, school, peers, and mass media each influence our political knowledge and attitudes. As I read through the description, I found myself thinking about how great our need is for a newer, truer, macro model of how political learning takes place. We need a more incisive 'big picture' to initiate thinking among post-secondary and high school students about how their own political perceptions are being shaped, especially as affected by the media.

In the old model of political socialization found in teacher education textbooks today, the mass media appears to be a discrete, disconnected influence on socialization. Much of the research cited above indicates that electronic media influences interact with other factors such as family and peer group. Today, we cannot study home and family influences without scrutinizing mass media in the household. Any study of the influence of peers would have to include some assessment of how mass media interact with, even dominate, interests, discussions, and activities of peer groups. Similarly, socialization studies would have to take into the account the interaction of mass media with school environments because electronic instruction is fast becoming part of the school scene.

Television News Broadcasts in Schools

In some schools the connection with television news broadcasts has been formalized. Channel One, which broadcasts a daily ten-minute news program for schools and includes two minutes of advertising, is produced by Whittle Communications. The arrangement made with schools is that they will receive free video equipment worth about $30,000 to $50,000. In return for the national 'captive' audience of eight million high school students, Whittle charges advertisers $157,000 per half minute, thus grossing $628,000 daily (Kubey, 1993). Advertisers are assured that products competing with their line will not gain advertising time. The ten minutes of news that schools contract for is not all news. It promotes other Whittle programs and contests that are also advertising promotionals. About 40 per cent of the secondary schools in the country reportedly subscribe. A few states like New York have objected to this kind of commercialism in schools and the lure of free equipment and have banned Channel One participation.

CNN also offers a news program for students. It provides a 15-minute news segment without advertising. Teachers can videotape it without cost during late-night broadcasts and use it in the classroom wherever they see fit. Teachers may also obtain free lesson plans from several computer networks to assist them in designing classroom activities around the broadcast. 'The CNN Newsroom' contains no promotionals. It is designed for instructional use with large colorful maps featured on the screen and with background information and vocabulary contained in the computer printout. The program, nevertheless, is set up in the brief capsule form of the CNN headlines program, familiarizing students to that format. Compared to the inimical teen ads that are sent into the schools in Channel One programming, CNN Newsroom is by far the better educational tool, and, for older students, C-SPAN news documents are a rich source of information and perspectives. However, if any of these student news broadcasts are used, teachers should be well equipped to teach students how the program is produced, funded, its stated goals, an inquiry into what is selected as news of the day, and to look for effects: 'Just what is this television program doing for us and to us?'

Video Screen Role Models

As educators and as social scientists we should maintain a sociological perspective on mass-media developments in society. Television tends to give viewers social perspectives on what is acceptable and what is not. Stereotyping is common. Portrayals of TV mothers, for example, usually show a caring and concerned but frequently shallow woman. Senators and politicians are often shown as unapproachable, pompous, and corrupt. Adolescents even learn dating behavior from viewing programs and films. By showing viewers daily the actions of people in various life roles the screen defines what is expected of them. There is plenty of evidence of the power and pervasiveness of TV, and it is also evident that consumers of all ages absorb role models and sometimes imitate them (Dominick, 1994). From many passive hours in front of television, what life roles are instilled in viewers, especially the more impressionable young viewers? What are the visions of heroism, leadership, family life, personal relationships, and public responsibility that they take from the images and voices they see and hear? We must continually ask what models the powerful images of electronic media are presenting to the public.

REVITALIZING CITIZENSHIP EDUCATION

Study of the public media's effects and effectiveness in a democracy fits the higher ideals of citizenship education that are geared to critical awareness and participation. If we examine the history of citizenship education in the US we find that, for a century, training for citizenship in the US was expected to be a by-product of years of study of history and the structure of government by a minority of the public. That early, indirect education for citizenship did not specifically address many of the ideal dimensions of citizenship outlined by Ichilov (1990). However, there is an articulated basis for critical, participatory citizenship education in the US that developed in the 20th century. In 1916 specific citizenship courses were proposed for the curriculum when a subcommittee of the National Commission on the Reorganization of Secondary Education of the National Education Association included in its recommendations a proposal for two new courses (Dunn, 1916). One course, 'Community Civics', was specifically designed for eighth or ninth grade to serve the needs of the many students who would leave school to take a job. It was recommended that the course focus on 'the elements of community welfare rather than upon the machinery of government'. Among 11 suggested significant topics were communication, health, protection of life and property, recreation, and education topics that are timely for the 1990s. The recommended teaching approach was informative, practical, and active: designed to prepare a young citizen for community life.

The second course proposed was a capstone course for the last year of high school, 'Problems of Democracy', which at that time was most likely to be taken by pre-college students. It would provide an opportunity to examine in some depth 'problems of vital importance to society and of immediate interest to the pupil'. The two new courses, like the relatively new term 'social studies', had a decidedly interdisciplinary approach. The stated aims were to educate individuals to be informed, socially responsible, critically aware, participating members of communities including city, state, national, and world communities.

The aims of the 1916 recommendations are still found within objectives of citizenship education in the United States today. Both thinking skills and practical participation skills are emphasized, and, although social and technological conditions have changed greatly, the objectives still have relevance. Professional support and public acceptance of these goals for citizenship education have declined during reactionary periods, but the basic commitment to informing young citizens about public affairs and teaching them skills of analysis and decision-making has persisted. (For a discussion of the rationales for citizenship education in the US, see Shaver, 1977.)

Utilizing many of the ideas and objectives of that 1916 foundation and applying broader perspectives from the present, educators can mold school and general public education programs that will make Americans more aware of their media environment and better equip them to deal with it. Those public and professional leaders who define directions for public education must often call up 'tradition' and the 'American way'. I am convinced that there is a strong supporting basis for the critical study of the mass media, its news disbursal, and its effects on democratic participation in the ideals of the past and the needs of the present.

CONCLUSION

We cannot roll back time and technological development, nor would we wish to. The electronic media by virtue of a broad reach to every level of society do have democratizing influences. This makes for a common experience and identity among all Americans, and which is pluralistic as seen in the diversity of actors, news broadcasters, and dramas representing many ethnic groups. Advances in technology, however, require advances in social development and responsibility. In the US, television has revolutionized communication by its fast and direct reach into every home. While it is a marvel of speed, convenience, and action, at the same time it encourages citizen passivity, models violent and corrupt behavior, gives a fragmented sense of reality, and blurs distinctions between news and entertainment, reality and fiction. If democratic participation is to survive, the citizenry must overcome the passive spectator mentality, the fascination with image, the steady diet of violence, and the overall mesmerizing effects of television to demand better quality from the media. Educators at every level can assist. Citizenship education and public discourse can play a pivotal role in motivating citizens to deal more intelligently with current communications issues and prepare for even greater technological changes in the future.

The issue of mass-media effects is at once public and personal. It is a topic that has the potential for honing skills beyond conventional patriotic themes to develop a broader sense of democratic expression. If we apply Ichilov's (1990) analytical framework to defining high-level purposes for studies of the media, we can hope to educate for evaluative, practical, world-minded participation. It is a logical and necessary part of democratic education to scrutinize the characteristics of the mass-media oriented society and analyze how television and other media influence perceptions and behaviors. This is a task for citizenship educators in the United States and perhaps all other modern societies that strive for democratic participation.

REFERENCES

Adatto, K. (1993). *Picture perfect: The art and artifice of public image making.* New York: Basic Books.
Banks, J. (1990). *Teaching strategies for the social studies.* White Plains, NY: Longman.
Belson, W.A. (1978). *Television violence and the adolescent boy.* Westmead, England: Saxon House.

Bowman, K.H and Ladd, E.C. (eds) (1993). 'Public opinion and demographic report', *The American Enterprise*, 4(3) (May–June), 91–5.

Centerwall, B.S. (1993). 'Television and violent crime', *The Public Interest*, 3, 56–71

Chaffee, S.H. and Tims, A.R. (1982). 'The development of news media use in adolescence: Implications for political cognition', in M. Burgoon (ed.), *Communication yearbook*. Beverly Hills, CA: Sage.

Davis, D.K. and Robinson, J.P. (1989). 'Newsflow and democratic society in an age of electronic media', in G. Comstock (ed.), *Public communications and behavior*, 2. San Diego, CA: Academic Press.

Dominick, J.R. (1994). *The dynamics of mass communication*. New York: McGraw Hill.

Dunn, A.W. (ed.) (1916). *The social studies in secondary education*, Report of the Committee on Social Studies of the Commission of the Reorganization of Secondary Education of the National Education Association. Washington, DC: Department of the Interior, Bureau of Education.

Ellis, A.K., Fouts, J.T. and Glenn, A.D. (1991). *Teaching and learning secondary social sudies*. New York: HarperCollins Publishers.

Gamson, W.A., Croteau, D., Hoynes, W. and Sasson, T. (1992). 'Media images and the social construction of reality', *Annual Review of Sociology*, 18, 373–93

Garramone, G.M. and Atkin, C.K. (1986). 'Mass communication and political socialization', *Public Opinion Quarterly*, 50, 76–86.

Graber, D.A. (1990). *Media power in politics*. Washington, DC: CQ Press.

Harwood, R. (1992). 'PBS vs. MTV: So many media, so little time', *Washington Post*, 2 September, A21.

Hepburn, M.A. (1990). 'Americans glued to the tube: Mass media, information, and social studies', *Social Education*, 54(4) (April/May), 233–7.

Hepburn, M.A. (1994). 'Public news media and political education in a democratic society', in G. Csepel, D. German, Kri, and I. Stumpf (eds), *From subject to citizen*. Budapest: Hungarian Center for Political Education.

Hepburn, M.A. (1995). 'TV violence: Myth and reality', *Social Education*, 59(4), 309–11.

Holroyd, H.J. (1985). 'Children, adolescents, and television', *American Journal of Diseases in Children*, 139(6), 549–50.

Hudson, R.V. (1987). *Mass media: A chronological encyclopedia of television, radio, motion pictures, magazines, newspapers, and books in the United States*. New York: Garland Publishing.

Huesmann, L.R. and Eron, L.D. (1986). 'The development of aggression in American children as a consequence of television violence viewing', in L.R. Huesmann and L.D. Eron (eds), *Television and the aggressive child: A cross-national comparison*. Hillsdale, NJ: Erlbaum Associates.

Ichilov, O. (ed.) (1990). *Political socialization, citizenship education, and democracy*. New York: Teachers College Press.

Institute for Social Research (1994). 'Televised violence and kids: A public health problem?', *ISR Newsletter*, 18, 1.

Iyengar, S. (1991). *Is anyone responsible? How television news frames political issues*. Chicago: University of Chicago Press.

Kubey, R. (1993). 'Whittling the school day away', *Education Week*, 1 December.

Martorella, P.H. (1991). *Teaching social studies in middle and secondary schools*. New York: Macmillan.

Matlack, C. (1992). 'We have met the anomie and he is us', *National Journal*, 24, 7 March, 600.

Milburn, M.A. and McGrail, A.B. (1992). 'The dramatic presentation of news and its effects on cognitive complexity', *Political Psychology*, 13(4), 613–32.

Nielsen Media Research (1993). *1992–1993 report on television*. New York: A.C. Nielsen.

Neumann, W.R. (1987). 'Knowledge and opinion in the American electorate', *Kettering Review*, Winter, 56–64.

Postman, N. (1982). *The disappearance of childhood*. New York: Delacorte Press.

Postman, N. (1990). 'Television and the decline of public discourse' (an interview), *The Civic Arts Review*, 3(1), 4–6.

Roper Organization (1985). *Public atitudes toward television and other media in a time of change*. New York: Television Information Office.

Roper Organization (1989). *America's watching*. New York: Television Information Office.

Shanahan, J. and Morgan, M. (1992). *Journal of Educational Television*, 18, 35–55.

Shaver, J.P. (ed.) (1977). *Building rationales for citizenship education*. Arlington, VA: National Council for the Social Studies.

Slaby, R.G. (1994). 'Combating television violence', *The Chronicle of Higher Education*, 40(18), 5 January, B1-2.

St Peters, M., Fitch, M., Huston, A.C., Wright, J.C. and Eakins, D.J. (1991). 'Television and families: What do young children watch with their parents?', *Child Development* 62, 1409–23.

Stanley, H.W. and Niemi, R.G. (1993). *Vital statistics on American politics*. Washington, DC: CQ Press.

Zevin, J. (1992). *Social studies for the 21st century: Methods and materials for teaching in middle and secondary schools*. New York: Longman.

Zuckerman, D.M. and Zuckerman, B.S. (1985). 'Television's impact on children', *Pediatrics*, 75(2), 233–40.

8

EDUCATION FOR DEMOCRACY IN ARGENTINA: EFFECTS OF A NEWSPAPER-IN-SCHOOL PROGRAM

STEVEN H. CHAFFEE,
ROXANA MORDUCHOWICZ
and HERNAN GALPERIN

Although the present democratic regime in Argentina is in its second decade, its infrastructure in terms of citizen participation and enthusiasm remains fragile. Voting turnout is deceptively high, because it is mandatory. In a poll conducted by a major national newspaper days before the October 1997 national elections, 51 per cent of Argentinians interviewed said that, if it were not mandatory, they would not cast their votes. Youngsters, many with the opportunity to exercise their democratic rights for the very first time, were even more apathetic: in the 18–29 age group, the percentage that would not bother to vote was 64. This represents a distinct downward trend: in a similar study carried out before the 1991 national elections, the percentage of 'apathetic voters' was 9 per cent.[1] Scarcely a dozen years after Argentina's transition to democracy, many of its citizens give indications that they do not value this system of government.

The roots of this problem are not readily identifiable. Since the process of redemocratization in Latin America started in the early 1980s, there has been considerable debate on how to sustain and consolidate democratic institutions in the region. Economic, political and cultural factors all seem to play a role in this process. Particular attention is now being paid to citizenship education, as scholars recognize that there is no immediate correspondence between institutional arrangements and political culture. A democratic system can coexist with a political tradition that harbors deep-rooted authoritarian elements (Diamond, 1993). Many of the 'new democracies' of Latin America govern peoples in which there is no widespread norm of political tolerance or democratic participation.

The problem of building a broadly democratic citizenry is especially acute in countries where the transition to democracy has generated high expectations – particularly in terms of economic growth and redistribution –

that democratically elected governments are often unable to meet. Ordinary results when compared with extraordinary demands generate popular feelings of inefficacy and distrust toward democratic institutions (Catterberg, 1991). Rosy predictions of the early 1980s that democratization of political institutions would automatically 'spill over' to the political culture were far too optimistic. Therefore, in contrast with the established democracies of North America and Western Europe, issues of citizenship and democratic education are regarded as crucial for the consolidation of democratic regimes in Latin America.

It should come as no surprise that the recent 'rebirth' of political socialization research has emerged from Third World countries that are struggling to build legitimacy for their democratic institutions (Niemi and Hepburn, 1995). As Ichilov (1990) argues, scholars working in new democracies have preoccupations that differ from those in more established regimes. While the latter focus on such issues as political apathy, decreasing voter turnout, political cynicism, and shrinking party affiliation, the issue for many political education scholars in the Third World is the very existence of democratic institutions. Focus is on practical interventions that could consolidate new political institutions through inculcation of normative values and development of skills of citizenship suitable for democratic processes.

The present chapter discusses the results of one such practical intervention, an experimental curriculum throughout Argentina called 'Newspaper-in-Schools'. Started in 1986, this program aims at strengthening democratic norms among primary and secondary school students by promoting open discussions of current political issues in the classroom. Contrary to many studies on similar school interventions in the US and other established democracies, the results in Argentina have been very encouraging. Morduchowicz *et al.* (1994) found in a 1992 evaluation that the Newspaper-in-Schools program contributed to students' knowledge of public affairs, and had some impact on use of news media and interpersonal discussion of politics by students. In this chapter, we explore how creative use of the newspaper in the classroom during an election year can also promote democratic value orientations and skills among students.

A second major concern in this chapter is the social structure underlying these values. Political scientists have long noted the allegiance of lower socioeconomic classes in Third World countries to populist regimes in which democratic principles were traded off for economic gains. We will examine specifically the impact of the newspaper intervention on pro-democratic norms among children in the lower SES (socioeconomic status) strata, where we expect to find such values most lacking.

Implementation of the program studied here varies widely among teachers, a source of variance not accounted for in the 1992 evaluation. Some teachers merely use the newspaper in class for routine learning assignments, while others incorporate its content for class discussions of current events or to stimulate their students to write essays on civic education topics such as freedom of the press. These different implementations of the program are thus a third concern in this chapter. We give special attention to three communication-related strategies in teaching (class debate, writing exercises and media education), evaluating how each can contribute to students' political education beyond mere exposure to the newspaper in class.

POLITICAL CULTURE IN ARGENTINA

In *Political culture and democracy in developing countries,* Diamond argues that 'political culture is better conceived not purely as the legacy of the communal past but as a geological structure with sedimentary deposits from many historical ages and events' (1993, p.428).[2] In the case of Latin America, these sedimentary deposits hardly encouraged the consolidation of democratic regimes. Lechner (1992) argues that pluralism did not develop historically in the region due to a holistic conception of society and order in which dissent and conflict were viewed as disintegrative and hence intolerable. As he puts it, 'Latin American democracy has always been permeated by a distrust of plurality, seen as improper questioning of national unity' (Lechner, 1993). In the same vein, Garretón (1994) contends that Latin American political culture is based on two main concepts, unity and subordination. Individual rights, community dialogue, and kindred pluralistic values have been relegated to secondary status.

Argentina, one of the world's richer nations at the turn of the century, experienced from 1930 to 1983 an incomplete process of late industrialization, under alternating populist governments, weak democracies, and oppressive military regimes. The result was a political culture of intolerance, marked by distrust of pluralism and of democratic debate as a legitimate means of conflict resolution. Tolerance for difference, pragmatism and willingness to engage in debate and compromise, a sense of efficient political institutions, a general climate of cooperation, and bargaining and accommodation between competing parties – all of which characterize most democratic political cultures (Almond and Verba, 1963; Diamond, 1993) – are to a large extent foreign to Argentina.

Empirical work by Catterberg (1989, 1991) supports this picture of deep-rooted anti-democratic elements in the Argentinian political culture. His findings also cast doubt on the socializing power of political democracy *per se*, at least in times of acute economic crisis. After eight years of oppressive military rule, democratic institutions were reinstated in Argentina in 1983. In a survey conducted immediately after the country's transition to democracy Catterberg (1989) found that 69 per cent of Argentinians interviewed disagreed with the statement, 'Democracy is dangerous because it can bring disorder and disorganization'; yet, in 1988 the number disagreeing had dropped to 52 per cent (Catterberg, 1991). And while in the 1984 survey 81 per cent disagreed that 'the majority has the right to eliminate the rights of the minority', only 50 per cent said that in 1988. Apparently, although the transition to democracy in 1983 brought immediate expression of democratic norms, the next few years of economic crisis and political turmoil seriously undermined these gains. It is likely that these losses in the normative realm were most acute in the lower socioeconomic classes, where support for dissent and debate were never strong and where hardship cuts deepest in times of economic distress.

In Argentina's political culture of 'clientelism', support for democracy as a system seems to depend heavily on its perceived capacity to meet immediate individual economic demands (Catterberg, 1989). Democratic orientations are less widespread and less stable among those who bear most of the impact of recurrent economic crises. This is not a surprising finding in a country characterized by dramatic polarization of wealth, as is the case in many Latin American countries. Social structure is hence a key factor to consider in evaluating any field intervention aimed at citizenship education in such a setting. If pro-democratic norms were strengthened in the upper SES sector and yet remain weak farther down the socioeconomic ladder, this widened gap could undermine support for the entire regime during times of trouble. Thus, much more is at stake in citizenship education in Argentina and similar young democracies than it is in established democracies where the main problem is to encourage new citizens to make full use of a political system that is itself not seriously in any jeopardy.

THE NEWSPAPER-IN-SCHOOLS PROGRAM

Argentina's political culture is reflected in many ways in its educational system. As Niemi and Hepburn (1995) point out, in new democracies transmission of democratic values from one generation to the next cannot be assumed. That is, schools do not necessarily promote democratic orientations among students, nor provide them with the critical skills necessary to participate in the public sphere. This was undoubtedly the case when Argentina regained democracy in 1983.

Education scholars agree that the Argentinian educational system bears footprints of authoritarianism and anti-pluralism (Braslavsky et al., 1989; Filmus, 1988). In particular, the educational project advanced by the last military regime (1976–83) pursued a non-participatory, disciplinary and authoritative pedagogical model that aimed to isolate students from political issues and prevent them from forming personal, critical perspectives. The learning process was conceived as expository, a one-way flow of information from teacher to student which hardly encouraged tolerance, independent thinking or participatory debate. The educational system inherited from the military regime was not only in critical financial condition but also completely ill-suited for the needs of consolidating democratic institutions. As Morduchowicz *et al.* (1994) have argued, the transition to democracy in 1983 did not guarantee that citizenship education would take place in the classrooms: 'there was no tradition of political debate in the schools; the lingering memory of the military regime hardly encouraged open expressions of feelings and preferences' (1994, p.3).

In response to this situation, a number of changes and new programs were implemented in order to accommodate the educational system to the requirements of a new democracy, with varying degrees of success.[3] Among them was the Newspaper-in-Schools program, started in 1986. It was first established in Buenos Aires and, with support from the national association of regional daily newspapers (ADIRA), it was extended to the rest of the country the following year. Three basic goals guide the program: first, to 'promote a reflexive reception of the media among students'; second, 'to incorporate current political affairs in class discussions by using the newspaper'; and third, 'to encourage students' political interest and participation by fostering the formation and expression of personal opinions' (ADIRA, 1995, our translation).

The program, as its name implies, is centered on use of the local newspaper in classes. Teachers cooperating with the program receive training in regional workshops, and a national conference is held once a year. Regional newspapers provide local schools with free copies once a week, and some papers also run a special weekly section featuring the program. Though teacher training provides guidelines for class activities with the newspaper, the curriculum varies in practice: some teachers mainly use the newspaper for grammar exercises, but others connect it to social studies lessons including writing exercises, and to discussion of current events and of the free press. The program is most pervasive in the sixth and seventh grades, when students are 11 to 13 years old. While some students at this age have limited understanding of public issues, there is a large drop-out rate after seventh grade, so this is the age when universal political education is most feasible in Argentina. The present study focuses on sixth and seventh graders.

The program faces some resistance by teachers and school authorities, for many reasons. To begin with, teachers in Argentina have little or no experience with media education. In general, they view the media as a competing form of socialization, one from which children need protection. Second, teachers find it easier to talk about the past than the present; unlike textbooks, newspapers deal with current controversies that some teachers find difficult to handle in class. Third, trained in expository teaching methods, many teachers lack the pedagogical skills to promote and coordinate debates in class; many perceive these activities as a threat to their control of the learning process. As a result, only some teachers have volunteered to join the program, and there is a great diversity in the ways they implement it. For purposes of evaluation, this limited participation is fortunate, because it provides a ready-made 'control condition' within virtually every school where the newspaper program is being used.

The program also raises some unusual questions for political socialization scholars. Although early studies on political socialization (Almond and Verba, 1963; Easton and Dennis, 1969) found that the school plays an important role in shaping children's political orientations, scholars later argue that schools are only instrumental in developing support for the existing political system and a sense of national loyalty. Educational institutions fail to provide a critical understanding of democracy and its functioning (Siegel and Hoskin, 1981; Langton and Jennings, 1968; Merelman, 1971; Patrick, 1972). As McLeod et al. put it in a recent US study, 'the effects of school curricula appear to be a strong sense of loyalty to the nation, combined with a vague understanding of democracy and an idealized view of political authority' (1995, p.4).

Chaffee et al. (1995) argue that the seemingly weak evidence on the socializing role of the school stems from evaluations grounded on a 'transmission' model of political education. The recent 'rebirth' of political socialization studies (Niemi and Hepburn, 1995) is based to a considerable extent on questioning this literal didactic instructional approach, reconceiving political education as a life-long process in which schools mainly provide students with critical tools that enable them to participate in the political sphere.[4] This reconceptualization offers a new view of all so-called socializing agents, including the family, the school, and the media. In recent studies, use of media and discussion with parents are as likely to be considered indicators of political socialization, as agents. In the present study, the school curriculum is the principal independent variable, even though earlier field experiments on interventions of this type have shown only limited effects beyond transmission of didactic knowledge (Williams, 1961; Litt, 1963; Elley, 1964).

In early political socialization studies, the enduring influence of the limited-effects model of communication (Lazarsfeld, 1965; Klapper, 1960) discouraged scholars from seriously taking the media and other communication factors into account. Political scientists accepted the assertion that the media had only 'minimal consequences' on political attitudes, and extended this premise uncritically to political socialization (e.g., Dawson and Prewitt, 1969). Empirical studies, however, asserted a socializing role for media by demonstrating their importance in ushering teenagers and immigrants into the world of politics (Chaffee et al., 1970;

Chaffee and Yang, 1990). Still, communication variables were generally interpreted as 'agents' of political socialization, interacting with families and schools in creating new citizens. Looking beyond the transmission model, researchers are now considering communication behaviors such as TV news watching, newspaper reading, and political discussion within the family or in the schools as themselves important outcomes of political education. Stimulation of communication habits is one important focus of evaluation, on the assumption that these behavioral skills persist long after a student's knowledge of a particular school lesson has faded into obsolescence.

STUDY DESIGN AND CONTEXT

The present study was conducted in the fall of 1995, near the end of Argentina's school year. It involved 3,387 students and 130 teachers in public elementary schools in 14 provinces across the country. The fact that implementation of the Newspaper-in-Schools program was voluntary upon the teacher made possible a quasi-experimental design: each teacher participating in the program was asked to fill out our teacher questionnaire and to administer the student questionnaire to his/her students (Program group). These teachers were also asked to administer both questionnaires to a second class and teacher, in the same grade and school, who were *not* using the curriculum (Control group). This is similar to the design used by Morduchowicz *et al.* (1994) for their 1992 evaluation, except for our addition of the teacher questionnaire.

Fieldwork was conducted between October and November of 1995, about five months after Argentina's general presidential elections, and many regional elections. This context maximized our opportunity to compare the treatment and control groups in terms of political discussion and attention to media coverage of political issues and campaigns. Indicators of political socialization were developed in three areas where we hypothesized that the Newspaper-in-Schools program might have some effects: communication behaviors, political cognitions, and political attitudes.[5] Each of these had been affected in some manner according to the results of Morduchowicz *et al.* (1994).

Previous studies of effects of school interventions with political implications (especially Chaffee *et al.*, 1995) have shown strong stimulation of communication behaviors. From our questionnaire we constructed the following indices:

1. Mass media use, which includes questions about frequency of newspaper reading and of attention to news on television.

2. Interpersonal discussion of political issues, divided into a general index

and separate indices for family and friends.

Political cognitions represent the area where strong effects of educational efforts in school are usually found. Our measures included three indices that we expected the Newspaper-in-Schools program to stimulate.

3. Political knowledge, which consisted of the number of correct answers to factual questions about current national and international political events.

4. Opinion-holding, an index constructed by summing the number of questions about political issues to which the student expressed an answer other than 'I don't know'.

5. Political interest, based on dispositional questions about willingness to vote and to take part in other political activities.

Finally, and perhaps most important in the context of Argentina's long-range need to establish broad support for a democratic regime, we evaluated normative attitudes involving support for democratic institutions and tolerance for diversity. These kinds of measures have rarely been found to be much affected by school interventions in established democracies such as the US or Canada.

6. The support for democracy index includes items on support for democratic institutions and party pluralism.

7. The tolerance index includes items on religious diversity, immigration, and freedom of expression.

Another measure of central interest in this study is socioeconomic status (SES), an index built from information about parental education and occupation, and family possessions. As in most Third World countries, there is a great deal of variance in SES within Argentina. The Program group (students who participated in the program) proved to be slightly below the Control group (students not involved in the program) on the family SES scale (Mp = 8.9, Mc = 9.2, t = 1.38, df = 3365, p < .01). This difference would, if anything, tend to counteract positive overall effects of the classroom intervention; when we later test for interactions between the intervention and SES, the latter variable will be controlled statistically. Since these two factors, the field intervention of teaching with vs without the newspaper and the measure of SES, are essentially uncorrelated with one another, we interpret the study as a field experiment (most exactly, a quasi-experiment per Cook and Campbell, 1979).

In addition to this dichotomous test of effects, we measured (in the teacher questionnaire) several methods by which teachers might use the newspaper in class. These teaching variables were grouped in four main indices:

1. Newspaper Use index, a measure of how often and for how much class time the teacher used the local newspaper.

2. Discuss Problems index, based on items about the use of the newspaper as a tool for carrying out class debate on current social and political issues that appeared in the local newspaper.

3. Writing index, based on questions about assigning students to produce and share written pieces about current social and political issues that appeared in the local newspaper.

4. Media Education index, including measures on class discussion about media-related issues such as freedom of the press, and on teacher's attempt to train students to read newspapers critically.

In summary, there are three main sources of variance to explain the students' political socialization levels: family SES; the field intervention of teaching with vs without the newspaper; and the four teaching method measures.

RESULTS

Our analysis is divided into three sections corresponding to the three sources of variance in students' political socialization measures identified above. While this approach is analytically useful at this juncture, we will in our conclusion attempt to integrate these sections into a more general discussion. We begin with the experimental intervention, and then add SES to that picture.

Program vs Control

Overall effects of the newspaper program are summarized in the form of group means in Table 8.1. There are significant differences for most measures, although not necessarily those we most expected.

All five of the communication measures were significantly affected by the Newspaper-in-School intervention, including at-home behaviors such as watching television news, and discussing politics with family. These effects are impressive both for their strength and consistency, and for the fact that they carried beyond the schoolroom into the students' daily lives. One important impact of the program seems to be to communicate more, both via news media and interpersonally.

Some of our results for political cognitions were, however, disappointing. Almost all prior studies evaluating the impact of school programs on political socialization report effects on knowledge of current events (Chaffee *et al.*, 1995; McLeod *et al.*, 1995; Morduchowicz *et al.*, 1994), if little else in some cases. But we did not find a significant knowledge difference despite our

TABLE 8.1
INDICES OF POLITICAL EDUCATION (MEANS) BY EXPERIMENTAL CONDITION

Index	Program	Control	Difference
Media use			
Newspaper reading	2.07	1.90	+.17***
	(.86)	(.86)	
TV news viewing	7.04	6.58	+.46***
	(2.69)	(2.64)	
Interpersonal discussion			
General	1.53	1.44	+.09**
	(.74)	(.79)	
With family	5.61	5.37	+.24***
	(2.12)	(2.20)	
With friends	5.11	4.87	+.24***
	(1.88)	(1.86)	
Political cognitions			
Political knowledge	2.31	2.26	+.05
	(1.21)	(1.19)	
Opinion-holding	6.40	6.12	+.28***
	(1.71)	(1.89)	
Political interest	1.92	1.83	+.09**
	(.94)	(.92)	
Political attitudes			
Support for democracy	1.25	1.08	+.17***
	(.99)	(.98)	
Tolerance index	3.21	3.00	+.21**
	(2.16)	(2.24)	
	$(N \leq 1626)$	$(N \leq 1761)$	

Entries are means. Standard deviations in parentheses.

* $p < .05$; ** $p < .01$; *** $p < .001$.

large sample size. On the other hand, Table 8.1 shows a sizable impact on the number of questions on which students express opinions. This behavioral indicator involves not only cognitions, but also affect and communication. It probably indicates a global expansion of the student's range of interpersonal political contacts. Self-reported communication measures on Table 8.1 support this broad interpretation.

Participation beyond voting is an essential characteristic of a healthy democracy, and our results encourage a future image of these students as adult citizens who will take active roles in political affairs. Detailed analyses show that students in the Program group were more interested in political issues and more likely to take part in political events ($p < .01$) than those in the Control group. This result is particularly important because many political scientists recognize that Argentina, like many other Latin-American political regimes, has strong tendencies to authoritarianism or to what O'Donnel (1994) has called 'delegative democracies' – a hybrid somewhere between formal democracy and de facto dictatorship. These tendencies can only be offset by active citizen involvement in the political sphere. In other words, unlike an established democracy, Argentine democracy cannot endure political apathy. By encouraging students to participate actively in politics, the program appears to provide an antidote to the prevailing apathy among emerging citizens.

Both of the normative attitudes, tolerance and support for democracy, were affected by the newspaper intervention. Students whose teachers used the newspaper expressed significantly greater tolerance for diversity, and stronger pro-democratic values. Such attitudinal results, which are rarely found in similar studies in established democracies, are very encouraging as an assessment of a program that typically involves no more than a few hours of school work per week.

Effects by Socioeconomic Status

In a seminal paper on rural development, Tichenor *et al.* (1970) coined the fortunate term, the 'knowledge gap'. A field intervention usually has significant positive effects on a total population on average, but these effects can be very different in higher and lower social strata. When a positive impact is limited to upper SES levels, the widening gap can be dysfunctional for the total system; when there are stronger effects in the lower SES range, the overall function is to bring the community closer together. In this study we are not simply concerned with the direct effects of SES on political socialization, which are undoubted, as with the interaction between SES and the Newspaper-in-School program.

Prior research in the US suggests that special civics curricula have greater impact on students from underprivileged family backgrounds (Jennings and Niemi, 1974). Evaluating a voting-centered curriculum, McDevitt *et al.* (1996) found clear gap-closing patterns in political communication and affect, helping low-SES students catch up with those from middle-class families, where political awareness is the norm.

Reasons why gaps close or widen are not well established (Viswanath and Finnegan, 1995); differing theories lead to opposing predictions (Ettema and Kline, 1977). The gap-widening prediction presumes that interventions activate latent predispositions, exaggerating differences that stem from structural factors. In this view, children from poor families come to school with structural deficits – weak verbal and attentional skills, for example – that predict they will fall farther behind their high-SES peers when everyone is

TABLE 8.2
INDICES OF POLITICAL EDUCATION, BY EXPERIMENTAL CONDITION AND SES

Index	Low-SES			High-SES			Net Difference[a]
	Program	Control	Difference	Program	Control	Difference	
Media use							
Newspaper reading	2.07	1.88	+.19***	2.07	1.94	+.13***	+.06
	(.87)	(.87)		(.84)	(.84)		
TV news viewing	6.85	6.44	+.41***	7.20	6.74	+.45***	−.04
	(2.68)	(2.61)		(2.72)	(2.66)		
Interpersonal discussion							
General	1.49	1.36	+.13***	1.58	1.51	+.06	+.07
	(.76)	(.81)		(.70)	(.76)		
With family	5.48	5.06	+.42***	5.78	5.66	+.12	+.30*
	(2.12)	(2.20)		(2.08)	(2.16)		
With friends	5.05	4.69	+.35***	5.18	5.05	+.12	+.23
	(1.88)	(1.79)		(1.86)	(1.88)		
Political cognitions							
Political knowledge	2.24	2.11	+.13*	2.39	2.40	−.01	+.14
	(1.17)	(1.19)		(1.24)	(1.17)		
Opinion-holding	6.26	5.85	+.41***	6.56	6.36	+.20*	+.21
	(1.79)	(1.99)		(1.60)	(1.76)		
Political interest	1.85	1.75	+.09*	2.00	1.91	+.08	+.01
	(.94)	(.92)		(.93)	(.90)		
Political attitudes							
Support for democracy	1.18	0.92	+.25***	1.34	1.22	+.11*	+.14*
	(.98)	(.90)		(.99)	(1.02)		
Tolerance index	2.93	2.49	+.43***	3.49	3.43	+.06	+.37**
	(2.14)	(2.24)		(2.13)	(2.15)		
	N ≤ 786	N ≤ 780		N ≤ 813	N ≤ 940		

Cell entries are means. Standard deviations are in parentheses. * $p < .05$; ** $p < .01$; ** $p < .001$.
Note: [a] Significance of net difference tested by analysis of variance. Positive sign (+) indicates that experimental effect was to close SES gap.

offered an intensive educational experience. The gap-narrowing prediction, to the contrary, assumes that all students can learn and that a special intervention can stimulate novel interests despite social background. This view stresses that *differences* between children from diverse backgrounds do not represent persistent *deficits* (Ettema and Kline, 1977). In the same vein, Chaffee *et al.* (1995) concluded that their gap-narrowing evidence supported a characterization of the educational program's impact as 'stimulation', rather than 'activation', of students' political behaviors.

Testing the 'gap' model takes the form of an interaction between SES and the experimental program. Table 8.2 compares the Program and Control groups' means on each dependent variable at two contrasting levels of SES, dichotomized at the median. The right-hand column tests the gap effect by comparing the Program–Control difference in low-SES to that in high-SES. As is evident from the table, the school program produced consistent gap-closing patterns, across the political socialization indicators we measured. While not every net difference is statistically significant, all but one (TV news viewing) indicate a narrowing of the SES gap; this is indicated by positive directional signs in the right-hand column of the table. This pattern is probably due to the fact that these indicators of political socialization tend generally to be lacking in lower-SES strata. Catterberg's findings (1991, 1989) about major differences of political culture between socioeconomic strata in Argentina – attributable to their different political experiences and opportunities – are clearly replicated here in the pre-teen sub-population.

A notable finding in Table 8.2 is that the largest net difference across SES strata is found for tolerance; this coincides with much other research on social stratification and political culture. It is vividly shown in the table, where the mean difference on our Tolerance index between the two SES levels was approximately one full scale position in the Control group (this finding is equivalent to a survey in an unperturbed population); in the Program group, this distance has been reduced by about one-half. While this encouraging result shows that norms of tolerance can be built through educational programs, the very size of the tolerance gap between SES strata reminds us how far a new democracy like Argentina has yet to go in building a citizenship culture where tolerance for diversity could be considered a stable norm.

Many scholars dealing with the problem of regime consolidation in new democracies (e.g., Catterberg, 1991; Alvaro-Moises, 1994; Linz, 1988) note that the lower classes waver in their acceptance of democratic principles. This is understandable in our case given Argentina's great polarity of wealth even after its formal transition to democratic institutions. Unease with democracy among those who are most affected by recurrent economic crises and restructurations should come as no surprise. Indeed, we would consider the political socialization of lower-SES students to be in some degree faulty if they were uncritically to embrace a political system that consistently reproduced their own disadvantaged socioeconomic position. More than schooling and newspaper exposure are needed to sell democracy to the very poor in Argentina. But the Newspaper-in-Schools program does seem to have closed somewhat an extremely wide structural gap in democratic norms, thus promoting their institutionalization across social strata.

The more privileged students did not remain unmoved by the newspaper intervention. Table 8.2 shows significant gains in the high-SES group on both measures of media use, and also statistically significant increases in expression of opinion (although not in interpersonal discussion) and in our index of pro-democratic norms. Some of our gap-closing results could be due to a 'ceiling effect' among students from high-SES families (Ettema and Kline, 1977). It is possible that these students come to school with such high initial levels on our measures that the intervention adds little to them. In other words, students whose families are already likely to subscribe to one or more newspapers probably do not find the newspaper at school an especially novel or stimulating experience. Overall, though, we have found in our gap analyses a general social leveling effect that could represent a small but important step in the building of an inclusive political sphere in Argentine society.

Effects of Classroom Teaching Methods

Results of different teaching methods for students' political socialization were in general weaker than the differences between program and control conditions, and between socioeconomic strata. We attribute this partly to demand characteristics inherent to the teacher survey. Since the questionnaire was administered through regional coordinators of the Newspaper-in-Schools program, it is likely that teachers – particularly those participating in the program – tried to give the 'correct' answer regarding class activities advocated for them. Some of the teacher measures produced little variance, leading to low correlations with the student measures. This in turn limits our ability to analyze interactions with the other independent variables, and we will limit our tests here to correlations that have been controlled only for one major predictor variable, the student's family SES.

Despite the vast literature on media education programs, there is scant empirical research on the relation between particular classroom procedures and political socialization outcomes. In particular, little is known about the use of media products such as the newspaper for purposes of developing citizenship skills and democratic orientations among students. Most research on media education programs concentrates either on students' acquisition of technical skills for media production, or on teaching them how to decode media messages critically (Bazalgette et al., 1992). These concerns leave larger questions of political socialization unexamined.

TABLE 8.3
TEACHERS' CLASS ACTIVITIES, BY EXPERIMENTAL CONDITION ($N = 121$)

	Treatment	Control	Difference
Newspaper use	6.2	4.3	1.9***
	(1.6)	(2.1)	
Discuss problems	4.6	3.8	0.8*
	(1.0)	(1.1)	
Writing	3.3	2.7	0.6*
	(1.0)	(1.2)	
Media education	4.7	3.9	0.8
	(1.1)	(1.4)	
	($N \leq 64$)	($N \leq 57$)	

Entries are means. Standard deviations in parentheses.
* $p < .05$; *** $p < .001$

Since implementation of the newspaper program varies greatly, our first step is to check whether teachers participating in it were carrying out the activities recommended in their training. This program check is summarized in Table 8.3. This table indicates that teachers participating in the program were significantly more likely to carry out these class activities, despite the upward bias in self-reports. Strong intercorrelations between self-reported use of recommended class activities (not shown) indicate that these activities form a coherent pattern of teaching methodology. In other words, teachers in the program were indeed carrying out citizenship education activities around the local newspaper, differentiating their classes from those of their colleagues who were using the regular curriculum. The high correlations between these methods, however, make it difficult for us to separate one from another in statistical analysis. We will examine each method separately, in evaluating its effectiveness in political socialization. Significant results are shown in Table 8.4.

The first teaching variable is simply the frequency of using the newspaper in class. Table 8.4 indicates that this activity strongly stimulated children to read the newspaper outside the school, hopefully creating in them an enduring readership habit. And while the mere presence of the newspaper in class did not predict public affairs knowledge (Table 8.1), there was a significant effect on students' knowledge of the amount of classroom newspaper usage by teachers. Otherwise, though, this quantitative measure predicts only one other criterion variable, political tolerance.

TABLE 8.4
CORRELATIONS BETWEEN TEACHERS' CLASS ACTIVITIES AND STUDENTS'
POLITICAL EDUCATION MEASURES ($N = 2,650$)

	Newspaper use	Discuss problems	Writing	Media education
Media use				
Newspaper reading	.07***	.06**	.04*	.07***
TV news viewing			.04*	.05**
Interpersonal discussion				
General				.04*
With family		.08***		.06**
With friends				.04*
Political cognitions				
Political knowledge	.07***		.05**	
Opinion-holding				.06**
Political interest		.06**	.05**	.07***
Political attitudes				
Support for democracy			.05**	.05**
Tolerance index	.04*		.04*	

Note: Only those correlations with significance level of $p < .05$ are shown.
* $p < .05$; ** $p < .01$; *** $p < .001$.

Many of our most encouraging results occurred when use of the newspaper in class was combined with the specific class activities prescribed by the program such as group debate or writing assignments. In other words, sheer exposure to the newspaper in class *per se* does not guarantee positive results. This underscores the need to train teachers in how to use the newspaper in ways conducive to development of citizenship skills, going beyond its common use as a teaching tool for such goals as enriching children's vocabulary or enhancing their reading proficiency.

Prior literature led us to expect strong effects of class discussion of problems highlighted in the local newspaper. Education scholars have long advocated classroom debate as a strategy for developing critical thinking among students (see Herrick, 1991). Group debate has been found to enhance students' comprehension and mastery of the subject discussed (Hill, 1969), and to lead to attitude change. For example, Fisher (1968) found that fifth graders who were asked to read stories about American Indians and later to debate them developed more positive attitudes toward this minority than did students who only read them. Miller and Biggs (1958) found similar results with secondary school students.

Table 8.4 shows that class debate on controversial news issues significantly affected just three of the ten outcomes we measured: students' discussion of political issues with their families, reading newspapers outside school, and general interest in politics. Encouraging as these results are, we were surprised to find that classroom debate did not affect normative attitudes or opinion formation. Given that debating skills are a central component of democratic citizenship, this rather weak result suggests that teacher training in leading class debate could be strengthened.

A more successful emphasis of the program was to have students produce and share written pieces about controversial issues that appeared in the newspaper. It is well established among education researchers that writing exercises require higher-order comprehension of the subject, as they force students to reconstruct the meaning of what they have read and to organize their ideas for presentation to others (Squire, 1983). Writing has been found to improve students' knowledge acquisition (Stotsky, 1983), comprehension (Doctorow et al., 1978) and recall of issues (Taylor and Berkowitz, 1980). Moreover, writing exercises invite students implicitly to argue for their own opinions, and to imagine the perspective of readers as an implicit audience. As Kohut suggests, 'the written dialogue forces students to anticipate the criticisms their own positions elicit and to be prepared to offer competent justifications for their claims' (1990, p.11).

The results in Table 8.4 offer considerable support for this positive view of writing exercises as part of the study of issues in the newspaper. Students whose teachers emphasized writing were significantly higher in a number of individual qualities that are desirable in citizens: interest in politics, political knowledge, tolerance for other perspectives, and support for democratic institutions. They were also more likely to turn to news media outside class, including television news as well as the newspaper. This teaching technique did not, though, stimulate the students to engage in interpersonal discussion.

In effect, teachers who assign writing exercises are giving their students experience much like that of the journalist. The broad effects of writing that we found suggest a skill akin to what Mead (1934) called 'ideal role-taking'. That is, forced to reflect on the justification of their own perspectives, students move from an egocentric position to a pluralistic understanding of others' points of view. Piaget (1960) also called attention to the importance of this 'decentration' in children's development. Through this process students learn the basic democratic principle that all opinions deserve consideration and respect. This would explain the observed increase in tolerance and support for democracy among those more intensively involved in writing activities.

Typical media education programs focus mostly on teaching media production techniques, and on critical reading skills such as deconstruction of covert meanings in popular texts. These foci overlook broader possibilities for citizenship education. As Kumar argues, what new democracies need are media education programs that 'move beyond textual criticism to social criticism and understanding of public policy' (1992, p.156). The Newspaper-in-Schools program was guided by the concept of using media education to help build democratic orientations and skills lacking in children's regular school experience. The results in Table 8.4 are encouraging in every respect.

It is apparent that teachers' use of the newspaper to educate their students about news media stimulated students' political communication habits, both interpersonal and mass-mediated. Increased understanding of media enhanced students' willingness to discuss politics with parents and friends, and their curiosity to look actively for political information both in newspapers and in television newscasts. In other words, educating students on how to read and understand the production and distribution of political messages seems to build in them an inclination to engage in both consumption and interpersonal processing of political news. Moreover, media education apparently stimulated students' interest in politics, and their level of opinionation on political issues. It is as if understanding the role of the media in modern democracy primes young people to engage in the political world.

Media education seems also to have affected key normative attitudes, increasing children's support for democratic political institutions. Media education clearly involves more than the honing of critical reading abilities. It is inseparable from education about political democracy and its basic assumptions, one of them being the functioning of a free-press system. It seems that educating about the role of the media in society by means of the newspaper allows students better to reflect on and to comprehend basic democratic principles.

EDUCATION FOR DEMOCRACY, DEMOCRACY *THROUGH* EDUCATION

The apparent success of the Argentine Newspaper-in-Schools program invites rethinking of some assumptions about media education and political socialization, particularly in fledgling democracies. School programs typically promote democratic practices *within* the school, but the research literature – based mostly on studies in countries with long-consolidated democratic institutions – has discouraged educators from attempting to influence young people in their future role as citizens; in other words, to build democracy *through* the schools. The program analyzed here is a notable experiment in the latter direction, and is particularly important in a country where students begin dropping out of school to assume adult roles soon after the grade levels we have studied here.

Our results discredit some common notions about civics education and political culture. It appears that curriculum interventions can be instrumental in enhancing political literacy among pre-teens, despite considerable prior findings that suggest the contrary. The Newspaper-in-Schools program helped students develop political communication habits, and stimulated their forming and voicing of personal opinions. It also fostered interest in political participation, pluralistic orientations, and support for democracy.

Our results also contradict the pessimistic view that prevails in most academic renderings of the 'knowledge gap' hypothesis. Gap-closing is in principle just as likely as gap-widening, as an outcome of a field intervention. Moreover, political socialization involves a good deal more than mere transmission of information. Although we in fact found no significant overall effect on political knowledge *per se*, the gap model led us to uncover a general leveling effect in the narrowing of numerous 'gaps' in other political behaviors of consequence. While SES was, as expected, highly correlated with most indicators of political socialization, the intervention reduced that correlation, helping students from low-SES families approach the levels of their high-SES peers. These results also lead us to reject the belief that the political culture of the lower classes, historically identified with populist leaders in Latin America, is inherently antithetical to democratic principles. Our analysis shows quite the opposite: students from low-SES families were more receptive to the program and benefitted most in terms of citizenship education.

Variations in the execution of the curriculum led us to analyze the specific ways in which teachers implemented the program, revealing some interesting points for media educators. First, it is apparent that mere exposure to the newspaper in class is not in itself likely to contribute much to education for citizenship; it must be accompanied by classroom activities conducive to larger objectives. For example, our results show that writing exercises can be effectively used to develop children's democratic skills. By forcing students to reflect on others' thoughts and to justify their own opinions, writing exercises provide a 'training ground' in perspective taking, widely considered a basic requirement for rational political debate (Habermas, 1990).

A participatory conception of democracy, one that conceives of citizens as permanently engaged in political dialogue, presupposes both political literacy on the part of individuals and a political system that encourages the formation of personal opinions and provides the channels for political participation. These conditions both remain lacking to a large extent in some new democracies. And though considerable progress has been made in the institutionalization of channels for citizenship participation since Argentina's transition to democracy, the apathy that has characterized recent elections reveals that many changes in the political culture are needed before Argentinians make full and wise use of their political system. Our purpose here has been a narrow one, to evaluate a school program based on the use of the newspaper in class. Typically, this involved no more than a few hours of class work per week, and while our findings encourage a very hopeful view of this educational tool, it is only one small indicator of the kinds of changes that are needed in the political culture of Argentinian citizens, young and old.

NOTES

This research was supported in part by grants to the first author from the Center for Latin American Studies and the Institute for International Studies at Stanford University, and from the Spencer Foundation. Data collection was supported by the Association of Dailies of the Interior Region of Argentina (ADIRA) under the direction of the second author.

1. Source: *La Nación*, 13 October 1997.
2. For further discussion on the concept of political culture, see Almond and Verba (1963), Linz (1988) and Weffort (1992).
3. For a review, see Braslavsky *et al.* (1989).
4. For a critique of the transmission model of political socialization, see also Sigel (1995), Flanagan and Gally (1995), Conley and Osborne (1988), Merelman (1990) and Westholm *et al.* (1990).
5. For details on index construction, see Appendix A.

REFERENCES

ADIRA (1995). *Programa 'El diario en la escuela'*. Buenos Aires: Asociación de Diarios del Interior de la República Argentina.

Almond, G. and Verba, S. (1963). *The civic culture*. Princeton, NJ: Princeton University Press.

Alvaro-Moises, J. (1994). 'A escolha democrática em perspectiva comparada', *Lua Nova*, 33, 17–38.

Bazalgette, C., Bevort, E. and Savino, J. (1992). *New directions: Media education worldwide*. London: BFI.

Braslavsky, C., Cunha, L.A., Filgueira, C. and Lemez, R. (1989). *Educación en la transición a la democracia*. Santiago de Chile: UNESCO/OREALC.

Catterberg, E. (1989). *Argentina confronts politics*. Boulder, CO: L. Rienner Publishers.

Catterberg, E. (1991). 'El balance de la transición: Percepciones de eficacia gubernamental en el Cono Sur', paper presented to the XV Political Science World Congress, Buenos Aires, July 1991.

Chaffee, S.H. and Yang, S.M. (1990). 'Communication and political socialization', in O. Ichilov (ed.), *Political socialization, citizenship, education and democracy*. New York: Teachers College Press.

Chaffee, S.H., Moon, Y. and McDevitt, M. (1995). 'Stimulation of communication: Reconceptualizing the study of political socialization', paper presented to the Association for Education in Journalism and Mass Communication, August 1995.

Chaffee, S.H., Ward, S. and Tipton, L. (1970). 'Mass communication and political socialization', *Journalism Quarterly*, 47, 647–59.

Conley, M.W. and Osborne, K. (1988). 'Civics, citizenship, state power and political education: The Canadian experience', in B. Claussen and S. Kili (eds), *Changing structures of political power, socialization and political education*. New York: Peter Lang.

Cook, T.D. and Campbell, D.T. (1979). *Quasi-experimentation: Design and analysis issues for field settings*. Chicago: Rand-McNally.

Dawson, R. and Prewitt, K. (1969). *Political socialization*. Boston, MA: Little, Brown.

Diamond, L. (1993). *Political culture and democracy in developing countries*. Boulder, CO: L. Rienner Publishers.

Doctorow, M., Wittrock, M.C. and Marks, C. (1978). 'Generative processes in reading comprehension', *Journal of Educational Psychology*, 70, 109–18.

Easton, D. and Dennis, J. (1969). *Children in the political system*. New York: McGraw-Hill.

Elley, W. (1964). 'Attitude change and education for international understanding', *Sociology of Education*, 37, 325.

Ettema, J.S. and Kline, F.G. (1977). 'Deficits, differences, and ceilings: Contingent conditions for understanding the knowledge gap', *Communication Research*, 4, 179–202.

Filmus, D. (1988), *Respuestas a la crisis educativa*. Buenos Aires: Cántaro.

Fisher, F.L. (1968). 'Influences of reading and discussion on the attitudes of fifth graders toward Indians', *Journal of Educational Research*, 62, 130–4.

Flanagan, C. and Gally, L. (1995). 'Reframing the meaning of "political" in research with adolescents', *Perspectives on Political Science*, 24(1), 34–42.

Garretón, M.A. (1994). *La faz sumergida del iceberg: Estudios sobre la transformación cultural*. Santiago de Chile: CESOC-LOM.

Habermas, J. (1990). *Moral consciousness and communicative action*. Cambridge, MA: MIT Press.

Herrick, J.A. (1991). *Critical thinking: The analysis of arguments*. Scottsdale: Gorsuch Scarisbrick.

Hill, W.F. (1969). *Learning through discussion*. Beverly Hills, CA: Sage.

Ichilov, O. (1990). 'Dimensions and role patterns of citizenship in democracy', in O. Ichilov (ed.), *Political socialization, citizenship, education and democracy*. New York: Teachers College Press.

Jennings, M.K. and Niemi, R.G. (1974). 'Social studies teachers and their pupils', in M.K. Jennings and R.G. Niemi (eds), *The political character of adolescence: The influence of families and schools*. Princeton, NJ: Princeton University Press.

Klapper, J.T. (1960). *The effects of mass communication*. Glencoe, IL: Free Press.

Kohut, K. (1990). *Developing critical thinking through the use of argumentation techniques*. ERIC document # 330001.

Kumar, K.J. (1992). 'Redefining the goals: Reflections from India', in C. Bazalgette, E. Bevort and J. Savino (eds), *New directions: Media education worldwide*. London: BFI.

Langton, K.P. and Jennings, M.K. (1968). 'Political socialization and the high school civics curriculum in the United States', *American Political Science Review*, 62, 862–7.

Lazarsfeld, P.F. (1965). *The people's choice*. New York: Columbia University Press.

Lechner, N. (1992). 'Some people die of fear: Fear as a political problem', in J. Corradi, P. Weiss-Fagen and M.A. Garreton (eds), *Fear at the edge*. Berkeley, CA: University of California Press.

Lechner, N. (1993). 'A disenchantment called post-modernism', *Boundary* 2, 20(3), 122–39.

Linz, J.J. (1988). *Democracy in developing countries*. Boulder, CO: L. Rienner Publishers.

Litt, E. (1963). 'Civic education norms and political indoctrination', *American Sociological Review*, 28, 69–75.

McDevitt, M., Chaffee, S.H. and Moon, Y. (1996). 'Closing gaps between rich and poor: Effects of an experimental curriculum on political socialization', paper presented to Instructional and Developmental Communication Division, ICA, Chicago, IL, May

1996.

McLeod, J., Eveland, W.P. and Horowitz, E.M. (1995). 'Learning to live in democracy: The interdependence of family, schools and media', paper presented to the Association for Education in Journalism and Mass Communication, August 1995.

Mead, G.H. (1934). *Mind, self and society*. Chicago, IL: University of Chicago Press.

Merelman, R. (1971). *Political socialization and educational climates*. New York: Holt, Rinehart & Winston.

Merelman, R. (1990). 'The role of conflict in children's political learning', in O. Ichilov (ed.), *Political socialization, citizenship, education and democracy*. New York: Teachers College Press.

Miller, K.M. and Biggs, J.B. (1958). 'Attitude change through undirected group discussion', *Journal of Educational Psychology*, 49, 224–8.

Morduchowicz, R., Catterberg, E., Niemi, R.G. and Bell, F. (1994). 'Teaching political information and democratic values in a new democracy: An Argentine experiment', paper presented to the XVI World Congress of the IPSA–Berlin, August 1994.

Niemi, R. and Hepburn, M.A. (1995). 'The rebirth of political socialization', *Perspectives on Political Science*, 24(1), 7–16.

O'Donnel, G. (1994). 'Delegative democracy', *Journal of Democracy*, 5(1), 55–69.

Patrick, J. (1972). 'The impact of an experimental course, "American Political Behavior", on the knowledge, skills, and attitudes of secondary school students', *Social Education*, 36, 168–79.

Piaget, J. (1960). *The moral judgment of the child*. Glencoe, IL: Free Press.

Sigel, R. (1995). 'New directions for political socialization', *Perspectives on Political Science*, 24(1), 17–22.

Sigel, R.S. and Hoskin, M. (1981). *The political involvement of adolescents*. New Brunswick, NJ: Rutgers University Press.

Squire, J.R. (1983). 'Composing and comprehending: Two sides of the same basic process', *Language Arts*, 60(5), 581–9.

Stotsky, S. (1983). 'Research on reading/writing relationships: A synthesis and suggested directions', *Language Arts*, 60(5), 627–42.

Taylor, B. and Berkowitz, S. (1980). 'Facilitating children's comprehension of content material', in M. Kamil and A. Moe (eds), *Perspectives on reading research and instruction*. Washington, DC: National Reading Conference, Inc.

Tichenor, P.J., Donohue, G.A. and Olien, C.N. (1970). 'Mass media and differential growth in knowledge', *Public Opinion Quarterly*, 34, 158–70.

Viswanath, K. and Finnegan, J.R. (1995). 'The knowledge gap hypothesis: Twenty-five years later', in B. Burleson (ed.), *Communication Yearbook 19*. Thousand Oaks: Sage.

Weffort, F. (1992). *New democracies, which democracies?* Washington, DC: Latin American Program, Woodrow Wilson Center.

Westholm, A., Lindquist, A. and Niemi, R. (1990). 'Education and the making of the informed citizen: Political literacy and the outside world', in O. Ichilov (ed.), *Political socialization, citizenship, education and democracy*. New York: Teachers College Press.

Williams, H.M. (1961). 'Changes in pupils' attitudes toward West African Negroes following the use of two different teaching methods', *British Journal of Educational Psychology*, 31, 292–6.

APPENDIX

Listed below are item wording and coding for the indices used in this chapter.

I. STUDENT QUESTIONNAIRE

Media Use

Newspaper reading
'Do you read the first page of the newspaper?' Yes = 1, No = 0, DK = 0.
'Do you read the inside pages of the newspaper?' Yes = 1, No = 0, DK = 0.
'Do you read the editorials or opinion articles?' Yes = 1, No = 0, DK = 0.

TV news viewing
'How many days a week do you watch news?' 0 = 1, 1 = 2, 2 = 3, 3 = 4, 4 = 5, 5 = 6, 6 = 7, 7 = 8.
'When was the last time you watched TV news?' Yesterday = 3, The past week = 2, More than 2 weeks ago = 1, Else = 0.

Interpersonal Discussion

General
'Do you talk with anyone about what is going on in the country and the world?' Yes = 1, No = 0, DK = 0.
'When you see or read news about what is going on in the country and the world, do you share it with other people?' Yes = 1, No = 0, DK = 0.

With family
'When you watch TV news, do you call your parents' attention to something to see?' Yes, very often = 2, Yes, at times = 1, No = 0.
'Do you recommend that your parents read interesting news?' Yes = 1, No = 0.
'How much do you talk with your parents about what is going on in the country and the world?' Almost every day = 3, Once/twice a week = 2, Almost never = 1, Else = 0.
'With whom do you share news about what is going on in the country and the world?' Father = 1, Mother = 1, Siblings = 1, Teacher = 0, Friends = 0.
'Who brings up, in general, discussion in your home about what is going on in the country and the world?' I do = 1, My parents = 0, My siblings = 0, DK = 0.

With friends
'With whom do you share news about what is going on in the country and the world?' Father = 0, Mother = 0, Siblings = 0, Teacher = 0, Friends = 1.
'Do you talk with friends about what is going on in the country and the world?' Yes, a lot = 2, Very little = 1, No = 0, DK = 0.
'How much do you talk with your friends about what is going on in the country and the world?' Almost every day = 3, Once/twice a week = 2, Almost never = 1, Else = 0.
'How much do you talk with your friends about the elections?' A lot = 3, A little = 2, Almost none = 1, Else = 0.

Political Cognitions

Political knowledge
'Which of these names is Minister of Foreign Affairs?' Correct = 1, Incorrect = 0.

'The privatization of which of these 3 services is currently being discussed?' Correct = 1, Incorrect = 0.

'In which country is there at terrible civil war?' Correct = 1, Incorrect = 0.

'Which of these presidents governs a country of the Mercosur?' Correct = 1, Incorrect = 0.

Political interest

'When a project is proposed by the government, do you ask yourself what your opinion is?' Yes = 1, No = 0, DK = 0.

'If the government proposed a project you considered bad for the country, would you do something to show your opposition?' Yes = 1, No = 0, DK = 0.

'Would you like to be able to vote?' Yes = 1, No = 0, DK = 0.

Opinion-holding

'Democracy is the best form of government for our country and the world.' DK = 0, Else = 1.

'In elections it is the same if either party wins, because they are all the same.' DK = 0, Else = 1.

'In a democracy every citizen should participate.' DK = 0, Else = 1.

'Do you approve of the optional military service?' DK = 0, Else = 1.

'Should illegal immigrants have a right to care in a public hospital?' DK = 0, Else = 1.

'Should others who think differently from you be allowed to express themselves?' DK = 0, Else = 1.

'Should other religions besides Roman Catholic be permitted?' DK = 0, Else = 1.

'Do you approve that newspapers criticize the government?' DK = 0, Else = 1.

Political Attitudes

Tolerance

'People don't have the right to criticize the government.' Agree = –1, Disagree = 1, DK = 0.

'Should illegal immigrants have a right to care in a public hospital?' Yes = 1, No = –1, DK = 0.

'What should be done with drug-addicts?' Re-education = 1, Put them in jail = –1, DK = 0.

'Should other religions besides Roman Catholic be permitted?' Yes = 1, No = – 1, DK = 0.

'Should others who think differently from you be allowed to express themselves?' Yes = 1, No = –1, DK = 0.

'Do you approve that newspapers criticize the government?' Yes = 1, No = –1, DK = 0.

Support for democracy

'Democracy is the best form of government for our country and the world.' Agree = 1, Disagree = 0, DK = 0.

'Who should govern the country?' Those for whom people vote = 1, Those who know the most = 0, The military = 0, DK = 0.

'What would be the best for the country?' If many parties exist = 1, If no political parties exist = 0, If only one political party exists = 0, DK = 0.

Socioeconomic Status (SES)

Father's education: completed primary school = 1, completed secondary school = 3, completed university = 5.

Mother's education: completed primary school = 1, completed secondary school = 2, completed university = 3.

Father's occupation: unemployed = 0; employed, general = 3; employed, professional/ manager/supervisor = 6.

Mother's occupation: unemployed = 1; employed, general = 2l; employed, professional/ manager/supervisor = 4.

II. TEACHER QUESTIONNAIRE

Newspaper use

'Do you use the newspaper in school?' Yes = 2, Very little = 1, No = 0.

'How often do you use the newspaper in school?' Almost every day = 3, Once a week, all year = 2, Once a month, as a curriculum unit = 1, Never used = 0.

'For how much class time do you use the newspaper?' The whole class hour = 3, Half of the hour = 2, Only a few minutes = 1, Never used = 0.

Discuss problems

'Do you analyze in class actual problems that face society?' A lot = 2, Sometimes = 1, No = 0.

'Have you ever discussed with students controversial or polemical issues published in the newspaper?' Yes, we investigate in depth = 2, Yes, but only in general = 1, No, I try to avoid = 0.

'Do students discuss current events that appear in the newspaper, in class with you?' Yes = 2, Very little = 1, No = 0.

Writing

'Do students produce writing about current events?' Yes, a lot = 2, Rarely = 1, No = 0.

'When students write about current events, do they share their work with other students, or with their parents?' Yes, a lot = 2, Rarely = 1, No = 0.

Media education

'Do you talk about communication media in class?' Yes, a lot = 2, Sometimes = 1, Almost never = 0.

'Do students learn to read the media critically, and to differentiate their positions?' Yes, a lot = 2, Sometimes = 1, Almost never = 0.

'Do you discuss with students the significance of freedom of the press?' Yes, a lot = 2, At times = 1, No = 0.

9

DEMOCRACY MINUS WOMEN IS NOT DEMOCRACY: GENDER AND WORLD CHANGES IN CITIZENSHIP

VIRGINIA SAPIRO

'Democracy minus women is not democracy.' This declaration, which became the slogan of the early post-communist Russian women's movement, caught the attention of women's movements around the world. At first blush it was generally read outside Russia as an expression of exhilaration and optimism about the implications of the construction of democracy for women's future. But, just as the world's initial optimism faded as it became clear that initiating the first stages of democratization was going to be a more difficult task than clinching the final stages of destroying the previous authoritarian regime, so the Russian women's movement reported that the creation of a new structure of gender relations was not going as well as many had hoped. This pattern repeated itself throughout the area covered by the former Soviet bloc (Einhorn, 1993).

The problem framing this essay is whether the phrase, 'democracy minus women is not democracy', is a statement of fact or a statement of hope, an analytical definition or a normative prescription. Is inclusion of women an essential definitional criterion of democracy? That is, could we not define a regime as democratic unless women are included in the same rights, responsibilities, and suppositions about political relationships that lead us to say – when we look at men – that a democracy exists? Or is this phrase merely one of many competing theories of democracy, the one that feminists and others who value inclusiveness prefer and hope to advocate in a way that will convince and become part of the basic cultural norms underlying the constructions of democracy that will evolve through the rigors of regime construction?

In either case, women's movements in these self-reconstructing nations are attempting to play important roles in citizenship education and socialization. In the former case, if it is indeed true that democracy minus women is not democracy, women's movements are acting to remind their fellow citizens of this democratic lesson, to make them aware of the ways in which practices are falling short of principles. If the latter, if women's movements are offering a contending definition of democracy – which I will argue is the case – then women's movements are attempting to play crucial roles in the creation of political culture by advocating and inculcating a specific set of democratic norms in the developing political culture. Social movements are not just interest groups; they are also agents of socialization and culture creation (Sapiro, 1990).

An interesting theoretical question to pursue, then, is how beliefs about gender and attitudes toward women do and will fit into the new political schemas, and particularly, mass and élite constructions of democracy. The crucial practical question linked to this theoretical issue is how will the female half of the population fit into the 'new democracies' as they are constructed. What difference will 'democracy', so called, make for women? What changes for women are implied by the term, 'democracy'? For those of us who focus on the political psychology of democracy, that is, on the relationship of identity, cognition, and affect to the development and maintenance of democracy, what association does gender have with democracy in the minds of the public and leaders?

The current waves of changes in the formerly authoritarian communist countries (and, indeed, the more subtle changes going on in the course of profound self-reassessment taking place in the older and various liberal social-welfare democracies) offer venues for observing political change from two different perspectives that are rarely integrated together. On the one hand are the transformations at the cultural and societal level. Basic assumptions about the relationships among citizens and those between citizens and leaders, understandings of the nature of law, notions of individual rights and responsibilities, and the purposes and potential uses of collective and individual political action must be restructured both in terms of widespread conventional norms or cultural values and as principles effected through reconstructed social and institutional practices. To investigate how these changes take place we generally focus on the process of institution building.

But, at the same time, these transformations also happen on the individual level. People who had grown up in one system must develop new practices, norms and, in many ways, a very new language of politics. Within the large community of scholars seeking to understand the current changes and the future potential of these rapidly changing political systems it is probably true that the dominant approaches to research will focus on the cultural and institutional levels. But it is also important to understand these transformations at the individual level, and focus on the processes by which people establish new patterns of political thinking and practices.

Certainly research on patterns of individual political thinking in the mass public has offered interesting insights into these transformations. A long tradition in the field of political psychology focuses on the political attitudes often thought to undergird democracy, such as political tolerance. But before scholars of the older democracies leap to seek evidence for 'democratic values' in the changing regimes, we need to remind ourselves of a common observation in past research: the citizens of 'democratic' nations do not always display the cognitive characteristics scholars have often expected democratic nations to have.

Beginning in the early 1960s, analysis of survey data showed that, in the main, the mass public does not seem to put different attitudes together in a way that coherently and consistently reflects the premises embedded in the writings of the intellectuals, theorists, and theoreticians of politics (Converse, 1964). A large proportion of citizens do not reach political judgments through the same ideological language their leaders – political, intellectual, and cultural – tend to use. Indeed, a significant portion of the citizenry often does not attach any meaning – or they attach erroneous meanings – to some of the most central words in élites' political vocabulary: 'liberal' and 'conservative'. The 'left-right continuum' appears not to be a single continuum, but multidimensional, and it alone is inadequate to capture the underlying structure of political thinking and political culture, at least in the United States. Just as the mass public does not seem to connect different attitudes and ideas together 'horizontally' in the way that élites used to expect, they also do not seem to make the 'vertical' connections as often as was expected. General principles and specific examples do not seem as nested together as political scientists once expected.

The public, in other words, is not at all agreed about what political attitudes fit together 'consistently' or 'coherently', or what specific acts are implied by some of the most basic political values. The weight of public opinion research over the last decade has shifted away from hypothesizing the existence of a single underlying structure to coherent political thinking toward talking in terms of multiple and variable schemas or frames that structure political thinking even in a single, relatively stable democracy.

The current realities of the political world should forcibly remind scholars that there are not 'natural' or 'universal' meanings to basic political terms such as 'democracy'. Certainly there has been a core of ideas conventionally agreed to be part of theories of democracy articulated by political and legal theorists throughout the West and to some degree elsewhere. But as arguments between 'liberal' and 'republican' or 'communitarian' democrats show, even in the circles most dominated by the traditions of seventeenth- and eighteenth-century canonical democratic theorists of the British Isles, France and Geneva, there are important differences in the ways democracy has been conceptualized. Comparing the political and legal systems of the various parliamentary and presidential, constitutional monarchy and republican, federal and unitary systems of democracy leads us to the same conclusion. In the midst of the current global debates over political transformation and democratization it is perhaps clearer than it used to be that there are many different 'democratic' models from which to choose. Even within particular 'stable democracies' such as the United States, there are disagreements about the meanings of basic political terms, and certainly, social movements and other groups crop up regularly that seek to alter these terms or advocate one view of politics over another. 'Democracy' does not exist in nature; the concept and practice must be constructed.

The fact that even the most basic political terms such as 'democracy' are socially and historically constructed and widely variable has implications that eluded feminists in the early days of political transformation in the late 1980s and early 1990s. These are becoming ever clearer as the struggles of building new regimes and civic cultures wear on. The transformation to 'democracy' does not imply any particular outcome for women or gender relations. Much as it may pain those of us with fundamentally inclusive notions of democracy to recognize it, democracy minus women can be democracy according to widely accepted norms and, indeed, throughout most of the history of 'democracy' it has been.

DEMOCRACIES MINUS WOMEN

In the past decade a very rich literature on the historical relationship of women to democratization and political development has shown that, although there is considerable variation across times and places, democratization has never seemed to have the same implications for women and men. As great as the transformations are that usually accompany the shift to democracy, or as great as are the ruptures when democratization is ushered in by revolution, the measures that are used to determine whether a nation has crossed the threshold of democracy have usually required looking at men's but not women's relationship to the state.

Thus, for example, the changes that allowed married (white) women to own property in the United States in the 1840s or in Britain in the 1880s generally go unremarked in histories of the development of the first-wave democracies despite the fact that these were probably the single most widespread programs of property redistribution that happened in either country and that some basic rights – e.g., any contingent on the ability to contract – are based on the right to own property. Universal 'manhood' suffrage is usually understood as the clincher in terms of citizenship rights, leaving the voting rights of the other half of the population as mere icing on the democratic cake. Switzerland, often touted as one of the world's most fundamentally democratic states, did not include its female citizens in the right to vote until 1972. The right to a trial by a jury of one's peers has long been considered an essential part of the edifice of democracy in many countries, but in the United States women could be intentionally and systematically excluded from juries until the middle of the 1970s.

The fact that the definition of 'minimal standards' for applying the term 'democracy' have shifted substantially over time or are different in different countries is not news. This easily observable fact is enough to tell us it is very possible for 'new democracies' to develop that could not only tolerate excluding women from its basic terms, but even prefer their exclusion.

Women's exclusion from the terms of democracy is not a mere matter of neglect or forgetfulness. The men who guided the construction of the terms and practices of democracy did not simply overlook women. Most of the major political theorists of democracy dealt with questions of women's citizenship and political roles at least up until this century, and most – Locke and Rousseau among them – noticed there was a contradiction between 'general' democratic principles (that is, those applying to men) and the treatment of women. Many political theorists devoted some energy to explaining why women's relationship to government and the state had to be different from men's without compromising the values for which men had fought.

It would be a mistake to attribute women's exclusion in any simple way to men declaring principles of democracy as simply inapplicable to women. Rather, as many feminist theorists and historians have pointed out, the principle theories and practices of democracy developed in the United States and West Europe during the past three centuries were very basically gendered, and depended on specific notions of the distinct but functionally interdependent roles and characters of women and men. Even apparently neutral and universalistic liberal democratic theory has almost always been profoundly gendered (Pateman, 1988; Phillips, 1991, 1993).

How could a nation that regards itself as democratic carefully exclude women from participation in many forms of conventional politics? How can it justify placing less value on women's political participation, especially as leaders, or the political representation of their views? As many historians and theorists have shown, the meanings of democracy, participation, influence, and representation are malleable enough that women's exclusion from politics can come to be identified as the very means toward their inclusion. The concept of 'republican motherhood' is a prime example of a means through which cultural doctrines of separate spheres could be reformulated to endow women's everyday activities as mothers and wives with political and patriotic meaning while at the same time, justifying the exclusion of women from more conventional politics and avenues of influence (Kerber, 1986; Landes, 1988; Evans, 1989; Phillips, 1991). Although variations differ, a theory of republican motherhood has as its core an argument as follows.

Democracy entails the right and, indeed, obligation for citizens to participate in the civic life of their country and to have a say in the way it is run. As compared with conventional liberal theories, in which politics is distinctly something that happens in public spaces, separated from private institutions and relationships such as the family, republicanism incorporates at least a bridging notion of the 'civic', in which apparently private character, acts and relationships have an important bearing on the whole.

For a culture encompassing an ideology of gender-based separate spheres, a doctrine of republican democracy can transform women's traditionally restricted and domestic roles not by moving women's activities 'out of the house', but by moving the ultimate significance of their domestic roles 'out of the house'. In the early nineteenth century women came to be seen increasingly as playing crucial roles in the development of the nation and its political system, especially through their function as educators and socializers of children, but also through their activities in voluntary civic organizations and networks. A republican mother did not just raise her child, she raised the next generation of citizens. She did not just help to feed, clothe, and comfort old and infirm neighbors through her church, she helped to cement the bonds of civic ties that undergirded the good society and polity.

Even as late as the 1960s United States courts continued to accept a gender-based 'separate spheres' argument about citizenship, especially in cases that had to do with citizenship obligations. In the 1961 case of Hoyt v. Florida the Supreme Court reflected on the practice of affirmative registration for juries, a system in which only women who specifically volunteered for jury duty could serve as compared with men, who were conscripted for jury service. Because few people ever volunteer, women virtually never appeared on juries. The Supreme Court found this practice constitutional for the following reason:

> Despite the enlightened emancipation of women from the restrictions and protections of bygone years, and their entry into many parts of community life formerly considered to be reserved to men, woman is still regarded as the center of home and family life. We cannot say that it is constitutionally impermissible for a State, acting in pursuit of the general welfare, to conclude that a woman should be relieved from the civic duty of jury service unless she herself determines that such service is consistent with her own special responsibilities.

In other words, women are exempted from this obligation to the state because they have others – motherhood and homemaking – that come first as duties of their citizenship. Only when those obligations are fulfilled need a woman participate in other acts of citizenship.

In a parallel decision in 1968, a US district court explained why men's citizenship required them to be conscripted into military service (in this case for duty in Vietnam) while women might only volunteer, although not for combat duty.

> Congress made a legislative judgment that men should be subject to involuntary induction but that women, presumably because they are 'still regarded as the center of home and family life (Hoyt *v.* State of Florida ...)' should not. In providing for involuntary service for men and voluntary service for women, Congress followed the teaching of history that if a nation is to survive, men must provide the first line of defense while women keep the home fires burning (US *v.* St Clair).

Notice that women's exclusion from the military is not in this case tied to any physical or character disability – the most common justification offered for the nearly universal absence of women from combat roles and conscription. The reason in this case has to do with alternative gendered citizen duties. Even in its most universalistic impulses liberal democrats have never argued that all citizens are exactly the same. Like the religious view that there are circumstances in which the apparent reinforcement or at least toleration of inequality on earth might undergird people's equality 'in the eyes of God', so a separate spheres theory of citizenship has often been the structure on which a theory of equal citizenship might depend.

The period since the demise of the communist governments of Europe has witnessed different kinds of movements toward a gender differentiated notion of democratic citizenship. Research on the gender basis of changes in the former Soviet Union and Eastern European countries shows that a norm that has widely accompanied and been an integral part of 'democratic' argument and democratizing efforts has been a move away from gender equality and some of the social support systems on which women in particular depend. Indeed, one common symbolic attack on the authoritarian communist regimes is that they denied the freedoms of the private realm, especially to women, who were unnaturally torn away from the home and domestic relationships to serve as workers. Many 'democrats' would argue that democracy can restore women's more proper place in the home with their children (Einhorn, 1993).

POLITICAL PSYCHOLOGY OF DEMOCRATIZATION

What has been perhaps most interesting about the development of democratic theory and practice from the point of view of political psychology is the degree to which its cognitive practices can flexibly encompass such a wide array of relationships depending on the material needs of the society, the current institutional arrangements, and persistent cultural values.

'Cognitive practices' refers to the ways in which people define their terms, package different ideas together, and generally make sense of the political world around them. I use this term rather than 'ideology' or 'belief systems', or 'schemas', terms more commonly used for a similar concept, to emphasize the dynamics of this process of 'making sense' of the world. Most public opinion researchers once seemed to assume that modal practices of putting ideas together in an informed public would be based primarily on logic. Thus, we expected specific statements to follow from more general statements in an obvious way. If an individual claimed to be in favor of government intervention generally, we would expect him to be in favor of government-sponsored health care plans. If an individual expressed belief in a general principle of tolerance, we would expect her to be in favor of tolerance toward any specific group, such as homosexuals, Nazis, or communists. Likewise we expected ideas to be connected 'horizontally' on the basis of logic; those in favor of civil rights for one group should be in favor or civil rights for others; those in favor of one kind of government sponsored social welfare program should be in favor of others.

Much of the field has abandoned the idea that the cognitive practices, even of an informed public, are based on logic alone. Critiques of the early belief systems and ideology literature pointed out that there might be many different useful and economical ways for individuals to frame their political ideas and responses. Particular packages of ideas may appear logically connected only in the context of specific cultural or subcultural systems, or in specific settings. Further, politics and political values presumably can be complex enough that 'logic' becomes increasingly contingent and subtle. Favorable attitudes toward a range of government social programs may not imply being favorable toward any specific one, such as health programs, if people have cultural 'reasons' to believe that health is a special category of service that cannot be done expertly or to appropriate cultural standards if done by the government. Attachment to the general principle of tolerance would not generally imply tolerance of a group one 'has reason' to believe will threaten the very existence of democratic processes. Those who are generally 'liberal' on social and moral issues may be opposed to abortion either if they have learned through their religion that abortion is murder, or if they have 'reason' to fear genocide.

Note that the term 'reason' is flagged here to refer not to reason as abstract logic, but reason as experience-driven understanding of causes and consequences.[1] Thus, as suggested above, political reasoning must be shaped in part by history, experience, and cultural values. In the case of republican motherhood, for example, the continuing cultural definition of women as private domestic creatures combined with the increasing strength of democratic values led to a reformulation of both concepts that allowed these two norms to coexist 'logically'. In a culture with either no strong normative preference for specifically female private roles, or no dominant view of women's domestic roles and public participation being psychologically or morally inconsistent, or in a society that has created institutional arrangements making women's domestic roles and public participation easy to juggle or integrate, there is presumably no 'motivation' for formulating a theory of republican motherhood.

Cognitive practices of politics are not limited to the development of reasons and logics. Political psychologists are becoming increasingly aware of the important dynamics of identity and affect in the way people make sense of and react to the political world. It is clear that many political reactions, including those that can be discussed in coherent terms of reason, are based on comfort and discomfort, fear, anxiety, liking, disliking, and attachment. Because gender identity and relations are profoundly linked to a basic sense of self and sexuality, there must be a strong emotional as well as cognitive basis to the political significance of gender (Sapiro, 1993).

We return, then, to the point that, taken as an empirical question of culturally defined practices, 'democracy' can encompass many different views of women. Consider a small bit of data taken from the 1992 American National Election Study. Unfortunately that study contains no measures of attachment to democratic values, but we can define a population that, arguably, has at least a basic attachment to functioning democracy. One of the core conventional definitions of democracy has been the existence of (competitive)[2] elections. Let us take as an extremely crude measure of attachment to basic norms of democracy those who both identified with one or the other major party and who voted in 1992, a year with a relatively large election turnout. This is not to say that those with some attachment to the Democratic or Republican party are necessarily more democratic than those who call themselves Independents; this would be an absurd proposition. But we can be more sure that those who are both associated with one of these parties and who vote have some attachment to the institution of elections and, indeed, are relatively more likely to take a role in this process. This definition is, after all, intended to indicate a clear but minimal attachment to 'democracy' as it is conventionally defined in the United States.[3]

Among the questions asked of respondents to the 1992 National Election Study is this:

> People have different opinions about how much power and influence women have in society compared to men. Thinking about the way things really are in government, business, and industry today, do you think men have more power and influence than women, or that men and women have about equal power and influence, or that women have more power and influence than men?

The majority of the respondents we have defined as minimally democratic – 86 per cent – look around them and believe that men have more power, although a small proportion – 11 per cent – think that this country has reached a position of equality.

These citizens also share a consensus that they would prefer greater equality of power and influence in public life. They were asked:

> People disagree about how much power and influence they think women ought to have compared to men. Thinking about how you would like things to be in government, business, and industry, do you think men should have more power and influence, or that men and women should have about equal power and influence, or that women should have more power and influence?

A full 86 per cent thought that women and men should have equal power and influence in public life, while 13 per cent thought that men should have more. These figures show consensus, but certainly not anything close to unanimity. A minority of these participants in democratic culture believe that one half the population should have more power and influence in public life than the other half. Interpretation becomes more complicated, however, when we note that these figures do not tell us what respondents mean by 'equality'. Do they mean that women and men should play the same roles? Or, as with the significance of republican motherhood, do they think there can be great divisions of labor that still amount to equality?

A partial answer is available from the 1991 ANES Pilot Study. That survey asked members of the public for their definition of gender equality:

> Some people say that the only way for men and women to be equal in society is if they play the same kinds of roles in government, business, and the family. Others say that equality can exist even if men and women play very different kinds of roles. Which would you say …?

Here again we find broad consensus. Eighty-five per cent of the respondents believed that women and men can be equal while playing different roles; only about 15 per cent say that women and men must play the same roles in order for sexual equality to be attained. Moreover, whether the respondents actually *favored* gender equality was not correlated with whether they thought that equality required similarity or difference. And even more interesting, whether the respondents thought that women and men were currently equal in their amount of public power and influence was not correlated with their definition of equality. In other words, in this democracy, in which the vast majority of people say they are in favor of basic equality in public life, most of the same citizens believe that women and men can nevertheless play very different roles, including in politics and, indeed, supporting democratic values for both women and men within the same political system can be related to diverse definitions of equality and diverse perceptions of the current situation.

A better test of the varieties of constructions of democratic values is available through analysis of the 1988 Euro-Barometer 30 study, which explored the theme of Immigrants and Out-Groups in Western Europe through parallel nationally representative sample surveys of 12 European nations. Here, again, we have at least an indirect way of looking at alternative 'democratic' orientations toward women's integration into political life. This survey included some very useful measures of democratic attachments and attitudes. For a measure of attachment to democratic values, respondents were asked which of the following statements 'comes closest to your own way of thinking?': (1) 'Democracy is the best political system in all circumstances.' (2) 'In certain circumstances a dictatorship could be a good thing.' (3) 'Whether we live in a democracy or under a dictatorship makes no difference to people like me.' In the 12 European nations, the proportion who expressed unqualified support for democracy (i.e., those who said that democracy is always the best form of government) ranged from a low of about 65 per cent in Ireland to a high of 93 per cent in Denmark.[4]

Of course, as I have been arguing, simple expression of democratic values is not enough; we also need to know what people mean by 'democracy'. For example, the history of both political theory and state and party ideology and practice shows that some major approaches to democracy emphasize the maximizing the underlying value of 'liberty' or 'freedom', while others emphasize 'equality'. These different constructions are reflected in the responses of the mass publics to the Euro-Barometer surveys. Respondents were asked which of the following two statements 'comes closest to your own opinion?': (1) 'I find that both freedom and equality are important. But if I were to make up my mind for one or the other, I would consider personal freedom more important, that is everyone can live in freedom and develop without hindrance' or (2) 'Certainly both freedom and equality are important. But if I were to make up my mind for one of the two, I would consider equality more important, that is that nobody is underprivileged and that social class differences are not so strong.' In the aggregate, across all nations included in the survey, 50.3 per cent picked freedom, 43.0 per cent picked equality, and only 6.7 per cent claimed neither statement represented their views. This aggregate figure, however, masks considerable international variation, as we shall see shortly.

What is the relationship between people's relative valuation of freedom and equality and their attachment to democratic values. Table 9.1 shows the answer, country by country. Respondents were divided into two groups according to their responses to their attachment to democracy, defining those who expressed unqualified attachment to democracy as the 'democrats'. Table 9.1 shows the proportion of those 'democrats' and others in each nation participating in the survey who chose freedom over equality in their own priorities.[5] The nations are displayed in two columns: those with some historical experience of nondemocratic regimes (including the fascist regimes

TABLE 9.1
WHICH IS MORE IMPORTANT – FREEDOM OR EQUALITY?
(BY NATION AND DEMOCRATIC ATTACHMENT)

	% Naming Freedom			% Naming Freedom	
	Not Democrats	Democrats		Not Democrats	Democrats
Belgium	45.2	59.6	Germany	41.7	50.6
Denmark	80.0	72.8	Greece	67.3	69.1
France	36.5	51.7	Italy	38.2	39.4
Ireland	42.1	50.3	Portugal	43.4	51.9
Luxembourg	42.0	44.8	Spain	31.2	44.6
Netherlands	55.1	60.3			
UK	55.3	63.1			

Source: 1988 Euro-Barometer 30 study.
Note: Cell entries are percentages; *italics* indicates statistically significant differences
($p < .05$) across levels of democratic support within nation.

of Germany, Italy, Portugal, and Spain, the communist regime of East
Germany, and the military junta of Greece) and those with no such
domestically created experience.[6] Two conclusions stand out clearly. First,
the difference among nations is very large, even once we divide people
according to their attachment to democracy. Second, people who are more
attached to democracy are more likely to choose freedom than equality as
their fundamental value in most countries, although the differences are only
statistically significant in Belgium, France, Ireland, the UK, and Spain. In
any case, we find some considerable difference in the definition of
fundamental values among those who are strongly attached to democracy,
even within countries.

  Finally, let us return directly to the question of gender equality.
Unfortunately the 1988 Euro-Barometer contains almost no useful variables
tapping gender ideology. However, respondents were given a list of different
goals and asked to identify 'which are the great causes which nowadays are
worth the trouble of taking risks and making sacrifices for?'[7] One of those
causes was 'sex equality'. Thus it is at least possible to look at the degree to
which democrats and others in different European nations identify sex
equality as one of these worthy causes in comparison with others. Table 9.2
shows the proportion of democrats and others in each of eight countries who
identify sex equality, protecting wildlife, ending racism, defense of the
country, eliminating poverty, freedom, and human rights as great causes
worth sacrifice. That table also shows what proportion of the sample in each
country are categorized as 'democrats'.

  There is a fair amount of variation in the degree to which many of these

TABLE 9.2
WHICH ARE THE GREAT CAUSES? (BY NATION AND DEMOCRATIC ATTACHMENT)

	DENMARK		FRANCE		NETHERLANDS		UK	
	Not Democrats	Democrats	Not Democrats	Democrats	Not Democrats	Democrats	Not Democrats	Democrats
Sex Equality	18.6	23.1	24.1	22.5	25.2	26.8	21.5	23.3
Wildlife	55.7	59.9	52.4	57.1	49.0	54.6	37.2	44.7
Racism	28.6	30.6	27.4	44.8	32.2	37.4	24.9	29.6
Defense	27.1	21.4	37.3	29.2	3.5	7.9	30.2	41.0
Poverty	35.7	34.9	69.8	71.3	49.0	45.4	50.8	59.6
Freedom	31.4	44.7	30.7	43.9	24.5	33.7	32.6	42.1
Human Rights	61.4	59.4	44.8	72.4	49.7	53.9	44.3	55.3
% Democrats	92.9		78.5		85.6		74.9	

	ITALY		GERMANY		PORTUGAL		SPAIN	
	Not Democrats	Democrats	Not Democrats	Democrats	Not Democrats	Democrats	Not Democrats	Democrats
Sex Equality	15.0	19.8	18.7	35.5	25.3	33.7	17.5	25.6
Wildlife	56.9	57.6	56.1	78.4	51.3	58.2	33.0	46.6
Racism	37.2	46.5	21.1	34.5	34.2	42.9	27.8	38.2
Defense	27.4	23.4	23.4	27.5	44.9	50.4	44.9	50.4
Poverty	52.9	56.3	33.3	46.1	77.8	80.5	77.8	80.5
Freedom	34.7	36.0	19.9	39.1	36.1	45.5	36.1	45.5
Human Rights	59.5	64.8	45.6	65.1	47.5	60.3	47.5	60.3
% Democrats	74.0		83.6		84.2		78.4	

Source: 1988 Euro-Barometer 30 study.
Note: Cell entries are percentages; *italics* indicates statistically significant differences ($p < .05$) across levels of democratic support within nation.

causes are picked by democrats and others across the nations, and in the ranking they are assigned. The rank orders are displayed in Table 9.3. Nevertheless, there is a remarkable degree of consistency as well. Human rights ranks in the top two choices for democrats in all countries. Reducing poverty appears in the top three among democrats in all countries as does protecting wildlife in all but one country. In most countries the rank ordering of great causes is not very different when we compare democrats with others. In two countries (the UK and Italy) the ordering does not change at all and in four others (Denmark, the Netherlands, Portugal, and Spain) no item moves more than one place up or down in ranking. But the relative consistency in ranking does not mean that democrats and others value these different causes in the same way. For example, a significantly larger proportion of democrats than non-democrats identify freedom as a great cause in all countries but Italy. Everywhere but Italy and the Netherlands democrats identify human rights as a great cause more than others do. Racism is more often identified by democrats than others everywhere but Denmark, the Netherlands, and the UK.

Sex equality does not rate very highly among causes. It is the last ranked cause for the French, British, Italians, Portuguese, and Spanish regardless of whether they identified themselves as democrats or not. In addition it is the last ranked cause among Danes and Germans who did not express unqualified attachment to democracy. At the same time, it should be noted that there are indeed substantial minorities within these European nations who identify sexual equality as a great cause, ranging from 15 per cent of the Italian non-democrats to almost 36 per cent of German democrats. On the whole, however, attachment to democracy was not substantially related to whether people identified sex equality as a goal worth sacrifice. Only in Germany, Spain and Portugal were these two attitudes significantly related, by far most impressively in Germany.

Asking whether the cause of sex equality is a 'great cause worth the trouble of taking risks and making sacrifices for' is probably far from the best measure of incorporation of gender into politics one could imagine. But in one sense, it is an excellent measure for the purposes of thinking about how transforming societies might construct their conceptions of democracy. As many nations are finding now, and as many have found before, constructing democratic regimes and democratic political cultures is a costly venture, and entails thinking carefully about costs and sacrifices along the way. As most cultures are currently constructed, including those most universally currently identified as democratic, gender equality is considered a 'great cause' by a relatively small proportion of people, and this does not tend to be a value on which conceptions of democracy commonly hinge.

TABLE 9.3

WHICH ARE THE GREAT CAUSES? (IN RANK ORDER BY NATION AND DEMOCRATIC VALUE)

DEMARK		FRANCE		NETHERLANDS		UK	
Not Democrats	*Democrats*	*Not Democrats*	*Democrats*	*Not Democrats*	*Democrats*	*Not Democrats*	*Democrats*
Human Rights	Wildlife	Poverty	Human Rights	Human Rights	Wildlife	Poverty	Poverty
Wildlife	Human Rights	Wildlife	Poverty	Wildlife*	Human Rights	Human Rights	Human Rights
Poverty	Freedom	Human Rights	Wildlife	Poverty*	Poverty	Wildlife	Wildlife
Freedom	Poverty	Defense	Racism	Racism	Racism	Freedom	Freedom
Racism	Racism	Freedom	Freedom	**Sex Equality**	Freedom	Defense	Defense
Defense	**Sex Equality**	Racism	Defense	Freedom	**Sex Equality**	Racism	Racism
Sex Equality	Defense	**Sex Equality**	**Sex Equality**	Defense	Defense	**Sex Equality**	**Sex Equality**

ITALY		GERMANY		PORTUGAL		SPAIN	
Not Democrats	*Democrats*	*Not Democrats*	*Democrats*	*Not Democrats*	*Democrats*	*Not Democrats*	*Democrats*
Human Rights	Human Rights	Wildlife	Wildlife	Poverty	Poverty	Poverty	Poverty
Wildlife	Wildlife	Human Rights	Human Rights	Wildlife	Human Rights	Human Rights	Human Rights
Poverty	Poverty	Poverty	Poverty	Human Rights	Wildlife	Defense	Defense
Racism	Racism	Defense	Freedom	Defense	Defense	Freedom	Wildlife
Freedom	Freedom	Racism	**Sex Equality**	Freedom	Freedom	Wildlife	Freedom
Defense	Defense	Freedom	Racism	Racism	Racism	Racism	Racism
Sex Equality	**Sex Equality**	**Sex Equality**	Defense	**Sex Equality**	**Sex Equality**	**Sex Equality**	**Sex Equality**

Note: * These two are ranked equally.

EDUCATING FOR INCLUSIVE DEMOCRACY

Social movements are not just agents of mobilization and conduits of pressure on political leaders; they are also agents of socialization and education (Sapiro, 1990). Most literature about social movements analyzes how they are formed in the first place, how they mobilize their constituents, and what are their means of influencing élites, usually regarding the institution of specific laws or policies. But much of what social movements also do is to promulgate and instill new or – probably more often – reformulated cultural and social values in key sectors of society that may lead to an acceptance of new laws and policies.

In relatively stable political systems, leaders and public alike act as though the fundamental definitions of democracy are not at issue. Thus the most rhetorically successful arguments social movements can offer is that their proposals, if enacted, will simply make laws and policy more consistent with well-accepted democratic values. Participants in these political cultures have reached broad consensus that they understand 'what goes with what' in terms of the logical connections within belief systems and ideology even if systematic empirical examination reveals considerably more variation in the 'cognitive practices' of these democracies. When feminists in these countries heard Russian feminists say 'Democracy minus women is not democracy', they heard it as one might hear a school teacher guiding us through our lessons, reminding us to clean up the grammatical errors that had crept into our writing despite our knowledge of the rules. We know the rules of 'agreement' within political grammar even if we don't always follow those rules.

In the case of the many societies currently undergoing dramatic transformations, the very definition of democracy itself is at the center of debate. Indeed, many Western social scientists, jurists, and others who have traveled to offer their expertise and assistance to those nations engaged in this self-transformation have often returned home profoundly disillusioned when they find that some of the major problems involve not just the practicalities of getting from authoritarianism to democracy, but the theoretical and cultural difficulties of arriving at a conception of democracy. In those contexts, when feminists declare that 'Democracy minus women is not democracy', they are trying to create or reformulate a political grammar, making a claim about 'what goes with what'. Certainly, leading traditions of democratic thinking have increasingly moved away from 'separate spheres' or gender-differentiated definitions of democracy. Relatively few democratic theorists in the older democracies would make a serious case that democracy minus women is democracy. But even in those countries, disagreements over some aspects of citizenship continue.

NOTES

I am grateful to the Graduate School of the University of Wisconsin-Madison for financial support for this project. My thanks also goes to Paul Martin for his assistance in this work and to Graham Wilson for his valuable comments and suggestions.

1. For a discussion of the different meanings of 'reason' that has important bearing both on political psychology and the philosophy of social science, see Toulmin (1970).
2. I indicate a hesitation about 'competitive' elections because, for example, neither Mexico nor Japan might fall into the category of 'democracies' throughout most of the last 50 years.
3. The total number of respondents who satisfy this criterion is 1,085.
4. The sample used here includes a total of 11,791 respondents.
5. The small proportion of respondents who said neither statement reflected their views were left out of this analysis. The category 'freedom' (rather than 'equality') was picked for display because in almost all countries 'freedom' is chosen more by 'democrats', even if the results are not always statistically significant.
6. One might further distinguish between the countries that had authoritarian regimes imposed on them through foreign invasion, including Benelux, Denmark, and France compared with the nations that were not occupied: the United Kingdom and Ireland.
7. Respondents were allowed to choose as many as they wanted.

REFERENCES

Converse, P.E. (1964). 'The nature of belief systems in mass publics', in David Apter (ed.), *Ideology and discontent*. New York: Free Press.

Einhorn, B. (1993). *Cinderella goes to market: Citizenship, gender, and women's movements in East Central Europe*. New York: Verso.

Evans, S.R. (1989). *Born for liberty: A history of women in America*. New York: Free Press.

Kerber, L.K. (1986). *Women of the Republic: Intellect and ideology in revolutionary America*. New York: Norton.

Landes, J.B. (1988). *Women and the public sphere in the age of the French Revolution*. Ithaca, NY: Cornell.

Pateman, C. (1988). *The sexual contract*. Stanford, CA: Stanford University Press.

Phillips, A. (1991). *Engendering democracy*. University Park, PA: Pennsylvania State University.

Phillips, A. (1993). *Democracy and difference*. University Park, PA: Pennsylvania State University.

Sapiro, V. (1990). 'The women's movement and the creation of gender consciousness: Social movements as social agents', in Orit Ichilov (ed.), *Political socialization, citizenship education, and democracy* (pp.266–80). New York: Teachers College Press.

Sapiro, V. (1993). 'The political uses of symbolic women: An essay in honor of Murray Edelman', *Political Communication*, 10 (April–June), 137–49.

Toulmin, S. (1970). 'Reasons and causes', in Robert Borger and Frank Cioffi (eds), *Explanation in the behavioural sciences* (pp.1–48). Cambridge: Cambridge University Press.

10

APOLITICAL PATRIOTISM AND CITIZENSHIP EDUCATION: THE CASE OF NEW ZEALAND

MATTHEW S. HIRSHBERG

New Zealand is a quiet, peaceful country, not a land of drastic changes. Conquered and settled by British colonialists in the nineteenth century, New Zealand gradually drifted into a separate identity during this century. The schools, which once were given the task of training loyal British subjects, have since tended to promote progressive, internationalist conceptions of New Zealand and world citizenship. In keeping with New Zealand's largely apolitical self-image, politics tend not to be emphasized in the schools. This may change, as significant reductions to the welfare state, combined with the introduction of proportional representation, promise to produce a more independent, politically active citizenry.

THE FADING IMPERIALIST SHADOW

New Zealand never broke away from its colonial roots; it has slowly drifted into a separate identity. New Zealand's foundation as an autonomous nation-state was so gradual and devoid of overt conflict with the British that it is difficult to refer to it as an experience. As a result, New Zealand nationalism is not based, as it is in many other countries, on an initial fight to exist. New Zealanders were never politicized by revolution. Instead, as the imperial aspects of New Zealand nationalism receded, a relatively apolitical patriotism developed.

New Zealand was 'discovered' in 1642 by Abel Tasman and again in 1769 by James Cook, but it was not until the 1840 Treaty of Waitangi that the British Empire assumed sovereignty over the islands. From the 1850s onward, New Zealand was a loyal, self-governing British colony. Free, compulsory and secular primary school education was mandated in the

Education Bill of 1877, male suffrage was introduced in 1879, and women were allowed to vote in 1893. Most New Zealanders were faithfully allegiant to the British Crown, and there was no significant movement or desire for independence (Gibbons, 1981).

The colonial period ended in 1907, when New Zealand was declared a Dominion. Still, writes Gibbons (1981), when Great Britain entered the First World War in 1914, 'There was no separate declaration of war, no debate in or out of Parliament ... New Zealand was placed at the disposal of the British authorities almost as if it were a part of the British Isles' (pp.312–13). William Massey, New Zealand Premier from 1912 to 1925, had opposed Dominion status in 1907, and viewed New Zealand as a loyal and very junior 'partner' in the British Empire. While salient war experiences such as Gallipoli laid foundations for a proud national 'Kiwi' consciousness, most New Zealanders remained patriotically attached to the Empire after the war (Sinclair, 1980, pp.245–7).

During the inter-war period, New Zealanders continued to refer to Great Britain as 'home' (Sinclair, 1986), and New Zealand remained economically dependent on the 'Mother Country'. While pressure from South Africa, Ireland and Canada elicited the Statute of Westminster, which in 1931 granted independence to the Dominions, New Zealand did not pass the Statute until 1947 (McKinnon, 1993).

New Zealand foreign policy became less dependent on the Empire with the election of the first Labour government in 1935. In 1939, New Zealand was the first Dominion independently to declare war on Germany (Lipson, 1948). By about this time, according to Sinclair (1980), 'most people born in New Zealand would, without hesitation, have said that they were New Zealanders' (p.329).

In 1940, the British let it be known that they would be unable to help New Zealand protect itself from possible Japanese attack. During the war, closer relations were formed with a new protector, the United States. The US continued in this role in the subsequent cold war era, and in 1951 a mutual security treaty (ANZUS) was signed by New Zealand, Australia and the United States. This event was particularly significant in its exclusion of Great Britain: New Zealand was clearly charting an independent foreign policy under American influence.

Still, a deep imperial connection to Britain survived in New Zealand hearts, minds and institutions. In the 1950s, for example, a British admiral ran New Zealand's navy, the Queen received an enthusiastic reception on her visit to New Zealand, and Prime Minister Holland repeatedly proclaimed, 'where Britain goes we go'. The Commonwealth remained central to New Zealand's self-perceived role in the political world (McKinnon, 1993, pp.112–14).

In fact, both Britain's and New Zealand's political and economic roles in world affairs were changing. The United Kingdom receded in power and importance under American hegemony, and became increasingly tied to Europe. New Zealand became, primarily, a small state in the Pacific, increasingly tied to the United States and the new world economic order. Trade was diversified after the Second World War, and Britain's share of New Zealand's exports steadily decreased from about 80 per cent immediately prior to the war (Sinclair, 1980, p.314) to 35 per cent in 1970. When Britain joined the EEC in 1972, then, New Zealand was not entirely unprepared. By 1980, only 14 per cent of New Zealand's exports were destined for Britain, and similar quantities went to the United States, Australia and Japan (McKinnon, 1993, p.220). With Britain, the retired great power, now submerged in the European Community, New Zealand finally came of age as an independent nation.

Thus New Zealand's separation from Britain was a slow, peaceful process. In fact, lingering British allegiance stunted the growth of full-fledged New Zealand nationalism. For example, indigenous national symbols have been slow to take over for symbols of the British Empire. In a 1973 study, many 13-year-old New Zealanders were confused about whether New Zealand's national anthem was 'God Save the Queen' or 'God Defend New Zealand' (Tower, 1978). Today New Zealand remains in the British Commonwealth, the Queen of England continues to adorn New Zealand money (although she has been banished from some denominations), and New Zealanders are of predominantly British stock. Because the Union Jack, the symbol of Empire, continues to dominate the New Zealand flag, the flag cannot function as the central icon of an independent nation. Aside from the flag, the closest things New Zealand has to established national icons are the silver fern worn on the chests of the national rugby team, and side-on likenesses of that shy, flightless and almost extinct national bird, the kiwi. Neither icon can approach the nationalistic potency of the Stars and Stripes, which hold deep meaning for even the most cynical American.

Had New Zealand's exit from British domination been a sudden, salient, or conflict-ridden one, imperialist indoctrination might have been replaced by a conscious educational effort to turn British subjects into loyal New Zealand patriots. As it is, 'Kiwi' patriotism is generally not pushed in the schools, and New Zealanders tend to reach adulthood remarkably free from the sorts of patriotic chauvinisms that characterize many countries. New Zealanders are patriotic in that they are proud of and loyal to their country, but that pride and loyalty is connected to landscape, lifestyle and exploits on the rugby field, more than political history, ideological chauvinism, or exploits in war.

Another result of New Zealand's gradual weaning away from imperialist domination has been a relatively apolitical national self-image. The basic attributes of New Zealand's self-image developed under the political shadow of the Empire. As imperialism faded, the national self-image was left without a salient political component. Thus, while the American national self-image, for example, is deeply rooted in politics and ideology, the New Zealand national self-image is based on lifestyle and geography. When New Zealanders think of their country, they think of small, isolated islands covered with mountains and green pastures full of sheep. Fundamentally, New Zealanders view their country as home – a warm, secure, relaxed place with family life at its center. While Americans view themselves as citizens of a political entity, New Zealanders see themselves as citizens of a place they call home (Hirshberg, 1994).

RECENT POLITICAL DEVELOPMENTS

The loss of British markets, combined with worldwide economic woes, seriously hampered the New Zealand economy's ability to sustain costly social entitlements which had come to define state–citizen relations. New Zealand's once impressive welfare state, in which each citizen could expect to be taken care of 'from cradle to grave', was built on economic success and an egalitarian ethic. The cradle-to-grave welfare state encouraged a paternalistic social compact: the state promised to look after the citizen when in need, while the citizen would leave the worries of governance to duly elected officials and their agents. Most New Zealanders came to combine an optimistic complacency with a healthy sense of entitlement.

Political participation, under such benign conditions, consisted of dutifully voting once every three years. Aside from voting, citizens were expected to obey the law and behave nicely, and they could expect their government to reward them with the necessities for secure, comfortable lives. This relaxed arrangement, with its de-emphasis of politics in everyday life, fits nicely with New Zealand's apolitical national identity. Active citizenship, in this context, tended to be directed toward social interaction rather than political participation. Citizen unrest was the exception rather than the rule.

This happy, if paternalistic state–citizenship relationship has been shaken by the economic woes that have plagued New Zealand over the last couple of decades. Economic necessity and more business-oriented policy making led to extensive cutbacks in social entitlement programs. Over the last decade governments from both major parties have pursued policies that have resulted in significant reductions in many health, education and welfare services and benefits. From the point of view of many citizens, the welfare reforms have constituted a betrayal by the state, a breaking of the social compact. This reaction was particularly evident in the early years of the reforms, when they were introduced by a Labour government. It has become evident that the state can no longer be relied upon to provide generously for citizen needs. In the new New Zealand, citizens will have to fight for policies which will benefit them.

The public response to the unpopular pillaging of the welfare state was to vote the offenders out of office. This proved ineffective, as both Labour and National governments pursued policies which reduced social entitlements. Protests by adversely affected interest groups also had little effect.

Shaken from their complacency, many New Zealanders saw, for the first time, an electoral system which was proving unresponsive to popular sentiments. In recent times, New Zealanders have elected 99 members to a single parliament through single-member district representation. Such systems tend to reduce electoral politics to a struggle between a small number of large political parties. Because smaller parties tend to be unable to win entire districts, voters tend to avoid 'wasting' their votes on them, and such parties rarely survive very long. Two-party systems often result, and, because the 'left' and 'right' fight over crucial votes in the middle, party stances often converge. This has certainly been the case on the New Zealand political scene, where it has become difficult to distinguish between the policies of the two major parties, Labour and National.

The two parties' tag-team assault on the welfare state highlighted the need for electoral reform, as the electoral process was proving unresponsive to public sentiments. An electoral system which would allow alternative parties representation in proportion to their public support would consequently allow voters to express effectively their dissatisfaction with the two major parties. Proportional representation was, of course, very much against the common interest of the two major parties, yet they nonetheless stumbled into allowing the electorate the opportunity to change the system.

New Zealand's electoral system was changed as a result of two successive referenda. In the first referendum, which took place in September 1992, voters were asked whether or not they wanted the electoral system changed, and were instructed to express a preference for one of four possible alternative systems. Referendum results showed a clear preference (85 per cent) for change, and the German-style 'Mixed Member Proportional' (MMP) system was preferred by 70 per cent of the voters.

MMP combines district with proportional representation. Voters choose both a candidate to represent their district and a preferred party. In the New Zealand version, half of the 120 members of Parliament will represent individual districts, and the rest will be taken from party lists so that party strengths in Parliament will be proportional to the party preferences of the overall electorate. The second referendum, which accompanied the November 1993 general election, consisted of a head-to-head contest between the *status quo*, 'First Past the Post' (FPP) system and the challenger, MMP. Business interests, concerned with maintaining a *status quo* in which they had a great deal invested, led a well-financed media campaign against change. In the end, the proposal for change was passed by the narrowest of margins, and New Zealand is now preparing to change the way it elects its parliament.

In asking the New Zealand electorate to choose their own electoral system, the government was putting an important decision in the hands of a public ill equipped to pass judgement. New Zealanders, most of whom had only a vague sense of how the old system worked, were being asked to choose between it and something new and entirely unknown. This required them to learn what the *status quo* consisted of, comprehend the alternatives, and have some sense of the relevant advantages and disadvantages of the various systems.

As it turned out, the referenda proved to be educational experiences in themselves. The government and other organizations distributed descriptions of the alternative systems which also attempted to explain the relative advantages of each. The electoral system became a subject for public discourse and debate, and while the average New Zealander did not develop a deep understanding of electoral systems and their relative merits, they at least gained a passing familiarity. Regardless of their outcomes, then, repeated referenda requiring public participation served an important socialization function, in that they increased public knowledge of and interest in the electoral process.

In addition, the changes in the electoral system serve the system maintenance function of effectively channelling discontent. The maintenance of a healthy, stable political system in the face of public frustration and discontent requires adjustments that increase the available avenues for positive public impact on policy making. If, under such conditions, the political system is unable to provide legitimate, conventional outlets for this increased citizen energy, that energy will manifest itself in social strife and disillusioned withdrawal.

It is likely that the new electoral system will provide exactly the sort of change necessary to absorb the increased citizen energy in a positive way. Even before the election reform was passed, alternative, pro-welfare parties amassed substantial public support. Under the new system, such parties will be strengthened and may well become important forces in Parliament. From a systemic point of view, the important point is that increased citizen participation will be channelled primarily into an expanded electoral system, rather than protest.

EMPIRE AND THE MEANING OF CITIZENSHIP

New Zealand's historically close connection to the British Empire played a crucial role in the development of citizenship and citizenship education. Rather than breaking forcefully away from its colonial roots as the United States did, New Zealand gradually drifted into a separate identity. During New Zealand's metamorphosis into a separate nation, citizenship took on ambiguous and shifting meanings.

Early in this century, New Zealanders tended to consider themselves British subjects. Citizenship education was intended to produce loyal, patriotic subjects of the Crown, and New Zealand's Education Department was dedicated to that purpose. The educational system, according to Olssen (1981), 'was designed to produce not only economically useful skills ... but also sound morals and loyalty to the British Empire. Education was seen as a method of socializing the young in order to produce good, productive, and efficient citizens' (p.270). In 1914, the use of the strongly imperialistic School Journal was made compulsory in public schools. Weekly worship of the Union Jack, usually accompanied by the singing of 'God Save the King', was made compulsory in 1921 (Sinclair, 1986, pp.232–4). In that same year, T. B. Strong (1921), Chief Inspector of Primary Schools, wrote, 'What higher aim can schools have than to implant in the minds of boys and girls those principles that will lead them to become worthy citizens of a great Empire!'

While its school children were learning political allegiance to the Crown, New Zealand was developing its own separate culture and social identity. As the New Zealand national identity developed, imperialist notions of citizenship became less influential in the schools. Imperial loyalty became decreasingly relevant to the New Zealand experience, and imperialist citizenship education gradually made room for the liberal internationalism which has continued to predominate since. As Archer and Openshaw (1992) argue, children began to be taught such progressive values as 'human brotherhood, international understanding, respect for other cultures', along with good old-fashioned 'obedience, loyalty and duty' (p.22). Openshaw (1992) succinctly describes these developments:

> The particular notions of citizenship favoured (in schools) are largely dependent on whichever group of educators is dominant at a particular time. In turn, the maintenance of such dominance is ultimately linked to wider social, economic and political factors. During the interwar period, for instance, history served as a forum for imperial-patriotic views, but by 1929 these views were being challenged by growing internationalist sentiment. Such views became more predominant with the gradual rise of left-liberal educators to positions of responsibility in the education system after the election of Labour in 1935. When social studies displaced history in the primary schools and in the lower secondary schools, it largely assumed the responsibility for citizenship transmission. (p.9)

According to Openshaw, social studies have been primarily a post-Second World War phenomenon in New Zealand (p.7). Shermis (1992) argues that, as in the United States, social studies developed in New Zealand 'as a means of training future citizens in a self-governing society' (p.101). While relatively progressive conceptions of citizenship now guide educators, they continue, claims Shermis, to 'indoctrinate students in the ways of a culture that no longer exists in the hope of creating a culture that has been only dimly glimpsed' (p.102).

Although Shermis draws some interesting parallels between New Zealand and the United States, he does this by de-emphasizing two crucial differences. First, citizenship education is strongly emphasized in American schools – it is far less salient and persistent in New Zealand. Because the New Zealand Ministry of Education, school administrators, and teachers put relatively little emphasis on political socialization, New Zealand students receive far less political indoctrination than their American counterparts. Among other effects, this makes teaching university-level political science a very different task in the two countries. In America it can be a difficult undertaking, as many students are quick to reject ideas that conflict with the cozy political truths they learned, among other places, in school. Because New Zealand school children are not bombarded with ideological orthodoxies to the extent that American children are, those who make it to the university level are remarkably open to a variety of perspectives on politics. The political science lecturer in New Zealand need spend little time de-indoctrinating, and can concentrate of the positive tasks of teaching about politics.

Second, conceptions of citizenship and nationhood are vastly different in the two countries. While American children learn to be proud observers of and participants in what they are taught is the greatest political entity ever to grace Planet Earth, New Zealand students are taught how to be worthy members of both their own society and the world community. While Americans view their nation as an ideologically sanctified political entity, New Zealanders view their country as a wonderful pair of islands they call home. As argued above, the relatively apolitical nature of New Zealand patriotism is a result, at least in part, of the gradual waning of imperialist influence.

Dimensions of Ichilov's (1990) structural model of citizenship roles shed light on the New Zealand case. While early citizenship education in New Zealand promoted a particularistic, nationalistic notion of the British subject, this was replaced by transnational universalism: school children are now taught that they are citizens, not just of New Zealand, but of a world consisting of a plurality of nations, values, and social structures. Because New Zealand notions of nationhood are more social than political, conceptions of citizenship tend to be diffuse and oriented toward social domains. 'Good citizenship' is practiced in daily interpersonal relations, obedience to laws and norms, concern and respect for the natural environment, and so on.

Political participation at the national level has tended to be passive and conventional: New Zealanders have expressed their consent to be governed once every three years through the ballot box, but otherwise they have tended to watch passively or even ignore public policy-making. Over the last decade, however, as successive governments from both major parties have proceeded to withdraw social benefits, dissent has been ineffectively expressed through voting. As was argued above, the shrinking welfare state, combined with a new, more responsive electoral system, may well result in a more active, involved citizenry.

CITIZENSHIP EDUCATION IN PRACTICE

Civics, *per se*, are not a prescribed area of study in New Zealand schools. There are no governmental programs or policies directly intended to teach children how a New Zealand citizen is supposed to think and act, and few schools give this task special attention. Instead, citizenship education is seen as one of the functions of the social studies curriculum, and the prescribed social studies syllabi (New Zealand Department of Education, 1962, 1978) suggest some relevant subject matter. Although these governmentally prescribed syllabi constitute the general social studies curriculum framework under which most schools have operated, reliance here on official documents would give only an idealized approximation of what actually gets taught. In order to obtain a more accurate picture, written inquiries were made to all of New Zealand's approximately 400 secondary schools and about 200 primary schools. Replies were received from principals and department heads representing about 200 schools, two-thirds of which were secondary schools.

To avoid leading respondents, the letter of inquiry was general and open-ended: it asked about any policies and practices related to citizenship education or political studies, and about educational responses to recent political changes in New Zealand. Responses ranged from a couple of sentences to several pages (plus documentation) in length. No rigorous quantitative analysis was conducted. Instead, all responses were read at least twice, and common responses and tendencies were noted.

Overall, schools in New Zealand lack specific policies or curricula for teaching about civics or political issues. Citizenship education occurs, to a greater or lesser extent, at all levels, depending on teacher inclinations, syllabi for related subjects, and current political events.

At the primary school level, citizenship education occurs incidentally in the pursuit of other educational goals. Current events lessons, which are part of the standard social studies syllabus, provide the most frequent forum for citizenship education. Such education is relatively haphazard, as its content is highly dependent upon the salient events of the day, that is, the news agenda. Within this context, children learn about electoral politics at least once every three years – when general elections are held. It is then that students tend to learn about elections, political parties, the Parliament, the cabinet, and other basic political realities. Teachers make use of educational material supplied by newspapers and government agencies, and often stage mock elections.

Outside of current events, citizenship education at the primary level is very variable. In some schools it is given further attention in social studies lessons, while others teach citizen roles, rights and responsibilities in such lessons as 'Life Skills' and 'Health'. A few of the principals who responded expressed frustrated concern about the lack of citizenship education in their schools. 'In general', wrote one, 'we follow the Social Studies syllabus and available curriculum and find that there is not a specific amount of time set for the teaching of political issues. One of the greatest difficulties would be in finding the time to introduce new topics such as these.' Another complained, 'As a primary school teacher with eighteen years' experience, I consider this area, namely civics, including local and central government, to be an area very poorly served in the education area in both official recognition and available resources ... At present the only reference in primary schools to civics and political issues are made if individual teachers show such an interest and bring it to children's notice.'

New Zealand school children tend to receive their largest doses of citizenship education at the intermediate level (Forms 3 and 4), when they tend to be between the ages of 13 and 15. This is because the social studies syllabus (New Zealand Department of Education, 1978; New Zealand Ministry of Education, 1991) suggests that relevant material be covered in those years (particularly in Form 3), and schools tend to implement these governmental guidelines in compulsory social studies lessons. The syllabus prescribes 'social control' as the central theme for Form 3 and suggests a unit on 'how systems of government operate in various societies today and in the past'. The teachers' handbook (New Zealand Ministry of Education, 1991, p.15) suggests that focus be placed on such questions as 'What is government? What were some systems of government in past times? How does a parliamentary system work? What systems of government operate in some socialist states? What impact have some systems of government had on people's lives?' Although schools are not required to duplicate syllabus guidelines in the classroom, many follow them quite closely, and most include a unit on government at this level. Such units tend to last up to about six weeks and concentrate on the New Zealand political system in a comparative context.

The Form 3 syllabus also proposes 'a study of social controls, such as beliefs and customs, and laws and rules that operate in societies'. The handbook suggests that teachers examine the beliefs, customs, laws and rules that structure and control their students' lives and compare them with those of other cultures. Another suggested topic consists of the processes by which laws are made and the manner in which offenders are dealt with in New Zealand (p. 16). In practice, this sort of material tends to be covered, in various altered forms, in many of the schools. The overall result is that most Form 3 students at least learn something about how their political and legal systems operate, what functions they serve, how New Zealand compares with some other societies, and what their political and legal rights and responsibilities as New Zealand citizens are.

Although citizenship education tends to reach its peak in Form 3, it continues into Form 4, as the focus shifts to social change. At this stage, for instance, many schools do units on the nature of and struggle for human rights. Units on the 1840 Treaty of Waitangi, the foundation agreement between native Maoris and British settlers, are also common. Such subjects (both of which are suggested in the syllabus) enhance students' understanding of citizen rights and political participation. Current events continue to play an important role in citizenship education in Forms 3 and 4. Teachers often make use of Newspapers in Education (NIE), a program sponsored by a number of local papers. The newspapers regularly distribute current events material to the schools, and NIE produce kits to help teachers cover general elections. NIE's central purpose is to protect the long-term interests of the newspaper industry in the video age by getting children into the habit of staying informed by reading newspapers. To this ultimately commercial end, they produce educational material which many teachers put to good use, particularly, though certainly not exclusively, at the intermediate level.

Thus the recent referenda on the electoral system was educational, not just for voters, but for students as well. The referenda and the alternative electoral systems were discussed during current events lessons and special election units, and teachers took advantage of relevant material provided by the government and NIE. These subjects also made their way into lessons on New Zealand government, usually in Form 3.

Now that MMP has been accepted as the new electoral system, it will have to be integrated into those sorts of lessons in an ongoing way. This will not be a problem in the long run, but transition will take time. One teacher explained:

> The text book that we have deals with the old system, and until we get something concrete on MMP and not just the theoretical it will be difficult for Third Formers to understand what is involved (I think most voters don't have too much idea either). We, therefore, are focusing on the aspects that will be relatively unchanged – the role of the governor general, what is physically involved in voting, how bills become laws … Teaching government is not easy to most students. They don't really care about how we govern ourselves and take their vote for granted …

There is a sense of resignation that they can do nothing to bring about change so why bother. I don't think it has always been like this and I can think back to really stimulating class 'election campaigns' run in conjunction with past general elections. Maybe MMP will increase involvement in the future.

At the senior high school level (Forms 5–7, ages 15–18), social studies tend to make way for history, and schools vary a great deal with regard to civics-related course material. Some schools, for example, offer history courses on social welfare in Form 5, and legal studies often appear in Form 6. While these and other courses teach citizenship lessons, most students, if their schools offer them the opportunity, will decline to take them. Students at this level have many options to choose from, including leaving school. There is tremendous variation, then, not just in the amount and type of citizenship education offered at the senior level, but also in the extent to which a given student will be exposed to relevant material. History students at schools with politically oriented history programs may learn a great deal, but citizenship education in the classroom all but ends for most students by the time they reach Form 5. As one teacher explained:

In Form 3, the teachers' handbook for Social Studies encourages teachers to cover the material in question ... and in Form 4, it does the same ... but difficulties sometimes arise over students' 'readiness' to learn such matters at that age.

In the senior school, when increased 'maturity' generally creates greater interest in 'Civics', the pressures of academic subjects and external examinations frequently make it difficult to ensure that all students have the opportunity to undertake citizenship studies. Furthermore, some schools and individual teachers may make a point of avoiding politics in case they are accused either of taking a political stance or of avoiding social action. Consequently, for many students, their knowledge of their 'rights and responsibilities' within the country's political framework is, at best, uneven.

Still, citizenship education in the schools is not limited to lessons in the classroom – it also has its active component. Not only do mock elections often occur around election time, but efforts are also made in many of the schools to teach democratic political participation through student elections, councils, committees, representation on boards, and the like. As one teacher put it:

School policy regarding students in school decision making is an inclusive policy. We run house councils and a school council, all democratically elected ... We (staff) see the value in house/school councils (and their various sub-committees) not so much in the various recommendations they make (usually petty) but rather in the training and example it provides in the democratic process.

At other, more traditionally run schools, student involvement in authoritarian power structures no doubt teaches lessons about power politics in non-democratic settings (such as the business world they are being trained to enter). Students also attend occasional assemblies during which outside speakers (such as politicians) teach political lessons. These sorts of extra-curricular citizenship training are particularly important at the more senior levels, where participation tends to be the greatest.

CONCLUSION

When New Zealand crept out of the imperial shadow, it emerged as a democratic welfare state on stunning, secluded South Seas islands. New Zealanders developed a relatively apolitical sense of nationhood, and while they have dutifully exercised their voting rights, they have generally left the job of governing to the state. Citizenship education has not been a major governmental or pedagogical concern in modern times, although it has been evident in social studies and current events tuition. In the last decade, however, economic scarcity and stingy public policy have sown the seeds of discontent that have helped New Zealand down the road toward a more active, demanding citizenry. As New Zealand approaches the twenty-first century, knowledge of political issues, electoral processes and possibilities for participation will be increasingly relevant to New Zealanders. It will be interesting to observe how the new social studies syllabus, to be released presently, will interact with these new political realities. In any case, increased attention to citizenship education is likely to play an important part in these developments.

REFERENCES

Archer, E. and Openshaw, R. (1992). 'Citizenship and identity as "official" goals in social studies', in R. Openshaw (ed.), *New Zealand social studies: Past, present and future* (pp.19–33). Palmerston North: The Dunmore Press.

Gibbons, P. (1981). 'The climate of opinion', in W. Oliver (ed.), *The Oxford history of New Zealand* (pp.302–30). Wellington: Oxford University Press.

Hirshberg, M. (1994). 'Land, lifestyle, and the New Zealand national self-image', paper presented at the New Zealand Studies Section of the Annual Meeting of the Western Social Science Association, Albuquerque, New Mexico.

Ichilov, O. (1990). 'Dimensions and role patterns of citizenship in democracy', in O. Ichilov (ed.), *Political socialization, citizenship education, and democracy* (pp.11–25). New York: Teachers College Press.

Lipson, L. (1948). *The politics of equality: New Zealand's adventures in democracy.* Chicago, IL: University of Chicago Press.

McKinnon, M. (1993). *Independence and foreign policy: New Zealand in the world since 1935.* Auckland: Auckland University Press.

New Zealand Department of Education (1962). *Suggestions for teaching social studies in the primary school.* Wellington: Government Printer.

New Zealand Department of Education (1978). *Social studies syllabus guidelines, Forms 1–4.* Wellington: Government Printer.

New Zealand Ministry of Education (1991). *Social studies forms 3–4, A handbook for teachers.* Wellington: Learning Media.

Olssen, E. (1981). 'Towards a new society', in W. Oliver (ed.), *The Oxford history of New Zealand* (pp.250–78). Wellington: Oxford University Press.

Openshaw, R. (ed.) (1992). *New Zealand social studies: Past, present and future.* Palmerston North: The Dunmore Press.

Shermis, S.S. (1992). 'Social studies in New Zealand and the United States: A cross-cultural comparison', in R. Openshaw (ed.), *New Zealand social studies: Past, present and future* (pp.89–106). Palmerston North: The Dunmore Press.

Sinclair, K. (1980). *A history of New Zealand.* London: Allen Lane.

Sinclair, K. (1986). *A destiny apart: New Zealand's search for national identity.* Wellington: Allen and Unwin.

Strong, T.B. (1921). 'The inculcation of patriotism', *Education Gazette*, 1 November.

Tower, M. (1978). 'The political socialisation of New Zealand schoolchildren', in S. Levine (ed.), *Politics in New Zealand.* Sydney: Allen and Unwin.

11

POLITICAL CULTURE, EDUCATION AND DEMOCRATIC CITIZENSHIP IN AFRICA

CLIVE HARBER

Wars will not cease, either on the ground or in people's minds, unless each and every one of us resolutely embarks on the struggle against intolerance and violence by attacking the evil at its roots. Education offers us the means to do this ... Education is what will enable us to move from a culture of war, which we unhappily know only too well, to a culture of peace.

(Director-General of UNESCO, quoted in Tedesco, 1994)

INTRODUCTION

It has long been felt that there is a relationship between the political system of a country, the character of its people and the way they are educated. This idea goes back as far as the ancient Greek philosophers. Aristotle (1962, pp.215–16), for example, in *The Politics* wrote:

> But of all the safeguards that we hear spoken of as helping to maintain constitutional continuity the most important, but most neglected today, is education, that is educating citizens for the way of living that belongs to the constitution in each case. It is useless to have the most beneficial rules of society fully agreed upon by all who are members of the politea if individuals are not going to be trained and have their habits formed for that politea, that is to live democratically if the laws of society are democratic, oligarchically if they are oligarchic.

Similar concerns can be found in the writings of Plato, Rousseau, Marx, Thomas More and John Stuart Mill. More recently, in the first half of this century, there emerged from psychology and cultural anthropology a 'culture and personality' school of thought which sought to explain political aspects of national character such as authoritarianism, aggression, ethnocentrism and fascism in terms of the patterns of early childhood socialization. In the 1950s and 1960s the study of the relationship between the political values, attitudes and beliefs of different societies (what became known as 'political culture') and political structures took place on a more systematic and empirical basis as did the study of where and how such values were learned (what became known as 'political socialization'). However, the influence of such studies in political science declined in the 1970s and 1980s in the light of the ascendancy of neo-Marxist and dependency theories on the one hand and of economic bargaining and market-driven models on the other (Diamond, 1993, pp.ix–xii).

The last few years, however, have witnessed something of a renewed interest in the idea of political culture and political socialization in the light of the collapse of the former communist regimes in eastern Europe and a developing international consensus on the need for democratic forms of government and the protection of human rights. Major questions now, therefore, are what sort of political values best support and facilitate democratic political systems and how are such values best transmitted to the population? At the individual level the questions can be rephrased in terms of what sort of values should a democratic citizen possess and how are these values best learned?

THE CIVIC POLITICAL CULTURE

Perhaps the most well known study of political culture is Almond and Verba's *The civic culture* (1963). This classified political cultures into three types according to the criterion of participation. 'Parochial' political cultures (now increasingly rare) could be found in those traditional and small-scale societies where there were no specialized political roles and where political orientation to these roles was the same as religious and social ones. In 'subject' political cultures, which is the type that has been most commonly found in developing countries, citizens are aware of specialized government authority but do not take part in it and are simply subject to the administrative, output side of the political system which tends to be ruled by an authoritarian regime. There is a top-down flow of information and the emphasis is on obedience and compliance. In the 'participant' political culture the citizen takes a much more active role in terms not only of voting but also of high levels of political interest, knowledge, opinion formation and organizational activity. Linked to this is the idea that citizens have a high level of political efficacy – both the competence to participate and the belief that political participation can change policy. For Almond and Verba, however, the 'civic culture' that best promotes democracy is a mixture of all three where the participant role is balanced by the subject role, thereby facilitating acceptance of political authority, and the parochial role so that membership of traditional, non-political groups absorbs some of the energy that might otherwise have been spent on politics and therefore decreases the intensity of participation.

Despite this emphasis on participation, an equally important issue for both Almond and Verba and other writers is the question of how citizens participate – the procedural values of politics in a democracy. A recent work on political culture and democracy in developing countries, for example, usefully summarizes the work of Alex Inkeles, which captures the key procedural dispositions of both authoritarian and democratic political cultures:

> Early in the development of the political culture literature, Inkeles portrayed democratic political culture as the inverse of the authoritarian personality syndrome that makes for political extremism. Inkeles identifies the components of this syndrome as including faith in powerful leaders; hatred of outsiders and deviates; a sense of powerlessness and ineffectiveness; extreme cynicism; suspicion and distrust of others and dogmatism. To list the components of the inverse syndrome is to comprehend much of what embodies a democratic culture: flexibility, trust, efficacy, openness to new ideas and experiences, tolerance of differences and ambiguities, acceptance of others. (Diamond, 1993, p.12)

While it must be remembered that not all 'developed' countries are necessarily doing that well in terms of the democratic basis of their political institutions (see, for example, Harber, 1992, on Britain), one textbook on politics in developing countries is in little doubt as to which of the two sets of Inkeles's components characterizes the political cultures of most developing countries. Kamrava (1993, pp.152–3) argues that such political cultures are marked by the intense emotional nature of political sentiments, the lack of meaningful discourse and mutual respect, the often dogmatic and rigid nature of ideology and the general lack of interpersonal trust. However, this is a very broad generalization given the fact that relatively little attention has been directed at how political culture presently affects the possibilities for democracy in less-developed countries. In particular, only limited attention has been paid to how such political cultures can be changed and shaped in a direction which would be more supportive of democratic political institutions through the education of citizens. The rest of this chapter examines these issues in relation to political culture and education for democratic citizenship in the context of one developing area – sub-Saharan Africa.

DEMOCRACY AND AUTHORITARIANISM IN AFRICA

When the majority of the countries of sub-Saharan Africa gained their independence from Britain and France in the 1950s and 1960s there was widespread hope about the institutionalization of democracy in the new states. Yet by the early 1970s most states were ruled either by one-party or military regimes. Moreover, neither the ex-Portuguese colonies of Angola, Mozambique and Guinea-Bissau, which became independent in the mid-1970s, nor Zimbabwe, which became independent in 1980, looked like following the path of multi-party democracy. Indeed, it became fashionable to argue that authoritarian regimes provided the necessary discipline for development. This 'developmental dictatorship' argument, as Sklar (1986) has called it, reasoned that the suppression of human rights and freedoms were justifiable if this led to more economic growth, more education, better housing and a higher standard of living.

Yet in the last four or five years there has been a renewed interest in democracy in Africa. In Zambia, Kenneth Kaunda became the first ever African head of state to lose his position through competitive democratic elections and there have now been multi-party elections in many African countries, the most recent, for example, bringing an end to apartheid in South Africa and the rule of the 'life President' of Malawi, Hastings Banda. Why is democracy back on the agenda in Africa?

Some factors have come from within Africa and some from outside. From inside Africa, opposition to apartheid in South Africa in terms of the principle of one person one vote not only influenced the nature of the independence struggles towards the goal of democracy in South Africa itself and in neighbouring Namibia, but also made other African governments appear somewhat contradictory when they denied the same right to their own citizens. Moreover, it has become increasingly clear that after 30 years of independence the previous tendency to explain poor economic, social and human rights performance solely in terms of the colonial regime and subsequent neo-colonial relationships now looks partly like shifting the blame. Moreover, authoritarian regimes have clearly not delivered the development promised.

Outside Africa the collapse of communism in eastern Europe undermined the Marxist-Leninist model of development favoured by the rulers of such countries as Ethiopia, Mozambique and Zimbabwe and meant that in the liberation war between Ethiopia and Eritrea the latter consciously chose a democratic ideology. The collapse of communism also meant that American, French and British governments stopped seeing African governments in cold war terms. It was no longer justifiable to support dictatorships solely because they were anti-communist and pro-Western. Western aid and loan organizations such as the World Bank and the IMF have, as a consequence, begun to add political strings to economic packages – no multi-party democracy, no money. The election in Kenya in January 1993, for example, came about as a direct result of the suspension of aid for six months.

The extent to which these new democratic political institutions can be made sustainable in Africa will depend partly on the political cultures in which they exist. Yet in the post-independence period African states have been faced with both widespread problems of ethnic tension and high popular expectations in severely restricted economic circumstances. Indeed, such 'ethnic' tension is itself often a vehicle in the fierce competition for the scarce resources of wealth and power. However, as a result of such conflict, African states have been fragile and potentially unstable and this fragility has often led in an undemocratic direction for, as Mazrui has noted, 'the African state is sometimes excessively authoritarian to disguise the fact that it is inadequately authoritative' (1983, p.293).

This authoritarian reaction to weak state legitimacy is also consistent with a great deal of African historical experience and traditional culture. While many pre-colonial societies established certain checks and balances to oversee rulers, monitor their actions and call them to account, the predominant pattern was probably more authoritarian with highly personalized rule, faith in the wisdom and justice of rulers rather than a belief in laws and procedures, unequal rights of citizenship and the absence of formal opposition (Chazan,1993, p.71). One writer, for example, has argued that whereas many African scholars and politicians have portrayed African societies before colonialism as harmonious and enjoying democratic tranquilities,

> what comes out of a careful examination and analysis of the political institutions and mechanisms of the pre-colonial African societies is a mixture of the rudiments of democratic tendencies and practices on the one hand and aristocratic, autocratic and/or militaristic tendencies, with varying degrees of despotism on the other ... However, colonialism unleashed such violence, discrimination and exploitation that Africans, young and old, educated and uneducated, soon forgot the violence and undemocratic practices of their traditional rulers. (Simuyu, 1988, pp.51–2)

As this quotation suggests, the tendency, with some exceptions, was for traditional authoritarian systems to be replaced by colonial authoritarian ones where colonial governors enjoyed wide powers with very few restrictions and dealt with opponents by jailing them, as many of the future leaders of Africa experienced for themselves. Moreover, the nationalist reaction to colonialism was itself not particularly democratic:

The decision to dismantle the colonial apparatus was the culmination of the call for liberation. But the by-products of democracy seen in terms of freedom were far more uncertain. Emphasis was put on consensus as opposed to tolerance, on loyalty in contrast to self-expression, on identity and not on individual rights, on political boundaries but hardly on procedures. Nationalism in many parts of Africa was not, in any fundamental sense, liberal. (Chazan, 1993, p.75)

Yet the outlook for democracy in Africa is not necessarily as negative as the above trends suggest. First, in Nigeria, for example, as in many other countries, there is strong popular support for the idea of democracy and choice of leaders, even though the corrupt and ethnically biased practices of politicians, institutions and the public themselves may leave much to be desired (Wiseman, 1990, p.x; Harber, 1989, p.89; Peil, 1976, p.45). Second, there are strong forms of cultural resistance to authoritarianism. Chazan, for example, refers to the resilience of the democratic ethos in Ghana in the face of virtually continuous abuse and corruption by civilian and military élites,

A deeply ingrained indigenous culture of consultation, autonomy, participation and supervision of authority ... has enabled Ghanaians to combat the uncertainties of state domination and the tyranny of its leaders. Lawyers, students, unions and traders have also evolved a culture of resistance to interference in their affairs. (Chazan, 1988, p.121)

Third, some countries, like Gambia and Botswana, have successfully retained democratic political structures. This has been facilitated in the case of Botswana, for example, by certain political and cultural factors which will be further discussed below.

The evidence therefore suggests that in Africa there is experience of both authoritarianism and democracy and both have failed to become fully institutionalized. However, in order to survive in the longer term, the newly formed democratic political institutions will need to be grounded in a more supportive political culture. The values of a political culture are not inherited genetically but must be learned socially and schools must therefore play an important part in this. Two books on democracy in Africa, for example, make this point briefly but emphatically:

Finally, without exhausting the list of possible useful changes, one may note the need for civic education to develop a more tolerant political culture, a deeper commitment to and understanding of political institutions, and a more mutually trustful political climate. (Diamond, 1988, pp.28–9)

the amount or degree of democracy in any given society is directly proportional to the degree of acculturation of the people in democratic values, attitudes and beliefs. For democracy to exist, survive and prosper, it requires that the people be bathed in and drenched with the democratic ethos! It is in this manner that education and culture constitute one of the most fundemental foundations of democracy ... education must preach the gospel of equality, freedom and human dignity. (Gitonga,1988, p.22)

Yet education is presently a paradoxical and contradictory factor in the development of a democratic political culture. It is an obstacle to democracy while at the same time it contains the potential to make a significant contribution to democratic development in the future.

EDUCATION AND AUTHORITARIANISM IN AFRICA

This section will explore some of the problems facing education as a potential mechanism for promoting democracy in Africa by examining two case studies of traditional political cultures in Africa and the patterns of child rearing in each. While such cultures can be termed 'traditional' in that they have existed for a long period of time, they are of considerable importance in understanding the contemporary nature of modern African states. The impact of modern education systems on existing political cultures and patterns of child rearing will then be explored. The first political culture, that of the dominant Hausa/Fulani ethnic group of northern Nigeria, fits firmly into Almond and Verba's 'subject' model, whereas the second, that of the various Tswana groups that go to make up Botswana, mixes this with some elements from a 'participant' model.

Diamond (1988b), in discussing the progress of democracy in Nigeria since independence in 1960, notes the dominance of the northern Hausa/Fulani in both civilian and military periods of politics and the general ethnic and political intolerance and repression that has marked political life. The nature of traditional Hausa political culture is therefore an important factor in the future of democracy in Nigeria as a whole, yet key aspects of Hausa culture do not seem to sit comfortably with democracy. This was and is a steeply hierarchical system in which the role of the citizen is seen in terms of loyalty, obedience and dependence on those in authority. It is a system that favours qualities of servility, respect for authority and allegiance to the powerful and rejects qualities of independent achievement, self-reliant action and initiative (Le Vine, 1966; Paden, 1973).

Eleazu (1977, pp.65–6) argued that family rearing patterns in northern Nigeria, which is predominantly Islamic, reflect the Islamic idea that people are in need of a hierarchical ordering of roles and he states that 'from early childhood, it is drummed into the child that obedience to the powers-that-be is the first duty of a person'. In a study of child-rearing practices in northern Nigeria, Hake found that fear was the dominant means that adults used to control youngsters, relying heavily on corporal punishment to induce respect, humility, obedience and submission. He notes that, in general, fear of punishment rather than positive reinforcement of good behaviour appears to be the dominant method of helping children learn proper behavioral controls. These fears eventually establish life patterns of servile submission to authority which extend into adulthood (1972, pp.41–2).

The Hausa child's experience of authority in the family is similar to that experienced in the Koranic school. It is usual for Hausa children to experience some Koranic education before attendance at primary school and many will continue with it at primary school by going to Koranic schools in the late afternoon and evening. As in the family, there is an emphasis on physical punishment, obedience and deference (Skinner, 1977; Sanneh, 1975). Hiskett (1975) characterizes as authoritarian the pedagogical style common to both Koranic schools for the young and the schools for higher Islamic learning for those who have achieved a certain proficiency in memorizing the Koran. Teaching is based on rote learning and the uncritical acceptance of a transmitted body of knowledge without argument or disagreement.

The retention of democratic political structures in Botswana on the other hand has been facilitated by certain cultural and political factors. The Tswana groups that go to make up Botswana share similar languages and cultural traditions and the ruling party has gone out of its way to treat all ethnic groups equally. The ruling party has also built on the tradition of the *kgotla*, a village communal assembly used to consult public opinion and gain local support for policies prior to implementation. Moreover, the emphases in Tswana traditional culture on moderation, non-violence and obedience to the law as well as public discussion and community consensus have also facilitated and helped to sustain democratic government. However, while these values have been helpful in sustaining democratic government:

> In some respects, they compensate for the lack of rigorous support for the legal rights of speech and press already mentioned. On the other hand, there is little in the traditional culture that supports the idea of the popular election of leaders. There is a presumption, particularly in the rural areas, that males from royal families ought to rule. As a consequence, outside the cities, the public shows little concern about the central government's appointments to local councils. It is presumed that the central government has the real power, that it is the new chief.

Thus:

> It is hard to say yet that this system of leadership is 'deeply institution-alised', given the fact that several centuries of autocratic political practice predated the present regime. (Holm, 1988, pp.198, 202)

Democracy in Botswana, therefore, cannot be said to be fully institution-alized or embedded in a political culture that will ensure its survival. Moreover, traditional child rearing practices have not necessarily been helpful in the further development of a political culture that fosters democratic citizenship:

> Much of child training consists in imparting the etiquette that an older individual (doing the instructing) feels should govern how a junior person acts towards a senior person. Basically this is training in deference ... The Tswana are rigid and authoritarian disciplinarians who enjoy teaching legalistic do's and don'ts in manners of public decorum, etiquette and role obligations ... Child training is directed toward producing a mannerly, conforming and industrious person. (Alverson, 1978, p.68)

What has been the impact of 'modern' schools on such traditional patterns of culture and child rearing? Unfortunately, schools in Africa, as in most other parts of the world, are presently essentially authoritarian institutions. This is because they are based on the bureaucratic model of organization inherited during colonialism and, as Fuller puts it, writing on Malawi:

> Even today, when political leaders and educators talk about 'modernising schools' or 'improving school effectiveness' they usually envision bureaucratic ways of organising – sharpening lines of authority, subdividing labour into more routinised (teaching or administrative) tasks, standardising what is learned, and tightening evaluation of uniform knowledge and action. (Fuller, 1991, pp.29–30)

Thus, the values which are supposed to be socialized by the school are those necessary for the functioning of bureaucratic organization and the maintenance of social order – obedience, abiding by the rules, loyalty, respect for authority, punctuality, regular attendance, quietness, orderly work in large groups, working to a strict timetable, tolerance of monotony, the ability to change readily from one situation to the next and the ignoring of personal needs when these are irrelevant to the task in hand (Shipman, 1972, Ch.2; 1975, pp.12–15).

The schools, by attempting to transmit 'modern' bureaucratic skills and values can provide a necessary, though not sufficient, basis for democracy, for without the spread of such skills it would be difficult for any large-scale political system to operate – including democracy. However, by excluding democratic values, school organization in Africa has probably done as much to contribute to the operation of military regimes as it has to the development of the values and skills supportive of a democratic regime. Indeed, in his study of African university students Barkan (1975, p.143) found that more students favoured a technocratic political order resembling the administrative state of the old colonial regime than any other. In the light of their experience of school, this is not altogether surprising.

Classroom authority patterns are congruent with those in the wider school:

> In most African countries the classroom is highly structured in terms of the formal distribution of space. The teacher in the classroom exercises unquestioned authority in such matters as seating arrangement and movement. He not only initiates the activities to be pursued by pupils, but also controls communication channels within the group. We do not know the extent to which this kind of classroom environment determines the political orientation of pupils but forced conformity to an authoritarian system throughout childhood and early adolescence, if supplemented by other factors, is likely to encourage passive acceptance of authority in later years. (Datta, 1984, p.40)

These general trends are, correspondingly, to be found in schools in the two case-study political cultures discussed above. In northern Nigeria, school and classroom organization also socializes towards authoritarianism, albeit of a more 'modern' bureaucratic variety, and the result is that pupils possess political values in keeping with a 'subject' political culture (Harber, 1989, Ch.5). Similarly, in Botswana:

> Students are perceived as passive recipients of vast amounts of information to be memorised and as apprentices in the acquisition of elementary skills required for the production of specific products. Learning is perceived to occur through repetition and drill, the effectiveness of which is assessed through the use of test questions requiring little more than simple recall. (Rowell and Prophet, 1990, p.24)

CHANGING POLITICAL CULTURE – EDUCATION FOR DEMOCRACY

Diamond (1993, pp.9–10) argues strongly against what he terms a 'deterministic' view of political culture which sees it as fixed and unchanging and determining the nature of political institutions. Instead, he favors a more 'plastic' and changeable view of political culture that both shapes and is shaped by the politics of its state and society. One of his reasons for so doing is one shared by the present writer, a 'bias towards hope': i.e., that not to do so would be to condemn many countries in the developing world and the ex-communist bloc to perpetual authoritarianism and praetorianism. This, as he argues, not only offends the sensibilities of democrats but also contradicts real and enduring cultural change in countries such as Germany, Japan, Spain, Italy and Portugal which were once written off as infertile soil for democracy.

If, however, schools in Africa in the future are going to educate for democracy in terms of peaceful debate, mutual respect and the protection of human rights and against ethnic prejudice, bias, hostility, mistrust and intolerance, then the organization of both classrooms and schools must be more congruent with these aims. In terms of classrooms this means that teaching methods across the curriculum will need to become more active, participant, cooperative, investigative and critical in order to develop democratic citizens. The curriculum will also need to contain time for a direct and explicit examination of political issues and structures. This is because democracy is based on a notion of choice, but choice based on political ignorance is no choice at all. Research by Osler (1993a) suggests that young people in Africa can be very well aware of this. Osler investigated the production and use in Kenyan schools of a magazine on environmental and development education called *Pied Crow*. When asked to give their opinions on suitable topics for future editions of the magazine, pupils in every school she visited demanded more information on politics. They particularly requested material on democracy, on multi-partyism and on the next President of Kenya and felt that they needed to be helped in developing the skill of identifying bias.

It is encouraging that there is evidence that more open, democratic classrooms making greater use of discussion and other participatory methods can foster a range of democratic political orientations such as greater political interest, less authoritarianism, greater political knowledge and a greater sense of political efficacy (Ehman, 1980). Research in Israel demonstrated that different forms of classroom relationship facilitate or impede the development of pupils' political efficacy and orientation to public forms of political involvement (Ichilov, 1991). Democratic and cooperative teaching methods have also been shown to reduce inter-ethnic conflict and promote cross-cultural friendship (Lynch, 1992, p.22). A recent study of ethnically mixed schools in the south-eastern United States compared two schools that stressed cooperative learning, the development of interpersonal relationships, values clarification and the heterogeneous grouping of students with three traditional schools where students were streamed by achievement and taught in a lecture-recitation style in predominantly same-race classes. The study found that cross-race interaction and friendships and a positive evaluation of different-race students were significantly higher in the former than in the latter (Conway and Damico, 1993).

There are also some encouraging signs that, despite problems of cultural resistance and resource shortages, attention is now being paid to the creation of more democratic classrooms in Africa. In Namibia there have been moves in recent years towards a more democratic form of pedagogy that actively involves pupils in making decisions about their own learning and work has begun on the in-service teacher education that will be necessary for this to happen (Rowell, 1995). In South Africa 'People's Education', developed by the African National Congress, seeks 'to restructure classroom relationships from the standard teacher-centred and authoritarian climate to a more student-centred, democratic form' (Jansen, 1990, p.67). In West Africa there are clear indications of a renewed interest in human rights education with programmes in junior secondary schools in Ghana and Nigeria. The defeat of the Mengistu regime in Ethiopia in 1991 and moves towards democratic government have meant that human rights education is seen as a curriculum priority and is regarded by the Minister of Education as the basis upon which to build education for a democratic state and citizenry (Osler, 1993b).

In neighboring Eritrea, during the war of liberation against Ethiopia which ended in 1991, democracy was a clear aim of political education. There was a conscious attempt to apply the ideas of Paulo Freire and introduce more investigative and participant teaching and learning methods. Following the end of the war of liberation there is a determination to change the authoritarian type of schools inherited from British, Italian and Ethiopian colonialism and to produce students with the ability to talk and discuss with self-confidence as a way of strengthening unity between ethnic groups (Teklu, 1993).

In the early 1980s the British Schools Council (1981) summed up well the case for organizing schools as a whole on a more democratic basis:

> Some values, like those of democracy, tolerance and responsibility grow only with experience of them. Social education arises from a school's ethos, its organisation and its relation with the community. The way a school organises its staff and pupils and its formal rules, says a great deal about its real values and attitudes. Schools need to practise what they seek to promote.

Moreover, research evidence suggests that democratic school structures can indeed help to foster democratic values and skills. One survey of five research studies in the United States, for example, concluded that democratic schools 'contribute to the participatory awareness, skills and attitudes fundamental to life in democratic societies' (Hepburn, 1984, p.261). Research in Britain comparing a democratic school with a traditional one also suggested that democratic attitudes, including support for gender and racial equality, were stronger in the democratic school (John and Osborn, 1992).

One country in Africa that has taken the idea of democratic schools seriously is Tanzania. In 1967 the then President of Tanzania, Julius Nyerere, announced that schools would follow a policy of education for self-reliance. One aspect of this policy would be that each school would have a school council which would be part of the decision-making structures of the school as 'only then can the participants practise – and learn to value – direct democracy ... the pupils must be able to participate in decisions and learn by mistakes' (Nyerere, 1967, pp.28–9). So, one important objective of education for self-reliance was 'to promote a sense of belonging together and enhance a spirit of cooperation by making pupils value work, practise their democratic rights, but also be accountable in their responsibilities' (Mosha, 1990, p.60).

However, despite encouragement and support at the political level, the extent to which functioning school councils actually exist is open to question (Saunders, 1982) and where they do exist they are perhaps better characterized as consultative participation than direct democracy since, although pupils are able to discuss and influence policy, the head retains the final veto (Kisanga, 1986). Nevertheless, pupils in some schools in Tanzania still expect to have an influence over school policy and are expected to do so by the staff, a significant improvement on the bureaucratic-authoritarian nature of school organization still prevalent in Africa and elsewhere. In interviews conducted by the writer in two schools in Tanzania in 1992, it was noted by both staff and pupils that participation, apart from improving certain aspects of school management, had helped to develop responsibility, confidence, problem-solving through discussion and a friendlier and more cooperative environment. It has also helped to avoid the violence that has erupted in schools from time to time in Africa and which has been caused primarily by authoritarianism and poor communications leading to suspicion and resentment (Harber, 1993).

During the war of liberation against Ethiopia, the Eritrean People's Liberation Front founded a school in one of the liberated zones which became known as the Zero School. In this school pupils were involved in democratic decision-making through membership of a series of key committees. As a result, according to one participant in the school, students were 'responsible, disciplined, tolerant and critical'. Since the establishment of an independent state of Eritrea in 1991 the Ministry of Education has promulgated a Legal Notice No.2 which lays down that every school must have a governing school committee onto which staff, pupils and parents are democratically elected (Tesfamariam, 1993).

CONCLUSION

The period 1989–94 has witnessed profound changes in global politics. During this period there has been a growing emphasis within international agencies on the need for political development towards democracy as well as the traditional emphases on economic indicators of development such as gross national product and social indicators such as life expectancy. In Africa this has manifested itself in a rapid series of multi-party elections across the continent. Yet, if such democratic political structures are to be sustainable, efforts must be made towards the development of more supportive political cultures. As an agency of mass socialization, education can play an important part in this process of creating citizens with democratic values, though at present it tends to hinder rather than help it. It may be, as Gloria Steinem once put it, that 'the first problem for all of us, men and women, is not to learn but to unlearn'.

REFERENCES

Almond, G. and Verba, S. (1963). *The civic culture.* Princeton, NJ: Princeton University Press.

Alverson, H. (1978). *Mind in the heart of darkness.* New Haven, CT: Yale University Press.

Aristotle (1962). *The politics.* Harmondsworth: Penguin.

Barkan, J. (1975). *An African dilemma.* Nairobi: Oxford University Press.

Chazan, N. (1988). 'Ghana: problems of governance and the emergence of civil society', in L. Diamond, J. Linz and M. Lipset (eds), *Democracy in developing countries: Africa.* London: Adamantine Press.

Chazan, N. (1993). 'Between liberalism and statism: African political cultures and democracy', in L. Diamond (ed.), *Political culture and democracy in developing countries.* Boulder, CO: Lynne Rienner.

Conway, M. and Damico, S. (1993). 'Facing up to multiculturalism: Means as ends in democratic education', paper delivered to the International Conference on Education for Democracy in a Multicultural Society, Jerusalem, Israel.

Datta, A. (1984). *Education and society: A sociology of African education.* London: Macmillan.

Diamond, L. (1988a). 'Introduction: Roots of failure, seeds of hope', in L. Diamond, J. Linz and S. Lipset (eds), *Democracy in developing countries: Africa.* London: Adamantine Press.

Diamond, L. (1988b). 'Nigeria: Pluralism, statism, and the struggle for democracy', in L. Diamond, J. Linz and S. Lipset (eds), *Democracy in developing countries: Africa.* London: Adamantine Press.

Diamond, L. (1993). 'Introduction: Political culture and democracy', in L. Diamond (ed.), *Political culture and democracy in developing countries.* Boulder, CO: Lynne Rienner.

Ehman, L. (1980). 'The American high school in the political socialisation process', *Review of Educational Research*, 50.

Eleazu, U.D. (1977). *Federalism and nation building.* Devon: Stockwell.

Fuller, B. (1991). *Growing up modern: The Western state builds Third-World schools.* London: Routledge.

Gitonga, A. (1988). 'The meaning and foundations of democracy.', in W. Oyugi *et al.* (eds), *Democratic theory and practice in Africa.* London: James Currey.

Hake, J. (1972). *Child rearing practices in northern Nigeria.* Ibadan: Ibadan University Press.

Harber, C. (1989). *Politics in African education.* London: Macmillan.
Harber, C. (1992). *Democratic learning and learning democracy.* Ticknall: Education Now.
Harber, C. (1993). 'Democratic management and school effectiveness in Africa: Learning from Tanzania', *Compare*, 23, 3.
Hepburn, M. (1984). 'Democratic schooling – five perspectives from research', *International Journal of Political Education*, 6.
Hiskett, M. (1975). 'Islamic education in the traditional and state systems in northern Nigeria', in G.N. Brown and M. Hiskett (eds), *Conflict and harmony in education in tropical Africa.* London: George Allen and Unwin.
Holm, J. (1988). 'Botswana: A paternalistic democracy', in L. Diamond, J. Linz and S. Lipset (eds), *Democracy in developing countries: Africa.* London: Adamantine Press.
Ichilov, O. (1991). 'Political socialisation and schooling effects among Israeli adolescents', *Comparative Education Review*, 35, 3.
Jansen, J. (1991). 'In search of liberation pedagogy in South Africa', *Journal of Education* 172, 2.
John, P. and Osborn, A. (1992). 'The influence of school ethos on pupils' citizen attitudes', *Educational Review*, 44, 2.
Kamrava, M. (1993) *Politics and society in the Third World.* London: Routledge.
Kisanga, M. (1986). 'On the implications of the principle of pupil, parent and community participation in the management of formal and non-formal educational institutions and activities survey for UNESCO', unpublished, Dar Es Salaam.
Le Vine, R. (1966). *Dreams and deeds: Achievment motivation in Nigeria.* Chicago, IL: University of Chicago Press.
Lynch, J. (1992). *Education for citizenship in a multicultural society.* London: Cassell.
Mazrui, A. (1983). 'Political engineering in Africa', *International Social Science Journal*, 25, 2.
Mosha, H. (1990). 'Twenty years of education for self-reliance: A critical perspective', *International Journal of Educational Development*, 10, 1.
Nyerere, J. (1967). *Education for self reliance.* Dar Es Salaam: Government Printer.
Osler, A. (1993a). 'Education for development and democracy in Kenya', *Educational Review*, 45, 2.
Osler, A. (1993b). 'Education for human rights and democracy in Ethiopia', *Human Rights Newsletter*, 5.
Paden, J. (1973). *Religion and political culture in Kano.* Berkeley, CA: University of California Press.
Peil, M. (1976). *Nigerian politics: The people's view.* London: Cassell.
Rowell, P. (1995). 'Perspectives on pedagogy in teacher education: The case of Namibia', *International Journal of Educational Development*, 15, 1.
Rowell, P. and Prophet, R. (1990). 'Curriculum-in-action: The "practical dimension in Botswana classrooms"', *International Journal of Educational Development*, 10, 1.
Sanneh, L. (1975). 'The Islamic education of an African child', in G.N. Brown and M. Hiskett (eds), *Conflict and harmony in tropical Africa.* London: Allen and Unwin.
Saunders, M. (1982). 'Productive activity in the curriculum: Changing the literate bias of secondary schools in Tanzania', *British Journal of Sociology of Education*, 3, 1.
Schools Council (1981). *The practical curriculum.* London: Methuen.
Shipman, M. (1972). *Education and modernisation.* London: Faber & Faber.
Shipman, M. (1975). *The sociology of the school.* London: Longman.
Simuyu, V. (1988). 'The democratic myth in the African traditional societies', in W. Oyugi *et al.* (eds), *Democratic theory and practice in Africa.* London: James Currey.
Skinner, N. (1977). *Alhaji Mohmadu Koki.* Zaria: Ahmadu Bello University Press.
Sklar, R. (1986). 'Democracy in Africa', in M. Doro and N. Stultz (eds), *Governing in Black Africa.* London: African Publishing Company.

Tedesco, J. (1994). 'Knowledge versus values', *Educational Innovation*, 78.
Teklu, M. (1993). 'Schools and political learning in Eritrea', unpublished MEd essay, University of Birmingham.
Tesfamariam, T. (1993). 'Democratic school practice in Eritrea', unpublished BPhil essay, University of Birmingham.
Wiseman, J. (1990). *Democracy in Black Africa*. New York: Paragon House.

12

PATRONAGE, DOMESTICATION OR EMPOWERMENT? CITIZENSHIP DEVELOPMENT AND CITIZENSHIP EDUCATION IN HONG KONG

WING-KWONG TSANG

The run-up to handing over Hong Kong to the People's Republic of China (PRC) in 1997 drastically radicalized the political scenery of Hong Kong. This last colony of the United Kingdom, situated on the doorstep of the largest socialist state in the world, had been characterized as a borrowed place in borrowed time (Hughes, 1976). However, time was rapidly running out for both the British, who had acquired the territory more than a century before, and for the Hong Kong Chinese, most of whom had come as refugees when the Chinese Communist Party rose to power in China in 1949.

Anticipating the inevitable hand-over of the colony back to the People's Republic of China, the British started to democratize the political system of Hong Kong by granting its residents political rights, such as the right to elect about one-third of the legislators during the 1991 general elections. These steps, which can be characterized, using Bryan Turner's distinction (1990), as passive and handed-down-from-above, were perceived by the Hong Kong Chinese as belated and patronizing. They remained estranged, as indicated by the surprisingly low voting turnout rates (44 per cent) in the 1991 maiden general election, and expressed strong feelings of distrust toward the colonial government (Tsang, 1993). These steps towards greater democratization also resulted in the proliferation of political organizations and activities during the past decade.

Hong Kong citizens' attitudes towards the PRC, their future sovereign state, were no more favorable (Tsang, 1993). In defiance of the Chinese Communist Party, two mass rallies were held before and after the 4 June massacre in Tiananmen Square in Beijing, in which more than one million people (about one-sixth of Hong Kong's residents) took to the streets. Confronted by such strong defiance, the PRC government has been trying hard in recent years to contain the development of democratic citizenship in Hong Kong.

Citizenship education, a subject which has been marginalized in the school curriculum for more than three decades, is emerging in the midst of this political turmoil. Citizenship education assumed its focal position in the public forum at exactly the time when the 1997 takeover became an inevitable fact. Its introduction in the schools was first advocated by local educators in the early 1980s, in the hope that it would empower citizens and serve as means for emancipation from colonial rule to self-government. The colonial government responded half-heartedly to this initiative by producing a document advocating the inculcation of 'responsible' citizenship. Following the 4 June massacre, nationalist patriotic citizenship education was advocated by pro-Beijing educators in Hong Kong as a means of diluting anti-Communist sentiments, and of taming the growing defiance of the PRC government.

It has been argued that the discourse concerning school knowledge as socially constructed reality, reflects the modes of social control and the socio-political configurations prevailing in a given society (Bernstein, 1971; Young, 1971a; Apple, 1979, 1982; Giroux, 1981, 1983; Aronowitz and Giroux, 1985; Whitty, 1985). The situation in Hong Kong confirms this. In the present chapter, I will show how conceptions of citizenship education in Hong Kong changed in the last four decades and illustrate how these changes relate to changes in the configurations of citizenship within Hong Kong society. I will first outline the trajectory of cultural and institutional development of citizenship in Hong Kong since the Second World War. I will then locate changes in the conceptions of citizenship education within the context of citizenship developments, and illustrate how the two nurture each other. I will argue that citizenship and citizenship education are empowering practices. As such, they can help citizens stand against political constraints imposed upon them in the form of patronage by the former colonial government and in the form of domestication by the PRC government.

In the present chapter, two aspects of citizenship development in Hong Kong will be explored, namely the institutional and the attitudinal aspects. Concerning the institutional aspect, I shall rely on the conceptions of citizenship which sprang from T.H. Marshall's theory of citizenship (Marshall, 1973; Giddens, 1982; Mann, 1987; Held, 1989; Turner, 1990). The development of various citizenship rights and their corresponding political institutions in Hong Kong will be delineated and evaluated. As for the attitudinal aspect, the research tradition of political culture and the study of attitudes in general will be employed (Abramson, 1983; Almond and Verba, 1963, 1980; Campbell et al., 1960; Inglehart, 1990; Milbrath and Goel, 1977). Through the review of the empirical work on political attitudes and culture of the Hong Kong Chinese in particular, I will try to depict changes over time in these domains. These two lines of inquiry will illustrate how the attitudinal and institutional aspects of citizenship interact with and nurture each other, and how they constitute particular political configurations at different periods in Hong Kong's history.

ATTITUDINAL AND CULTURAL DEVELOPMENT OF CITIZENSHIP IN HONG KONG

Hong Kong Political Culture before the 1990s

The study of the political culture of the Hong Kong Chinese can be traced back to the early 1970s. Based on data generated from a poll conducted in 1966–67, Hoadley (1970) characterized the political culture of Hong Kong as parochial, using Almond and Verba's (1963, 1980) conceptual framework. Similar findings were reported in a survey conducted in 1971 at Kwun Tong, then a newly developed industrial and residential area: 'the political culture of the ordinary people is predominantly a parochial one ... The political culture of the leaders is predominantly a subject political culture ... In general ... it might not be too wrong to say that the political culture of Kwun Tong is mixed parochial-subject' (King, 1981, p.164). The most comprehensive exposition of the political culture of the Hong Kong Chinese is the series of studies conducted over a period of a decade by Lau and his colleagues. Their initial study in 1977 revealed 'apparent traces of subject political culture' (Lau, 1982, p.106). Lau demonstrated how subject political culture is built upon a particular relationship between the colonial state and Chinese society. The Hong Kong Chinese society contributes its share by remaining estranged and by acting as 'a minimally-integrated social-political system' (Lau, 1982, pp.157–63). This behavior has been characterized as the 'social accommodation of politics', i.e., relying on traditional familial social networks rather than on state bureaucracy to accommodate own needs (Lau and Ho, 1982). The colonial government and state bureaucracy on their part act as a 'secluded bureaucratic polity' (Lau, 1982, p.65). They enjoy an autonomous and superior status and can remain secluded from the civil society.

In the 1980s, the relationship between the state and civil society underwent substantial change. Following the economic success of the 1970s, the colonial regime began to take a more active role in regulating economic and social affairs, and in the provision of goods and services to the community. Thus, social programs on housing, education and medicine were implemented in the 1970s. Growing state intervention in communal affairs activated the politically aloof Chinese society, leading to a proliferation of pressure groups since the mid-1970s, and a growing normative orientation of political participation among the Hong Kong Chinese (Cheung and Louie, 1991; and Lau and Kuan, 1986). However, Lau reports that, owing to the lack of effective institutional means to participate, and the legacy of political aloofness, the 'actual participatory behavior [of the Hong Kong Chinese], nevertheless, lags behind normative orientation' (1986, p.50; Lau and Kuan, 1986). On the whole, in the early 1980s, the Hong Kong Chinese were moving away from subject political culture, which, however, had not been replaced with a full-fledged participatory political culture. Hong Kong was said to be involved in 'an early "modern", and hence "immature", form of participatory political culture' (Lau and Kuan, 1986, p.50).

As the issue of the 1997 reunion with the PRC unfolded in the fall of 1982, and the subsequent negotiation between the British and Chinese governments began, the political culture of Hong Kong Chinese underwent another substantial change. Hong Kong Chinese sense of powerlessness, in spite of the progressive democratization of the political system since 1984, grew stronger (Lau and Kuan, 1988, p.94). This could be attributed to the fact that the Hong Kong Chinese themselves could take no part in the on- going Sino-British negotiations concerning the future of Hong Kong. A survey conducted in 1985 revealed that 54.3 per cent of the respondents agreed or strongly agreed with the statement: 'As an ordinary citizen, I find it even more difficult than it was in the past to influence the decisions of the Hong Kong government at a time when Hong Kong is governed by the Chinese, British and Hong Kong governments' (Lau and Kuan, 1988, p.95). Distrust in the PRC and Hong Kong governments increased from 1985 to 1988, as can be seen in Table 12.1.

The Hong Kong Chinese feeling of being ignored, if not betrayed, by the two governments no doubt reinforced their distrust of them. Following the 4 June massacre, the Hong Kong government regained some public trust, while the PRC government suffered a substantial loss of confidence. This was also due to the different reactions of the two governments to the massacre. The Hong Kong government attempted to pacify the fears of their Hong Kong Chinese, putting forth an airport construction project, and granting British nationality to 50,000 Hong Kong families. By contrast, the PRC government accused the Hong Kong Chinese of being the world's strongest hold of anti-Communist and unpatriotic feelings. Among the Hong Kong Chinese there is also 'a growing sense of dependence on the government for a variety of services related to daily living' and 'an increasing perception of government as the benefactor and primary solver of social and even private problems' (Lau and Kuan, 1988, p.72). Hong Kong Chinese have also become more prepared for political participation. However, political participation is seen mainly as instrumental and materialistic in nature, and as a means to enhance private interests (Lau and Kuan, 1988).

TABLE 12.1
DISTRUST OF THE HONG KONG AND PRC GOVERNMENTS, 1985–90

	1985 (%)	1988 (%)	1990 (%)
Hong Kong government	16.8	18.2	15.1
PRC government	42.9	43.6	62.5

Sources: Lau and Kuan (1988), p.84; Lau, Kuan and Wan (1991), p.199; Lau (1992), p.138.

Political Culture of Hong Kong in the 1991 Maiden General Elections

The process of democratization of the legislature began in 1985 with the introduction of 24 indirectly elected seats of functional constituencies and electoral colleges, which constituted less than one-third of the legislative council. The other two-thirds of the council were either ex-official or governor-appointed members. It was not until 1991 that the Hong Kong residents were granted, for the first time in more than a century, the right to elect one-third of their legislators in direct general elections. A territory-wide survey of a sample of registered voters was carried out between October 1991 and January 1992 using face-to-face interviews with 939 registered voters (Louie, 1993). The guiding framework of the study (Tsang, 1993) was based on the Michigan model (Campbell *et al.*, 1954; Campbell *et al.*, 1960; Miller and Traugott, 1989). The study provides updated measures of the political attitudes and political culture of the Hong Kong Chinese, such as voters' decisions and actions concerning participation in the elections.

The study measured both internal and external political efficacy, the former being defined as the individual's belief that means of influence are available to her/him, and the latter as the belief that the authority or regime is responsive to influence attempts (Balch, 1974, p.24). The data revealed the continuing prevalence of powerlessness feelings towards the colonial political system. Only 8.8 per cent of the respondents agree or strongly agree that 'I can influence government policy', and only 11.4 per cent felt similarly about the statement 'I understand what politics is all about'. Furthermore, a majority of the electorate expressed skepticism toward appointed legislators, and 64.8 per cent of the respondents agreed and strongly agreed that 'appointed councillors vote in line with the government's will rather than with the public interest'. However, the Hong Kong electorate expressed a stronger sense of efficacy concerning the emerging representative democracy. They held high expectations of democratic principles such as the presence of elected councillors and political groups, and voting itself. For example, 58.9 per cent of the respondents agreed or strongly agreed that

TABLE 12.2
SENSE OF CITIZENSHIP DUTY (IN PERCENTAGES)

	Strongly Agree	Agree	Undecided	Disagree	Strongly Disagree	N
So many other people vote that it does not matter much whether I vote or not	3.1	15.4	13.1	57.1	11.3	884
I will vote even if the candidate I support has the least chance of winning	38.9	29.1	13.2	10.4	8.4	843
I will vote in the Legislative Council election even though I recognize the Council's limited influence on Hong Kong affairs	15.7	56.7	12.8	14.3	0.5	833
I will not vote unless it concerns my vested interest	1.5	11.2	8.7	67.9	10.7	866

Sources: Lau and Kuan (1998); Lau, Kuan and Wan (1991); Lau (1992).

'voting is an effective means to express my opinion to the government'. Similarly, 49 per cent agreed or strongly agreed that 'elected councillors are responsive to people's opinions'. Finally, 49.1 per cent agreed or strongly agreed that 'political groups can enhance the government's accountability'. Taken together, it seems that the Hong Kong electorate perceives the emerging democratic system as an escape from a situation of political powerlessness.

As for political estrangement, the 1991 study basically confirmed Lau and Kuan's (1986) assertion that normative orientations of political participation are on the rise among the Hong Kong Chinese. This is indicated by the findings presented in Table 12.2. It is apparent that the Hong Kong electorate holds a strong normative orientation towards electoral participation and a sense of citizenship duty. In all four items, over two-thirds of the respondents endorsed the belief that, under all circumstances, voting is a citizen's duty.

Nonetheless, when it comes to actual electoral participation, lack of involvement and apathy seem to remain strong. In our 1991 study, we adopted two of the conceptions of Verba *et al.* (1987) of political participation which are directly related to electoral participation.

We also included items indicating 'unconventional' or 'confrontational' modes of political participation, such as petitions, rallies and marches commemorating the 4 June massacre. The study revealed that most of the Hong Kong voters remained at the spectator level of political participation, watching the TV news (68.1 per cent) and privately discussing electoral issues with relatives and friends (45.8 per cent). Furthermore, more than 90 per cent did not take part in the election campaign, and 98 per cent reported that they did not make a donation to the candidates.

As for the confrontational mode of political participation, what is most conspicuous is that a substantial portion (20.7 per cent) of the electorate participated in the 1989 activities commemorating the 4 June massacre. However, this political passion cooled off quickly in subsequent years, and only 6.4 per cent and 2.6 per cent of the respondents participated in the same kind of activities in 1990 and 1991, respectively. It must be stressed, however, that the Hong Kong electorate are not totally indifferent. They are quite attentive to news coverage of the elections on TV (70 per cent), in newspapers (56.6 per cent) and on the radio (36.5 per cent), and are well informed.

By employing refined measurement (Miller and Traugott, 1989) we were able to differentiate two dimensions of trust in government: trust in the government's efficiency and trust in the government's integrity. The Hong Kong electorate expressed a strong trust in its government's efficiency. However, they were divided in their responses to the statement that 'the Hong Kong Government is a lame duck government': 33.3 per cent agreed, 32.2 per cent disagreed and 34.4 per cent were undecided. This could mean that the recently received PRC interference in Hong Kong's affairs damaged the Hong Kong government's perceived efficiency. The Hong Kong electorate expressed a strong sense of distrust in the government's integrity. Many voters agreed or strongly agreed with the following two statements: 'most of the government policies are for the benefit of the rich' (70.5 per cent) and 'Hong Kong government misused public funds' (66.3 per cent).

Our 1991 survey revealed that there were strong, defiant attitudes towards the PRC government, especially concerning civil rights and related issues. Voters' response to the issue of the Hong Kong Alliance in Support of the Patriotic Democratic Movement in China (HKASPDM) is indicative of these trends. HKASPDM came into existence in May 1989, in support of the students' democratic movement in Beijing. It subsequently became the symbol for, as well as the organization of, the Hong Kong Chinese's defiance of the 4 June massacre. The Chinese government repeatedly proclaimed HKASPDM an anti-Chinese and anti-Communist organization which must be dissolved. However, only 7.3 per cent of the electorate supported this view.

The Hong Kong Chinese expressed their support for continuing democratization under the PRC in several ways. A majority of 73.7 per cent agreed with the statement that 'the Bill of Rights should be carried over beyond 1997'. The PRC had already proclaimed that it would not endorse the Bill of Rights passed by the Hong Kong Legislative Council. Furthermore,

68.8 per cent of the respondents supported the statement that 'SAR [the government of the Special Administrative Region] chief executive should be directly elected', and 50.2 per cent agreed that 'all members of the Legislative Council should be directly elected'. Both these political rights have been denied already by the mini-constitution for the future SAR government (Basic Law), which was drafted and endorsed by the PRC government. The Hong Kong electorate expects candidates who run for political office to express independent views (84.5 per cent), and courageously to express their dissent with regard to both the PRC (80.5 per cent) and the Hong Kong (HK) (85.9 per cent) governments. However, a substantial portion of the voters expressed more accommodating views. They wished their candidates to be 'moderate in views' (65.1 per cent), and 51.5 per cent favored a 'candidate accepted by the Chinese government'.

Confronted by these seemingly contradictory attitudes towards both governments, one may ask are they held simultaneously by the Hong Kong electorate, or rather taken by different segments within Hong Kong society. The correlations among the expected attributes of candidates in Table 12.3 reveal that the Hong Kong electorate, in fact, simultaneously holds these apparently contradicting attitudes.

TABLE 12.3
PEARSON CORRELATION COEFFICIENTS AMONG EXPECTED ATTRIBUTES OF
CANDIDATES

	V1	V2	V3	V4
V1 Candidate moderate in views	1.000			
V2 Candiate dares to dissent from HK government	.1284**	1.000		
V3 Candidate dares to dissent from PRC government	.1145*	.6266**	1.000	
V4 Candidate accepted by PRC government	.2447**	.1723**	.1233**	1.000

$* p < .05; ** p < .01.$

In my opinion, these apparent contradictions vividly reflect the Hong Kong Chinese fears of the Chinese government. A considerable portion of the Hong Kong Chinese still have memories of fleeing mainland China in the 1950s through the 1970s. To a greater portion, their fears reflect their witnessing of the 4 June massacre on their television screens. It is these fears that lead the Hong Kong electorate to look for daring politicians to stand against the Chinese government on their behalf. However, the same fears also caused them to expect their chosen political representatives not to provoke the Chinese regime, and to be acceptable to it. The Hong Kong Chinese seem unready to take an aggressive or even confrontational stance towards their future sovereign. In conclusion, our 1991 voting-behaviour study revealed that the democratization process has mobilized the Hong Kong Chinese to move away slowly from a subject political culture of powerlessness and detachment.

INSTITUTIONAL DEVELOPMENT OF CITIZENSHIP IN HONG KONG

In this section, I will illuminate the relationships between the attitudinal and institutional aspects of citizenship in Hong Kong. The particular political attitudes found among the Hong Kong Chinese have been attributed to the inheritance of traditional Chinese political culture (Hsiao, 1979; Lau, 1982; Lau and Kuan, 1988; Pye, 1968; Solomon, 1971). In addition to this type of explanation, I would like to put forth an institutional explanation by looking into the institutional configurations of citizenship in Hong Kong and relating it to the attitudinal dimension of the political culture of the Hong Kong Chinese.

Citizenship should not be construed solely as a status endowing the individual with a set of rights and obligations. It also consists of a set of institutions within which the endowed rights and obligations are guaranteed and practiced. According to T.H. Marshall's (1973) formulation, there are three major institutions which constitute citizenship within modern states: the courts of justice, the parliamentary system, and the educational system and social services. The courts of justice are custodians of 'the rights necessary for individual freedom' (Marshall, 1973, p.78). The parliamentary system secures the political element of citizenship, i.e., 'the right to participate in the exercise of political power, as a member of a body invested with political authority or an elector of the members of such a body' (p.78). As for the educational system and social services, they form the institutional context within which the social element of citizenship is materialized. The social element of citizenship consists of 'the whole range from the right to a modicum of economic welfare and security to the right to share to the full in the social heritage and to live the life of a civilized being according to the standards prevailing in the society' (p.78).

While Marshall's classification of citizenship rights has been well received in the field of the sociology of citizenship, his formulation of the stages of development of these rights was criticized as being 'Anglophile' and 'evolutionary'. Giddens (1982) points out that the trajectory of citizenship development is not a natural and peaceful evolutionary process but a trail full of struggles and battles because 'each set of the three citizenship rights referred by Marshall had to be fought for, over a long span of historical time' (p.171). Furthermore, the development of citizenship rights is neither 'a one-way phenomenon' nor 'an irreversible trend of development' (p.172). These rights must be defended against resurgence time and again. Mann (1987) points out that the trajectory of citizenship development is not a universal process. Looking at the developmental experiences of six countries (the US, Britain, Germany, Austria, Russia and Japan), Mann concludes that each underwent different citizenship developments and arrived at different configurations of the institutions embodying citizenship rights. Mann attributes these variations to a number of factors. One is the differences in the points of departure of the various national citizenship movements, i.e., differences in the nature of the traditional regimes governing each country in the early nineteenth century, when citizenship movements first emerged. The other factor is the difference in strategies used by the ruling class in each country to cope with the rising citizenship movements. Finally, the outcomes of the struggle between the citizenship movements and the ruling class also depends on the geopolitical context and on the ethic composition of each of these six countries. Citizenship developments are, therefore, perceived as the historical product of the interplay among socio-political, cultural, ethic and geopolitical forces within a particular nation-state.

Turner (1990) makes a distinction between citizenship movements initiated 'from below' and 'from above'. Citizenship movements which are activated by subordinate classes, represent active citizenship and emerge from below. Citizenship movements which are initiated by the ruling classes, represent a passive citizenship movement and emanate from above. According to Turner, citizenship movements in France and the US in the eighteenth century are examples of citizenship movements from below, while citizenship movements in England and Germany in the eighteenth century are examples of citizenship movements from above.

Turner (1990) classifies the arenas in which the contest for citizenship rights takes place, into the public and private realms. Citizenship movements in the public realm are often engaged in direct conflicts with the state apparatus. The actions of movements in the private realm take the form of gradual transformation of both the state and civil society. Citizenship movements in France and England are examples of the former, while those in the US and Germany are examples of the latter.

With reference to these distinctions, we can proceed to look into the developmental trajectory of citizenship rights and their corresponding institutions in Hong Kong. Owing to its being a colony, citizenship rights in Hong Kong have never fully developed, nor have the various elements of citizenship developed to an equal extent. The colonial regime kept a tight control over the development of citizenship rights. Such developments had to be under the patronage of the colonial government or to be initiated 'from above'. Under these circumstances only passive citizenship could develop in Hong Kong.

Institutionalization of Civil Citizenship

Of the three elements of citizenship specified by Marshall (1973), civil rights are the most developed in Hong Kong. The Supreme Court of Hong Kong was established as early as 1844, two years after Hong Kong became a British colony (Endacott, 1964). The British system of common law and an independent judiciary was instituted during the first decade of British rule. As a military and trade base for British merchants to exploit the growing commercial prospects in China, Hong Kong's rational and stable legal foundation was of vital importance. Thus, the establishment of a court of justice to ensue protection of civil rights, especially property rights, was a top priority of the colonial regime. The rule of law that was instituted mainly out of commercial interests, became over the years a custodian of civil rights: 'a measure of respect for civil liberty certainly exists and the means to enforce one's rights are certainly available' (Wesley-Smith, 1988, p.11). Lau and Kuan (1988) describe the existence of the civil component of citizenship in Hong Kong as follows:

> The government has no need to resort to suppression to sustain colonial rule. Consequently, while there is a dearth of positive channels of political participation, the people of Hong Kong are still able to enjoy a tremendous amount of negative political freedom (freedom from government oppression). A case in point is the relatively free press in Hong Kong, which stands in stark contrast to the absence of an all-powerful propaganda apparatus in the hands of the government. In fact, Hong Kong's compact society possesses a highly developed mass media structure which spans a wide spectrum of political colorations. Even though the government retains suppressive power (enshrined in the harsh press law still existent in Hong Kong), it is rarely used except in crisis situations. As such, freedom of speech and expression is largely taken for granted and is difficult to rescind. (pp.32–3)

Kuan's survey (1992) reveals that the court of justice gained the highest vote of confidence among the Hong Kong Chinese. Kuan reports that in 1990, while 70.8 per cent of the respondents expressed trust in the courts, only 58.4 per cent reacted similarly towards the Legislative Council, and only 42.2 per cent expressed confidence in various advisory committees appointed by the Hong Kong government (p.171). The survey also revealed that the Hong Kong Chinese lend strong support to the idea and practice of the rule of law, although these ideas are totally foreign to China's legal traditions (Kuan, 1992).

Institutionalization of Social Citizenship

In comparison with civil citizenship, the institutions securing social citizenship were less developed in terms of both scale and pace before the Second World War. Maintaining law and order was much more important to the colonial regime than the provision of educational and social services. Bowring, the fourth governor of the colony, was quoted as saying in 1854 that, 'It is quite monstrous to see a charge of 8,620 for police ... by contrast with an expenditure of 120 for the instruction of the people' (Endacott, 1964, p.138). A laissez-faire policy and minimal state interference characterized the handling of all social services (Scott, 1989). Throughout the nineteenth century, for example, the expenditure on education constituted on average only 2 per cent of the total government expenditure (Ng, 1984, pp.167–8). Educational, medical and social-welfare services were mainly provided by missionaries and Chinese communal associations (Scott, 1989; Ng, 1984; Sweeting, 1990).

The institutionalization of social citizenship began after the Second World War, more than a century after the British had colonized the territory (Sweeting 1993; Chow 1994). Post-war recovery and the rise of the Chinese Communist Party to power in mainland China triggered a huge influx of refugees into the colony in the late 1940s and the early 1950s. According to one estimate, 'there were 1,285,000 people arriving in the Colony between September 1945 and December 1949' (Podmore, 1971, p.25). According to the first post-war census of 1961, the population growth rate between 1945 and 1961 was more than 500 per cent, and the population totalled 3,130,000 in March 1961. This drastic increase of population elicited huge demands for housing, medical care, welfare, and education. These social demands imposed a heavy burden on the colonial regime that lacked both the motivation and capacity to respond adequately in the late 1940s and early 1950s. The inactive and apathetic attitude of the colonial government was inspired by several factors. First, the threat of the Chinese Communist government in mainland China caused uncertainty concerning the future of the colony. Second, a trade embargo imposed upon the PRC by the United Nations during the Korean War ended abruptly Hong Kong's century-long status as an entry port to China trade, and obliterated the primary financial source of Hong Kong economy. Social services in Hong Kong found themselves in a chaotic situation. A study conducted by the United Nations Commission for Refugees in mid-1954 revealed that 'the number of children aged from 5–14 years who do not attend schools can be estimated at 175,000, the majority being girls' (Sweeting, 1993, p.95). The educational system consisted mainly of private schools, and in 1955 'only 37 per cent of the schools in the territory were government-run or government-funded' (Scott, 1989, p.73). The housing situation was acute as well: 'In 1956, ... 35 per cent of the households had less than 15 sq. ft of living space per person ... In the most overcrowded district, the average living space was only 12 sq. ft, 6 ft by 2 ft per person' (Hopkins, 1971, p.276). Furthermore, 'squatters in 1956 formed about one-seventh of the metropolitan population, the proportion rose quickly to around 20 per cent and reached its peak in 1964–65' (Hopkins, 1971, p.278). Relief and welfare services were mainly provided by 'voluntary or non-government welfare organizations ... Most of these welfare organizations were linked to their parent-bodies overseas; only a few were the outcome of efforts made by the local people like the kaifong and clansmen associations. During this emergency period, the internationally linked welfare organizations had probably done much more than the Government in meeting the welfare needs of the people' (Chow, 1994, p.324). To make things worse, a fire broke out at one of the largest squat areas, Shek Kip Mei, on Christmas Eve in 1953, and left 53,000 people homeless overnight (Castells *et al.*, 1990; Chiu, 1994; Fong, 1987).

The colonial government had to abandon its apathetic laissez-faire policy and to intervene in the situation. A large emergency housing project was launched on top of the ashes at Shek Kip Mei. Though the colonial government began to shoulder a bigger share of responsibility in providing social services in the mid-1950s, its efforts have been characterized as reactive and limited (Chiu, 1994; Chow, 1994; Scott, 1989; Sweeting, 1993). It was not until 1973 when Murry MacLehose took office as the 25th Governor of Hong Kong, that a real change in policy began. In his first policy speech, MacLehose announced his intention to launch large-scale and long-term projects to improve education, public housing, and medical and welfare services. His speech was seen by many observers as the starting point of the process of institutionalization of social citizenship in Hong Kong.

This policy shift was the result of GDP growth that averaged 11.3 per cent annually throughout the 1960s (Ho, 1986, pp.166–70). As a result, the fiscal reserves of the colony by the early 1970s had accumulated to about 1,500 million Hong Kong dollars (Sung, 1986, p.133). No less influential were the two riots which broke out in 1966 and 1967 consecutively. The 1966 riot was triggered by a fare raise for a cross-harbor ferry, and lasted for less than a week. The participants in the riot, especially those who were arrested and convicted, were typically young males under 25 years old, and 'poorly-educated, poorly-paid, inadequately-housed, over-worked' (Scott, 1989, p.89). The colonial regime realized that the riot was not provoked by external political forces, but was the result of internal 'anomie, mindless violence sparked by vague, unarticulated resentment, a product of the existing social structure ... [and] the causes of the riot, at root, probably lie in the common experiences of the rioters and the social conditions under which they had been living' (Scott, 1989, p.88). It became apparent that the riot was the result of a social policy of long neglect. Indeed, the report of a commission set up by the colonial government to inquire into the 1966 Kowloon disturbances recommended:

to stress the need for better education and employment opportunities, better housing, more youth services and recreation facilities, as well as the development of a sense of belonging through participation in community affairs. (Commission of Inquiry on Kowloon Disturbances, 1967, p.147)

In contrast to the 1966 riot, the riot in 1967 was premeditated and provoked by external forces. It was initiated by so called 'leftists' or anti-imperialist, anti-colonialist, and pro-Communist activists (Scott, 1989). The riot which took the form of labor disputes during March and April 1967, escalated in June into a total confrontation between local pro-Communist organizations and the colonial government with demonstrations and a general strike. The conflict reached its peak between August and November 1967 when indiscriminate bomb attacks were launched in the streets. The forceful suppression of the riots by the colonial regime and the aloofness of the Beijing government dissolved these movements towards the end of December 1967. The leftist riots had, ironically, mobilized the support of the Hong Kong Chinese for the colonial government (Scott, 1989). The reaction of the Chinese government implied that the colonial regime of Hong Kong had the endorsement and blessing of the PRC government to govern and to maintain stability and prosperity in the colony.

Within the decade following MacLehose's first policy speech in 1973, the colonial government covered considerable ground in the provision of social services. However, the institutionalization of social citizenship in Hong Kong can be characterized as passive and patronized 'from above'. To a large extent it was not the result of overt and deliberate political articulation and action of citizens, but rather an outcome of the reaction of the colonial regime to the deteriorating social condition in post-war Hong Kong.

The Institutionalization of Political Citizenship

The political component of citizenship is the most underdeveloped in Hong Kong. Basic political rights, such as the rights to elect chief executives and members of the legislature, have never been fully granted to Hong Kong citizens. In fact, the issue of democratization did not appear on Hong Kong's political agenda for over a century. It was not until the summer of 1984, when the Sino-British negotiation on the future of Hong Kong approached its conclusion, that the colonial government began to introduce political rights. From then on, heated debates concerning the institutional developments of political citizenship in Hong Kong took place. The controversies centered around three sets of documents, reflecting the three stages of institutional development of political citizenship in Hong Kong. The first set consisted of the green and white papers entitled 'Further Development of Representative Government in Hong Kong', and were issued in July 1984 and November 1984 respectively. These documents, which signify the initial stage of political reform in Hong Kong, stipulate the creation of an electoral system and composition of the 1985 Legislative Council. The focal issue was the introduction of indirectly elected councillors into the Legislative Council which had been dominated by governor-appointed councillors and government officials. The controversy between the colonial regime and the fairly unorganized general public was mainly focused on the number of indirectly elected members to be introduced in the 1985 Legislative Council. A concession was made by the Hong Kong government to increase the indirectly elected legislators from 12 to 24 but at the same time to increase the total number of legislators from 48 to 56. In other words, elected members were still the minority in the 1985 Legislative Council.

The second stage of political reform was activated by the green paper entitled 'The 1987 Review of Developments in Representative Government', published in May 1987 and the subsequent white paper entitled 'The Development of Representative Government: The Way Forward' issued in February 1988. These documents stipulated the creation of an electoral system and the composition of the 1988 and 1991 Legislative Council. The contestants in this round of the debate over the reform were the Hong Kong government, the Hong Kong general public, which became much more mobilized and well organized, and the PRC government. The main issues were when and how many directly elected members were to be introduced into the Legislative Council. The largest political alignment was the Joint Committee on the Promotion of Democratic Government whose primary objective was to fight for direct election for the 1988 Legislative Council. It was able to bring together 190 organizations, most of which were grass-roots pressure groups, labour unions and student federations (Scott, 1989). The most prominent political action taken by the Joint Committee was a campaign in which 220,000 signatures were collected together with the names and identity card numbers of those who signed. This behavior of the Hong Kong public was considered 'a significant development in a society which had traditionally avoided personal identification with a particular course of political action' (Scott, 1989, p.292). The position of the PRC government was that there should not be drastic changes in the political system of Hong Kong during the transitional period, as this could cause political, social and economic unrest. Such potential sources of disturbance included direct election for the 1988 Legislative Council. Consequently, supporters of the PRC government organized and 60,706 written submissions were made to the Hong Kong government objecting to the 1988 direct election. Of these, '50,175 came on cyclostyled forms and 22,722 of those were from the communist-controlled Hong Kong Federation of Trade Unions' (Scott, 1989, p.294). Confronted by these contradictory or even antagonistic demands, the Hong Kong government requested the Survey Office to collect data and analyze public opinion. The Survey Office released its report in October

1987, and concluded that 'among submissions to the Survey Office from individuals, groups and associations, more were against than in favour of direct elections in 1988' (The Survey Office, 1987, p.8). This was considered by some observers as 'a highly dubious conclusion' (Scott, 1989, pp.286–97), for whom it represented a concession to the PRC demands, suppressing the desire of Hong Kong citizens for direct election to the Legislative Council in 1988. Direct elections were postponed until 1991.

The third stage of the institutional development of political citizenship in Hong Kong concerned the drafting of the Basic Law for the future SAR government. The Basic Law Drafting Committee commenced its work in April 1985 and concluded in April 1990, when the document was endorsed by the National People's Congress of the PRC. The Committee released a consultative draft of the Basic Law for the solicitation of opinions in April 1988. However, the opinions on the political structure of the future SAR government were so diverse and incompatible that the final document included a list of options. The massive support of the Hong Kong Chinese for and their identification with the students' hunger strike at Tiananmen Square, and the protest following the massacre, came as a shock to the PRC government. In retaliation, the final version of the Basic Law was orchestrated by the PRC government to include the most conservative option that was listed in the consultative draft. Only one-third of the members (20 out of 60) would be directly elected for the 1997 Legislative Council. The proportion would increase to two-fifths (24 out of 60) in 1999, and to half of the Council in the year 2003. As for the election of the chief executives for the SAR Government, both nomination and elections would be the responsibility of an electoral college comprising 800 representatives of different sectors of the community, half of them representing professional business interests. The method of forming the electoral college has not yet been determined. All this indicated clearly that the people of Hong Kong would not be granted full and universal franchise either under colonial or under PRC rule. Nevertheless, the decade-long empowering endeavor produced some prominent political leaders and aligned some political organizations and parties. Though these organizations and leaders have been marginalized and constantly criticized by the PRC government, they won massive support in the 1991 general elections (Tsang, 1993). In conclusion, the empowering efforts have not been totally fruitless. They have erected the infrastructure for political participation in Hong Kong, and set the stage for the next round, which was due to take place in 1997.

Citizenship Education in Hong Kong

The present analysis of citizenship education in Hong Kong will be done from the vantage point of the sociology of educational knowledge (Apple, 1979, 1982; Aronowitz and Giroux, 1985; Bernstein, 1971; Giroux, 1981, 1983; Mannheim, 1963; Wexler, 1982, 1987; Young, 1971a). The basic premise is that a relationship exists between the social-historical context, and the selection, organization, and transmission of educational knowledge. Educational knowledge consists of curriculum, pedagogy and evaluation. The curriculum 'defines what counts as valid knowledge, pedagogy defines what counts as valid transmission of knowledge, and evaluation defines what counts as a valid realization of this knowledge on the part of the taught' (Bernstein, 1971, p.47). Bernstein asserts that 'how a society selects, classifies, distributes, transmits and evaluates the educational knowledge it considers to be public, reflects both the distribution of power and the principles of social control'. Consequently, 'school knowledge is analyzed as a meaningful text' (Wexler, 1982, p.277), which signifies a particular representation of meanings. The process of selection and organization of school knowledge can be considered as the 'social practice of signification' and 'the process through which meaning is produced' (Wexler, 1987, p.125). Basic to this approach are questions such as 'what kind of culture system does school knowledge legitimate?' and 'whose interests are served by the production and legitimation of school knowledge?' (Aronowitz and Giroux 1985, p.145).

Citizenship education in Hong Kong will be taken as one form of educational knowledge constructed within the colonial school system. I will analyze the particular conceptions of citizenship signified by it. Furthermore, I will trace changes in these conceptions at different periods of time. Finally, I will analyze how these different conceptions of citizenship are related to, or even serve, the various cultural and institutional configurations. My analysis will focus on the citizenship curriculum only, because no empirical data are available recording pedagogical or evaluative practices.

In the last five decades several school subjects taught in Hong Kong explicitly stated citizenship education as their objective. These included 'Civics' at the secondary school level from 1948 to 1964, which was replaced by 'Economic and Public Affairs' (EPA) in 1965. In 1987, another school subject, 'Government and Public Affairs' (GPA), was introduced into the senior forms (Form 4 and Form 7) of the secondary school. The syllabi of these three school subjects for Forms 4 and 5 will be analyzed, i.e., the syllabi for the Hong Kong Certificate of Education Examination (HKCEE), which is the public examination for Form 5 graduates. The reason for this choice is that data on all three subjects are available for these forms only. The analysis will make a distinction between three periods: (1) citizenship education from 1948 to 1956, (2) from 1957 to 1984, and (3) from 1984 onward.

Citizenship Education from 1948 to 1956: Lifeboat on the High Tide of the Cold War

In 1948, the colonial government suddenly devoted substantial efforts to citizenship education (Sweeting, 1993). In the Education Department Annual Report 1948–49, a special section was devoted to 'Education for Citizenship'

(Education Department, 1948–49); training courses were organized in both English and Chinese for school teachers; and 'Civics', a new subject, was introduced into the Hong Kong School Certificate examination. For the first time in more than a century of colonial rule, citizenship education entered into the the main stream of the colonial school system. The colonial government's sudden enthusiasm came as no surprise, in view of the influx of refugees into the colony, following the rise to power of the Chinese Communist Party in China.

The Civics syllabus consisted of the following sections, and a paragraph was devoted to explain the meanings of each of them: (1) Introduction, (2) Our Community, (3) How Hong Kong is Governed, (4) Public Health, (5) Housing, (6) Communications, (7) Education, (8) Other Public Services, (9) Livelihood, (10) Work, (11) Industry, (12) Money, (13) Insurance, (14) The Press, (15) Politics, (16) War and Peace, and (17) The Future.

What are the themes in each section, and what messages do they convey? The first essential message conveyed in the syllabus is that Hong Kong is under British rule and is a community fundamentally different from China. The section 'Our Community' emphasizes that 'Hong Kong – the community in which we live … [is] connected racially with China and politically with Britain' (The Hong Kong School Certificate Syndicate, 1950, p.47). A comparison between the British system of justice and the judiciary system of China is made in the section on 'How Hong Kong is Governed', stating also that 'Order is the first condition of a happy and prosperous community … Laws are intended to protect rather than to punish' (p.48). In the section 'The Press', the contrast between the political situation in Britain and China is reiterated, in a more subtle manner:

> The primary function of a democratic press is to give full and fair information, and to criticize public affairs within the bounds of justice and good taste. Freedom of the Press is safeguarded by law. Its abuse is restricted by the law of Libel. What happens when the press becomes corrupt or falls under the control of one political party, or of the ruling polity. (p.49)

Another important distinction is that between a citizen and a subject:

> Man as an individual and as a member of society: today he is a 'citizen' rather than a 'subject'. Active association in community life is the mark of a citizen; mere obedience to community laws is the mark of a subject. Democracy requires that all citizens should participate in its activities. (The Hong Kong School Certificate Syndicate, 1950, p.47)

The syllabus presents Britain as a polity of citizens, and China as a polity of subjects. This message was clear to most of the Hong Kong Chinese, who had just fled from mainland China in which the Communist party practised the Marxist doctrine of proletarian dictatorship. The message was that to be able to live under British rule and to enjoy certain rights was a blessing in comparison to the political situation in China. Hence, everyone is gratefully obliged to abide by law and order, 'the first condition of a happy and prosperous community'. The exposition of citizenship in Britain, however, selectively presented only the two elements of civil citizenship which people in Hong Kong could also enjoy under British rule: 'system of justice' and 'democratic press'. No mention was made of political and social citizenship rights in Britain. This was a deliberate choice, because both political and social citizenship rights were absent in Hong Kong. Nevertheless, the syllabus included 'social' topics such as 'Public health', 'Housing', 'Education', and 'Other public services'. Yet a careful reading of the contents of these topics reveals that they have nothing to do with social rights. Instead, these sections simply present a way of life in urban areas, as opposed to that in the rural areas from which most of the Hong Kong Chinese had recently emigrated (Wong, 1981). The 'social' sections also include an irrelevant if not distorted depiction of the social situation in Hong Kong in the early 1950s. For example, the section on 'Housing' included: 'Housing. Modern ideas on housing. Comfort, health, and utility housing schemes. Examples from Europe and America' (p.48). This contrasted sharply with the fact that a quarter of a million of Hong Kong's residents lived in slums at that time, making the exposition on 'Housing' ridiculously irrelevant. It vividly reflects the irresponsible attitude of the colonial government in the early 1950s towards the housing problem in particular and social problems in general.

The syllabus also conveys a broader political view by including the following subjects: 'American capitalism, Russian Communism, and British Socialism' (The Hong Kong School Certificate Syndicate, 1950, p.50). It is obvious that the syllabus reflects the political position of the West during the Cold War. On the one side, there were British democratic socialism and American liberal capitalism. On the other, there were the Russian and Chinese Communist, authoritarian regimes. This Cold War message becomes much sharper if one takes into account the historical context of the early 1950s. China was at war with the United States in Korea; the United States stationed its Seventh Fleet in the Taiwan Straits and South China Sea to blockade the so-called Communist aggression; Hong Kong was flooded with refugees and the colonial government was busy suppressing the rising nationalism among the Hong Kong Chinese. The Cold War message is also seen in the way nationalism is presented in the syllabus. In the section 'War and peace', the following statements are found:

The causes of war. Intellectually, socially, and economically, we are largely cosmopolitan, but politically we have not advanced far beyond

> a narrow form of nationalism. War is caused largely by the retardation of our political development. Peace as a positive and creative force. How it can be secured. The United Nations Organization as an ideal of world-wide Government to which all nations owe ultimate obedience. The British Commonwealth as an example of what can be done to achieve the peace, happiness and co-operation of nations. (The Hong Kong School Certificate Syndicate, 1950, p.50)

The messages 'to owe ultimate obedience to the United Nations' and 'to advance beyond a narrow form of nationalism' are clearly intended to tame nationalist sentiments among those Hong Kong Chinese loyal to the PRC. The PRC was after all 'disobedient', being involved in a military conflict with the United Nations. The message is further strengthened in the syllabus by appealing to cosmopolitan rather than national loyalty. In the section 'The future', the syllabus states:

> Citizens of the World. How science and knowledge have broken the old barriers of isolationism. ... Every individual is now virtually concerned with events happening throughout the world. Our first concern and first loyalty are with our own immediate surroundings, but they, in turn are bound up with world conditions. The ultimate loyalty of all is humanity as a whole. (The Hong Kong School Certificate Syndicate, 1950, p.50)

It is obvious that the conception of citizenship the syllabus strives to convey is that of a nationless citizen, loyal to the British Commonwealth and to the United Nations.

In summary, the messages conveyed in the Civics syllabus can be described metaphorically as follows. Hong Kong is a lifeboat and China is the rough sea. The Hong Kong Chinese must be grateful for the blessing to be able to climb onto the lifeboat during the high tide of the Cold War. They should be compliant and should not rock the boat.

Citizenship Education from 1957–84: Constitution of a Subject Political Culture

The underlying theme of citizenship education in this period was the constitution of an autonomous economic community supported by a subject political culture. From the end of the 1950s to the early 1980s, there were several changes in the citizenship education curricula. The Civics syllabus was substantially amended in 1957. It was later replaced by a new school subject – Economic and Public Affairs – which remained generally intact until the mid-1980s.

A comparison between the Civics syllabi of 1950 and 1957 indicates fundamental differences. A number of essential political messages conveyed in the 1950 Civics syllabus totally disappeared from the 1957 syllabus. These included the Cold War rhetoric about American capitalism, Russian Communism, British Socialism, narrow nationalism, isolationism, etc. Comparisons between Chinese and British rule were also deleted from the 1957 syllabus. 'China' and 'The Chinese' vanished completely from the 1957 syllabus. These deletions reflected British intentions to develop Hong Kong into an independent community, isolated from the Cold War confrontation between the PRC and the US, while nationally and politically secluding the Hong Kong Chinese from the PRC.

The democratic, participatory conception of citizenship in the 1950 syllabus was replaced by 'responsible citizenship', defined as a set of relationships between citizens and the community, including 'Obeying laws; civic duties; active participation in its [the community's] affairs ... service; the value of character and initiative' (The Hong Kong School Certificate Syndicate, 1957, p.32). The 1957 syllabus emphasized the social component of citizenship, which had been missing in the 1950 version. Under the section 'Man and his institutions', the following topics are included in the 1957 syllabus: 'citizens' opportunities for service', 'governmental and voluntary agencies of social services', 'relief work', 'youth work', etc. (p.28). In contrast to the exposition on the housing problem in the 1950 syllabus which I characterized above as 'ridiculously irrelevant', the 1957 syllabus presents the problem realistically under the topic 'Shelter', stressing the following points: (1) Overcrowding in Hong Kong, its causes and effects; provision for the safety, comfort and health of the individual and community; (2) Resettlement and low-cost housing; the squatter problem, emergency and long-term measures. Voluntary and government housing project.

There was also a substantial increase in the coverage of economic affairs in the 1957 syllabus, especially regarding trade and industry. Taken together, the differences between the 1950 and 1957 syllabi signify changes in the social, economic and political context of Hong Kong during the 1950s. The British colony had come out of the uncertainty concerning its future, as it became clear that the newly established PRC was unlikely to reclaim its sovereignty over Hong Kong in the foreseeable future. Hong Kong had gradually recovered from its economic crisis and developed into an industrial colony. The colonial government began to cope with the social turmoil caused by the huge influx of immigrants, by gradually developing social service programmes. All these themes are present in a section entitled 'Hong Kong Today': (1) What Hong Kong is: commercial and industrial centre, community of free individuals, example of tolerance, e.g., racial, religious. (2) Main reasons for growth: geographic position; trade; the overcoming of early difficulties; just and stable government; periodic influx of population; enterprise and industry of population; influx of capital (p.31).

In 1964, Civics was replaced by Economic and Public Affairs (EPA), and half of the syllabus was dedicated to economic affairs. The 1968 syllabus for the Hong Kong Certificate of Education, stipulated that 'a candidate must show knowledge of both economic and public affairs' (Hong Kong Certificate of the Education Board, 1966, p.26). The expansion of economic affairs was at the expense of the political aspects of citizenship education. The latter were marginalized in the only section of the 1968 syllabus designated to deal with the relationships between the 'Government and the citizen'. The section covered the following topics:

(a) The government's responsibility to provide necessary services and to protect the citizen.

(b) The citizen's duty to co-operate, the importance of the individual's work, character and service.

(c) Aid given by voluntary societies. (Hong Kong Certificate of Education Board, 1966, p.28)

The administrative output of the colonial state, mainly in the forms of social services, took up more than one-third of the topics in the 1968 syllabus. Taken together, the various orientations characterize a subject political culture. In other words, citizens were relegated to the role of a subject who is the recipient of and abider by governmental administrative outputs (Almond and Verba, 1963).

The 1975 EPA syllabus, published in 1973, underwent some further amendments. The term 'colony' was replaced by 'community' and, after more than 20 years, China made its re-entrance in the syllabus. China was mentioned in the section 'Hong Kong's international setting', which included 'social and political links with other countries, with particular reference to Britain and China' (Hong Kong Certificate of Education Board, 1973, p.52). The changing attitude toward China had to do with the PRC's resumption of its permanent membership in the United Unions in 1972, and its subsequent demand that Hong Kong be removed from the list of territories under the purview of the Special Committee on Colonialism. The introduction of the concept of 'community' was part of a project designed to inculcate a sense of belonging in the young generation in Hong Kong. It came at first as a response to the 1966 riot (Scott, 1989, pp.82–96), and was designed as a means to contain the growing dissent among the young. Student movements in Hong Kong proliferated in the early 1970s and campaigned for various causes: a campaign for Chinese to become the official language in Hong Kong, and an anti-corruption movement in 1975 (Leung, 1993). Political messages which could encourage active political participation were deleted from the 1975 syllabus, together with the topic 'Citizens', which was replaced by the 'Role of youth'. It included the following topics:

(a) The size of the youth population in Hong Kong and the rights and responsibilities of youth *vis-à-vis* the community.

(b)   The importance and problems of youth in relation to Hong Kong public affairs. (Hong Kong Certificate of Education Board, 1973, p.52)

Overall, the 1975 syllabus did not contain any message relating to the role of citizens as political actors, nor was there any exposition of channels of political input available to the Hong Kong residents. The syllabus emphasized the community, the constitutional structure of the government, and the provision of governmental services such as education, welfare, housing and communications. Citizens were regraded as recipients of services patronized by the colonial government. The 1975 syllabus is a typical example of citizenship education for a subject political culture.

The EPA syllabus, which was published in 1980, underwent additional amendments in 1982, reflecting a more liberal approach. The topic 'Government and the people' reappeared, and included an exposition of liberal democracy and of the political inputs available to the Hong Kong citizenry. However, these inputs represented passive forms of citizenship, such as 'consultation' and 'redress of grievances'. The 1982 syllabus also included the treatment of the current social problems of Hong Kong, emphasizing the government's role in the provision of social services.

Citizenship Education since 1984: Under the Imperative of the 1997 Run-up to Self-Rule

In response to the 1997 run-up to British withdrawal, and to reunion with the People's Republic of China, citizenship education in Hong Kong underwent significant changes. First, in 1985 the Education Department issued Guidelines on Civic Education in Schools, and in 1987 a new school subject – Government and Public Affairs – was introduced and became a requirement for the Hong Kong Certificate of Education Examination in 1989. The EPA syllabus also underwent a major amendment in 1992.

Ever since the 1997 issue became public concern and the Chinese government proclaimed that a high degree of autonomy would be granted to Hong Kong Chinese after 1997, there has been a mounting demand for strengthening citizenship education in the schools' curriculum, to prepare future citizens for self-government after 1997. The initial response of the colonial regime was 'unwilling' and 'dismissive' (Morris, 1992). For example, in reply to Legislators' queries concerning the government's policy stance on citizenship education, the Director of Education bluntly replied that there were plenty of opportunities available to young people going through the education system to develop their political awareness and knowledge (Hong Kong Hansard, 1983–84, pp.920–2). On another occasion he went even further and 'criticized those who had argued for the inclusion of political studies in the curriculum on the ground that it was "too risky"' (Morris, 1992, p.128). As public demand for promoting citizenship education in schools gathered momentum, the government finally compromised and announced that 'a comprehensive set of guidelines ... to assist teachers and school authorities to implement the plan' would be published (Hong Kong Hansard, 1983/84, p.1283).

However, a careful examination of the guidelines reveals the remains of a subject political culture. The section 'Political socialization' indicates this trend:

> Socialization is usually understood as a process through which new or immature members of society are induced to accept and conform to traditionally established ways of life. To this end, civic education, with the promotion of social responsibility as its main aim, becomes a method of political socialization. However, there are those who consider that civic education should not be used in this way, claiming that its 'products' become merely passive, consenting adults all too ready to 'toe the government line'. Critics of political socialization would prefer to see young people grow up with a reforming zeal, prepared to question established authority and introduce radical changes. (Curriculum Development Committee, 1985, p.9)

It is apparent that the guidelines identify with the conception of a citizen who 'conformed to traditionally established ways of life' as opposed to the conception of a citizen who dares to question established authority. The questioning of established authority is, nonetheless, a responsible act of democratic citizenship. Hence, the cited paragraph indicates that the government was not yet prepared to be criticized by its colonial subjects.

The conservative stance of the colonial government concerning citizenship education indeed becomes visible through the interpretation of democracy and education for democracy in the guidelines. In the section entitled 'Education for democracy', the following expositions can be found:

> Democracy means different things to different people. As the American president Abraham Lincoln put it, it means 'Government of the people, by the people, for the people'. Alternatively, it may also be interpreted as a way of life in which the decision-making process is characterized by majority control. There are many brands of democracy in the political arena – some pluralistic, some centralist and various combinations of both. So education for democracy *per se* would be difficult to interpret. Although some basic understanding of the concept of democracy may be introduced according to the intellectual level and experience of pupils, for the purpose of the guidelines the term 'civic education' will be used. (p.8)

Both these statements and the logic behind them are problematic. I would query whether the meaning of democracy was as ambiguous as the paragraph suggested; and if the interpretation of 'education for democracy' was as difficult as the paragraph implies. Even if one accepts these assertions about democracy and education for democracy, this does not allow one to conclude that education for democracy should be introduced solely as an intellectual, academic exercise in conceptual analysis. The paragraph reveals the government's dismissive attitude towards education for democracy.

The guidelines include a framework for teaching civic education through the formal curriculum, specifying that

> Civic education ... should be merged into the widest possible programme of interdisciplinary or 'integrated' studies but not to the extent that it loses its focus and identity in the minds of teachers and pupils. Teachers of social subjects will continue to play a central role in the school's civic education programme but teachers in other areas of experience should be aware of the social and political dimensions and incorporate these in their teaching. (p.25)

The paragraph indicates that the colonial government does not intend to introduce civic education as a distinct subject into the existing school curriculum. Instead, teachers will be asked to integrate elements of citizenship education into existing school subjects. Such an arrangement has been criticized by local educators and scholars as conservative or even irresponsible, leaving the school curriculum intact (Tsang, 1985; Yu, 1986; Morris, 1992; Morris and Sweeting, 1991). The existing secondary school curriculum is apolitical and anationalist in nature, and does not provide teachers with the opportunity to foster democratic citizenship (Luk, 1991; Morris, 1992; Morris and Sweeting, 1991; Tsang, 1985). Furthermore, the pragmatic examination-oriented approach of both teachers and students in the competitive schooling system of Hong Kong makes it very unlikely that time be dedicated to citizenship education as part of other school subjects. Such a proposal therefore only indicates that the colonial regime intended to maintain the *status quo*. This conservative attitude towards citizenship education is in total congruence with the government's stance concerning political reform in Hong Kong.

A new syllabus, the GPA, was introduced into the school curriculum at the 'A' level (i.e., matriculation level). However, this was not a novelty. In fact, 'during the 1970s several attempts were made to introduce an "A" level subject in Politics. These initial efforts were not fruitful as the subject was viewed by the Education Department as too specialized and unsuitable for school children who might be susceptible to undue political pressure' (Morris and Sweeting, 1991, p.161). In response to public pressure, the Education Department and the Director of Education announced in the Legislative Council in May 1984 that the subject GPA would be introduced in the 'A' level examination. They went even further, to proclaim the introduction of the subject into the Hong Kong Certificate of Education Examination (i.e., examination for Form 5 school leavers) was also under serious consideration. Subsequently, the syllabus of 'A' level GPA was published in 1986, and students took the examination for the first time in 1988. The GPA syllabus for the Hong Kong Certificate of Education Examination was published in 1987 and students were examined in 1989.

Analysis of the contents of the GPA syllabus on the Hong Kong Certificate of Education Examination level reveals that, in comparison with the previous EPA syllabus, a number of improvements had been made. For example, in the section 'Government and the People', detailed expositions on topics such as 'rights of citizens' and 'representative government and elections' are found:

(a) fundamental rights and obligations of citizens
    (i) civil rights, e.g., freedom of speech, freedom of association and freedom of belief
    (ii) political rights, e.g., the right to vote, to be elected and to voice opinion on government policies
    (iii) obligations, e.g., to obey laws and to pay taxes;

(b) representative government and elections
    (i) meaning and characteristics of representative government
    (ii) meaning and role of elections; accountability of government
    (iii) direct and indirect elections and their relative merits
    (iv) a basic knowledge of two major forms of representative government: liberal democratic, e.g., UK, USA. and democratic centralist e.g., China
    (v) the development of representative government in Hong Kong.

(Hong Kong Examination Authority, 1987, p.202)

Two essential aspects of citizenship long neglected in citizenship education in Hong Kong were incorporated, namely, citizens as political actors and citizens' political inputs.

Another significant improvement in the GPA syllabus is the way social problems and services are handled. In previous syllabi social services were treated as part of the administrative outputs and patronage granted by the colonial government to its subjects. In contrast, the 1989 GPA syllabus treats education, medical and health services, housing, public order, social welfare and transport as 'public policy areas' and students are encouraged to study these areas by adopting a reflective and participatory approach. For example, the GPA syllabus suggests that in studying social issues and policies:

Pupils are expected to acquire the basic knowledge, and to develop the appropriate skills and attitudes in approaching local social issues:

(i)   location, gathering, organizing, analyzing and evaluating information
(ii) evaluating the public policies concerned and suggesting possible alternatives
(iii) participating effectively and responsibly in social and political processes relating to the social issues and public policies concerned. (p.204)

Another feature of the 1989 GPA syllabus worth underlining is the way China is presented. A specific section is devoted to 'Hong Kong and China', discussing the following topics: (1) relationships between Hong Kong and China, (2) political institutions of the People's Republic of China, and (3) recent developments in China and their impact on Hong Kong. Under these topics, a wide range of concepts and principles are discussed, such as the Sino-British agreement, the idea of 'one country – two systems', state institutions of the PRC, party institutions of the Chinese Communist party, etc. These represent an attempt to provide students with a comprehensive understanding of the relationships between Hong Kong and China for the first time in Hong Kong's history.

The Economic and Public Affairs syllabus for the Hong Kong Certificate of Education Examination also underwent a major revision in 1992, with regard to both content and the teaching approach. These changes were implemented in the 1994 examinations.

The structure of the syllabus was changed. Instead of being divided into two parts, Economic Affairs and Public Affairs, it is divided into the six following sections: (A) The Individual as a Consumer, (B) The Individual as a Producer, (C) Consumer, Producer and Their Interactions, (D) The Individual as a Citizen, (E) The Economic and Political Environment of Hong Kong, and (F) Controversial Issues..

In the 1994 syllabus an 'institution approach' is replaced by a 'role approach': that is, economic and public affairs are no longer presented as the outputs of economic and political institutions. Instead they are treated as outcomes of activities and roles performed by consumers, producers and citizens. The rights and obligations of these actors have also assumed a central position in the new syllabus. In addition to the exposition of 'consumer rights and protection', and 'the function of labor unions in promoting labor welfare', the syllabus presents the most detailed exposition of citizenship rights ever. These are included in the section 'The Individual as a Citizen':

4.1. Civil rights: the rights necessary for individual freedom, e.g., freedom of speech, freedom of belief, freedom of association and assembly, Habeas corpus and the right to be tried fairly and impartially.

4.2. Political rights: the rights to participate in the exercise of political power, e.g., the right to vote, to be elected and to dissent.

4.3. Social rights: the rights to a minimal economic and social well-being, e.g., the right to education and to social services.

4.4. Bill of Rights in Hong Kong: a brief understanding of the importance of the Bill of Rights in Hong Kong.

4.5. Obligations: e.g., to respect others' rights, to obey laws, to pay taxes. (Hong Kong Examination Authority, 1992, pp.150–1)

The approach proposed in the 1994 EPA syllabus for teaching controversial issues resembles the practices of Western democracies, notably the UK and US, in the last three decades (Bank, 1985; Barr *et al.*, 1978; Cherryholmes, 1980; Crick and Porter, 1978; Engle and Ochoa, 1988):

Framework for approaching the controversial issues:

(i) identify the values embedded in the issues. The issues involve different values which lead to differences in the goals, methods and results of public policies, thus controversies arise.

(ii) establish the facts related to the issues. It is important to clarify the facts around which the controversies have developed.

(iii) clarify the meanings or use of words which describe the controversies.

(iv) evaluate the proposals for solving the controversies and examine the possible consequences of the proposals. (p.155)

However, examination of the rate of students' exposure to these syllabi is not encouraging. Both school subjects are not central in the Hong Kong Certificate of Education Examinations. In 1994, for example, only 905 candidates sat for the GPA examinations, and 1,151 sat for the EPA examinations, constituting less than 2.5 per cent of the total number of candidates for the HKCEE. Furthermore, after the revised 1994 syllabus was published in 1992, no appropriate textbooks were made available. Textbook publishers do not consider it profitable to launch a major revision of existing textbooks for small numbers of students, let alone publishing a new textbook.

CONCLUSION

Since 1984, citizenship education in Hong Kong has taken large strides in the direction of democratic education, focusing on civil, political, and social rights of citizens, and of their active participation in the political process. The developments which are discussed in this chapter, and their relationships to

TABLE 12.4
CULTURAL AND INSTITUTIONAL DEVELOPMENT OF CITIZENSHIP AND CITIZENSHIP
EDUCATION IN POST-WAR HONG KONG

Period	Characteristics of Political Culture	Institutionalization of Citizenship	Citizenship Education
1945–1950s	Parochial / Parochial-Subject Political Culture	Civil Citizenship and Institutions	Citizenship Education for the 'Lifeboat' Situation
1960s–1984	Subject Political Culture	Institutionalizing Social Citizenship	Citizenship Education for Subject Political Culture
1984–present	Participatory Political Culture	Institutionalizing Political Citizenship	Citizenship Education in a Triangle of Tensions: Patronage, Domestication or Empowerment

the situation regarding educational and social reforms are summarized in Table 12.4.

These developments were displeasing to the PRC and its supporters in Hong Kong, who propagated nationalist and patriotic citizenship education, stressing the idea of China as the mother country. This approach is congruent with the domesticating stance which has been taken by the PRC government towards political and social developments in Hong Kong, in anticipation of the 1997 change of political regime.

In the spring of 1995, the Hong Kong government announced that the second edition of the guidelines on Civic Education in the Schools would be issued in November 1995. The announcement resulted in heated debates among local educators. Once more the triangle of tensions, namely, between the patronage of the colonial regime, the domestication strategies of the PRC, and the desire of citizens and local educators for empowerment and emancipation, came into play.

It must be emphasized that the analysis presented in this chapter is far from complete. The scope of analysis was limited to syllabi, overlooking other aspects of the curricula, such as textbooks and other teaching materials. Furthermore, I did not analyze the other two elements of educational knowledge, namely pedagogy and evaluation. The collection of vital information from the designers of the syllabi, and from teachers and students, was clearly beyond the scope of the present study. I also did not explore the syllabi of related subjects such as history and geography. However, given all these constraints, the analysis illuminated several basic features of citizenship education in Hong Kong. It also revealed how these features are related to changes in the economic and political situation of Hong Kong society at large.

REFERENCES

Abramson, P.R. (1983). *Political attitudes in America: Formation and change.* San Francisco, CA: Freeman.

Almond, G. and Verba, S. (1963). *The civic culture: Political attitudes and democracy in five nations.* Princeton, NJ: Princeton University Press.

Almond, G. and Verba, S. (1980). *The civic culture revisited.* Boston, MA: Little, Brown.

Apple, M.W. (1979). *Ideology and curriculum.* London: Routledge & Kegan Paul.

Apple, M.W. (1982). *Education and power.* London: Routledge & Kegan Paul.

Aronowitz, S. and Giroux, H. (1985). *Education under siege: The conservative, liberal, and radical debate over schooling.* London: Routledge & Kegan Paul.

Balch, G.I. (1974). 'Multiple indicators in survey research. The concept: sense of political efficacy', *Political Methodology*, 1, 1–43.

Bank, J.A. (1985). *Teaching strategies for the social studies: Inquiry, valuing and decision making* (3rd edn). New York: Longman.

Barr, R., Barth, J.L. and Shermis, S.S. (1987). *The nature of social studies.* Palm Springs, CA: ETC.

Bernstein, B. (1971). 'On the classification and framing of educational knowledge', in M.F.D. Young (ed.), *Knowledge and control: New directions for the sociology of education* (pp.47–69). London: Collier Macmillan.

Bottomore, T. (1992). 'Citizenship and social class, forty years on', in T.H. Marshall and T. Bottomore (eds), *Citizenship and social class* (pp.55–93). Concord, MA: Pluto Press.

Burbaker, W. Rogers (1990). 'Immigration, citizenship, and the nation-state in France and Germany: A comparative historical analysis', *International Sociology*, 3, 379–407.

Campbell, A., Gurin, G. and Miller, W.E. (1954). *The voter decides.* Evanston, IL: Row, Peterson.

Campbell, A., Converse, P.E., Miller, W.E. and Stokes, D.E. (1960). *The American voter.* New York: John Wiley.

Castells, M., Goh, L. and R.Y.-W. Kwok (1990). *The Shek Kip Mei syndrome: Economic development and public housing in Hong Kong and Singapore.* London: Pion.

Cherryholmes, C.H. (1980). 'Social knowledge and citizenship education: Two views of truth and criticism', *Curriculum Inquiry*, 10, 115–41.

Cheung, A.B.L. and Louie, Kin-shuen (1991). *Social conflict in Hong Kong, 1975–1986: Trends and implications.* Hong Kong: Hong Kong Institute of Asia-Pacific Studies, The Chinese University of Hong Kong, Occasional Paper No.3.

Chiu, R.L.H. (1994). 'Housing intervention in Hong Kong: From laissez faire to privatization', in B.K.P. Leung and T.Y.C. Wong (eds), *25 years of social and economic development in Hong Kong* (pp.336–56). Hong Kong: Centre of Asian Studies, Occasional Paper and Monograph No.111.

Chow, N. (1994). 'Welfare development in Hong Kong: An ideological appraisal', in B.K.P. Leung and T.Y.C. Wong (eds), *25 years of social and economic development in Hong Kong* (pp.317–21). Hong Kong: Centre of Asian Studies, Occasional Paper and Monograph No.111.

Commission of Inquiry on Kowloon Disturbances (1967). *Kowloon Disturbance 1966, Report of Commission of Inquiry.* Hong Kong: Government Printer.

Crick, B. and Porter, A. (eds) (1978). *Political education and political literacy.* London: Longman.

Curriculum Development Committee (1985). *Guidelines on civic education in schools.* Hong Kong: Government Printer.

Education Department (1948–49). *Education department annual report.* Hong Kong: Government Printer.

Endacott, G.B. (1964). *A history of Hong Kong.* Hong Kong: Oxford University Press.

Engle, S.H. and Ochoa, A.S. (1988). *Education for democratic citizenship: Decision making in the social studies.* New York: Teachers College Press.

Fong, P.K.W. (1987). 'A historical analysis of housing policies in Hong Kong', *Urban India,* 7 (2), 1–9.

Giddens, A. (1982). 'Class division, class conflict and citizenship rights', in A. Giddens, *Profiles and critiques in social theory* (pp.164–80). London: Macmillan.

Giroux, Henry A. (1981). *Ideology, culture, and the process of schooling.* Philadelphia, PA: Temple University Press.

Giroux, Henry A. (1983). *Theory and resistance in education: A pedagogy for the opposition.* South Hadley, MA: Bergin & Garvey.

Habermas, J. (1973). *Legitimation crisis.* Boston, MA: Beacon Press.

Held, D. (1989). 'Citizenship and autonomy', in D. Held and J.B. Thompson (eds), *Social theory of modern society: Anthony Giddens and his critics* (pp.162–84). Cambridge: Cambridge University Press.

Ho, Tin-pin (1986). 'Hong Kong's trade and industry: Changing patterns and prospects', in J.Y.S. Cheng (ed.), *Hong Kong in transition* (pp.165–207). Hong Kong: Oxford University Press.

Hoadley (1970). 'Hong Kong is the lifeboat: Notes on political culture and socialization', *Journal of Oriental Studies,* 8, 206–18.

Hong Kong Certificate of Education Board (1966). *Handbook of syllabuses for the 1968 examination.* Hong Kong: Government Printer.

Hong Kong Certificate of Education Board (1973). *Handbook of syllabuses for the 1975 examination.* Hong Kong: Government Printer.

Hong Kong Examination Authority (1980). *Hong Kong Certificate of Education Examination regulations and syllabuses 1982.* Hong Kong: Hong Kong Examination Authority.

Hong Kong Examination Authority (1987). *Hong Kong Certificate of Education Examination regulations and syllabuses 1989.* Hong Kong: Hong Kong Examination Authority.

Hong Kong Examination Authority (1992). *Hong Kong Certificate of Education Examination regulations and syllabuses 1994.* Hong Kong: Hong Kong Examination Authority.

Hong Kong Hansard: Reports of the Sitting of the Legislative Council of Hong Kong, Session 1983/84. Hong Kong: Government Printer.

Hong Kong School Certificate Syndicate (1950). *Hong Kong School Certificate Examination regulations and syllabuses for 1950.* Hong Kong: Ye Olde Prinyerie.

Hong Kong School Certificate Syndicate (1957). *Hong Kong School Certificate Examination regulations and syllabuses for 1957.* Hong Kong: Government Printer.

Hopkins, K. (1971), 'Housing the poor', in K. Hopkins (ed.), *Hong Kong: The industrial colony* (pp.271–335). Hong Kong: Oxford University Press.

Hsiao, Kung-chuan (1979). *A history of Chinese political thought.* Princeton, NJ: Princeton University Press.

Hughes, R. (1976). *Hong Kong: Borrowed place, borrowed time* (2nd edn). London: André Deutsch.

Ichilov, O. (1990). 'Dimensions and role patterns of citizenship in democracy', in O. Ichilov (ed.), *Political socialization, citizenship education and democracy* (pp.165–207). New York: Teachers College Press.

Inglehart, R. (1990). *Culture shift: In advanced industrial society*. Princeton, NJ: Princeton University Press.

King, A.Y.C. (1981). 'The political culture of Kwan Tong: A Chinese community in Hong Kong', in A.Y.C. King and R.P.L. Lee (eds), *Social life and development in Hong Kong* (pp.147–68). Hong Kong: The Chinese University of Hong Kong.

Kuan, H.K. (1992). 'Legal culture: The challenge of modernization', in S.K. Lau, M.K. Lee, P.S. Wan and S.L. Wong (eds), *Indicators of social development: Hong Kong 1990* (pp.159–72). Hong Kong: Hong Kong Institute of Asia-Pacific Studies, The Chinese University of Hong Kong.

Lau, Siu-kai (1982). *Society and politics in Hong Kong*. Hong Kong: Chinese University of Hong Kong.

Lau, Siu-kai (1992). 'Political attitudes', in S.K. Lau, M.K. Lee, P.S. Wan and S.L. Wong (eds), *Indicators of social development: Hong Kong 1990* (pp.129–57). Hong Kong Institute of Asia-Pacific Studies, The Chinese University of Hong Kong.

Lau, Siu-kai and Ho, Kam-fai (1982). 'Social accommodation of politics: The case of the young Hong Kong workers', *Journal of Commonwealth and Comparative Politics*, 20, 172–88.

Lau, Siu-kai and Hsin-chi Kuan (1986). 'The changing political culture of the Hong Kong Chinese', in J.Y.S. Cheng (ed.), *Hong Kong in transition* (pp.26–51). Hong Kong: Oxford University Press.

Lau, Siu-kai and Hsin-chi Kuan (1988). *The ethos of the Hong Kong Chinese*. Hong Kong: The Chinese University Press.

Lau, Siu-kai, Kuan, Hsin-chi and Wan, P.S. (1991). 'Political attitudes', in S.K. Lau, M.K. Lee, P.S. Wan and S.L. Wong (eds), *Indicators of social development: Hong Kong 1988* (pp.173–205). Hong Kong: Hong Kong Institute of Asia-Pacific Studies, The Chinese University of Hong Kong.

Leung, Kwan-kok (1993). 'Student politics in Hong Kong: Democracy and transition', in D.H. McMillen and M.E. DeGoeger (eds), *One culture, many systems: Politics in the unification of China* (pp.159–72). Hong Kong: The Chinese University Press.

Louie, Kin-sheun (1993). 'Who voted in the 1991 election?: A demographic profile of the Hong Kong electorate', in S.K. Lau and K.S. Louie (eds), *Hong Kong tried democracy: The 1991 election in Hong Kong* (pp.1–40). Hong Kong: Hong Kong Institute of Asia-Pacific Studies.

Luk, Bernard H.K. (1989). 'Education', in T.L. Tsim and B.H.K. Luk (eds), *The other Hong Kong report* (pp.151–88). Hong Kong: The Chinese University Press.

Luk, Bernard H.K. (1991). 'Chinese culture in the Hong Kong curriculum: Heritage and colonialism', *Comparative Education Review*, 35, 650–68.

Mann, M. (1987). 'Ruling class strategies and citizenship', *Sociology*, 2 (3), 339–54.

Mannheim, K. (1963). *Ideology and utopia: An introduction to the sociology of knowledge*. London: Routledge & Kegan Paul.

Marshall, T.H. (1973). 'Citizenship and social class', in T.H. Marshall, *Class, citizenship and social development*. Chicago, IL: The University of Chicago Press.

Milbrath, L.W. and Goel, M. (1977). *Political participation* (2nd edn). Chicago, IL: Rand McNally.

Miller, W.E. and Traugott, S.A. (1989). *American national election studies data sourcebook, 1952–1986*. Cambridge, MA: Harvard University Press.

Morris, Paul (1992). *Curriculum development in Hong Kong* (2nd edn). Hong Kong: Faculty of Education, University of Hong Kong, Education Paper No.7.

Morris, P. and Sweeting, A.E. (1991). 'Education and politics: The case of Hong Kong from an historical perspective', *Oxford Review of Education*, 17, 249–67.

Ng, Lun Nagi-ha (1984). *Interactions of East and West: Development of public education in early Hong Kong*. Hong Kong: The Chinese University Press.

Podmore, D. (1971). 'The population of Hong Kong', in K. Hopkins (ed.), *Hong Kong: The industrial colony* (pp.21–54). Hong Kong: Oxford University Press.

Pye, L. (1968). *The spirit of Chinese politics*. Cambridge, MA: Harvard University Press.

Scott, I. (1989). *Political change and the crisis of legitimacy in Hong Kong*. Hong Kong: Oxford University Press.

Solomon, R. (1971). *Mao's revolution and the Chinese political culture*. Berkeley: University of California Press.

Sung, Y.W. (1986). 'Fiscal and economic policies in Hong Kong', in J.Y.S. Cheng (ed.), *Hong Kong in transition* (pp.120–41). Hong Kong: Oxford University Press.

Survey Office (1987). *Public response to Green Paper: The 1987 review of development in representative government: Report of the Survey Office*. Hong Kong: Government.

Sweeting, A. (1990). *Education in Hong Kong pre-1984 to 1941: Fact and opinion*. Hong Kong: Hong Kong University Press.

Sweeting, A. (1993). *A phoenix transformed: The reconstruction of education in post-war Hong Kong*. Hong Kong: Oxford University Press.

Tsang, Wing-kwong (1985). 'A study on the direction and approach of the guidelines on civic education', *Chung Pao Monthly*, 71, 47–52 (Chinese).

Tsang, Wing-kwong (1993). 'Who voted for the Democrats? An analysis of the electoral choice of the 1991 Legislative Council election', in S.K. Lau and K.S. Louie (eds), *Hong Kong tried democracy: The 1991 election in Hong Kong* (pp.115–85). Hong Kong: Hong Kong Institute of Asia-Pacific Studies.

Turner, B.S. (1990). 'Outline of a theory of citizenship', *Sociology*, 24(1), 189–217.

Verba, S., Nie, N.H. and Kim, J. (1978). *Participation and political equality: A seven-nation comparison*. Chicago, IL: University of Chicago Press.

Wesley-Smith, P. (1988). 'The method of protecting civil liberties in Hong Kong', in Raymond Wacks (ed.), *Civil liberties in Hong Kong* (pp.11–30). Hong Kong: Oxford University Press.

Wexler, P. (1982). 'Structure, text, and subject: A critical sociology of school knowledge', in M.W. Apple (ed.), *Cultural and economic reproduction in education: Essays on class, ideology and the state* (pp.275–303). London: Routledge & Kegan Paul.

Wexler, P. (1987). *Social analysis of education: After the new sociology*. London: Routledge & Kegan Paul.

Whitty, G. (1985). *Sociology and school knowledge: Curriculum theory, research and politics*. London: Methuen.

Wong, Ping-man (1981). 'Hong Kong post-war economic and public affairs curriculum and citizenship education in comparative perspective', unpublished MA thesis, School of Education, Chinese University of Hong Kong (Chinese).

Young, M.F.D. (1971a). 'An approach to the study of curricular as socially organized knowledge', in M.F.D. Young (ed.), *Knowledge and control: New directions for the sociology of education* (pp.19–46). London: Collier Macmillan.

Young, M.F.D. (ed.) (1971b). *Knowledge and control: New directions for the sociology of education*. London: Collier Macmillan.

Yu, Shiu-tak (ed.) (1986). *Selected works on civic education* (Vols 1 and 2). Hong Kong: Professional Teachers' Union, Hong Kong (Chinese).

13

CITIZENSHIP AND CITIZENSHIP EDUCATION IN BRITAIN

IAN LISTER

INTRODUCTION

In considering citizenship and citizenship education in Britain there are several key factors which need to be highlighted:

1. Britain had, and still has, a monarchy, and it is *not* a republic. Some argue that citizenship is essentially a republican concept (and cite the US and France as the main examples). The future of the monarchy is now a topic for open debate.
2. Britain has no written constitution, and no bill of rights, and, thus, no authoritative and official code to which citizenship might be related in terms of rights and responsibilities. Constitutional reform is now on the agenda of the political parties.
3. Britain is made up of four parts – England, Scotland, Wales and Northern Ireland. The 'United Kingdom' might be a declaration of intent rather than a statement of fact. There is on-going civil strife in Northern Ireland. The question now asked is: How *united* is the United Kingdom?
4. In 1900 Britain possessed an empire on which the sun never set. The return of Hong Kong to China by Britain on 30 June 1997 marked the end of the empire (if not of lingering imperial mentalities). During the period 1945–97 Britain was 'losing an empire' and 'not finding a role' (Acheson, 1962). In particular, British leaders now seem uncertain about how to relate to the new Europe.
5. Citizenship is usually associated with nation-building (as with the US, Israel and Australia). In Britain the nation is supposed to be 'the British' (according to Colley, 1992, 'a nation forged on the anvil of war'). The British were four nations, and Britain may be a multinational state made

up of the English, the Welsh, the Scots and the Irish, and other peoples. They were smelted in the furnace of war and some internal conflict might have been avoided through the out-relief (for the 'Celts') provided by the British Empire. Since 1945, with the settlement of former colonial peoples in 'the Mother Country', Britain has become a multiethnic, multifaith and multicultural society. (In this it has become like the US, Canada and Australia – its former colonies.) This raises questions of multiple moral codes (each with its own integrity) within the same society.

6. The 'English' (themselves, in Defoe's words, 'a mongrel breed') were the apparent victors of the regional wars of the centuries. The English language was the language of power and of government. (Scots, Welsh and Irish who wanted to make it in Britain spoke and wrote the language, and some spoke it – Lloyd George, Aneurin Bevan – and some wrote it – Wilde and Yeats – better than the English themselves.) History in the schools, presented as the shared folk myth, was *English* history (and the ultimate triumph of humanity's labours since the world began was the parliament in London). The Scots, the Welsh, the Irish – and the German-named royal family – were Anglicized. This raises problems for citizenship as 'a shared identity'.

7. English society has been, and still is, class-conscious and class-divided. The formal education system has been a dual system – of élite and mass institutions – with differential provision for leaders and led. Progressive educational reformers have striven to democratize access to knowledge (with good success) and to democratize the institutions (with less success). Education in England is still riven by the élite–mass divide.

8. Britain was the first modern industrial society and it is also the first post-industrial society. The classic industries – coal, steel, textiles and shipbuilding – have virtually passed away, as has the classic 'working class'. Britain is now faced by the challenges of the globalization of the economy, of communications and information. British political leaders have shown much more interest in how they might create workers for the economy than citizens for the polity. They want to compete with other peoples (competitors include the Germans, the Japanese – the economic victors of the post-war period – and the 'Asian tigers') rather than to cooperate with them, or understand their cultures.

As in many other countries, political educators in Britain are confronted by the problems of creating a coherent character for citizenship in a semiotic society (of sound bites, signs and symbols, and 'disassociated impacting') and of sustaining 'the grand narrative' of 'the Enlightenment Project' (the alleviation of human suffering by the use of reason and the accumulation of knowledge, the celebration of life through active citizenship and common culture) against the pessimism of the post-modernists (for whom the grand narrative is dead and citizenship an eighteenth-century archaism and a forlorn enterprise).

1918 – 1944 – 1974

Between the landmark Education Acts of 1918 and 1944 most people in Britain had only elementary school education and they left school by the age of 14. They had *training* in the 'three Rs' – Reading, Writing and Arithmetic – but they had little *education*. Their lessons in 'Civics' aimed to create obedient and passive subjects, not active, democratic citizens. There was mentality formation in imperial ideals, with the wall map of the British Empire (stretching from Canada in the west to India and Australia in the east) and there was annual celebration of 'Empire Day'. The church schools offered moral education through Christianity. In the élite schools (fee-paying boarding and day schools) there were also the war memorials listing the 'old boys' who had fallen in the Great War of 1914–18 and who, as doomed youth, 'would grow not old' . The system of school prefects taught how to lead others. The élite schools produced leaders for the government, the army and the navy, and the law. There was political education through the hidden curriculum of roles and rituals. There was little explicit teaching about politics or for citizenship. The system seemed to produce leaders and achieve sufficient civic cohesion for a divided society to hold together. In his classic study, *The Making of Citizens*, Merriam, writing about England in 1931, said: 'an examination of the English school system in its relation to civic training reveals a general denial of any conscious attempt to engender national sentiment through the agency of education. In fact, one finds an indignant repudiation of any such unbecoming purpose' (p.96). Of course, in a country made up of four possible nations (English, Scots, Welsh and Irish) to promote 'English' nationalism could have undermined 'Britain', which had been reinvented to overcome petty nationalisms.

In 1922 the Christian Socialist R.H. Tawney wrote *Secondary Education for All* and that was the major policy objective of progressive educational reformers until it was achieved with the Education Act of 1944. In a sense, 'Education' had come before 'citizenship education', in a country where the educational provision was divided and unequal, and in a polity which remained (and still remains) an exotic combination of monarchy, aristocracy and democracy.

The period 1918–44 saw some important initiatives in the field of adult education, first through the programmes of the Workers' Educational Association (where political economy was a central feature) and later, during the Second World War, through the programmes of the Army Bureau of

Current Affairs (ABCA), which taught British soldiers about the political system, the economy and the ideals of a commonwealth of nations. It published *British Way and Purpose* bulletins which, even today, impress by their clarity, concision and balance. (It is a debate among historians of the period whether the activities of ABCA – soldiering for Socialism? – were a major cause of the landslide victory of the Labour Party in the general election of 1945.)

In 1935 a (voluntary) Association for Education in Citizenship (AEC) was founded to promote the ideals of democracy in a Europe in which the potentially great powers of Germany and the Soviet Union both had one-party rule. In the dark days of 1939 a Council for Education in World Citizenship was established.

During this period there were some rare voices, crying in the wilderness, for some political education in schools. The voices included those of Victor Gollancz (who wrote *Political Education at a Public School* in 1914), Michael Stewart (who wrote a book *Bias and Education for Democracy*, in 1938), Hugh Gaitskell (in *Educating for Democracy*, 1939) and Margaret Cole (*Educating for Democracy*, 1942). They were all Socialists of some sort, and they all believed in the redistribution of wealth, power and knowledge. Of course, they were opposed by those whose positional goods (wealth, power and knowledge-as-power – which are all relative) would have been altered by any implementation of their proposed programmes.

In general, official attitudes towards 'education for citizenship' were wary and towards political education negative. Citizenship education was acceptable as long as 'the good citizen' was well behaved, law abiding, and conforming. For a minority of school students teaching *about* politics (a limited kind of political education) was offered in the form of 'British Constitution'. It had twin foci of Whitehall (central government) and Town Hall (local government). Its perspectives were institutional, constitutional and legal. The classic textbook, written by Benemy, *Whitehall – Town Hall* (eight editions between 1960 and 1974) had chapters on the electorate; the nature of the constitution; the House of Commons; the government; the party system; the House of Lords; the Crown; the Commonwealth (could it hold together?); and the future. The 'missing curriculum' (a concept I learned from Ruth Firer) included trade unions; issue-based groups (formed around concern for the environment, housing, human rights); and extra-parliamentary politics. Bernard Crick made two trenchant remarks about 'British constitution'. If you wanted to teach about the British constitution, first you would have to invent it. To offer the British constitution instead of political education was like teaching anatomy instead of the nature of sexuality. To be fair, the focus of Benemy was formal political structures, and it was politics with the issues played down (and not politics with all the issues left out). For the majority of school students (in the low-status secondary modern schools) there were lessons on 'Civics'. These were concerned with the mechanics of central and local government and encouraged conformity and deference – for subjects, not citizens, for whom participation was passive – voting in periodic elections. This was politics with the issues left out – depoliticized politics or no-politics.

In the period 1967–74, between the time when I was first active in the field of political education and the start of the Programme for Political Education (PPE), a snapshot of the condition of political education and education for citizenship in Britain would show the following:

1. Education for citizenship was promoted by voluntary and non-governmental organizations and where it existed in schools it had low status and was for the 'less able' pupils. (The academic schools offered scholarship, not citizenship.)
2. Elements of political education could be found in British Constitution courses and in 'General Studies' for students aged 16–18. These are two of the areas where Schleicher quarried materials for his study *Politische Bildung in England: 1939–65* (1970).
3. Explicit approaches to political education and education for democratic citizenship had been opposed by people like Sir Cyril Norwood (head of a government commission on education in 1943): 'Nothing but harm can result from attempts to interest pupils prematurely in matters which imply the experience of an adult' and by people recommending the indirect approach – political education should be provided *through history*.
4. If teachers knew of John Dewey it was for his child-centred philosophy, not for *Democracy and Education*.
5. Workers in the field of political education and education for democratic citizenship were becoming aware of pioneering work in political socialization done in the US by people like Herbert H. Hyman, Fred I. Greenstein and Judith V. Torney. The 'new universities' of the 1960s, such as the universities of Essex, Sussex and York, were producing graduates in the newly established Social Sciences (particularly Politics and Sociology) who would have a vested interest in the promotion of politics and citizenship in the schools. Two voluntary associations were founded to support the teaching and teachers of politics and sociology: the Politics Association was founded in 1969, and the Association for the Teaching of the Social Sciences (ATSS) was founded in 1965.
6. In short, there were some factors working *against* and some factors working *for* the development of political education and education for citizenship in Britain. In 1974 the Nuffield Foundation granted funds for a Programme for Political Education, a curriculum development and research project, which aimed to promote 'Political Literacy' and democratic values for all students in the secondary schools.

POLITICAL LITERACY AND DEMOCRATIC DISCOURSE: 1974–

The Programme for Political Education (PPE) aimed to promote political literacy and democratic values for all secondary school students. Its image of 'the citizen' was of someone with the knowledge, attitudes and predisposition to be active in the polity – in 'everyday life', in the locality and at the national level. Its view of politics was characterized by the inevitability and centrality of *issues*, to be analyzed, discussed and debated and, where appropriate, acted on. It focused on developing 'the politically literate person' – where 'literate' meant 'reading', understanding, *and acting* – rather than on 'the citizen', as such. However, it was argued that the politically literate person, with democratic values, would, in consequence, be 'an active citizen'.

In reviewing the book on the PPE (*Political Education and Political Literacy*, edited by Bernard Crick and Alex Porter, 1978) I am struck, first, by how rarely the words 'citizen' and 'citizenship' appear and, second, by how often 'active citizenship' is obviously implied. The PPE was searching for a form of political education which would be above party politics, be able to answer accusations of 'indoctrination', and be acceptable to schools and politicians. It had its critics – from the traditional and authoritarian right and left (who both argued that school students up to the age of 16 – the age when most left school – were too young for political education) and from the radical left, who argued that an effective and liberating political education through the schools was an impossibility (as schools were elements of the oppressive state apparatus and, therefore, part of the problem, not part of the solution). The PPE also had its friends, supporters and achievements. Its supporters included leading politicians of all the main political parties (including Sir Keith Joseph, later to become a Minister of Education). Some local education authorities made special efforts to promote political literacy education, and Sheffield appointed an advisor to encourage it in its schools. Her Majesty's Inspectors supported it, and two HMIs wrote a document on 'Political Competence' to help spread it. Two leading universities in the field of education – London and Birmingham – set up lectureships in political education. A number of head teachers supported it and some set up their own project, in the north-east of England. In short, political education in the form of political literacy, to produce democratic and active citizens, had been legitimated. This may have been the major achievement of the project.

Case-study research in six institutions providing courses in political literacy showed that good practice was possible. It also revealed problems still to be overcome. In particular, it became clear that the problems of working with issue-based courses and a broad definition of politics (to include the politics of 'everyday life') – two key elements of the PPE – had been seriously underestimated. The notion that politics is a gladiatorial contest, fought in far-away Westminster between the leader of the government and the leader of the opposition (the would-be leader of government) was, and still is, hard to overcome. It is deep in the culture and is constantly reinforced by the British adversarial style of politics, the two-party system, and the confrontational seating arrangements in the House of Commons. Also deep in the culture, embedded in the language, is the notion that 'there are *two* sides to a question' (and other sides of the question are lost in the missing curriculum of the mind). A major barrier to political education in schools – the fear that teachers would indoctrinate their students – remained (in spite of lack of evidence that it happened in Britain). And, although legitimated at the official level, political education remained for teachers 'a low status: high risk' activity. (For teachers of political education there are few extrinsic rewards and no career structure. A contrast would be the security, status and career prospects enjoyed by teachers of English, Mathematics and Science.) Opportunities for school students to be active citizens were limited and, sometimes, controversial. Opportunities for activism were likely to be local, rather than national, and sometimes threatened to involve 'the school' or 'the teacher' in local politics. Schools then, and now, in general lack teachers who are good role models of active citizens.

The PPE was influenced by John Dewey, Bernard Crick and Paulo Freire and looking back on it I am impressed by its ambition and its ideals. Somehow, it ran out of steam (partly because it ran out of money) and by 1980 the new dynamic for political education was coming from vanguard educators promoting, first, world studies and, then, global education. Their search was for global citizenship, with the whole world viewed as the polity.

GLOBAL EDUCATION AS EDUCATION FOR GLOBAL CITIZENSHIP

Political literacy offered a political education without explicit attention to citizenship, without the promotion of 'Britishness'. It assumed that the actions of the politically literate, operating within a framework of democratic values, would be those of 'good citizens'. Global educators wanted to promote global consciousness, in an interdependent world, and local action. 'Think globally, and act locally' was one of their precepts. The vanguard educators who pioneered 'the new educations' had high aspirations for the global citizen. The global citizen would be skilled in the arts of peace-making; would have intercultural understanding; would be environmentally aware; would recognize human rights issues, and act on them; and would be able to imagine, and work for, alternative futures. For schools this meant that knowledge should have a social purpose. Books like *Learning for Change in World Society* (Richardson, 1979) and *Teaching Geography for a Better World* (Fien and Gerber, 1986) give some indication of the shift away from traditional school practice. The curriculum should contain major issues – such as questions of war and peace, poverty and development, and human rights – and should have international and global, and not essentially national and regional, perspectives. Activity-based, and student-centred learning, should promote action skills. The global educators were particularly adept at working with school teachers, and helping them to employ new forms of teaching and learning (such as problem-solving exercises, cooperative games, and simulations). However, the kind of global citizenship they were promoting could not relate to an established polity, and their philosophy and their activities set off a backlash by traditional and conservative groups. Their work in peace education was characterized as 'propaganda for defencelessness' and they were accused of offering indoctrination, not education. The attackers of their work also included political education in their targets. The classic collection of critiques of the new movements – *The Wayward Curriculum* (O'Keefe, 1986) – included critiques of peace studies ('no true subject' and, at school level, 'mere opinion-making of a propagandist kind'); sociology and politics ('unsuitable subjects for schools', with the 'literature too profound for the average school child'); and political education ('so many of its advocates are hostile to the democratic political tradition', and 'immature minds are vulnerable to extremist propaganda').

During the 1980s there were continuing attempts to promote political education in schools within a framework of agreed guidelines. In 1986, in the House of Lords' debate on 'Education and the Avoidance of Politicization', the Earl of Swinton said that government policy was to issue guidelines for the handling of controversial issues in schools, not to ban them. He stated: 'The education service has a long and honourable tradition of upholding the principles of a free and open society.' Guidelines for political education were issued by Her Majesty's Inspectorate, by the Inner London Education Authority, and by local education authorities (such as Derbyshire).

The national political context within which these developments were taking place was one in which the post-war settlement, including the welfare state, was running out of steam, and in which consensus about education was being replaced by dissension. In 1979 Margaret Thatcher became Prime Minister and subsequently Britain had a Conservative government for a period of almost two decades. Thatcher was convinced that the government needed to raise the standards of the schools and, to that end, in 1988 passed the Education Reform Act (ERA), which aimed to transform the schools and the educational administration system. A National Curriculum was established, with three core subjects – English, Mathematics and Science – and with other foundation subjects, including History and Geography. These were all compulsory, by law. In addition, some cross-curricular themes and dimensions were proposed, of which Citizenship was one. These were non-statutory and low status. The top priority for the schools had to be the implementation of the National Curriculum in English, Mathematics and Science and head teachers I talked with at the time told me that they might 'get round to Citizenship some time later'.

In 1990 the National Curriculum Council (also established by the 1988 Act) produced a document *Education for Citizenship*. This was a 'political' document, seeking a consensus of support from politicians, some of whom were hostile to 'political education'. It ignored previous research in the field and offered no examples of established practice. It seemed to stress responsibilities, rather than rights. However, it did suggest that areas of study might include Britain as a multicultural, multiethnic, multifaith and multilingual society; the diversity of cultures in other societies; and international and global issues. Scholars skilled in the arts of exegesis would find something from many political traditions in it.

A Centre for Citizenship Studies in Education was established at the University of Leicester, under Professor Ken Fogelman, who wrote *Citizenship in Schools* (1991). A Citizenship Foundation was set up in London, and it publishes a journal *Citizenship*. A National Conference on Education for Citizenship, addressed by the Minister of Education (John MacGregor) and the Shadow Minister of Education (Jack Straw) was held in Northampton in February 1990. A National Commission on Citizenship, an all-party body whose members were appointed by the Speaker of the House of Commons (and hence known as 'The Speaker's Commission'), was set up and it produced working documents which were collected in its report *Encouraging Citizenship* (1990). At a general level, there was formal support for citizenship education. In reality there were, and are, disagreements about the nature of citizenship and the model of 'the good citizen'. For some 'the good citizen' was 'the good Samaritan'. For some 'the good citizen' was the law-abiding citizen who did voluntary community work and did not drop litter in the street (or the school playground). Only for a few was 'the good citizen' someone actively working on issues in the public domain. Under Thatcher, and her successor, there was an attempt to present the good citizen as the consumer of services provided by the central and the local government. It was a long way from the Great Charter (1215) to the Citizen's Charter of Prime Minister Major. If Civics had offered politics without the issues, this offered citizenship without the politics.

Since 1988 there has been an abundance of excellent writing on citizenship by political scientists, in general, and by political philosophers, in particular. These have included works by Ralf Dahrendorf, David Held, Michael Ignatieff and Raymond Plant. In 1990, Dahrendorf was confidently asserting that the 1990s would be the decade of citizenship.

In the field of citizenship education three traditions now compete and co-exist: political education as political literacy; global education (which now includes 'futures education'); and citizenship education. There is also a growing area of 'Education for European Citizenship'. At present this is fragmented, and tends to lack clear characterizations of 'citizenship' and of 'Europe'. Its advocates include teachers of foreign languages who see multilingual ability as a desirable feature of the European citizen. Others stress human rights and democracy as core features of the European heritage. Of course, there is a European polity, a European parliament, and a European Court of Human Rights. There is also a European market (and the market preceded the polity). Economics, politics and the law are ahead of education. However, as before, *practice* is difficult to find. It is almost certainly varied and patchy. At government level there is now more interest shown in moral education – with a search for a common framework of values – than in citizenship education. In 1997, as in 1974, would-be educators for democracy and active citizenship are confronted by a number of problems and possibilities. The main obstacles and possibilities now are:

1. The National Curriculum (NC) of 1988 was an affirmation of traditional knowledge forms, with Sociology and Politics excluded and with History and Geography included as the 'social subjects'. On the face of it this was an obstacle to a genuine political and social education, which might encourage critical reflection. However, both History and Geography had been transformed in the previous decades. 'Drum and trumpet' history, and the history of dates, kings and queens and prime ministers were themselves largely things of the past. So, too, was 'capes and bays', 'placename' geography. In fact, Geography had become the most 'political' subject of the school curriculum – teaching about 'North–South' development *issues*, environmental *issues*, and town planning *issues*. The 'New' Geography, which was promoted from the 1960s on, viewed the use of land space as a disputed question – that is, as an *issue*. This is a long way from the environmental determinism in which explanations were once offered – Australia had so many sheep because it provided an environment in which sheep were happy. Also, some pioneering work has been done in teaching about citizenship through established and high-status subjects – such as English. One example was the project to teach about citizenship issues through literature carried out by Christopher Spurgeon in schools in the Midlands, and reported in a practitioner research doctoral thesis in 1995.

2. The National Curriculum supported education for citizenship, but gave it a low status and made it a marginal activity. However, it also gave it legitimation. In 1993 the Dearing Committee, which was set up to review the NC, reduced its size and areas of compulsion and, thus, created some free space for schools and teachers to make their own initiatives. Curriculum time now exists.

3. Whereas the dearth of teaching materials for political education and

education for democratic citizenship was a problem two decades ago, there is now an abundance of teachers' handbooks, guides and teaching and learning materials – many of them produced by the vanguard educators (such as David Hicks, Graham Pike and David Selby). Appropriate materials now exist.

4. Since their foundation in 1965 and 1969, respectively, the Association for the Teaching of the Social Sciences and the Politics Association have secured the teaching of Sociology and Politics in the schools. They are boom subjects at the 16+ level. With the 1993 reduction of the NC, sociology is flourishing again. However, for neither of these two associations was political education their main concern. Now, with the establishment of the Citizenship Foundation and the Centre for Citizenship Studies in Education, there are two organizations which might have an existential commitment to education for democratic citizenship.

5. The current concern about moral education – there is a National Forum on Values in Education and the Community, searching for a common code of values – offers opportunities to those who, like the ancient Greeks, see citizenship as a moral enterprise. Schools are now developing codes of practice, based on procedural values, for staff and for students. Some of these codes of practice arise from the managerial culture which was linked with the Thatcher reforms, and the production of school 'mission statements'. However, some of these now speak the language of political education and citizenship. Opportunities exist for the creative adaptation of these codes of conduct to promote education for democratic citizenship.

6. Partly because of the work of the global educators we are now aware of the possibilities of *multiple citizenships*. For example, I am a citizen, firstly, of the City of York; secondly, of Great Britain; and thirdly, of the European Union. My 'global citizenship' may be more of an aspiration than a realization (yet), but the language of human rights helps me to search for a shared human identity. Educators in Britain can plan programmes to support multiple citizenships – and in Scotland, Wales and Ireland these may also provide for peoples within a wider British nation.

7. Current items on Britain's agenda – the constitution, a bill of rights, the future of the monarchy, Britain's relationship to Europe, and Britain's place in the world – afford rich material for citizenship education. Long-term issues of education, health, transport and the environment provide questions for discussion and debate (which are essential elements of democratic discourse).

8. In the General Election of 1 May 1997, the Labour Party was victorious, with a landslide majority of 179 seats. This ended 18 years of Conservative Party rule. Thatcherism seems to have run its course, and to have run out of steam. John Gray, a previous supporter, is now looking

beyond neo-liberalism. George Soros now warns of the dangers of unleashed capitalism. Some search for ways to reconnect individuals to community, and to society (the existence of which Thatcher denied – 'There is no such thing as society', she said). There are attempts to build consensus (whereas Thatcher said: 'Consensus is the negation of leadership'). In an age of uncertainty, and of anxiety, there is a search for social cohesion and for shared identity and a sense of belonging. There are many would-be citizens in search of a city, and a form of modern citizenship, appropriate to our democratic and pluralistic society, might help them find it.

REFERENCES

Acheson, D. (1962). 'Great Britain has lost an empire and not yet found a role', speech at West Point Military Academy, 5 December 1962.

Ascherson, N. (1996). 'National identity.', in G. Radice (1996) (ed.), *What needs to change: New visions for Britain.* London: HarperCollins.

Benemy, F.W.G. (1960). *Whitehall – Town Hall.* London: Harrap.

Brown, C. (1991). 'Education for citizenship – Old wine in new bottles?', in *Citizenship*, 1(2), 6–9.

Colley, L. (1992). *Britons: Forging the nation.* New Haven, CT, and London: Yale University Press.

Crick, B. and Lister, I. (1975). 'Political literacy', in B. Crick and A. Porter, *Political education and political literacy.* Harlow: Longman.

Dahrendorf, R. (1990). 'The coming decade of citizenship', *The Guardian*, 1 August 1990.

Davies, I. (1992). 'Guidelines for political education', unpublished doctoral thesis. University of York, England.

Dewey, J. (1916). *Democracy and education.* New York: Macmillan.

Fien, J. and Gerber, R. (1986). *Teaching geography for a better world.* Brisbane: Jacaranda Press.

Fogelman, K. (1991). *Citizenship in schools.* London: Fulton.

Gray, J. (1993). *Beyond the new right.* London and New York: Routledge.

Heater, D. (1992). 'Education for European citizenship', *Westminster Studies in Education*, 15, 53–67.

Heater, D. (1996). *World citizenship and government.* London: Macmillan, and New York: St Martin's Press.

Ignatieff, M. (1996). 'There's no place like home: The politics of belonging', in S. Dunant, and R. Porter (eds), *The age of anxiety.* London: Virago.

Lister, I. (1987). 'Global and international approaches in political education', in C. Harber (ed.), *Political education in Britain.* Lewes and Philadelphia, PA: Falmer Press.

Lister, I. (1991a). 'Civic education for positive pluralism', in R. Sigel (ed.), *Civic education in multiethnic societies.* Hillsdale, NJ: Lawrence Erlbaum.

Lister, I. (1991b). 'Research on social studies and citizenship education in England', in J.P. Shaver (ed.) (1991), *Handbook of research on social studies: Teaching and learning.* New York: Macmillan.

Lister, I. (1995a). 'Conscientisation and political literacy', in P.L. McLaren and C. Lankshear (eds) (1991), *Politics of liberation.* London and New York: Routledge.

Lister, I. (1995b). 'Educating beyond the nation.', *International Review of Education*, 41(1–2), 109–18.

Marshall, T. H. (1950). *Citizenship and social class*. Cambridge: Cambridge University Press.

Merriam, C.E. (1931). *The making of citizens*. Chicago: Chicago University Press.

National Curriculum Council (1990). *Education for citizenship*. York: NCC.

O'Keefe, D. (ed.) (1986). *The wayward curriculum*. Exeter: Short Run Press.

Osler, A., Rathenow H.-F. and Starkey, H. (eds) (1995). *Teaching for citizenship in Europe*. Stoke-on-Trent: Trentham Books.

Plant, R. (1990). 'Citizenship: Dilemmas of definition', paper submitted to the Speaker's Commission on Citizenship.

Richardson, R. (1979). *Learning for change in world society*. London: World Studies Project.

Schleicher, K. (1970). *Politische buildung in England: 1939–1965*. Heidelberg: Quelle & Meyer.

Scruton, R. (1985). *World studies: Education or indoctrination?* London: Institute of Defence and Strategic Studies.

Soros, G. (1997). 'Capital crimes', *The Guardian: The Week*, 18 January, 1–3.

Speaker's Commission (1990). *Encouraging citizenship*. London: HMSO.

Spurgeon, C. (1995). 'Teaching and learning about citizenship issues through literature', unpublished doctoral thesis. University of York, England.

Spurgeon, C. and Lister, I. (1996). 'Teaching and learning about citizenship issues through literature', *New Era in Education*, 77(2), 34–9.

Taylor, R. (1996). 'Democracy in the workplace', in G. Radice (ed.), *What needs to change: New visions for Britain*. London: HarperCollins.

Wringe, C. (1989). 'The ambiguities of education for active citizenship', *Journal of Philosophy of Education*, 26(1), 29–38.

Wringe, C. (1996). 'The role of foreign language learning in education for European citizenship', *Evaluation and Research in Education*, 10, 2.

14

CONCLUSION: THE CHALLENGE OF CITIZENSHIP EDUCATION IN A CHANGING WORLD

ORIT ICHILOV

Preparing the younger generation for the citizenship role is a formidable objective in our kaleidoscopic and rapidly changing world. Political socialization research, which was carried out primarily within Western societies and fairly stable political settings, provides only limited guidance in this respect (Ichilov, 1990; Sears, 1990). The present volume offers a glimpse at the landscape of citizenship in various parts of the world. However incomplete and selective, it demonstrates the great variety of political contexts in which children grow up today, and the diversity of issues which have a bearing upon citizenship education. The various case studies represent parts of a fascinating and dynamic global mosaic. In countries like Russia and Hungary, which have been part of the former Soviet Union, youngsters witness attempts to construct civil society and democracy in the face of eroding social services, economic crises, ethnic conflicts, rising crime rates, political apathy, and an ideological vacuum which is being quickly filled up by selfish consumerism. In the turbulent Middle East, Palestinian children on the West Bank and the Gaza Strip grow up under a contested regime – Israeli occupation – and participate both as spectators and actors in the Palestinian uprising (Intifada). Israeli Jewish and Arab children, although citizens of the same Jewish nation-state, cannot share a common Israeli identity and commitment to the state. Israeli-Arabs still consider the establishment of Israel an illegitimate and tragic event which violates their national aspirations. The issue of collective identities within the Israeli-Jewish population is also salient, given the fact that Israel is a new state and democracy, which has been built by massive waves of immigrants from all over the world. British children grow up in a multinational state made up of English, Welsh, Scots and Irish. Despite English dominance, the persisting conflict in Northern Ireland reveals fractures in the unity of the United

Kingdom. In many African countries children are exposed to a renewed interest in democracy following periods of military regimes or one-party rule, but also to wars, hunger and diseases. Across the globe, Chinese citizens of Hong Kong are caught between their desire to break away from British colonialism, and their fears regarding the consequences for human and civil rights of becoming again part of the People's Republic of China. In veteran and relatively stable democracies, such as the US, a growing concern about the future of democracy is evident. Some scholars worry that civil competence, knowledge and attitudes of youth may prove insufficient for sustaining the democratic creed. Others worry that the simplistic and shallow coverage, which often characterizes TV reports of political occurrences, may have a negative effect for citizens' information acquisition and processing. This is especially alarming since broadcasting media, especially TV, have gained precedence over newspapers, books and other sources of information. Gross inequalities within Western democracies, on the basis of gender and other personal and social characteristics, raise the issue of how viable these democracies are. Even in politically less eventful places such as New Zealand, citizens gradually become more aware and better informed about politics.

It is evident that present-day societies are highly diverse, and are becoming increasingly more ethnically, nationally and racially hetero-geneous, more regionally fragmented, more pluralistic culturally, and more strongly linked with global affairs. Citizenship education limited to inculcation of traditional patriotism or conventional nationalist ideology is obviously insufficient in a highly dynamic, complex and interdependent world.

CITIZENSHIP EDUCATION: DEVELOPMENT AND TRENDS

Several terms are presently used interchangeably to refer to institutionalized forms of political knowledge acquisition which take place within formal educational frameworks (such as schools and universities) and informal settings (such as youth movements). These include 'political education', 'civic education', 'citizenship education', and 'political literacy'. While the choice of terms can be a matter of fashion, they usually represent different intellectual traditions concerning the goals, nature, and practices of political education, as well as adaptation to changing citizenship circumstances (Ichilov, 1994).

Civic education and citizenship education are frequently associated with the ideas of liberal democracy. They often focus upon individuals' relations with the civic/social realm, rather than on their affinity with the political arena. The civic curriculum associated with these approaches reflects mainly the structural, procedural and the legal aspects of political institutions, avoiding the discussion of controversial issues, and stressing consensus, harmony and compliance. Civic education and citizenship education are often considered conservative and inadequate by more recent approaches such as peace education, multicultural education, human rights education, developmental education, environmental education, and global education.

'Political literacy' is associated with more radical traditions (Tarrant, 1981). It is related to the ideas of participatory democracy, and aims at 'raising the levels of participation by trying to reveal the political dimensions of everyday life. It is about empowering people' (Lewis, 1987, p.2). 'It is not to be limited to or confused with ... "civics" ... political literacy can be advanced through other subjects, for instance, History, English, Geography, Social Studies, Sociology and Economics' (Porter, 1984, pp.1–2). The curriculum tends to be issue-based, confronting controversies on the local, national and international levels. Activity-based teaching methods, such as role play, sociodrama, simulations, community action and games, are often employed (Ichilov, 1994).

Several trends have characterized the development of political education in Western democracies. Needless to say that not all trends equally apply to any given society, nor have they been fully and uniformly implemented everywhere. As a matter of fact, the works presented in this volume suggest that civic education often focuses primarily on the legal and structural aspects of politics, neglecting controversial and global issues, and fostering mainly compliance.

First, there was a shift from formally differentiated education for leadership and for followership roles, to mass education for democratic citizenship. In Britain, for example, the élite public schools Eton and Harrow prepared a selected few for leadership, while the elementary schools produced followers. The creation of mass education systems after the Second World War is considered a revolution which enabled modernization and democratization processes to occur. In this respect it is considered to be as significant as the 'industrial revolution' (Parsons, 1971; Mannheim, 1992; Turner, 1997). Education as a human right has been formally established in the UN Declaration of the Rights of the Child in 1959, and in the UN Covenant of the Rights of the Child of 1989. Neo-Marxist and neo-Weberian theories of education and society, however, dispute the extent to which mass education reinforces democracy. They advance the argument that the progressive force of mass education in furthering democracy, tolerance and welfare has been undermined by its use as part of the apparatus that perpetuates a class system based on economic and cultural dependence (Bowles and Gintis, 1976; Carnoy and Levin, 1985; Collins, 1979).

The second phase was the introduction of political education as part of the school curriculum. This revolutionary step was accompanied by public debates in many Western democracies. It was especially feared that political education might turn into manipulation, indoctrination, and the teaching of political partisanship. It was also considered unadvisable to involve students prematurely in matters related to adult experiences.

Thirdly, there was a shift from a narrow to a broader definition of political education. Political education, narrowly defined, provided mainly factual knowledge about political institutions and avoided the discussion of controversial issues. It was normative rather than analytical. Gradually, political education is being expanded to include the discussion of issues related to the environment, gender egalitarianism, multiculturalism, and global affairs (Ichilov, 1990).

Finally, there was a movement away from learning processes in which the students were passive, and a transition to their more active involvement, for instance in role-play, community action, and computer simulations.

Citizenship education is also closely linked to other traditions which have been proliferating in recent years, such as 'moral education', 'character education' or education for virtue, and 'education for critical thinking'. The concept of moral education is probably most closely associated with the names of Emile Durkheim, a French sociologist considered one of the founding fathers of modern sociology, and Lawrence Kohlberg, who articulated a cognitive-developmental theory of moralization. Durkheim considered discipline, attachments to social groups, and autonomy as key elements of morality that should be inculcated through education (Durkheim, 1961). Kohlberg advocated the 'just community approach' to moral education in schools, focusing on 'the moral issues arising in day-to-day concerns of staff and students, governed by democracy, and motivated by an altruistic commitment to community' (Power et al., 1989, p.2). 'Education for critical thinking' is a generation-old movement of philosophers and educators who seek to transform education in general, and turn educational institutions into 'smart schools' which inculcate critical thinking in their students. It is linked, however, with citizenship education and other current educational traditions (Barens, 1992; Lipman, 1988, 1991; McPeck, 1981, 1990; Paul, 1993).

Other approaches address more specific problems within modern democratic societies. 'Education for conflict resolution' and 'multicultural education' were proposed to address problems within pluralistic societies (Carnegie, 1994; Kymlicka, 1995). 'Character education' was intended to withhold moral decline in an era of deteriorating morality, by teaching moral behavior to school children who are 'without such teaching in local communities or in the home' (Lo and Si-wai, 1996, p.xx). 'Citizenship' contains a clear notion of the civic virtues which are regarded as necessary for the functioning of democracy (Turner, 1997). Citizenship education is expected to inculcate in the younger generation citizenship competences which embrace a profusion of qualities of intellect. These enable the individual to collaborate fully in the enterprise of creating and sustaining a viable and healthy democracy (Porter, 1996). However, how solid and definite have these virtues and competences remained over the years, especially with regard to trends of 'postmodernism' in the West? Have the practical demands of those virtues persisted unchanged? Furthermore, cultural variations exist regarding what constitute civic virtues. In China, for example, the unflagging support for respect for labor and the collective, as well as patriotism and loyalty to the Party, constitute an enduring theme in the content of moral education (Lo and Si-wai, 1996, p.xix).

The critical approach prescribes entirely different goals for civic and moral education. Its advocates acknowledge that state intervention is needed to provide full social and public status to citizenship rights, and to secure the means for their effective fulfillment. However, citizenship also entails the protection of citizens against the arbitrary exercise of state power. Therefore, citizens must be emacipated from the constraints imposed on them by various societal forces. They should be able to make independent and critical judgements, express dissent, not just consent, and develop a reformist spirit and 'civic courage' sometimes to resist the authorities (Giroux, 1983; Turner, 1997; Lo and Si-wai, 1996; Ichilov, 1990; Etzioni, 1970).

Citizens should also become aware that 'in principle the rights of citizenship are not conditional but categorical. What citizenship offers does not depend on the readiness of people to pay the price in the private domain. Citizenship cannot be marketed' (Dahrendorf, 1996, p.33). Social rights are not merely 'entitlements' which can be revoked as a result of changing social policies. They are as essential for democratic citizenship as political rights and civil liberties are. Social rights promote human dignity, equality, justice and solidarity.

The extent to which these various traditions will penetrate the main stream of school curriculum and educational practices remains to be seen.

CITIZENSHIP EDUCATION IN A CHANGING WORLD

Citizenship education is, perhaps, needed more than ever to provide a sense of purpose, solidarity, and guidance in a fragmented and a rapidly changing world (Pratte, 1988). In many Western democracies there is a trend among citizens to claim their rights and to retreat into their own privacy. However, a neglect of the community, of the national public place as well as of the international public space results in the loss of the sense of trust, efficacy and neighborliness. There are rising levels of crime and violence, homeless people, racism, social inequality, abuse of the environment, violations of human rights, etc., which all pose problems, nationally and internationally.

Citizenship education should help to redefine the public place, and to create conscientious, efficacious, interested, caring, and active citizens. Youngsters must be made aware that the 'public place is not only physical space ... it is social space ... [it] is action space, where we can tend to the arrangements that enhance our mutual well-being as society' (Boulding, 1988). Citizenship education should also promote global awareness, and the realization that circumstances that affect our immediate moral and physical well-being are located on the transnational arena as well. Many objectives which should affect the quality of life of each citizen on the planet cannot be accomplished without global awareness and cooperation.

REFERENCES

Barens, C.A. (ed.) (1992). *Critical thinking: Educational imperative*. San Francisco: Jossey-Bass.

Boulding, E. (1988). *Building a global civic culture*. New York: Teachers College Press, Columbia University.

Bowles, S. and Gintis, H. (1976). *Schooling in capitalist America*. New York: Basic.

Carnegie Corporation (1994). *Annual report of the Carnegie Corporation of New York*. New York: Carnegie Corporation.

Carnoy, M. and Levin, H.M. (1985). *Schooling and work in the democratic state*. Stanford, CA: Stanford University Press.

Collins, R. (1979). *The credential society*. New York: Academic Press.

Dahrendorf, R. (1996). 'Citizenship and social class', in M. Blumer and A.M. Rees (eds), *Citizenship today: The contemporary relevance of T.H. Marshall* (pp.25–49). London: UCL Press.

Durkheim, E. (1961). *Moral education*. Glencoe, IL: Free Press.

Etzioni, A. (1970). *Demonstration democracy*. New York: Gordon & Breach.

Giroux, H.A. (1983). *Theory and resistence in education: A pedagogy for the opposition*. Boston, MA: Bergin & Garvey.

Ichilov, O. (1990). 'Dimensions and role patterns of citizenship in democracy', in O. Ichilov (ed.), *Political socialization, citizenship education, and democracy* (pp.11–25). New York: Teachers College Press, Columbia University.

Ichilov, O. (1994). 'Political education', in T. Husen and T.N. Postlethwaite (eds-in-chief), *International encyclopedia of education* (2nd edn, Vol. 8) (pp.4568–71). New York: Pergamon Press.

Kymlicka, W. (1995). *Multicultural citizenship: A liberal theory of minority rights*. New York: Oxford University Press.

Lewis, L. (ed.) (1987). *Social education and political literacy*. Monograph Series No.3. Melbourne: Social Education Association of Australia.

Lipman, M. (1988). *Philosophy goes to school*. Philadelphia, PA: Temple University Press.

Lipman, M. (1991). *Thinking in education*. New York: Cambridge University Press.

Lo, L.N.K. and Si-Wai, M. (1996). 'Introduction: Nurturing the moral citizen of the future', in L.N.K. Lo and Man Si-wai (eds), *Moral and civic education* (pp.ix–1). Hong Kong: Hong Kong Institute of Educational Research.

Mannheim, K. (1992). *Essays on the sociology of culture*. London: Routledge & Kegan Paul.

McPeck, J.E. (1981). *Critical thinking and education*. New York: Martin.

Robertson, R. (1990). *Teaching critical thinking: Dialogue and dialect*. New York: Routledge.

Parsons, T. (1971). *The system of modern societies*. Englewood Cliffs, NJ: Prentice-Hall.

Paul, R. (1993). *Critical thinking: How to prepare students for rapidly changing world*. Santa Rosa, CA: Sonoma State University.

Porter, A. (ed.) (1984). *Principles of political literacy: The working papers of the programme for political education*. London: University of London Institute of Education.

Porter, A. (1996). 'The aims of education for citizenship', in L.N.K. Lo and Man Si-wai (eds), *Moral and civic education* (pp.1–11). Hong Kong: Hong Kong Institute of Educational Research.

Power, F.C., Higgins, A. and Kohlberg, L. (1989). *Lawrence Kohlberg's approach to moral education*. New York: Columbia University Press.

Pratte, R. (1988). *The civic imperative*. New York: Teachers College Press, Columbia University.

Sears, D. (1990). 'Whither political socialization research? The question of persistence', in O. Ichilov (ed.), *Political socialization, citizenship education, and democracy* (pp.69–98). New York: Teachers College Press, Columbia University.

Tarrant, J.M. (1981). 'The implications for education of different conceptions of democracy', PhD thesis, University of London.

Turner, B.S. (1997). 'Citizenship studies: A general theory', *Citizenship Studies*, 1(1), pp.5–19.

NOTES ON THE CONTRIBUTORS

Richard G. Braungart is Professor of Sociology and International Relations in the Maxwell School of Citizenship and Public Affairs at Syracuse University where he teaches courses in political sociology, international political psychology, life-course and generations, and collective behavior and social movements. He received his PhD from the Pennsylvania State University in 1969, and taught at the Pennsylvania State University and the University of Maryland. He served as Research Director for the President's Commission on Campus Unrest in 1970 and is currently the President of the Committee on Political Sociology, an international organization jointly affiliated with the International Sociological Association and the International Political Science Association. He is the author and editor of 11 books and has published over 100 articles and chapters.

Margaret M. Braungart is Professor of Psychology and Chairperson of the Liberal Arts and Science Department of the State University of New York Health Science Center at Syracuse where she teaches courses in educational psychology, developmental psychology, gerontology, and illness and death. Receiving her PhD from Syracuse University in 1980, she has co-authored a number of articles in the area of life-course and generations, most recently related to the topics of youth and citizenship, and political socialization and education. She is Co-Director of the Center for Research on Life-Course and Generational Politics, and Margaret and Richard's works have been translated into eight languages.

Steven H. Chaffee is Janet M. Peck Professor of International Communication, Professor of Political Science (by courtesy), and Chair of the Department of Communication at Stanford University. His publications include *Political Communication* (1976), *Television and Human Behavior* (1978), *Handbook of Communication Science* (1986), *To See Ourselves: Comparing Traditional Chinese and American Cultural Values* (1994), *The Beginning of Communication Study in the United States* (1997) and more than 60 research articles in academic journals.

Hernan Galperin is a PhD student at the Department of Communication at Stanford University. He received his Bachelor degree in Sociology from the University of Buenos Aires, and his Masters in Communication from Stanford University. His research interests include political communication and international media policy.

Clive Harber is Professor of Education at the University of Natal, South Africa where he is on leave of absence from the University of Birmingham in the UK. He has a long-standing interest in both education in Africa and education for democracy, and in recent years has been able to combine the two. He has published intensively in these areas.

Mary A. Hepburn is Head of the Citizen Education Division of the Vinson Institute of Government, University of Georgia, Athens, Georgia, US. She is Professor of Social Science Education and writes and teaches about political socialization and civic education. She has directed a number of projects on democratic education involving international information exchanges and comparative research.

Matthew S. Hirshberg received his PhD in Political Science from the University of Washington in Seattle, US. His areas of interest include political belief systems and perceptions, and political socialization. He is a lecturer in the Department of Political Science at the University of Canterbury in Christchurch, New Zealand. Dr Hirshberg is the author of *Perpetuating Patriotic Perceptions: The Cognitive Functions of the Cold War* (1993), and of many articles published in professional journals.

Orit Ichilov chaired the Department of Educational Sciences at Tel Aviv University, and is Vice-President of the International Society of Political Psychology. Her research has focused on political socialization, citizenship education, and youth sub-cultures in Israel. She is the author of *The Political World of Children and Adolescents* (1984, in Hebrew); *Citizenship Education in Israel: Current and Pre-State Trends of Development* (1993, in Hebrew); editor of *Political Socialization, Citizenship Education, and Democracy* (1990); and co-author (with

André Elias Mazawi) of *Between State and Church: Life History of a French-Catholic School in Jaffa* (1996). Her publications also include encyclopedia entries, chapters in books, and articles in professional journals in Israel and abroad.

Ian Lister is Professor of Education and Director of the Centre for Global and International Education at the University of York, England. He set up the Political Education Research Unit at the University of York, and was Co-Director of the Programme for Political Education. His work in political education includes case-study research on multicultural education and human rights education. His present interests include the internationalization of education; 'educating beyond the nation'; education and moral order; and educating for human future. In 1995 he was made a Fellow of the Politics Association in recognition for services to political education.

Zsuzsa Mátrai is Director of the Center for Evaluation Studies and Examinations at the Hungarian National Institute of Public Education, Budapest, and Associate Professor of Education at Miskole University, Hungary. Her research areas include social science education, civic education, curriculum development, and comparative studies of examination methods. She is the author of the *History of American Social Science Education*, of four social studies textbooks, and editor of *Curriculum and Examinations* (all in Hungarian). Her publications also include articles in professional journals.

André Elias Mazawi is teaching at the School of Education, Tel Aviv University. He recently received his PhD degree with distinction from Tel Aviv University. His dissertation dealt with the issue of equality of educational opportunities within the Arab public school system in Israel. Dr Mazawi has already established himself as a student of Arab society in Israel, and has been invited to present his work in international academic conferences. His studies have been published in professional journals such as *The British Journal of Sociology of Education, Higher Education, Compare: A Journal of Comparative Education* and *Studi E Documentazione Di Vita Universitaria* (Italy). He has also authored several book chapters, and is co-author (with Orit Ichilov) of *Between State and Church: Life History of a French Catholic School in Jaffa* (1996).

Roxana Morduchowicz is Professor in the School of Communication in the University of Buenos Aires, and Director of the Newspaper in the School Program for the Association of Dailies of the Interior Ministry of Argentina.

Virginia Sapiro is the Sophonisba P. Breckinridge Professor of Political Science and Women's Studies at the University of Wisconsin, Madison. Her teaching and research interests include the areas of political psychology, political participation, gender politics, and feminist theory. Sapiro is the author of *Women in American Society* (1994); *The Political Integration of Women: Roles, Socialization, and Politics* (1983), and *A Vindication of Political Virtue: The Political Theory of Mary Wollstonecraft* (1992), which won the American Political Science Association Victoria Schunk Award. Professor Sapiro has also published articles in professional journals and chapters in books.

Vladimir Shlapentokh is a Professor of Sociology at Michigan State University, East Lansing. Before migrating from the Soviet Union to the US in 1979, he was a Senior Fellow in the Sociological Institute in Moscow, where he conducted the first public opinion surveys in the Soviet Union. In the USSR he published ten books and dozens of articles pertaining to a wide variety of social and methodological issues. Since 1982, he has been consultant to the US government, regularly reporting on social processes, ideology, and public opinion in Russia and other former USSR states. In the US Professor Shlapentokh has published 12 books and dozens of professional articles about Soviet issues. In addition he has written columns for the editorial pages of the *New York Times*, *Los Angeles Times*, *Washington Post*, and *Christian Science Monitor*. His latest books include: *The New Russian Diaspora: Russian Minorities in the Former Soviet Republics* (1994, co-editor); *Soviet Cinematography 1918–1991: Ideological Conflict and Social Reality* (1993, co-author); *The Last Years of the Soviet Empire: Snapshots of 1985–1991* (1993); *State Organized Terror: The Case of Violent Internal Repression* (1991, co-editor); and *Soviet Intellectual and Political Power* (1990).

Wing-Kwong Tsang is Associate Director of the Hong Kong Educational Research Institute at the Chinese University of Hong Kong, and lecturer in the Department of Educational Administration and Policy. He received his PhD in Sociology from the Chinese University of Hong Kong in 1990. Tsang's research has focused on Hong Kong society. He has carried out research and published articles and chapters in books in the areas of citizenship education, voting behavior, and political developments in Hong Kong.

INDEX

Africa: democracy promotion, 8–9, 208–18, 268; developmental dictatorship, 208; education systems, 211–14; political culture, 215–18; pre-colonial systems, 209; schools, 213–14

Almond, G., 206–77

Alverson, H., 213

Arab world: nationalism, 15

Argentina: democracy through education, 166–8; education system, 152–3; Newspaper-in-Schools program, 7, 149–68; political apathy, 149–50; political culture, 151–2; political education indices, 160; political socialization, 154–5; socioeconomic status (SES), 150, 152, 156, 159–62, 167; study of newspaper program effects, 155–68; teaching methods, 162–6, 167

Army Bureau of Current Affairs (ABCA), 256–77

Association for Education in Citizenship (AEC), 257

authority: Hausa traditional culture, 212; Palestinian perceptions, 90–11

Barber, B., 19

Belgium: democracy views, 184–5; sex equality views, 185–8

Bell, D., 20

Benemy, F.W.G., 257

Bernstein, B., 237

Botswana: democracy, 210; Tswana political culture, 9, 212–14

Britain: adult education, 256–7; 'British Constitution' teaching, 257; citizenship, 9–10, 254–6; citizenship education (1918–74), 256–8; citizenship education (1974-80), 259–60; citizenship education (1980–), 260–5; Civics teaching, 258; democracy views, 184–5; democratic schools, 217; élitism, 269; European citizenship, 263; Geography curriculum, 263; global citizenship education, 260–1; multinationalism, 254–5, 267–8; National Curriculum, 261–2, 263; political education, 257–61; Programme for Political Education (PPE), 10, 258, 259–60; propaganda claims, 261; sex equality views, 185–8; special factors, 254–5; television violence, 138

British Schools Council, 216

Brzezinski, Z., 12–13, 17, 20

Bush, George, 104

Chazan, N., 210

Chechnya conflict, 42

children: Palestinian uprising, 5, 87–93, 267

China see People's Republic of China

citizens: obligations, 14

citizenship: Britain, 9–10, 254–6; definitions, 11–12, 52–3, 69, 229–30; democratic, 15–20; global, 260–1, 267–8; Hong Kong, 9, 229–36; Ichilov's model, 23–4, 58–60, 77, 146, 198; multidimensional, 23–4; New Zealand, 196–9; postmodernism, 20–3; technology impact, 17; United States, 98, 100, 101–17

citizenship movements, 230

civic consciousness, 14–15

civics teaching: Britain, 258; definition, 268–9; Hong Kong, 238–42; Hungary, 56–65; New Zealand, 199, 202; United States, 99–100, 119

civil citizenship: Hong Kong, 231

Books of Related Interest

International Review of History Education, Volume 2
Learning and Reasoning in History

Edited by **James F. Voss**, *University of Pittsburgh and*
Mario Carretero, *University of Madrid*

Series Editors: **Alaric Dickinson, Peter Gordon, Peter Lee**

The second volume in this series is a major contribution to both history education and the developing cognitive psychology of specific disciplines. It consists entirely of the proceedings of an international conference held near Madrid in 1994 on cognition and instruction in history, and is guest edited by Jim Voss and Mario Carretero.

Learning and Reasoning in History is divided into four sections. The first is especially concerned with a central matter in contemporary debate about history — historical narrative. Its five chapters discuss the nature of narrative, the impact of official and unofficial histories on students, and history and identity. The four chapters in Section II examines students' understanding and use of texts and sources in history, including the way in which such texts are used in facing historical controversies. Section III consists of five chapters on students' explanations in history, dealing with both causal and intentional explanation. Finally, the six chapters in Section IV are concerned with the teaching of history, and with students' understanding of some important substantive concepts.

The range and quality of the contributions, many from eminent researchers in the field, and the importance of the issues they discuss, make this book an indispensable tool for anyone interested in history education or cognitive psychology.

1998 432 pages
0 7130 0204 2 cloth   ISSN 1362-4822

WOBURN PRESS
Newbury House, 900 Eastern Avenue, Newbury Park, Ilford, Essex, IG2 7HH
Tel: +44 (0)181 599 8866 Fax: +44 (0)181 599 0984
NORTH AMERICA
c/o ISBS, 5804 NE Hassalo Street, Portland OR 97213 3644
Tel: (800) 944 6190 Fax: (503) 280 8832 E-mail: orders@isbs.com
Website: http://www.woburnpress.com E-mail: sales@frankcass.com

International Yearbook of History Education, Volume 1

Edited by **Alaric Dickinson, Peter Gordon, Peter Lee** and **John Slater,** *all at the Institute of Education, University of London*

This international academic and professional yearbook contains articles and reviews on matters of interest to all concerned with history in education from contributors throughout the world. The yearbook will encourage rigorous exploration of philosophical, psychological, sociological and historical perspectives upon history in education and their relation to practice where appropriate. The theme of the first edition is centralisation and decentralisation of national curricula.

Contributors: G. Cuthbertson, A. Grundlingh, I. González, C. Guimerà, G. Zaragoza, J. Domínguez, P. Lee, M. Chau, S. Ahonen, H.S. Nielsen, Y. Larsson, J. Slater, P. Rogers.

1995 232 pages
0 7130 0188 7 cloth

A Guide to Educational Research

Edited by **Peter Gordon,** *Institute of Education, University of London*

The Education Reform Act of 1988 had a major effect on the content of the curriculum and the process of educational assessment. This book, which gives a clear account of recent developments in educational research, is intended as a guide to possible research areas, both fundamental and policy-related, for students in colleges and higher education institutions, and will also be of interest to those engaged in curriculum planning and administration.

Contributors: Bill Marsden, Martin Booth, Tony Burgess, Piers Spencer, Leslie J. Francis, Jon Ogborn, Richard Kimbell, David J. Whitehead, Colin Wringe, Stewart Ranson, John Elliott, Kathy Sylva, Seamus Hegarty, Sara Delamont and Keith Watson.

1996 424 pages
0 7130 0192 5 cloth
0 7130 4024 6 paper

WOBURN PRESS
Newbury House, 900 Eastern Avenue, Newbury Park, Ilford, Essex, IG2 7HH
Tel: +44 (0)181 599 8866 Fax: +44 (0)181 599 0984

NORTH AMERICA
c/o ISBS, 5804 NE Hassalo Street, Portland OR 97213 3644
Tel: (800) 944 6190 Fax: (503) 280 8832 E-mail: orders@isbs.com

Website: http://www.woburnpress.com E-mail: sales@frankcass.com

Elementary School Teachers: Professional Identity and Classroom Practice 1918–1939

Peter Cunningham *and* **Philip Gardner,** *both at the School of Education, University of Cambridge*

There is an extraordinary gap in the published history of schooling in the twentieth century. Nowhere is the voice of the teacher, telling his or her own story, extensively to be heard. This book, drawing not only upon the official documentary record, but also upon the previously untapped recollections of more than 100 former classroom teachers, aims to fill this gap. In *Elementary School Teachers*, the nation's teachers from more than half a century ago tell what twentieth century education has looked like and felt like from their side of the classroom. The book concentrates particularly on the years between the end of the First World War and the passing of the landmark 1944 Education Act. All of the former state school teachers whose testimony stands at the centre of the book began their teaching careers in this period, and most completed the bulk of their classroom teaching in these years.

Oral testimony is set alongside more conventional documentary sources and thematic analysis and individual life histories are brought together. In this respect, the work will break new ground in terms of its methodological approach as well as in terms of its substantive historical concerns.

1999 c288 pages
0 7130 0213 1   cloth £32.50/$49.50
0 7130 4032 7 paper £17.50/$27.50

WOBURN PRESS
Newbury House, 900 Eastern Avenue, Newbury Park, Ilford, Essex, IG2 7HH
Tel: +44 (0)181 599 8866 Fax: +44 (0)181 599 0984
NORTH AMERICA
c/o ISBS, 5804 NE Hassalo Street, Portland OR 97213 3644
Tel: (800) 944 6190 Fax: (503) 280 8832 E-mail: orders@isbs.com
Website: http://www.woburnpress.com E-mail: sales@frankcass.com

The Values Debate

A Voice from the Pupils

Leslie J. Francis, *Trinity College, Carmarthen*

The debate about values among the young has generated many
opinions, but very little real evidence from young people
themselves. This new authoritative study provides the essential
evidence.

The Values Debate: A Voice from the Pupils presents findings from a
survey conducted among 30,000 13–15 year olds throughout
England and Wales, giving particular attention to social, personal
and moral issues. The analysis begins with an overview of what
teenagers really think. What are their views on sex, family, AIDS
and homosexuality? What stand do they take on tobacco, alcohol
and drugs? What values do they hold on pollution, poverty and
responsibility for the developing world? What value do they place
on themselves and on their future lives?

The analysis then examines the factors which shape these
fundamental values. How do values differ between male and
female teenagers? What difference does social class make? How
important is the family? Does religion continue to play a part? Does
private schooling shape a different set of values? How important is
the experience of being bullied at school?

1999 c192 pages
0 7130 0209 3 cloth
0 7130 4029 7 paper

WOBURN PRESS
Newbury House, 900 Eastern Avenue, Newbury Park, Ilford, Essex, IG2 7HH
Tel: +44 (0)181 599 8866 Fax: +44 (0)181 599 0984

NORTH AMERICA
c/o ISBS, 5804 NE Hassalo Street, Portland OR 97213 3644
Tel: (800) 944 6190 Fax: (503) 280 8832 E-mail: orders@isbs.com

Website: http://www.woburnpress.com E-mail: sales@frankcass.com

The Private Schooling of Girls

Past and Present

Edited by **Geoffrey Walford**, *University of Aston*

'This is a tantalizing volume of essays for those interested in the dynamics of gender, power, and socialization.... The social and intellectual values that have resulted in the lavishing of so much attention upon the reproduction of ruling elites in the English public schools are reflected in every chapter in this collection.'
Christine M. Heward,
History of Education Quarterly

'It provides fascinating glimpses into the generation, rhetoric and processes of the independent schooling of girls, and elicits....the strong desire for more... The book is truly post-modern in the range and eclecticism of disciplines, epistemologies and methodologies presented in its nine chapters.'
British Educational Research Journal

1993 224 pages
0 7130 0186 0 cloth £24.00/$35.00

WOBURN PRESS
Newbury House, 900 Eastern Avenue, Newbury Park, Ilford, Essex, IG2 7HH
Tel: +44 (0)181 599 8866 Fax: +44 (0)181 599 0984

NORTH AMERICA
c/o ISBS, 5804 NE Hassalo Street, Portland OR 97213 3644
Tel: (800) 944 6190 Fax: (503) 280 8832 E-mail: orders@isbs.com

Website: http://www.woburnpress.com E-mail: sales@frankcass.com

Teaching Science

Edited by **Jenny Frost** *with contributions from* **Arthur Jennings, Tony Turner, Sheila Turner** *and* **Leslie Beckett**. *Preface by* **Jon Ogborn** *all at the Institute of Education, University of London*

This book is packed with practical ideas and advice on the art of teaching science. The use of exposition, demostrations, practical work, investigations, circuses, independent learning, simulations and discussion are explored in detail through a wide variety of richly illustrated examples, alongside the reasons teachers have for choosing one strategy rather than another. The examples are taken from recent classrooms, made more vivid by a large collection of photographs and pen sketches.

1995   192 pages illus.
0 7130 0185 2 cloth
0 7130 4015 7 paper

WOBURN PRESS
Newbury House, 900 Eastern Avenue, Newbury Park, Ilford, Essex, IG2 7HH
Tel: +44 (0)181 599 8866 Fax: +44 (0)181 599 0984

NORTH AMERICA
c/o ISBS, 5804 NE Hassalo Street, Portland OR 97213 3644
Tel: (800) 944 6190 Fax: (503) 280 8832 E-mail: orders@isbs.com

Website: http://www.woburnpress.com E-mail: sales@frankcass.com